Suicide

Contemporary Issues

Series Editors: Robert M. Baird
Stuart E. Rosenbaum

Other titles in this series:

Suicide
Right or Wrong?

Second Edition

edited by **John Donnelly**

Contemporary Issues

Prometheus Books
59 John Glenn Drive
Amherst, New York 14228-2197

Published 1998 by Prometheus Books

01 00 99 98 97   5 4 3 2 1

Library of Congress Cataloging-in-Publication Data

Suicide : right or wrong? / edited by John Donnelly. — 2nd ed.
     p.   cm.
    Includes bibliographical references.
    ISBN 1-57392–186–6 (paper : alk. paper)
    1. Suicide—Moral and ethical aspects. I. Donnelly, John, 1941–
II. Series: Contemporary issues series (Amherst, N.Y.)
HV6545.S8426   1998
179.7—dc21   97–35042
                                                   CIP

Printed in the United States of America on acid-free paper.

Contents

Part Three: Is Suicide Moral? Is It Rational?

Appendix: The Supreme Court on Physician-Assisted Suicide

Introduction

There is but one truly serious philosophical problem, and that is suicide. Judging whether life is or is not worth living amounts to answering the fundamental question of philosophy.

—Albert Camus

Whoever is oppressed with the burden of life, whoever desires life and affirms it, but abhors its torments, such a man has no deliverance to hope from death, and cannot right himself by suicide.

—Arthur Schopenhauer

Free to die and free in death, able to say a holy No when the time for Yes has passed; thus he knows how to die and to live.

—Friedrich Nietzsche

Suicide (and euthanasia) are now center-stage on the public agenda. Derek Humphry's suicide manual *Final Exit* published in 1991 made the *New York Times* best-sellers list. Various opinion polls reveal considerable support for a person's right to die, and several legal proceedings invoked against people who assist in suicide (or euthanasia) usually result in verdicts that are mere slaps on the wrist (e.g., innocent because of temporary insanity, guilty of involuntary or voluntary manslaughter, or not guilty, often by virtue of jury nullification). Even the rock singer Kurt Cobain, who committed suicide in 1994, is memorialized by our youth, recently having a church named after him in Seattle. And, of course, the extraordinary epidemiological changes in medicine, advances in biomedical technology, and assorted preventive health measures have enabled people to live longer and, in turn, raise complex end-of-life decisions about the quality versus quantity of the life so prolonged. Contemporary public sentiment seems to be catching up with the long-standing view of many philosophers that suicide can sometimes be the quintessential free, rational act, something often noble and heroic.

In May 1996, Admiral Jeremy Boorda, chief of U.S. Naval Operations, committed suicide. It seems clear that this suicide was prompted by a *Newsweek* magazine inquiry into whether Boorda had truly earned two Vietnam wartime ribbons of valor that he wore on his uniform. In addition, the Navy was already beset from the sexual escapades of Tailhook, some Annapolis scandals, and assorted fighter-jet crashes. Boorda had recently been upbraided by a former secretary of the navy for alleged failure of leadership and excessive political correctness. In a one-page suicide note to his command, Boorda wrote positively of the core naval values of honor, courage, and commitment. I suppose one person's reckless suicide is another person's act of heroism. Some Americans reacted to Boorda's suicide with great anger and dismay, viewing it as a senseless tragedy that could only give aid and comfort to the enemy. Other Americans saw his action as the very embodiment of the military values of courage and honor, somewhat analogous to the captain going down with his ship (a comparison which would suggest, inadvertently, that the navy itself is sinking).[1]

The reality of suicide knows no demographic boundary. It occurs in all cultures, nationalities, races, age groups, and professions. Suicide rates appear relatively high in Hungary, Germany, Sri Lanka, Austria, Denmark, and among American Indians, college-age students, and psychiatrists. Where the bonds of family and socioeconomic cohesion are fragile, evidence suggests a higher incidence of suicide, whether among the childless, the divorced, the widowed, the unemployed, the dispossessed, the alienated, the emotionally distraught, alcoholics, substance abusers, or whomever.[2]

Theories abound regarding the conditions that influence people in their decision to commit suicide. Some insist that it results from a biochemical imbalance (e.g., low serotonin levels in individuals suffering from depression), while others cling to psychoanalytic explanations, sociocultural influences, and a whole host of other psychological, social, and biological variables. At the present time, no theory has risen above the rest. Any suicidal person is faced with perceived psychological pain that may take the form of anxiety, guilt, despair, hostility, etc., resulting in hopelessness, haplessness, and helplessness. Suicide is a multifaceted phenomenon, resulting from what Shneidman terms "psychache." Obviously, any mortality table that suggests suicide is not widely practiced would be considered deceptive. The United States Center for Health Statistics doesn't list a death as suicide unless there is proof that it was intentional, i.e., premeditated—a condition all the more difficult to establish given the paucity of suicide notes. Along with the fact that suicide is frequently underreported, euphemisms proliferate to soften the harshness of what the philosopher Immanuel Kant termed "the intention to destroy oneself." Indeed, intimations of suicide can appear "magical" and "consoling." Nietzsche said that "by means of it one gets successfully through many a bad night."

The situation of the would-be suicide is notoriously ambivalent. Often it isn't death as such that is so devoutly wished for; it is relief from physical pain and/or mental anguish. There are suicide prevention centers in over two hundred cities in the United States. The fact that so many people seek help at such centers strongly suggests that they are looking for a solution to their respective plights.

Surprisingly, suicide occurs at an alarming rate among the young, persons supposedly in the prime of their lives. Adolescent suicide in the United States rose by 300 percent in the twenty years between 1955 and 1975, and has stabilized somewhat since. In May 1993, the San Diego City Schools surveyed 1,788 students at twenty-five high schools regarding a number of behavioral matters. Even making allowances for teenage bravado, one cannot but be alarmed by the responses that indicated 21.1 percent of the males and 30.3 percent of the female students had seriously considered committing suicide in the past year; and that 7 percent of the males and 12.8 percent of the females allegedly attempted it. A more extensive study in 1991 by the National Center for Disease Control of some 11,631 high school students in all fifty states produced similar findings: 27 percent thought seriously of killing themselves and 8 percent attempted it. (The San Diego survey provoked considerable controversy and concern within and for the Filipino-American community when 39 percent of the female Filipino students spoke of serious suicide ideation and 23 percent of them had allegedly tried to kill themselves.) In 1995, a survey of San Diego middle school students found that 30 percent thought of committing suicide, 16.2 percent planned it, and 11.7 percent attempted it. On the San Diego high school level in 1995, 27 percent thought of it, 20 percent drafted a plan, and 10 percent attempted it. Much higher rates of teen suicide are reported in Switzerland and Austria. Only car accidents cause more deaths among adolescents than suicide, and many of these may well be "autocides." Yet despite a number of recent federal, state, and local programs attempting to address this problem, suicide remains a taboo subject for many parents. Sons and daughters may die by their own hands, but the deaths are often rationalized as Russian roulette gone awry, accidental poisoning, or attributed to alcohol or drug abuse. Nonetheless, studies indicate that most teen suicides occur in the home, usually during early evening when parents are close by. Experts view such suicides as desperate pleas for love and attention or spiteful acts of revenge. Yet, critics of suicide education programs in our schools claim the statistical data are skewed, and accuse suicidologists of seeking to hawk their theories for personal gain and publicity. Critics contend that such programs would inadvertently serve to increase the number of suicides as they heighten public awareness.

In 1994, the U.S. Department of Health and Human Services reported some 12.4 deaths by suicide per 100,000 population in this country. In 1994, some 5,350 people between the ages of fifteen and twenty-four committed suicide in the United States. On a global level there are approximately 730,000 suicides annually. Of course, millions of people unsuccessfully attempt suicide every year. Males seem to commit suicide more often than females and by more violent means. However, women attempt suicide more frequently than men. (Both male and female African-Americans commit suicide less than white males and females, with female African-Americans the least of all racial groups.) Doubtless, these figures are statistically inaccurate, inasmuch as respect for the dead and the deceased's family often influence physicians (when officially certifying the death) to list genuine suicides as deaths by some other cause. The practice of euphemistic coroners' reports has often reached peaks of morbid, if not comical, absurdity, as in the case of a

British report that described the "accidental" death of a man who just happened to shoot himself while cleaning the muzzle of his gun with his tongue!

This volume deals with the topic of suicide and not euthanasia. The two terms are often treated synonymously by the media and the public at large. However, suicide involves the preternatural or preemptive extinction of one's life, as opposed to genuine euthanasia (whether active or passive) that involves the killing or allowing to die of the terminally ill. Euthanasia—it might be claimed—is an alleged solution for the ills of dying, whereas suicide is an alleged cure for the ills of living.

Despite the word's etymology, suicide need not be self-inflicted, a point nicely made by R. G. Frey in this volume. And the distinction between suicide and euthanasia becomes very blurry in the case of physician-assisted suicide or death. Clearly, many cases of the latter involve terminally ill patients and perhaps should be spoken of as euthanatic suicides (or possibly active euthanasia). In the typical case of physician-assisted suicide, the doctor is merely the facilitator or conveyor of drugs or machinery, such that the chronically ill or severely disabled patient actually kills himself or herself. In less typical cases, the physician directly brings about the patient's voluntary death or suicide by, say, a lethal intravenous injection of potassium chloride.

Obviously, perplexing questions can arise about the exact meaning of expressions like "terminally ill." Full-blown AIDS (Acquired Immune Deficiency Syndrome) always leads to death; but do we want to call an HIV-positive victim who kills himself or is assisted in doing so in the early stages of the illness a suicide? What are we to make of the case of David Rivlin, a thirty-eight-year-old quadriplegic who wanted to die because of his condition and his reliance on a respirator? Since he had been judged fully competent, a court order was issued so that his ventilator could be removed. He was given valium and morphine, and then his respirator was turned off. He died some thirty minutes later. Had he not opted for this death, Rivlin might have lived for many more years. Is this assisted suicide, a type of euthanasia, or simply an attempt to gain control over one's own life by refusing life-sustaining treatment, the choice of which ultimately ended in death? If we are to put some reasonable restraints on the time factor involved in a terminal illness, it would seem that Rivlin might well have been a suicide.

Unless we are all absurdly declared to be terminally ill simply because every day we are a minute closer to death (existentialists sometimes speak of humans as "beings-unto-death"), it would seem sensible to reserve talk of terminal illness for the time frame of a year or less to live, given the best available medical prognosis about one's physical condition. Accordingly, despite the publicity surrounding the alleged "suicide" in 1981 of Nico Speijer, a prominent Dutch suicidologist, his death was probably more accurately described as a case of self-administered voluntary active euthanasia, for Speijer was terminally ill with intestinal cancer that was rapidly metastasizing. The situation of his wife, who died with him, is less obviously a case of euthanasia. By contrast, the suicide pact of Henry Pitney Van Dusen, the former president of Union Theological Seminary, and his wife, Elizabeth, both of whom died from deliberate overdoses of sleeping pills, seems genuine, for while he suffered from the aftereffects of stroke and she from arthritis, neither could reasonably be described as terminally ill, although they were chronically ill.

On the whole, civilized society still frowns upon and shudders at suicide. For example, in 1987, the convicted state treasurer of Pennsylvania committed suicide at a televised press conference, the day before he was to be sentenced to prison for fraud. While the media covered the story, few reputable television stations or newspapers would show the graphic event itself. Yet those same media outlets would not have hesitated to show footage of war scenes, plane crashes, gang shootouts, assassinations, or some violent, homicidal Hollywood film.

What exactly counts as a suicide? Is suicide ever rational or morally justified? Is it ever obligatory? Are suicidal actions—or patterns of self-negligent behavior that result in death—also bona fide suicides? Is it psychiatrically accurate to label successful or unsuccessful suicides as mentally deranged or seriously depressed and, in the case of the unsuccessful, in need of confinement or treatment? Should people who assist or abet others to commit suicide be criminally prosecuted? Is the notion of self-murder an oxymoron? Are cases of altruistically motivated self-killing really suicides? Are self-annihilations prompted by honor or loyalty—i.e., choosing death over dishonor—genuine suicides? Do autonomous individuals have a right to die? Do they have a right to assistance in their deaths? These and a host of related matters will be explored in this volume.

Since the foundations of many contemporary philosophical arguments, either for or against suicide, can be traced back to various important historical thinkers, I thought it appropriate to include two classic essays against suicide (those of Aquinas and Kant), balanced by two classic selections in support of suicide (those of Seneca and Hume).

The historical selections on suicide begin with a prosuicide essay by Lucius Annaeus Seneca (4 B.C.E.–C.E. 65), a Roman philosopher and Stoic who was accused of conspiring to kill Nero and who subsequently committed suicide upon the emperor's command. Seneca emphasizes considerations of quality of life over mere existence and recommends dying well as an escape from the ills of living. Human beings have the power and liberty (the right) to exit life when they so choose, and as his gladiator example illustrates, even "the foulest death is preferable to the cleanest slavery." If the vicious can "insult death," all the more appropriate for the virtuous to put a period to their lives. Seneca believed it was criminal to live by robbery, but noble to die by stealing one's own life.

St. Thomas Aquinas (1225–1274) argues against suicide, which he claims is a violation of self-love, love of neighbor or society, and a breach of God's sovereignty over us. Paradoxically, like Seneca, he sees suicide as having features analogous to theft—but the suicide steals God's gift of life and so misappropriates the property that belongs to God.

Like Seneca, Aquinas prizes human freedom, but the responsible use of it renders no person "judge of himself." Unlike the stoical Seneca, Aquinas fears death and the subsequent judgment of God. Suicide is viewed as a greater sin (moral wrong) than those sins which in time can be repented. Interestingly, Aquinas opposed the martyrdom via suicide of chaste women who were about to be raped; he argues that they need not consent to such violence and hence can morally avoid being violated because "evil must not be done that good may come" (or evil be avoided).

David Hume (1711–1776) wholly disagrees with Aquinas, arguing that suicide is not contrary to love of self, of neighbor, or of God. Hume claimed that even assuming the truth of Aquinas's theism, one need not preclude suicide from being rational and moral. That is, if it is religiously permissible to encroach on divine providence by disturbing the operations of various natural laws (by curing diseases and the like), then, by parity of reasoning, it ought to be similarly permissible to commit suicide. Moreover, couldn't a person commit suicide while expressing gratitude to God for the good she has enjoyed and for the ability to escape her current misery? After all, Aquinas allowed self-inflicted killings when one is divinely commanded to do so!

Hume, a known skeptic on religious matters, is being ever so ironical and sardonic in his essay.

> When I fall upon my own sword, therefore I receive my death equally from the hands of the deity as if it had proceeded from a lion, a precipice, or a fever.... There is no being which possesses any power or faculty, that it receives not from its Creator, nor is there any one, which by ever so irregular an action, can encroach upon the plan of his providence, or disorder the universe. Its operations are his works equally with that chain of events which it invades; and whichever principle prevails, we may for that very reason conclude it to be most favored by him.

Readers of Hume's *Dialogues Concerning Natural Religion* will be aghast at how his alter ego, Philo, could ever countenance such thoughts as presented in his essay on suicide. Secular humanists will appreciate Hume's pungent satire but find themselves taken aback by his bold claim that "the life of a man is of no greater importance to the universe than that of an oyster." Like Seneca, Hume wants to emphasize our liberty to kill ourselves. It's no more "playing God" to take one's life than it is to preserve one's life. Hume would clearly approve of the suicides of the Van Dusens and David Rivlin. And suicide is not necessarily opposed to the common good. A person is not obligated to do a small good for society at the cost of great harm to himself. Indeed, suicide can even be "laudable" (and required on utilitarian grounds) when continued existence is a burden to society. On March 27, 1984, then Governor of Colorado, Richard Lamm, said: "We've got a duty to die and get out of the way with all of our machines and artificial hearts and everything else like that and let the other society, our kids, build a reasonable life." He went on to say that he would "take the money we could save in reforming the health-care system and put it into... restarting America's industrial engine and in the education system."[3] Thus, a person is acting in her own rational self-interest (and could be maximizing value for society) when she prudently and courageously kills herself to avoid the sickness and misfortunes of life.

Defenders of St. Thomas will want to argue that Hume's maneuver has over-looked the important distinction between *laws of nature* and *natural laws.* The former are descriptive regulations based on uniform regularities in nature; the latter, the focus of Aquinas's animus toward suicide, are prescriptive rules, ostensibly based on the essential aspects of human nature.

Immanuel Kant (1724–1804), in opposition to both Seneca and Hume, claims that the exercise of freedom in self-destruction is self-contradictory. He seems to favor, however, the moral heroism of Cato (a Roman statesman who killed himself rather than surrender to Julius Caesar), but does not label it a suicide, since Cato was presumably attempting to rescue his personal integrity and not intending to destroy himself. That is, despite his antisuicide stance, Kant claims that there are times when life ought to be sacrificed. "If I cannot preserve my life except by violating my duties towards myself, I am bound to sacrifice my life rather than violate these duties." He views "humanity in one's own person" as "inviolable." Suicide, by contrast, treats our personhood as a thing, it reduces us to the level of a beast. Persons, for Kant, are ends-in-themselves, having the capacity for autonomy and rationality that constitute their humanity. (The reader might ask himself or herself how Kant would view Glenn Graber's cases of Irene and Jeremy.) Life is not more important than virtue. "To live is not a necessity; but to live honorably while life lasts is a necessity." Unlike Hume, Kant maintains that the fabric of society is undermined by those who advocate a right to suicide and romanticize it somewhat in the process. Nonetheless, pace his categorical imperative, it seems suicide can be universalized on Kantian grounds, e.g., anyone whose situation in life is such that his or her continued existence would cause others a greater amount of suffering than his or her suicide ought to commit suicide.

In his critique of suicide, Kant makes some interesting and controversial psychological claims. For example, he avers that a person lacking integrity and self-worth places greater value on biological life, unlike the person of "inner worth" who will sacrifice biological life to retain his or her personhood. In an ingenious thought experiment, Kant asks us to imagine a group of people, some vicious, some virtuous, all of whom are unjustly accused of a crime and given the choice of death or life imprisonment. He hypothesizes that they would choose as follows: "A man of inner worth does not shrink from death: he would die rather than live as an object of contempt, a member of a gang of scoundrels in the galleys; but the worthless man prefers the galleys, almost as if they were his proper place." Kant is offering the caveat that people shouldn't surrender their personhood to the will of others and shouldn't preserve their lives at the cost of disgraceful conduct. Kant would appear to approve of the self-killings of hostages held captive in sadistic terrorist quarters, as well as the suicide of Judas Iscariot.

From a distinctly religious perspective, Kant sides with Aquinas over Hume in viewing suicide as "abominable." It violates the purpose of creation and is a throwing of the gift in the giver's face, a rebellion against God. "Human beings are sentinels on earth," Kant writes, and "God is our owner, we are His property; His providence works for our good. A bondsman in the care of a beneficent master deserves punishment if he opposes his master's wishes."

Joseph Fletcher, the famed situation ethicist (no actions are intrinsically right or wrong, but judged according to the context, which determines what maximizes human fulfillment), provides a humanist defense of suicide. Whereas Western cultural influences (as well as the Islamic tradition) have opposed suicide, non-Western cultures have long been tolerant of it, as in the Japanese rite of *seppuku* or *hara-kiri,* and the Hindu *suttee.* (*Seppuku* or *hara-kiri* was the Japanese method of disembowelment with a sword. It was often performed by Samurai warriors who were disgraced, defiant of their superiors, or condemned to death. *Suttee* was the ritual in India's caste system where the widow of a nobleman threw herself upon his funeral pyre and was immolated.) St. Augustine probably lent the most authoritative weight against suicide, as he opposed the Donatists, who held that dying in a state of grace via suicide was better than living with the risk of lapsing back into sin.

Fletcher contends that "human rights are not self-validating," but, rather, human needs validate rights. Favoring the values of self-determination and liberty, he believes that suicide can often be morally right provided it isn't outweighed by harm to others, for persons are not the mere instruments or property of the church or the state.

In ancient times suicide was a tragic option. It then evolved under the influence of Christianity into a sin. Later it became a crime and is now often viewed as a sickness. Fletcher prefers to regard suicide as "the signature of freedom," one's last autonomous act.

It would be difficult to discuss the morality and legality of physician-assisted suicide (PAS) without some mention of Dr. Jack Kevorkian, a sixty-eight-year-old retired pathologist, who as of September 1996 has helped at least forty persons die, not all of whom were terminally ill. His thirty-second victim, Shirley Cline, traveled from Southern California to Michigan to die with Kevorkian's assistance on July 4, 1996. She had cancer. According to her son, Dennis Garling, she was given a sedative (by whom?) to put her asleep, then drugs were administered (by whom?) to kill her.

Kevorkian had for years been interested in the macabre, particularly the use of scientific experimentation on criminals and the dying, and harvesting organ transplants from executed prisoners. His first client involving PAS was Janet Adkins, age fifty-four, who suffered from early stage Alzheimer's disease. She had left Oregon to see Kevorkian in Michigan, since at that time the Wolverine state had no law against assisted suicide. On June 4, 1990, Adkins died on a cot in Kevorkian's 1968 van, from his death-machine, the "mercitron." That machine consisted of three intravenous bottles hanging from a frame. Kevorkian connected an IV line to her filled with saline solution, and then Adkins herself switched on the thiopental bag, and then the potassium chloride line, and she was dead in some six minutes.

Adkins was soon followed in death by Sherry Miller (age forty-three) and Marjorie Wantz (age fifty-eight). Miller had multiple sclerosis and Wantz had chronic vaginal pain. While Wantz had had an earlier operation to remove some noncancerous growths from her vagina, an autopsy after her suicide revealed no organic cause for her recurring pelvic pain. Apparently all three of these women would rather have erred on the side of exiting too soon than departing too late.

Kevorkian had his medical license suspended in November 1991, resulting in his inability to obtain sodium pentothal and potassium chloride and causing him to turn to carbon monoxide as his lethal instrument. In February 1993, Michigan outlawed PAS.

On May 2, 1994, a Detroit jury acquitted Kevorkian in the death of thirty-year-old Thomas Hyde, who suffered from amyotrophic lateral sclerosis (i.e., Lou Gehrig's disease). Hyde yanked the string that released carbon monoxide into his face mask. In a nutshell, the jury perceived Kevorkian as merely ameliorating Hyde's medical condition by supplying palliative care to relieve his suffering and agony.

On March 8, 1996, Kevorkian was again acquitted of homicide, being found not guilty of the deaths of Merian Frederick (age seventy-two) and Dr. Ali Khalili (age sixty-one). The former had amyotrophic lateral sclerosis, the latter bone cancer. (Interestingly, Dr. Khalili specialized in pain control, wore a morphine pump, but still found no relief from his pain and suffering.) Here once again, the jury believed that Kevorkian's intent was to relieve pain and suffering and not to kill his clients. Kevorkian's feisty lawyer, Geoffrey Fieger, viewed the verdict as more about the patient's right not to suffer than about the right to die.

On March 6, 1996, the U.S. Court of Appeals for the Ninth Circuit (which ranges over nine Western states) ruled in an 8 to 3 vote that competent, terminally ill adults have a right to die under the Fourteenth Amendment's due process guarantee of personal liberty. This decision overturned the state of Washington's ban on PAS. Speaking for the majority, Judge Stephen Reinhardt upheld a "constitutionally protected liberty interest in determining the time and manner of one's own death." Previously the Washington statute had made it a criminal act to knowingly cause or aid another person to attempt or commit suicide, and the Ninth Circuit's ruling retained only the criminal prohibition on the "knowingly cause" phrase. (In a dissenting opinion, Judge Robert Beezer of the Ninth Circuit claimed that the current Washington standard proscribing suicide doesn't violate the constitution's substantive due process or equal protection rights of a mentally competent, terminally ill adult. He argued that government interests outweigh a person's right to PAS, because society must preserve the sanctity of human life, protect the interests of innocent third parties, prevent suicide, and maintain the integrity of the medical profession.) This ruling also overrides a lower court decision to block the implementation of Measure 16 that Oregon voters approved in November 1994 by a 52 to 48 percent plurality. That Oregon measure allows a physician to indirectly aid a terminally ill patient to die by prescribing medication that the patient could take to end his or her life, provided that patient is a competent adult having six months or less to live, a diagnosis and prognosis backed by a second physician, and the patient made three separate requests to die. One of those patient's requests must be in writing, supported by two witnesses. The physician must wait at least forty-eight hours after the written request and provide information to the patient about feasible alternatives (e.g., hospice, palliative care, etc.). The physician can be present at the suicide.

On April 2, 1996, the U.S. Court of Appeals for the Second Circuit unanimously ruled that physicians may help terminally ill patients kill themselves. Judge Roger Miner ruled that a New York law against PAS failed to offer equal protection of the law for its citizens. That is, if terminally ill patients on life support can refuse medical treatment, then so too should those terminally ill patients not on life support be able to hasten their deaths. And if a competent terminally ill person has a strong liberty interest in choosing a dignified death by refusing even life-aiding hydration and nutrition, then surely such a person has a constitutionally protected right to die. The point made by advocates of assisted death seems to be that merely to interpret narrowly the right to die as the right to refuse unwanted medical care so that one is allowed to die is to undercut the full scope of the right to die, which involves more than legalized advanced directives such as living wills, durable powers-of-attorney, or other withholding and withdrawing techniques.

On June 26, 1997, the United States Supreme Court ruled that competent, terminally ill persons do not have a constitutionally protected right to PAS. The unanimous vote (with six separate opinions) overturned the New York and Washington Circuit Courts of Appeals' rulings that had claimed a right to die.

Chief Justice William Rehnquist claimed that to refuse medical treatment is to die from an underlying pathology; but in PAS, it would be the medication that kills the patient. He also found inherent slippery-slope problems in the Appeals Courts' rulings, arguing that the state has an interest in banning PAS to protect vulnerable groups like the mentally ill, the aged, the chronically ill, etc. To assist a suicide, Rehnquist avers, is to "necessarily and indubitably, intend primarily that the patient be made dead." Moreover a patient who has PAS intends suicide; not so necessarily for the patient who refuses or discontinues medical treatment. The latter may wish to live, but unencumbered with intrusive medical treatment. Granting the "absence of omniscience," the Chief Justice invokes the principle of double-effect, noting a distinction between acts that artificially sustain life and acts that artificially curtail life. He believes palliative care measures are designed to alleviate a patient's pain and suffering, and not to cause death.

Opponents of the Supreme Court decision find some hope in the Court's observing that states can still try to craft right-to-die legislation, such as Measure 16 in Oregon, which will be reconsidered in the fall of 1997, and see if such legislation can pass constitutional muster. Justice John Paul Stevens has clearly invited such public debate in holding that "it is clear that the so-called 'unqualified interest in the preservation of human life' is not itself sufficient to outweigh the interest in liberty that may justify the only possible means of preserving a dying patient's dignity and alleviating her intolerable suffering." Critics also allege that the Court's outlawing PAS seems inconsistent with other recent rulings, such as the 1992 *Planned Parenthood* v. *Casey* abortion ruling of the Court that held "choices central to personal dignity and autonomy are central to the liberty protected by the 14th Amendment. At the heart of liberty is the right to define one's own concept of existence, of meaning, of the universe and of the mystery of human life." It's difficult to see how the right to die doesn't follow from that Court decision.

Opinion polls indicate that Dr. Kevorkian, despite his often bizarre behavior, is viewed favorably by a significant number of Americans. Indeed, seven Michigan physicians have recently joined Kevorkian in proposing guidelines for PAS that involve the following elements: (1) the patient makes the request in writing. The notarized request must be signed also by any physician involved in the case as well as by two competent adults who have no financial interest in the patient's life or death; (2) the request is then sent to a qualified obitiatrist who will refer the patient to a specialist in that patient's illness, a pain management specialist if relevant, and a psychiatrist; (3) in turn, that medical team must verify that the patient is mentally competent, inflicted with an incurable illness, and beyond the bounds of palliative care; (4) the obitiatrist or some designated physician reviews the consultants' report; (5) within three weeks of that review, the patient must decide when and where the PAS is to take place; (6) the PAS must be performed within twenty-four and seventy-two hours after the patient's informed consent; (7) the patient can call off the PAS at any time; and (8) the obitiatrist performs the PAS for no fee.

Indeed, Kevorkian has envisioned obitariums—death clinics—where PAS could be performed. He opened one briefly in 1995, named after his sister—the Margo Janus Mercy Clinic—and Erika Garcellano, a sixty-year-old woman, died there as his twenty-fourth suicide overall. Indeed, after his most recent acquittal in May 1996, Kevorkian seems invincible, even helping someone commit suicide during that trial, and following that by three more cases on June 11, 18, and 20, 1996.[4]

Opponents of PAS often raise slippery-slope arguments, such as what starts out as (legalized) voluntary PAS may create a cultural ambiance in which nonvoluntary or involuntary PAS becomes discussable and possibly enactable. These critics sense that too much judicial activism is already afoot, such as finding (or inventing) a constitutional right to die in the Fourteenth Amendment but apparently unable or unwilling to find, say, a constitutional right to health care. There are checks and balances on personal autonomy, so that paternalistic interference can be warranted to prevent harm to the agent or others, especially where that harm avoided is greater than any harm of paternalism. Indeed the cry for PAS could have the reverse effect of suppressing individual autonomy so that the physician becomes the lord and master over life, and the traditional rule of physician qua healer is replaced by physician qua executioner.

Moreover, given the political climate's mood for cost containment in medicine, might not this medical rationing lead to more deaths of the aged, the senile, and the chronically ill as part of this economics? Shouldn't more imaginative emphasis be placed on hospice alternatives? Is it empirically true that pain often cannot be controlled or relieved? Isn't it a much further step from the right to refuse medical treatment to the right to die? And even if there is a right to die, the exercise of it may not be rational or moral. And if there is a right to die, does such a right confer a duty on others to assist in your death? Or merely not to interfere with your right? A person may have a *liberty*-right to die, but not a *claim*-right. The Patient Self-Determination Act of 1991 grants a patient a claim-right to medical information about his/her care and permits such instruments as advanced directives, living wills, and durable power of attorney. But, as yet, there is no physician who is duty-bound legally to obey those directives.

In his interview with philosopher Paul Kurtz, Dr. Jack Kevorkian states his opinions on some end-of-life issues. He claims to prize personal autonomy and espouses a situation ethic not unlike that of Joseph Fletcher. Kevorkian wants a medical system that not only allows competent adult persons to die humanly, but, in addition, makes allowances for organ transplantation and medical experimentation—all designed to make death a positive value. Ironically, Kevorkian doesn't think there is a right to die (like his antagonist Leon Kass), only a "right to choose when, how, and where."

The interview by Celeste Fremon of famed psychoanalyst Bruno Bettelheim in his Santa Monica condo offers an intriguing insight or psychological autopsy into why the octogenarian committed suicide some months later, cross-continent, in a Maryland nursing home, having taken barbiturates and suffocating from a plastic bag over his head. Having survived the brutalities of two Nazi concentration camps, Bettelheim had gone on to achieve fame at the University of Chicago where he treated numerous children throughout his career as a psychologist, offering hope to their emotional despair.

Bettelheim shares with Fremon his intention to go to Holland to die and the travails of old age. He felt like he was living on borrowed time, dealing with the death of his wife a few years earlier, himself victimized by strokes, and his estrangement from his oldest daughter. Fremon notes how his conversation, which is so somber, is yet laced with amusing anecdotes (e.g., the crestfallen Austrian soldier who attempted suicide, the old man who complained to his doctor about his loss of sexual prowess), as if Bettelheim is using humor to wrench from the chaos of his current existence the secret of its nothingness. Bettelheim is wrestling with the problem of aging, of no longer feeling useful or wanted, an alienation further exacerbated by professional criticisms of his earlier treatment methods at the Orthogenic School in Chicago. He nicely links loving and being loved as life-affirming, and the loss of it to a kind of death. It seems Bettelheim's libido is absent, and he finds it increasingly difficult to find any meaning in life if (as he believes) there is no God or rational apotheosis to it all.

Herbert Hendin, a psychiatrist, is highly critical of the recent selling of death that attempts to normalize euthanasia and suicide in our culture. He analyzes two recent marketing techniques of the prosuicide movement that are designed to utilize medical case descriptions to sympathetically display the heroic autonomy of the patient serviced by the bountiful ethical sensibility of the physician and others who participate in these suicides. Hendin seeks to expose the ruse of these prosuicide supporters who use snippets of medical cases that seem to justify suicide (and euthanasia) and then extrapolate from these putative rational cases to a general legal, moral, and medical acceptance of it all.

Hendin centers his critique on a recent Dutch film, *Death on Request*, and on a *New York Times Magazine* essay. The Dutch film describes the elected death of Cees van Wendel, who suffered from amyotrophic lateral sclerosis (ALS). Far from showing the dignified autonomy of Cees, the film largely centers on the physician and Cees's wife, Antoinette, who coldly speaks for Cees and deals with the physician. Hendin believes "the doctor and wife took away Cees's personhood before ALS had claimed it."

The newspaper piece describes the assisted suicide of an American woman, Louise, and her relationship to her physician, to a clergyman head of "Compassion in Dying," and to the journalist. Louise suffers from an unspecified neurological disease and seems ambivalent about her suicide. The physician will provide Louise with sufficient barbiturates to kill her but will be absent at the actual suicide because of possible legal liability. Since the physician will soon be going out of town (and the reporter needs a story), the Reverend Mero, Louise's mother, and a friend seem anxious for a hesitant Louise to act quickly. Hendin finds no compassionate death with dignity here; instead he perceives a rush to death and the selling of it as empowerment to Louise's rather acquiescent autonomy. " 'Empowerment' flows toward the relatives, the doctor who offers a speedy way out if he cannot offer a cure, or the activists who have found in death a cause that gives meaning to their lives. The patient, who may have said she wants to die in the hope of receiving emotional reassurance that all around her want her to live, may find that like Louise she has set in motion a process whose momentum she cannot control."

This section concludes with an American Medical Association (AMA) report on assisted suicide. While the AMA recognizes the value of patient autonomy, it wants to insist that there is a difference between "refusing life-sustaining treatment and demanding a life-ending treatment." Physicians in their professional role are to be healers and comforters affirming life and not death. To alter this traditional role would be to grant physicians authority to judge the quality of a person's life. Indeed, the fact that PAS is being requested should signal that the patient's physical and psychological needs are not being fully met and in turn need to be addressed by several modalities to provide optimal treatment for the patient's pain and anxiety.

From the historical underpinnings, we shift to a discussion of what counts as suicide. Granted, there may be no ideal platonic definitional essence to be discovered for suicide. Nonetheless, one cannot possibly deal with the complex moral, epistemic, and legal issues involving suicide until there is some generally agreed upon (however conventional or ad hoc) operational definition of suicide. That definition may not be able to handle all borderline cases, but it should at least have some plausible, determinate meaning. The current lack of a generally received definition of suicide seriously undermines annual statistical mortality charts (where suicide is listed as the eighth leading cause of death in the United States, but may well be higher) and hampers medical taxonomic determinations of death in the four broad modal categories found on death certificates of accidental, natural, homicide, and suicide.

Any proposed definition of suicide must be as precise as the topic allows and capable of reconciling with our pretheoretical intuitions most of the examples of self-annihilating acts calling for legal, moral, and epistemic assessment. Clearly, suicide cannot be defined (somewhat etymologically) as "self-killing" or even "self-murder." The former is so wide in scope that it would entail calling an action suicide if one died because of overwork (e.g., Japanese *karoshi*) or died while inadvertently overdosing on some medication; and the latter definition would too stipulatively and facilely settle in advance the complex moral issues involved in suicide.

The famed sociologist Émile Durkheim spoke of suicide as "all cases of death resulting directly or indirectly from a positive or negative act of the victim himself, which he knows will produce this result."[5] This definition fudges the difference between suicidal conduct and suicide and would label by its behavioral analysis as a suicide a physician who dies, say, while fighting a plague, or a patient who refuses medical treatment and dies.

My own personal (somewhat tentative) definition of suicide might be formulated as such: S commits an act of suicide if and only if S intentionally and deliberately strongly wills, either through his or her own causal efficacy or that of others, that his or her life be totally or partially preternaturally extinguished (S might believe in some form of personal postmortem existence), for reasons of an egocentric and/or altruistic sort, such that S willingly causes or generates his or her own death more or less according to his or her action plan, except in cases where S can preserve his or her life only by performing a morally dishonorable act where such an act is likely adjudged impermissible by anyone who is willing to take the moral point of view (i.e., by being impartial, conceptually clear, factually informed, willing to universalize such a decision, etc.), and/or cases in which S is in a state of terminal illness such that without extraordinary medical support to prolong life or an improbable cure, S would die in a year or less.

The proposed definition of suicide excludes cases of euthanasia and morally heroic action or martyrdom. Regarding the former, my definition would classify the apparent suicide of a person suffering from a rapidly metastasizing sarcoma of the peritoneum and all the physical and emotional torment attendant to that medical condition as voluntary active euthanasia (euthanatic suicide) whether other-performed or self-delivered. Regarding the heroic, my definition would not count as a suicide the case of the marine platoon leader who jumps on a grenade to save his fellow soldiers.

One of the most vexing issues in any attempted definition of suicide is how to handle the problem of "deviant causal claims." This problem may be intractable. It concerns the matter of the causal history of the agent's intentions and the eventual outcome. For instance: Smith wants to kill himself by jumping from the Coronado Bridge. But in driving there, he is killed in the crossfire of a gang drive-by shooting. This death would doubtless be listed as homicide, but is it suicide also? Note also that on the matter of causal efficacy, suicide need not be self-inflicted (i.e., victim-precipitated homicide where, say, an individual instigates a SWAT operation and dies in the ensuing shootout). The matter of altruistic suicide is also highly problematic. Some philosophers deny there are such suicides. I do not. I think Bobby Sands was one, but not Maximilian Kolbe. Sands, an Irish Republican Army provisional jailed in Northern Ireland, persisted in a well-publicized hunger strike that led to his death by starvation, despite knowing how futile his demands were in light of the British government's intransigency to them. Kolbe, a Franciscan priest, substituted himself for a father at Auschwitz, who was to be starved to death. Kolbe was canonized a saint in 1982, and his starvation was not only not self-inflicted, but he was injected by the Nazis with phenol when he hadn't died after two weeks of being starved. My definition also speaks of the strong intention to die. It is widely accepted by suicidologists that many "suicides" are ambivalent about their situation, as much desperately crying for help with their lives as self-engineering their deaths. Suppose a person takes an overdose of sleeping pills, with such ambivalence, and dies before any assistance is forthcoming. Is this suicide? I think not, because the intention is not strong enough.

William Tolhurst attempts to shed some light on exactly what constitutes suicide. The notion of suicide is presently very much open-textured,[6] and cases of apparent suicide are often ambivalent. Agencies reporting mortality rates need to be clear about what constitutes suicide, otherwise their statistical data will be hopelessly skewed. Insurance policies, religious burial rites, and issues of societal stigma on families and reputations all hinge on greater clarity in defining suicide. Without linguistic precision, we are left with the unsettling relativism inherent in the claim that one person's suicide is another person's heroic act or risk-taking venture resulting in death.

Tolhurst rejects Émile Durkheim's classic definition of suicide, and he also rejects Richard Brandt's proposal, since both accounts make a person's foreknowledge that death will result from one's actions into a sufficient condition of suicide. Tolhurst continues by rejecting the respective definitions of suicide proposed by Joseph Margolis and Tom Beauchamp, who deny that altruistic motivation or coercion can be compatible with suicide. In rejecting Beauchamp, Tolhurst tries to show how coercion is compatible with suicide, as in the case of a person who decides to kill himself by jumping into a ravine, only to encounter on the way an avalanche that kills him.

Tolhurst seeks a definition of suicide that will be both intuitive and plausible. He favors the view that suicide is "successfully implementing a course of action in order to bring about one's death." The reader will have to decide how much in accord with ordinary language Tolhurst's paradigm cases prove to be. He seems to regard the case of a captured soldier about to be tortured to death and who, to avoid this, bites and swallows a capsule of cyanide lodged in his dentures as a clear case of suicide. Granted, a choice is involved here, but it is so constrained that it is hard to see how Tolhurst could consider it a *free* choice.

Since the concept of intention enters into almost all definitions of suicide, Tolhurst explores a *weak* and *strong* sense of the term "intentional." He claims that for a self-caused death to be suicide it must be strongly intentional. In other words, some act x will be considered strongly intentional if and only if there is an act y that the agent wants to perform and x either generates or is y, and the agent's performance of x is caused in an appropriate way by the agent's desire to do y along with the agent's beliefs about the generation of y. Tolhurst believes that most altruistically motivated, self-caused deaths are not strongly intentional, and hence not suicides.

Tolhurst also takes up the topic of whether Socrates committed suicide. Since

Tolhurst believes that an intentional action requires the correct sort of causal history resulting from the person's beliefs and desires, the question comes down to Socrates' act-generating beliefs. Socrates was faced with (a) drinking hemlock, (b) causing his own death, and (c) complying with Athenian law. If we assume that Socrates believed that (a) would generate (b) and (c), and he wanted to do (c), then (a) and (c) do seem strongly intentional, and (b) at least weakly intentional. However, Socrates would not be a suicide if he believed the law required him to drink the hemlock, so that (a) would generate (c) directly, but not that (c) would be generated by (b). However, if Socrates believed that causing his own death was necessary to comply with Athenian law, and that drinking the hemlock would generate that compliance through his death, then Socrates was a suicide.

Tolhurst takes up the complicated matter of deviant causal chains involved in the logic of act-generating beliefs.[7] There can be situations where a person has the appropriate beliefs and desires to kill himself yet doesn't commit suicide, precisely because the actual causal chain does not conform to his action plan. For example, a person wants to commit suicide by jumping from an overhead bridge onto the traffic below, but in the excitement of the moment suffers a fatal myocardial infarction while still standing on the edge of the bridge. If this is not to be considered suicide, the causal deviations have to be considerable to avoid having it fall into that category. An "exact fit" is not required. One cannot avoid the verdict of suicide by wanting to shoot oneself in the head but out of nervousness shooting oneself instead in the heart. However, until the matter of deviant causal chains is resolved, Tolhurst believes we cannot definitively "say whether particular self-caused deaths which result from causal chains which do not exactly coincide with the agent's action-plan are suicides or not."

Some suggest that Socrates was not the only historically significant suicide; Jesus may well have been one also. More recently, questions have been raised about the death in 1981 of Bobby Sands. Were any of these persons suicides? Suzanne Stern-Gillet thinks that none of them was. She views their deaths as induced and suggests that how one decides the matter of responsibility-ascription here is very often politically motivated. She reminds us that inherent in the descriptive meaning of suicide is a normative component—the ascription of moral responsibility—that is "inextricably intermingled" with the descriptive meaning. In short, in making decisions on whether a particular self-engineered death was a suicide or not, one is also making a value judgment.

Stern-Gillet, unlike Tolhurst, seems to think that a definition, or an assessment, of suicide cannot be conclusively settled in any empirical way. Stressing the inherent responsibility-ascription in suicide assessment, there are bound to be intractable disputes over whether Socrates or Bobby Sands committed suicide. Some will argue that in such cases the victims brought on their own deaths; others will say instead that the Athenian or British government bears responsibility for these killings. Given such normative disputes, moral praise or blame will vary accordingly, and the issue of suicide or martyrdom will turn on how one views the responsibility ascribing function.

R. G. Frey challenges the widely accepted belief that suicide must be self-inflicted. He contends that there are cases where a person wants to die (either as an end or as a means) and so knowingly and willingly places himself in a perilous situation that results in death. The polar explorer Captain Oates would seem to be a suicide, although his death is other-inflicted by the Antarctic blizzard. Frey develops some interesting scenarios to show how suicide can be other-inflicted (e.g., the actor who puts real bullets in a gun that he knows will be fired at him in a play). Frey is making the important point that just because death is other-inflicted doesn't mean that the victim isn't a suicide, provided the suicide wanted and contrived the death by exploiting and manipulating the other party to do it. It should come as no surprise that a number of suicides are disguised in this manner.

Terence O'Keeffe focuses on the religious prohibition of suicide, especially the "life as a gift" thesis and its corollary, the divine ownership theory, as elucidated by such philosophers as Augustine, Aquinas, Locke, and Kant. From this religious perspective, suicide has also been condemned by such modern writers as Gilbert Chesterton, who compared suicide to omnicide (the killing of everything), and Ludwig Wittgenstein, who called suicide "the elementary sin."

O'Keeffe also considers cases of heroic self-sacrifice such as Maximilian Kolbe and Captain Oates. He thinks they are not suicides since there was no overriding intent to die. They are instead cases of instrumental self-killings where the act is performed for some paramount altruistic and overriding purpose. To be genuine suicides persons must intend to kill themselves, and there must be no other primary, independent objective involved in the action. In short, the self-engineered death must be noninstrumental.

Like many philosophers, O'Keeffe takes up the principle of double effect, but he interprets it as being primarily about acts and their effects, and not about intentions as such. He defines the principle of double effect as follows: "(1) the action must itself be a good action or at least morally neutral; (2) the performance of the action must bring about at least as much good as evil; (3) the evil effect must not be a means to achieving the good effect; and (4) the agent must have a justifying and sufficient reason for acting rather than refraining from acting." He seems to suggest that some cases of heroic, altruistic self-killing would escape the potentially harsh verdict of suicide by use of the principle of double effect.[8]

O'Keeffe offers an interesting thought experiment, a sort of postmortem verification test, to determine if a person's death was really a suicide. He asks us to imagine that these "suicides" are momentarily revived. Genuine suicides (i.e., noninstrumental self-killers) would be distressed and want to die again. But instrumental self-killers would take delight in being revived and be tempted to redo their deaths only if the paramount causes for which their lives were offered remained unaccomplished.

O'Keeffe admits that on his account the religious sin of suicide is "an almost inconceivable act." This is so because in order to be a genuine suicide, one must kill oneself from a sheer hatred of self, of world, of life, or of God. Suicide, for O'Keeffe, is the ultimate nihilistic act. Moreover, his account does not justify all instrumental self-killings, for the cause served must itself be noble and worthy. He believes the hunger strikes in Northern Ireland during the early 1980s were not justifiable; although he seems to suggest that Bobby Sands, and those of like mind, were not genuine suicides, however imprudent their actions may have been.

Glenn Graber defines suicide as "doing something that results in one's death in the way that was planned, either from the intention of ending one's life or the intention to bring about some other state of affairs (such as relief from pain) that one thinks it certain or highly probable can be achieved only by means of death." The intention in question must be *strong* as specified in the earlier analysis of Tolhurst. Interestingly, Graber would not label as genuine suicides cases in which an agent attempts suicide as a desperate plea for help rather than a desire to die, but who nonetheless does die as a result. Persons could hang themselves or take an overdose of sleeping pills and still not be properly classified as suicides, for they lacked the strong intention to die.

Graber, like Brandt, believes that suicide can sometimes be rational when "a reasonable appraisal of the situation reveals that one is really better off dead," that is, "the value of the benefits of which immediate death would rob them is outweighed by the disvalue of the pain from which death would spare them." On the whole, Graber, like Seneca, grants final authority regarding the rationality of suicide to the first-person judgment of the individual contemplating suicide, provided that the person is factually and conceptually clear about the situation and is not so nihilistic as to see no value in life or any disvalue in death.

Joseph Kupfer concludes this section by attempting to clarify the concept of suicide so that the subsequent work of moral evaluation can be undertaken. (He wisely reminds us that some so-called rational suicides discussed in the literature are really cases of "auto-euthanasia" as the individual is terminally ill and faced only with a choice between modes of death.) To determine what constitutes suicide involves getting clear about what it is that the individual strictly intends regarding the end and the means to that end, and what that person merely foresees as the result of the action performed but doesn't strongly will. The monk who self-immolates is a suicide, although calling it such needn't entail a negative moral assessment of such an act. By contrast, the airplane pilot faced with the choice of crashing at sea to certain death or parachuting out so that the pilotless plane crashes inland, killing many people, and who chooses the former, is viewed by Kupfer as heroic but not a suicide, as his death is foreseen but not intended.

Suicides can range in moral evaluation from the praiseworthy, obligatory, or heroic (where the suicidist puts other people, principles, ideals, or causes ahead of the agent's self-interest) to the immoral sort where the suicidist so acts to make others feel guilty, or to frame someone, or to cowardly avoid moral responsibility for one's previous actions. Kupfer reminds us that to describe an act as suicide is not to automatically settle the moral evaluation of it.[9]

Edwin Shneidman, the famed suicidologist, begins the discussion in Part Three on the rationality and morality of suicide. He is convinced that suicide is wrong and urges us to identify and treat various would-be suicides. He compares suicide prevention techniques to those of fire prevention and cautions us to be on the lookout for various "clues" that indicate a likely suicide attempt. He assumes that those who attempt suicide are really ambivalent about their wishes and at heart want to be rescued. Paternalistic intervention to salvage potential suicides is not a source of concern: "only by being free to see the possibility of suicide potential in everybody can suicide prevention of anybody really become effective." We must err on the side of vigilance. The reader must decide if Shneidman's paternalism is warranted, especially in light of the various suicidal symptoms he identifies in numerous verbal, behavioral, and situational contexts. To be sure, many attempted suicides (parasuicides) are dramatic cries for help, desperate attempts to manipulate others into addressing the would-be suicidist's needs and desires. But, pace Shneidman, given the inherent fallibility of suicide prediction methods, where false-positives can and do surface, isn't this an infringement on the liberty of those mistakenly identified?

Thomas Szasz, a psychiatrist, regards the attitude of suicidologists like Shneidman as both "erroneous" and "evil." The antisuicide posture is erroneous because it views any suicide as an event and not an action, and evil because it legitimizes force and fraud in suicide prevention under the guise of medical treatment. "Suicide is medical heresy. Commitment and electroshock are the appropriate psychiatric-inquisitorial remedies for it."

Szasz claims that the suicidal person is not necessarily mentally ill. Ever-vigilant suicidologists mistakenly treat a desire to die and to exercise autonomy over one's death as if it were a disease. Physicians do not involuntarily hospitalize patients who refuse to take their life-sustaining medications, yet they think nothing of intervening with potential suicides and incarcerating them if need be.

Szasz, like Seneca and Fletcher, holds the libertarian notion that the individual has a right to commit suicide (his or her person neither belongs to the state nor is owned by God). Just as there is no self-theft, so there is no self-murder (assuming that our lives belong to us) where alleged criminal and victim are the same person. Szasz grants that some medical interventions without the patient's consent are warranted, as when treating a fractured limb or in other purely mechanical acts on the body. But suicide prevention is more a political act than a medical one, depriving persons of their liberty and dehumanizing them in the process. The suicidologist reacts with involuntary confinement, electroshock, and slavish psychopharmaceutical interventions. Szasz offers a striking comparison of the way the medical community treats a potential suicide and how various totalitarian governments treat would-be emigrés.

Victor Cosculluela seeks a golden mean between Shneidman and Szasz regarding coercive suicide prevention measures. He thinks that suicide prevention is permissible when (assuming we know the potential suicidist's mental framework and his/her duties to others) any of the following situations hold: (1) the suicidal ideation is based on factual ignorance; (2) the potential suicidist is not in control of his/her actions; (3) committing suicide would involve a greater injury to others; and (4) the potential suicidist has irrational ethical beliefs. Intervention is *obligatory* when any of the above conditions hold and the agent of prevention is under no equally pressing duty requiring him or her to refrain. However, if none of the above conditions hold and the preventive measures employed involve long-term personal degradation to the suicidal patient, then prevention and intervention is not justified.[10]

The essay by Milton Gonsalves is a classic statement of the theistic position against suicide, which is defined as the "direct killing of oneself on one's own authority," wherein "death is intended either as an end or as a means to an end." Reminiscent of the methodological style of Aquinas, Gonsalves begins by considering six plausible and persuasive arguments for suicide and attempts to respond to each. To those who claim that it is rational to kill oneself when life becomes so burdensome that the individual is useless to himself and to society, Gonsalves responds by emphasizing how suffering can be redemptive and character-building. To those who stress the right to commit suicide as a last dignified act of self-mastery, Gonsalves counters that it violates our duty to love ourselves and to preserve our existence. The third argument underscores that death can be the lesser of two evils; but for Gonsalves it is wrong to choose the lesser of two physical evils when moral evil is involved.

The fourth prosuicide argument claims that God's gift of life is unrestricted and so can be relinquished when to continue it is more harmful than beneficial. Gonsalves responds by claiming that God's gift is restricted, and we are meant to be stewards over life, not lords and masters. To the fifth argument, Gonsalves responds that while an omniscient God cannot be defrauded by those who return the gift of life via suicide, it is wrong to seek to defraud God. The sixth argument emphasizes the allowing of killing in self-defense as well as the state's legal killings in war and capital punishment; but Gonsalves retorts by pointing out that the suicide is both attacker and the attacked, executioner and murderer, so the analogies drawn with self-defense and state executions are not appropriate.

David Holley, in the tradition of Aquinas and Gonsalves, explores the principal metaphors behind the theistic ethical-religious rejection of suicide. One of these metaphors is the property one, wherein we are said to be God's property and may not dispose of our life without divine permission. Holley finds the property metaphor unsatisfactory, for it suggests humans are mere chattel.

A more promising metaphor for proscribing suicide is the life as a gift metaphor, so that to commit suicide is a grave act of ingratitude, a throwing of the gift back into the Giver's face. Instead we are to be good stewards over the life given us, a life that is more like a training ground for character than an amusement park. This leads the theist to further usage of metaphors, such as our existence in the world is like being a student in school or a patient in a hospital. None of these metaphors rule out martyrdom, heroic self-sacrifice, or even euthanasia.

Holley reminds us that metaphorical thinking is regularly used in moral evaluation (cf. Hume's life as a burden) and that the employed metaphors circumscribe "what facts are seen as significant, what questions are important, and what principles are relevant." It is often the case that moral disputes seem unresolvable because of the power of differing dominant metaphors used in the debate. Perhaps we cannot objectively assess all our metaphorical patterns of thought, but we can try to critically examine them to see if we are consistent in our use of metaphors and alter them if they do not cohere with our basic beliefs and values.

Richard Brandt believes persons may have a prima facie rather than an absolute obligation not to commit suicide. He reminds us that even if a particular

suicide is morally wrong, it may nonetheless be excusable (if, for example, the suicide acted out of a misplaced sense of duty or was in an unsound state of mind).
Brandt finds fault with the arguments of Aquinas, Locke, and Kant, who reject suicide, especially via the divine ownership argument.

Brandt, a utilitarian, contends that suicide involves a "choice between future
world-courses." Those contemplating suicide must use the very best empirical
information available about their situation and take all their desires into account.
Agents' future desires and preferences are to count as much as their present ones.
The decision to kill oneself should never be made in a state of depression, which
tends "to primitivize one's intellectual processes," repressing one's memory of
countervailing evidence and affecting one's judgment about probable future
events. However, if it becomes clear beyond a reasonable doubt that future existence is not preferable to eliminating one's present misery, it is rational for the
agents to kill themselves, i.e., to choose a world-course that contains their early
demise. In short, Brandt, like Graber, defends the notion of balance-sheet suicide.

Brandt also offers some reflections on the role of an advisor to the potential
suicide. He thinks it is appropriate at times for paternalistic intervention to stop
the suicide. However, on other occasions, it may be appropriate to help a person
commit suicide, provided it doesn't involve any great cost to the advisor.

In contrast to Brandt, Philip Devine argues that it is not rational to choose
death via egocentric suicide (given the assumption that there is no life after death),
because one can have no knowledge about the choice to die, either through self-
experience or through the testimony of others. In short, death manifests a "logical
opaqueness," so that the option for death is not a genuine alternative. Rational
choice between life and death requires considerable knowledge about both
options; and since death is unknowable, suicide involves pathetic risk taking. Quite
obviously, there is no opportunity, once suicide is committed, to check one's losses.
So Devine rejects Brandt's limited defense of the morality and rationality of suicide because the world-course of death cannot be experienced. Devine reminds
us that there is a big difference between a painless existence that (while alive) we
prefer versus freedom from pain when we are nonexistent. (The reader might ask
whether given Devine's thesis about death's opaqueness, the choice not to commit
suicide can, by contrast, be rational.)

Joyce Carol Oates would disagree with Seneca, Hume, Graber, Brandt,
Fletcher, and Szasz. She regards as foolish, if not immoral, most suicides of an egocentric sort. She faults the literary and philosophical tradition for romanticizing
suicide and viewing it as the quintessentially free, rational, and creative act. The
fundamental error of justifications offered for suicide is an aesthetic one, because
the victim is misled by metaphors. Death is not liberating, but a mere brute inar-
ticulateness. It is sheer, unwarranted romanticism to describe death as the last
journey, everlasting sleep, perpetual rest, eternal peace, the absence of life, or the
Jungian "profound peace of all-knowing nonexistence." The suicide as artist is
rightly labeled neurotic or deranged. If there is no life after death, then death
cannot be rationally chosen, because it remains unexperienced and unimaginable.

Robert Weir analyzes the arguments both for and against physician-assisted suicide and concludes reluctantly that PAS is sometimes morally justified as a compassionate medical procedure. He contrasts the medical treatment of "Diane" by Dr. Timothy Quill with that of Janet Adkins by Dr. Kevorkian and finds the former a justified case of PAS. Weir offers some criteria under which PAS can be morally acceptable, recognizing the fine line between physicians as accomplices to a death and as agents of death. He grants that abuses could develop if PAS were legalized, but the same could be said of any legal medical practice. Tragically, there are some cases where a patient's life seems meaningless to them, suffering as they do from incurable or intractable pain and anxiety, so that there are some fates worse than death.

Leon Kass criticizes the right to die movement. He traces this postliberal cause to the Nietzschean idea of a right found not in nature or in reason, but voluntarily generated by the self-creative will. Kass offers an overview of the notion of a right and nicely picks up on the nuances of the Nancy Cruzan case and its relationship to the liberty clause of the Fourteenth Amendment.[11] Is the right to die (or its variants: a right to lethal injection, a right to assisted suicide, a right to die with dignity, a right to choose the time and manner of one's death, a right to be mercifully killed) a justifiable liberty claim? If so, does such a right entail an obligation on the part of other people to kill? Kass answers in the negative and suspects that the right to die advocates are often masking their true intention under the mantle of feigned compassion (e.g., grown children unwilling or unable to care for their aging parents, government social welfare programs and insurance companies concerned about their economic interests, etc.). The rise of individualism in our wants-demanded-as-rights society, advances in medical technology that can often prolong the dying process, the corresponding decline of the family, the widespread preaching of moral relativism—all of these elements have led, Kass believes, to the public clamor for right to die legislation. Should such a right be recognized and legalized, then Kass predicts: "Vulnerable life will no longer be protected by the state, medicine will become a death-dealing profession, and isolated individuals will be technically dispatched to avoid the troubles of finding human ways to keep company with them in their time of ultimate need."

Lastly, Margaret Battin, unlike Kass, contends that suicide is a right. While she takes issue with the libertarian notion of suicide as a property right (the private ownership of one's life) because it seems incoherent (unlike ordinary property one owns, there can here be no separation of the owner from her property, i.e., one can literally transfer ownership of one's car to someone else, but only figuratively one's life), she proceeds to locate suicide as a natural right. And if suicide is a fundamental right of humankind (like the right to life, liberty, the pursuit of happiness, etc.), then there is a prima facie reason at least for the agent to do as she chooses, with a corresponding obligation on the part of others not to interfere or prevent the exercise of that right, and possibly to even assist her in carrying out her right.

Battin feels that at least in some cases, suicide need not be pathological but instead can promote human dignity. Granted, there are circumstances under which that right can be overridden, but as a fundamental right the burden of proof to so override shifts to others to justify any abridgement of that right.

Søren Kierkegaard, reflecting on death in his *Concluding Unscientific Postscript* —albeit not on suicide per se—writes about students taking an exam that they have four hours to complete. The students have the option of taking the whole four hours allotted. The task of finishing the exam is one matter, time itself is another. However, when time itself is the very assignment, i.e., the task of life, then it is wrong to finish before the time has transpired. That is, if life constitutes the task, then "to be finished with life before life has finished with one, is precisely not to have finished the task."[12]

Is suicide right? Is it wrong? Is it noble? Is it ignoble? Each reader must grapple for an answer to these and a host of other queries raised in the essays and selections that follow. It is my personal hope that no reader will find it necessary to opt for suicide.[13] But if reason fails to convince, then perhaps we can all find some ironic distance to appreciate the sardonic ditty of Dorothy Parker, who advised:

> Razors pain you;
> Rivers are damp;
> Acids stain you;
> And drugs cause cramp;
> Guns aren't lawful;
> Nooses give;
> Gas smells awful;
> You might as well live.[14]

Notes

1. Margaret Pabst Battin ("Suicidology and the Right to Die," in *Suicidology*, ed. Antoon A. Leenaars [Northvale: Jason Aronson, Inc., 1993], pp. 390–94) points out how the German language seems more suitable to express and nuance the various senses of *suicide* than the English language. In German, there are some four different terms used to convey the connotation of the single English term *suicide*. They are: (1) *Selbstmord*, a very negative term morally and legally, akin to our self-murder; (2) *Selbsttötung*, a less negative but still disapproving term, akin to our self-killing; (3) *Suizid*, a more neutral term that suggests pathology in the agent's act; (4) and *Freitod*, a positive term that conveys the sense of a freely willed, voluntary self-deliverance, motivated by high personal integrity. Pace Battin, I'm not sure how this helps matters in assessing, say, Boorda's suicide. Those that approve of it would term it *Freitod*; those opposed would opt for one of the other three terms for suicide. Again, we are left with the unsettling result that one person's commendation is another person's condemnation.

2. Hungary has the rather dubious distinction of being the annual world leader in reported suicides. Is it due to genetics? Is it an acquired behavior brought about by repeated losses in war? The result of governmental change from communism to a form of capitalism? Are the Magyars, the original ethnic Hungarians, prone to suicidal melancholy? Ironically, Hungary's most well-known song is "Gloomy Sunday," a 1930s tune that espouses suicide and whose composer, Rezsoe Seress, committed suicide! Baffling questions also surface for suicidologists as to why in these high-risk groups some people do commit or attempt sui-

cide while others do not. Among other perplexing issues, one wonders why there is a high rate of suicide in such Scandinavian countries as Finland, Sweden, and Denmark, but a much lower rate in Norway. Do media coverage and school instructional programs about suicide actually generate a greater propensity for suicidal behavior, as in the phenomenon of "copy-cat" suicides?

3. *U. S. News and World Report* (April 9, 1984): 18. Consider the case of Richard (age seventy-nine) and Helen (age seventy-six) Brown, who died in their garaged Cadillac of carbon monoxide poisoning in December 1994. He suffered from arthritis and asthma; his wife had Alzheimer's disease. They decided to commit suicide because they wanted to leave their ten-million-dollar estate to charity rather than waste it on prolonged medical expenses for themselves. Couldn't they have donated the money and still lived? Is this a case where their perturbation constricted their reasoning?

4. On August 15, 1996, Kevorkian helped Judith Curren (age forty-two) commit suicide as his thirty-fifth victim. She was suffering from chronic fatigue syndrome and no longer wanted to take her antidepressant medicine. Allegedly unknown by Kevorkian, her psychiatrist husband was arrested three weeks earlier on charges of domestic abuse to his wife. Clearly, Judith wasn't terminally ill, and serious doubts could be raised about her competency to so opt for suicide.

On July 1, 1996, PAS became legal in the Northern Territory of Australia. Bob Dent, who suffered from prostate cancer, died on September 22, 1996, in Darwin, Australia. Dent, who was sixty-six, was connected by intravenous tubes to a computerized death machine that poured a mix of barbiturates and muscle relaxants into his bloodstream upon his touching the computer keyboard to give a *yes* answer to the question "Are you ready to die?" In March 1997, the federal Australian parliament overturned the law.

5. Émile Durkheim, *Suicide* (Glencoe: Free Press, 1951), p. 44.

6. Many words are linguistically imprecise or indeterminate in meaning. Such terms (e.g., "bald," "tall," "middle-aged," "rich," "poor," etc.) aren't really vague but they are prone to borderline cases.

7. Like Tolhurst, Michael Wreen (in "The Definition of Suicide," *Social Theory and Practice* 14 [1988]: 1–23) deals with the logic of deviant causal chains and intentions. In general, Wreen thinks that most cases of heroic self-sacrifice are similar to typical refusal-of-treatment cases that result in death and so should not be regarded as suicide. According to Wreen, a person commits suicide at time t if and only if: (1) the person strongly intends to kill himself (or strongly wants to let himself die) at t; (2) the person killed himself at t; (3) the intention in (1) caused (2) via the intermediary of a number of generated actions; (4) the causal route from (1) to (2) was more or less in accord with his action plan; and (5) the person acted voluntarily in killing himself.

8. O'Keeffe's formulation of the principle of double effect differs from many other such formulations, especially with respect to the second condition. Often that second condition states that the agent's intention is not directly to do the evil that results since it is only foreseen. No matter how it is formulated, the principle (representing the epitome of casuistry) is designed to offset the consequential harm often involved in dutiful adherence to a moral rule. Some ethicists have believed the principle could be used at least to condone suicide.

9. The reader might ask herself how, given Kupfer's analysis of suicide, one would evaluate the recent suicide of Terrance Yeakey, who killed himself just three days before he was to receive a medal of valor for his rescue efforts in saving four lives in the Oklahoma City federal building bombing. He left no suicide note, but friends said he was despondent because of his recent divorce and his inability to share custody of his two young daughters.

10. The issue of suicide prevention, intervention, and postvention raises the spectre of paternalism. Paternalism occurs when someone interferes with the liberty or autonomy of an individual either to promote that person's welfare or to prevent that person's being harmed, despite that person's current beliefs, desires, interests, etc. What is often overlooked in discussions of suicide prevention and the issue of paternalism is that, as Margaret Battin puts it, paternalism is a "two-edged sword." That is, paternalism may at times be used to counsel, abet, facilitate, or enforce the choice of suicide. While we shudder at the unjustified paternalism of Jim Jones and the mass suicide at Jonestown in 1978, we are more tolerant of Eleazar's paternalistic call in 73 C.E. for the mass suicide of Jews at Masada to be spared from the Roman soldiers. It seems to be an open question whether paternalism can justify suicide facilitation in cases of debilitating old age, chronic pain, insanity, situations of enforced degradation, etc.

11. Nancy Cruzan was in a persistent vegetative state after a car accident in 1983. Her parents sought to disconnect her feeding tube. The Missouri Supreme Court eventually denied the parental request, citing lack of clear and convincing evidence of Nancy's wishes prior to the accident (and, who now being comatose, was not competent to decide). The United States Supreme Court (in *Cruzan* v. *Director, Missouri Department of Health,* 110 S. Ct. 2841, 1990) took up the case. The Court ruled that a competent patient has the liberty interest to have life-sustaining treatment withdrawn. But Nancy's feeding tube wasn't allowed to be removed. After that famous decision, three of her former coworkers testified that a precomatose Nancy would have wanted her feeding tube to be removed. A Missouri probate judge agreed, and her tube was removed. Nancy died in December 1990. In August 1996, her father committed suicide by hanging.

12. Søren Kierkegaard, *Concluding Unscientific Postscript* (Princeton: Princeton University Press, 1968), p. 147. Like the Stoics, Kierkegaard thinks it is mistaken to speak of suicide as a cowardly act. In fact, he suspects cowardice often masquerades as courage in motivating people to refrain from suicide. And, while Kierkegaard's antisuicide stance is largely motivated by religious considerations (suicide is viewed as a "rebellion" against God), he is rather novel in treating suicide as a "jailbreak" from the prison of existence. Unlike many religious philosophers, Kierkegaard doesn't view suicide as ingratitude against God. To think so is "a lie and rubbish, the swindle which the prison has invented for mutual support in the notion that it is a splendid world" (*Journals and Papers,* #4733). Rather, eternal salvation awaits those who patiently endure their respective premortem, suffering lives. Unlike Kierkegaard, C. G. Prado in *The Last Choice: Preemptive Suicide in Advanced Age* (New York: Greenwood Press, 1990) argues for the rationality of preemptive suicide for "reflective aging" persons who are not yet inflicted with any terminal illness. Prado regards suicide as preferable to the prospects of self-diminishment and finds dignity in the assertion of will and value via self-inflicted death. Prado admits that preemptive suicide for his reflective aging individual (who is at least sixty-five years old) involves choosing self-inflicted death when one has a lot to lose. It involves a refusal to grow old beyond a certain point, after considerable deliberation about chronological age and its ramifications. His somewhat facile comparison of suicide to leaving a party at the right moment before it becomes banal and unenjoyable is unfortunate. Life isn't a party, and Prado gives new meaning to taking the life out of the party.

13. Anyone who may be interested in my own position and arguments against suicide might read *Language, Metaphysics, and Death* (New York: Fordham University Press, 1978), pp. 88-105.

14. John Morreall, *Taking Laughter Seriously* (Albany: State University of New York Press, 1983), p. 129.

PART ONE

Some Historical Background

The Stoic View
Seneca

Life has carried some men with the greatest rapidity to the harbor, the harbor they were bound to reach even if they tarried on the way, while others it has fretted and harassed. To such a life, as you are aware, one should not always cling. For mere living is not a good, but living well. Accordingly, the wise man will live as long as he ought, not as long as he can. He will mark in what place, with whom, and how he is to conduct his existence, and what he is about to do. He always reflects concerning the quality, and not the quantity, of his life. As soon as there are many events in his life that give him trouble and disturb his peace of mind, he sets himself free. And this privilege is his, not only when the crisis is upon him, but as soon as Fortune seems to be playing him false; then he looks about carefully and sees whether he ought, or ought not, to end his life on that account. He holds that it makes no difference to him whether his taking-off be natural or self-inflicted, whether it comes later or earlier. He does not regard it with fear, as if it were a great loss; for no man can lose very much when but a driblet remains. It is not a question of dying earlier or later, but of dying well or ill. And dying well means escape from the danger of living ill.

That is why I regard the words of the well-known Rhodian[1] as most unmanly. This person was thrown into a cage by his tyrant, and fed there like some wild animal. And when a certain man advised him to end his life by fasting, he replied: "A man may hope for anything while he has life." This may be true; but life is not to be purchased at any price. No matter how great or how well-assured certain rewards may be, I shall not strive to attain them at the price of a shameful confession of weakness. Shall I reflect that Fortune has all power over one who lives,

"On the Proper Time to Slip the Cable," reprinted by permission of the publishers and the Loeb Classical Library from Seneca, *Epistulae Morales*, Vol. IV, R. M. Gummere, trans. (Cambridge, Mass.: Harvard University Press, 1917).

rather than reflect that she has no power over one who knows how to die? There are times, nevertheless, when a man, even though certain death impends and he knows that torture is in store for him, will refrain from lending a hand to his own punishment; to himself, however, he would lend a hand.[2] It is folly to die through fear of dying. The executioner is upon you; wait for him. Why anticipate him? Why assume the management of a cruel task that belongs to another? Do you grudge your executioner his privilege, or do you merely relieve him of his task? Socrates might have ended his life by fasting; he might have died by starvation rather than by poison. But instead of this he spent thirty days in prison awaiting death, not with the idea "everything may happen," or "so long an interval has room for many a hope" but in order that he might show himself submissive to the laws and make the last moments of Socrates an edification to his friends. What would have been more foolish than, scorning death, at the same time to be afraid of poison?

Scribonia, a woman of the stern old type, was an aunt of Drusus Libo.[3] This young man was as stupid as he was well born, with higher ambitions than anyone could have been expected to entertain in that epoch, or a man like himself in any epoch at all. When Libo had been carried away ill from the senate-house in his litter, though certainly with a very scanty train of followers—for all his kinsfolk undutifully deserted him, when he was no longer a criminal but a corpse,—he began to consider whether he should commit suicide, or await death. Scribonia said to him: "What pleasure do you find in doing another man's work?" But he did not follow her advice; he laid violent hands upon himself. And he was right, after all; for when a man is doomed to die in two or three days at his enemy's pleasure, he is really "doing another man's work" if he continues to live.

No general statement can be made, therefore, with regard to the question whether, when a power beyond our control threatens us with death, we should anticipate death, or await it. For there are more arguments to pull us in either direction. If one death is accompanied by torture, and the other is simple and easy, why not snatch the latter? Just as I shall select my ship when I am about to go on a voyage, or my house when I propose to take a residence, so I shall choose my death when I am about to depart from life. Moreover, just as a long-drawn-out life does not necessarily mean a better one, so a long-drawn-out death necessarily means a worse one. There is no occasion when the soul should be humored more than at the moment of death. Let the soul depart as it feels itself impelled to go,[4] whether it seeks the sword, or the halter, or some draught that attacks the veins, let it proceed and burst the bonds of its slavery. Every man ought to make his life acceptable to others besides himself, but his death to himself alone. The best form of death is the one we like. Men are foolish who reflect thus: "One person will say that my conduct was not brave enough; another, that I was too headstrong; a third, that a particular kind of death would have betokened more spirit." What you should really reflect is: "I have under consideration a purpose with which the talk of men has no concern!" Your sole aim should be to escape from Fortune as speedily as possible; otherwise, there will be no lack of persons who will think ill of what you have done.

You can find men who have gone so far as to profess wisdom and yet maintain that one should not offer violence to one's own life, and hold it accursed for a man to be the means of his own destruction; we should wait, say they, for the end decreed by nature. But one who says this does not see that he is shutting off the path to freedom. The best thing which eternal law ever ordained was that it allowed to us one entrance into life, but many exits. Must I await the cruelty either of disease or of man, when I can depart through the midst of torture, and shake off my troubles? This is the one reason why we cannot complain of life: it keeps no one against his will. Humanity is well situated, because no man is unhappy except by his own fault. Live, if you so desire; if not, you may return to the place whence you came. You have often been cupped in order to relieve headaches. You have had veins cut for the purpose of reducing your weight. If you would pierce your heart, a gaping wound is not necessary; a lancet will open the way to that great freedom, and tranquillity can be purchased at the cost of a pin-prick.

What, then, is it which makes us lazy and sluggish? None of us reflects that some day he must depart from this house of life; just so old tenants are kept from moving by fondness for a particular place and by custom, even in spite of ill-treatment. Would you be free from the restraint of your body? Live in it as if you were about to leave it. Keep thinking of the fact that some day you will be deprived of this tenure; then you will be more brave against the necessity of departing. But how will a man take thought of his own end, if he craves all things without end? And yet there is nothing so essential for us to consider. For our training in other things is perhaps superfluous. Our souls have been made ready to meet poverty; but our riches have held out. We have armed ourselves to scorn pain; but we have had the good fortune to possess sound and healthy bodies, and so have never been forced to put this virtue to the test. We have taught ourselves to endure bravely the loss of those we love; but Fortune has preserved to us all whom we loved. It is in this one matter only that the day will come which will require us to test our training.

You need not think that none but great men have had the strength to burst the bonds of human servitude; you need not believe that this cannot be done except by a Cato,—Cato, who with his hand dragged forth the spirit which he had not succeeded in freeing by the sword. Nay, men of the meanest lot in life have by a mighty impulse escaped to safety, and when they were not allowed to die at their own convenience, or to suit themselves in their choice of the instruments of death, they have snatched up whatever was lying ready to hand, and by sheer strength have turned objects which were by nature harmless into weapons of their own. For example, there was lately in a training-school for wild-beast gladiators a German, who was making ready for the morning exhibition; he withdrew in order to relieve himself,—the only thing which he was allowed to do in secret and without the presence of a guard. While so engaged, he seized the stick of wood, tipped with a sponge, which was devoted to the vilest uses, and stuffed it, just as it was, down his throat; thus he blocked up his windpipe, and choked the breath from his body. That was truly to insult death! Yes, indeed; it was not a very elegant or becoming way to die; but what is more foolish than to be over-nice about dying?

What a brave fellow! He surely deserved to be allowed to choose his fate! How bravely he would have wielded a sword! With what courage he would have hurled himself into the depths of the sea, or down a precipice! Cut off from resources on every hand, he yet found a way to furnish himself with death, and with a weapon for death. Hence you can understand that nothing but the will need postpone death. Let each man judge the deed of this most zealous fellow as he likes, provided we agree on this point,— that the foulest death is preferable to the cleanest slavery.

Inasmuch as I began with an illustration taken from humble life, I shall keep on with that sort. For men will make greater demands upon themselves, if they see that death can be despised even by the most despised class of men. The Catos, the Scipios, and the others whose names we are wont to hear with admiration, we regard as beyond the sphere of imitation; but I shall now prove to you that the virtue of which I speak is found as frequently in the gladiators' training-school, as among the leaders in a civil war. Lately, a gladiator, who had been sent forth to the morning exhibition, was being conveyed in a cart along with the other prisoners; nodding as if he were heavy with sleep, he let his head fall over so far that it was caught in the spokes; then he kept his body in position long enough to break his neck by the revolution of the wheel. So he made his escape by means of the very wagon which was carrying him to his punishment.

When a man desires to burst forth and take his departure, nothing stands in his way. It is an open space in which Nature guards us. When our plight is such as to permit it, we may look about us for an easy exit. If you have many opportunities ready to hand, by means of which you may liberate yourself, you may make a selection and think over the best way of gaining freedom; but if a chance is hard to find, instead of the best, snatch the next best, even though it be something unheard of, something new. If you do not lack the courage, you will not lack the cleverness to die. See how even the lowest class of slave, when suffering goads him on, is aroused and discovers a way to deceive even the most watchful guards! He is truly great who not only has given himself the order to die, but has also found the means.

I have promised you, however, some more illustrations drawn from the same games. During the second event in a sham sea-fight one of the barbarians sank deep into his own throat a spear which had been given him for use against his foe. "Why, oh why," he said, "have I not long ago escaped from all this torture and all this mockery? Why should I be armed and yet wait for death to come?" This exhibition was all the more striking because of the lesson men learn from it that dying is more honorable than killing.

What, then? If such a spirit is possessed by abandoned and dangerous men, shall it not be possessed also by those who have trained themselves to meet such contingencies by long meditation, and by reason, the mistress of all things? It is reason which teaches us that fate has various ways of approach, but the same end, and that it makes no difference at what point the inevitable event begins. Reason, too, advises us to die, if we may, according to our taste; if this cannot be, she advises us to die according to our ability, and to seize upon whatever means shall offer itself for doing violence to ourselves. It is criminal to "live by robbery"; but, on the other hand, it is most noble to "die by robbery." Farewell.

Notes

1. Telesphorus of Rhodes, threatened by the tyrant Lysimachus.

2. I.e., if he must choose between helping along his punishment by suicide, or helping himself by staying alive under torture and practicing the virtues thus brought into play, he will choose the latter,—*sibi commodare*.

3. For a more complete account of this tragedy see Tacitus, *Annals,* ii 27 ff. Libo was duped by Firmius Catus (C.E. 16) into seeking imperial power, was detected, and finally forced by Tiberius to commit suicide.

4. When the "natural advantages" of living are outweighed by the corresponding disadvantages, the honorable man may, according to the general Stoic view, take his departure. Socrates and Cato were right in so doing, according to Seneca; but he condemns (*Ep.* xxiv. 25) those contemporaries who had recourse to suicide as a mere whim of fashion.

2

The Catholic View
St. Thomas Aquinas

We proceed thus to the Fifth Article:

Objection 1. It would seem lawful for a man to kill himself. For murder is a sin insofar as it is contrary to justice. But no man can do an injustice to himself, as is proved in Ethic. v. 11.[1] Therefore no man sins by killing himself.

Obj. 2. Further, It is lawful, for one who exercises public authority, to kill evildoers. Now he who exercises public authority is sometimes an evildoer. Therefore he may lawfully kill himself.

Obj. 3. Further, It is lawful for a man to suffer spontaneously a lesser danger that he may avoid a greater Thus it is lawful for a man to cut off a decayed limb even from himself, that he may save his whole body. Now sometimes a man, by killing himself, avoids a greater evil, for an example an unhappy life, or the shame of sin. Therefore a man may kill himself.

Obj. 4. Further, Samson killed himself, as related in Judges xvi, and yet he is numbered among the saints (Heb. xi). Therefore it is lawful for a man to kill himself.

Obj. 5. Further, It is related (2 Mach. xiv. 42) that a certain Razias killed himself, *choosing to die nobly rather than to fall into the hands of the wicked, and to suffer abuses unbecoming his noble birth.* Now nothing that is done nobly and bravely is unlawful. Therefore suicide is not unlawful.

On the contrary, Augustine says *(De Civ. Dei i 20): Hence it follows that the words "Thou shalt not kill" refer to the killing of a man, not another man; therefore, not even thyself. For he who kills himself kills nothing else than a man.*

I answer that, It is altogether unlawful to kill oneself, for three reasons. First,

From volume 2 of Thomas Aquinas, "Whether It Is Lawful to Kill Oneself?" *Summa Theologica* (New York: Benziger Brothers, Inc.; London: Burns & Oaks, Ltd., 1925), Part 2, Question 64, A5. Reprinted by permission of the publishers.

because everything naturally loves itself, the result being that everything naturally keeps itself in being, and resists corruption as far as it can. Wherefore suicide is contrary to the inclination of nature, and to charity whereby every man should love himself. Hence suicide is always a mortal sin, as being contrary to the natural law and to charity.

Secondly, because every part, as such, belongs to the whole. Now every man is part of the community, and so, as such, he belongs to the community. Hence by killing himself he injures the community, as the Philosopher declares (*Ethic.* v. ii).

Thirdly, because life is God's gift to man, and is subject to His power, Who kills and makes to live. Hence whoever takes his own life, sins against God, even as he who kiss another's slave, sins against that slave's master, and as he who usurps himself judgment of a matter not entrusted to him. For it belongs to God alone to pronounce sentence of death and life, according to Deut. xxxii. 39, *I will kill and I will make to live.*

Reply Obj. 1. Murder is a sin, not only because it is contrary to justice, but also because it is opposed to charity which a man should have towards himself: in this respect suicide is a sin in relation to oneself. In relation to the community and to God, it is sinful, by reason also of its opposition to justice.

Reply Obj. 2. One who exercises public authority may lawfully put to death an evildoer, since he can pass judgment on him. But no man is judge of himself. Wherefore it is not lawful for one who exercises public authority to put himself to death for any sin whatever: although he may lawfully commit himself to the judgment of others.

Reply Obj. 3. Man is made master of himself through his free-will: wherefore he can lawfully dispose of himself as to those matters which pertain to this life which is ruled by man's free will. But the passage from this life to another and happier one is subject not to man's free-will but to the power of God. Hence it is not lawful for man to take his own life that he may pass to a happier life, nor that he may escape any unhappiness whatsoever of the present life, because the ultimate and most fearsome evil of this life is death, as the Philosopher states (*Ethic.* iii. 6). Therefore to bring death upon oneself in order to escape the other afflictions of this life, is to adopt a greater evil in order to avoid a lesser. In like manner it is unlawful to take one's own life on account of one's having committed a sin, both because by so doing one does oneself a very great injury, by depriving oneself of the time needful for repentance, and because it is not lawful to slay an evildoer except by the sentence of the public authority. Again it is unlawful for a woman to kill herself lest she be violated, because she ought not to commit on herself the very great sin of suicide, to avoid the lesser sin of another. For she commits no sin in being violated by force, provided she does not consent, since *without consent of the mind there is no stain on the body,* as the Blessed Lucy declared. Now it is evident that fornication and adultery are less grievous sins than taking a man's, especially one's own, life; since the latter is most grievous, because one injures oneself, to whom one owes the greatest love. Moreover it is most dangerous since no time is left wherein to expiate it by repentance. Again it is not lawful for anyone to take his own life for fear he should consent to sin, because *evil must not be done that good may come* (Rom. iii. 8) or that evil may be avoided, especially if the evil be of small account and an uncertain event, for it is uncertain whether one will at some future time consent to a sin, since God is able to deliver man from sin under any temptation whatever.

Reply Obj. 4. As Augustine says (*De Civ. Dei* i.21), *not even Samson is to be excused that he crushed himself together with his enemies under the ruins of the house, except the Holy Ghost, Who had wrought many wonders through him, had secretly commanded him to do this.* He assigns the same reason in the case of certain holy women, who at the time of persecution took their own lives, and who are commemorated by the Church.

Reply Obj. 5. It belongs to fortitude that a man does not shrink from being slain by another, for the sake of the good of virtue, and that he may avoid sin. But that a man take his own life in order to avoid penal evils has indeed an appearance of fortitude (for which reasons some, among whom was Razias, have killed themselves, thinking to act from fortitude), yet it is not true fortitude, but rather a weakness of soul unable to bear penal evils, as the Philosopher (*Ethic.* iii. 7) and Augustine (*De Civ. Dei* i. 22, 23) declare.

Note

1. The reference is to Aristotle's *Nicomachean Ethics.*

3

Reason and Superstition
David Hume

One considerable advantage that arises from philosophy, consists in the sovereign antidote which it affords to superstition and false religion. All other remedies against that pestilent distemper are vain, or at least uncertain. Plain good sense, and the practice of the world, which alone serve most purposes of life, are here found ineffectual: history, as well as daily experience, furnish instances of men endowed with the strongest capacity for business and affairs, who have all their lives crouched under slavery to the grossest superstition. Even gaiety and sweetness of temper, which infuse a balm into every other wound, afford no remedy to so virulent a poison, as we may particularly observe of the fair sex, who, though commonly possessed of these rich presents of nature, feel many of their joys blasted by this importunate intruder. But when sound philosophy has once gained possession of the mind, superstition is effectually excluded; and one may fairly affirm, that her triumph over this enemy is more complete than over most of the vices and imperfections incident to human nature. Love or anger, ambition or avarice, have their root in the temper and affections, which the soundest reason is scarce ever able fully to correct; but superstition being founded on false opinion, must immediately vanish when true philosophy has inspired juster sentiments of superior powers. The contest is here more equal between the distemper and the medicine; and nothing can hinder the latter from proving effectual, but its being false and sophisticated.

It will here be superfluous to magnify the merits of Philosophy by displaying the pernicious tendency of that vice of which it cures the human mind. The superstitious man, says Tully,[1] is miserable in every scene, in every incident in life; even sleep itself, which banishes all other cares of unhappy mortals, affords to him

Reprinted from David Hume, "On Suicide," *The Philosophical Works of David Hume* (London: Adam and Charles Black, 1826).

matter of new terror, while he examines his dreams, and finds in those visions of the night prognostications of future calamities. I may add, that though death alone can put a full period to his misery, he dares not fly to this refuge, but still prolongs a miserable existence, from a vain fear lest he offend his Maker, by using the power with which that beneficent being has endowed him. The presents of God and nature are ravished from us by this cruel enemy; and notwithstanding that one step would remove us from the regions of pain and sorrow, her menaces still chain us down to a hated being, which she herself chiefly contributes to render miserable.

It is observed by such as have been reduced by the calamities of life to the necessity of employing this fatal remedy, that if the unseasonable care of their friends deprive them of that species of death which they proposed to themselves, they seldom venture upon any other, or can summon up so much resolution a second time, as to execute their purpose. So great is our horror of death, that when it presents itself under any form besides that to which a man has endeavored to reconcile his imagination, it acquires new terrors, and overcomes his feeble courage; but when the menaces of superstition are joined to this natural timidity, no wonder it quite deprives men of all power over their lives, since even many pleasures and enjoyments, to which we are carried by a strong propensity, are torn from us by this inhuman tyrant. Let us here endeavor to restore men to their native liberty, by examining all the common arguments against suicide, and showing that that action may be free from every imputation of guilt or blame, according to the sentiments of all the ancient philosophers.

If suicide be criminal, it must be a transgression of our duty either to God, our neighbor, or ourselves. To prove that suicide is no transgression of our duty to God, the following considerations may perhaps suffice. In order to govern the material world, the almighty Creator has established general and immutable laws, by which all bodies, from the greatest planet to the smallest particle of matter, are maintained in their proper sphere and function. To govern the animal world, he has endowed all living creatures with bodily and mental powers; with senses, passions, appetites, memory, and judgment, by which they are impelled or regulated in that course of life to which they are destined. These two distinct principles of the material and animal world continually encroach upon each other, and mutually retard or forward each other's operation. The powers of men and of all other animals are restrained and directed by the nature and qualities of the surrounding bodies; and the modifications and actions of these bodies are incessantly altered by the operation of all animals. Man is stopped by rivers in his passage over the surface of the earth; and rivers, when properly directed, lend their force to the motions of machines, which serve to the use of man. But though the provinces of the material and animal powers are not kept entirely separate, there results from thence no discord or disorder in the creation; on the contrary, from the mixture, union, and contrast of all the various powers of inanimate bodies and living creatures, arises that sympathy, harmony, and proportion, which affords the surest argument of Supreme Wisdom. The providence of the Deity appears not immediately in any operation, but governs every thing by those general and immutable laws which have been established from the beginning of time. All events, in one

sense, may be pronounced the action of the Almighty; they all pro[...]
powers with which he has endowed his creatures. A house which fa[...]
weight, is not brought to ruin by his providence, more than one destroy[...]
hands of men; nor are the human faculties less his workmanship than the [...]
motion and gravitation. When the passions play, when the judgment dictates, w[...]
the limbs obey, this is all the operation of God; and upon these animate principles,
as well as upon the inanimate, has he established the government of the universe.
Every event is alike important in the eyes of that infinite Being, who takes in at
one glance the most distant regions of space, and remotest periods of time. There
is no event, however important to us, which he has exempted from the general laws
that govern the universe, or which he has peculiarly reserved for his own immediate action and operation. The revolution of states and empires depends upon
the smallest caprice or passion of single men; and the lives of men are shortened
or extended by the smallest accident of air or diet, sunshine or tempest. Nature
still continues her progress and operation; and if general laws be ever broke by
particular volitions of the Deity, it is after a manner which entirely escapes human
observation. As, on the one hand, the elements and other inanimate parts of the
creation carry on their action without regard to the particular interest and situation of men; so men are entrusted to their own judgment and discretion in the various shocks of matter, and may employ every faculty with which they are
endowed, in order to provide for their ease, happiness, or preservation. What is the
meaning then of that principle, that a man, who, tired of life, and hunted by pain
and misery, bravely overcomes all the natural terrors of death, and makes his
escape from this cruel scene; that such a man, I say, has incurred the indignation
of his Creator, by encroaching on the office of divine providence, and disturbing
the order of the universe? Shall we assert, that the Almighty has reserved to himself, in any peculiar manner, the disposal of the lives of men, and has not submitted that event, in common with others, to the general laws by which the universe is governed? This is plainly false: the lives of men depend upon the same
laws as the lives of all other animals; and these are subjected to the general laws
of matter and motion. The fall of a tower, or the infusion of a poison, will destroy
a man equally with the meanest creature; an inundation sweeps away every thing
without distinction that comes within the reach of its fury. Since therefore the
lives of men are forever dependent on the general laws of matter and motion, is a
man's disposing of his life criminal, because in every case it is criminal to encroach
upon these laws, or disturb their operation? But this seems absurd: all animals are
entrusted to their own prudence and skill for their conduct in the world; and have
full authority, as far as their power extends, to alter all the operations of nature.
Without the exercise of this authority, they could not subsist a moment; every
action, every motion of a man, innovates on the order of some parts of matter, and
diverts from their ordinary course the general laws of motion. Putting together
therefore these conclusions, we find that human life depends upon the general
laws of matter and motion, and that it is no encroachment on the office of Providence to disturb or alter these general laws: has not everyone of consequence the
free disposal of his own life? And may he not lawfully employ that power with

which nature has endowed him? In order to destroy the evidence of this conclusion, we must show a reason why this particular case is excepted. Is it because human life is of such great importance, that it is a presumption for human prudence to dispose of it? But the life of a man is of no greater importance to the universe than that of an oyster: and were it of ever so great importance, the order of human nature has actually submitted it to human prudence, and reduced us to a necessity, in every incident, of determining concerning it.

Were the disposal of human life so much reserved as the peculiar province of the Almighty, that it were an encroachment on his right for men to dispose of their own lives, it would be equally criminal to act for the preservation of life as for its destruction. If I turn aside a stone which is falling upon my head, I disturb the course of nature; and I invade the peculiar province of the Almighty, by lengthening out my life beyond the period, which, by the general laws of matter and motion, he had assigned it.

A hair, a fly, an insect, is able to destroy this mighty being whose life is of such importance. Is it an absurdity to suppose that human prudence may lawfully dispose of what depends on such insignificant causes? It would be no crime in me to divert the Nile or Danube from its course, were I able to effect such purposes. Where then is the crime of turning a few ounces of blood from their natural channel? Do you imagine that I repine at Providence, or curse my creation, because I go out of life, and put a period to a being which, were it to continue, would render me miserable? Far be such sentiments from me. I am only convinced of a matter of fact which you yourself acknowledge possible, that human life may be unhappy; and that my existence, if further prolonged, would become ineligible: but I thank Providence, both for the good which I have already enjoyed, and for the power with which I am endowed of escaping the ills that threaten me.[2] To you it belongs to repine at Providence, who foolishly imagine that you have no such power; and who must still prolong a hated life, though loaded with pain and sickness, with shame and poverty. Do not you teach, that when any ill befalls me, though by the malice of my enemies, I ought to be resigned to Providence; and that the actions of men are the operations of the Almighty, as much as the actions of inanimate beings? When I fall upon my own sword, therefore, I receive my death equally from the hands of the Deity as if it had proceeded from a lion, a precipice, or a fever. The submission which you require to Providence, in every calamity that befalls me, excludes not human skill and industry, if possibly by their means I can avoid or escape the calamity. And why may I not employ one remedy as well as another? If my life be not my own, it were criminal for me to put it in danger, as well as to dispose of it; nor could one man deserve the appellation of *hero*, whom glory or friendship transports into the greatest dangers; and another merit the reproach of wretch or miscreant, who puts a period to his life from the same or like motives. There is no being which possesses any power or faculty, that it receives not from its Creator; nor is there anyone, which by ever so irregular an action, can encroach upon the plan of his providence, or disorder the universe. Its operations are his works equally with that chain of events which it invades; and whichever principle prevails, we may for that very reason conclude it to be most favored by him. Be it animate or inanimate; rational or irrational; it is all the same case: its power is still derived from the Supreme Creator, and is alike comprehended in the order of his providence. When the horror of pain prevails over the love of life; when a voluntary action anticipates the effects of blind causes; it is only in consequence of those powers and principles which he has implanted in his creatures. Divine Providence is still inviolate, and placed far beyond the reach of human injuries.[3] It is impious, says the old Roman superstition, to divert rivers from their course, or invade the prerogatives of nature. It is impious, says the French superstition, to inoculate for the smallpox, or usurp the business of Providence, by voluntarily producing distempers and maladies. It is impious, says the modern European superstition, to put a period to our own life, and thereby rebel against our Creator: and why not impious, say I, to build houses, cultivate the ground, or sail upon the ocean? In all these actions we employ our powers of mind and body to produce some innovation in the course of nature; and in none of them do we any more. They are all of them therefore equally innocent, or equally criminal. *But you are placed by Providence, like a sentinel, in a particular station; and when you desert it without being recalled, you are equally guilty of rebellion against your Almighty Sovereign, and have incurred his displeasure*—I ask, Why do you conclude that Providence has placed me in this station? For my part, I find that I owe my birth to a long chain of causes, of which many depended upon voluntary actions of men. *But Providence guided all these causes, and nothing happens in the universe without its consent and cooperation.* If so, then neither does my death, however voluntary, happen without its consent; and whenever pain or sorrow so far overcome my patience, as to make me tired of life, I may conclude that I am recalled from my station in the clearest and most express terms. It is Providence surely that has placed me at this present moment in this chamber: but may I not leave it when I think proper, without being liable to the imputation of having deserted my post or station? When I shall be dead, the principles of which I am composed will still perform their part in the universe, and will be equally useful in the grand fabric, as when they compose this individual creature. The difference to the whole will be no greater than betwixt my being in a chamber and in the open air. The one change is of more importance to me than the other, but not more so to the universe.

It is a kind of blasphemy to imagine that any created being can disturb the order of the world, or invade the business of Providence? It supposes, that that being possesses powers and faculties which it received not from its Creator, and which are not subordinate to his government and authority. A man may disturb society, no doubt, and thereby incur the displeasure of the Almighty: but the government of the world is placed far beyond his reach and violence. And how does it appear that the Almighty is displeased with those actions that disturb society? By the principles which he has implanted in human nature, and which inspire us with a sentiment of remorse if we ourselves have been guilty of such actions, and with that of blame and disapprobation, if we ever observe them in others. Let us now examine, according to the method proposed, whether Suicide be of this kind of actions, and be a breach of our duty to our *neighbor* and to *society*.

A man who retires from life does no harm to society: he only ceases to do good; which, if it is an injury, is of the lowest kind. All our obligations to do good to society seem to imply something reciprocal. I receive the benefits of society, and therefore ought to promote its interests; but when I withdraw myself altogether from society, can I be bound any longer? But allowing that our obligations to do good were perpetual, they have certainly some bounds; I am not obliged to do a small good to society at the expense of a great harm to myself: why then should I prolong a miserable existence, because of some frivolous advantage which the public may perhaps receive from me? If upon account of age and infirmities, I may lawfully resign any office, and employ my time altogether in fencing against these calamities, and alleviating as much as possible the miseries of my future life; why may I not cut short these miseries at once by an action which is no more prejudicial to society? But suppose that it is no longer in my power to promote the interest of society; suppose that I am a burden to it; suppose that my life hinders some person from being much more useful to society: in such cases, my resignation of life must not only be innocent, but laudable. And most people who lie under any temptation to abandon existence, are in some such situation; those who have health, or power, or authority, have commonly better reason to be in humor with the world.

A man is engaged in a conspiracy for the public interest; is seized upon suspicion; is threatened with the rack; and knows from his own weakness that the secret will be extorted from him: could such a one consult the public interest better than by putting a quick period to a miserable life? This was the case of the famous and brave Strozzi of Florence.[4] Again, suppose a malefactor is justly condemned to a shameful death; can any reason be imagined why he may not anticipate his punishment, and save himself all the anguish of thinking on its dreadful approaches? He invades the business of Providence no more than the magistrate did who ordered his execution; and his voluntary death is equally advantageous to society, by ridding it of a pernicious member.

That Suicide may often be consistent with interest and with our duty to ourselves, no one can question, who allows that age, sickness, or misfortune, may render life a burden, and make it worse even than annihilation. I believe that no man ever threw away life while it was worth keeping. For such is our natural horror of death, that small motives will never be able to reconcile us to it; and though perhaps the situation of a man's health or fortune did not seem to require this remedy; we may at least be assured, that anyone who, without apparent reason, has had recourse to it, was cursed with such an incurable depravity or gloominess of temper as must poison all enjoyment, and render him equally miserable as if he had been loaded with the most grievous misfortunes. If Suicide be supposed a crime, it is only cowardice can impel us to it. If it be no crime, both prudence and courage should engage us to rid ourselves at once of existence when it becomes a burden. It is the only way that we can then be useful to society, by setting an example, which, if imitated, would preserve to everyone his chance for happiness in life and would effectually free him from all danger or misery.[5]

Notes

1. Cicero, *De Divinatione* [II. 149-50.]
2. Agamus Deo gratias, quod nemo in vita teneri potest. Seneca, *Epistles* XII. 10.
3. Tacitus, *Annals* I. 74.
4. [Filippo Strozzi (1488–1538), wealthy Florentine merchant, captured after organizing an abortive revolt against Cosimo de' Medici. He was not strong, and incapable of withstanding torture; one day he was found dead in his cell, lying between two bloodstained swords, with a note that read in part "If I have not hitherto known how to live, I will know how to die." Unfortunately for Hume's argument, it is now believed that Cosimo staged the "suicide" to rid himself of his enemy.]
5. It would be easy to prove that suicide is as lawful under the Christian dispensation as it was to the Heathens. There is not a single text of Scripture which prohibits it. That great and infallible rule of faith and practice which must control all philosophy and human reasoning, has left us in this particular to our natural liberty. Resignation to Providence is indeed recommended in Scripture; but that implies only submission to ills that are unavoidable, not to such as may be remedied by prudence or courage. *Thou shalt not kill*, is evidently meant to exclude only the killing of others, over whose life we have no authority. That this precept, like most of the Scripture precepts, must be modified by reason and common sense, is plain from the practice of magistrates, who punish criminals capitally, notwithstanding the letter of the law. But were the commandment ever to express against suicide, it would now have no authority, for all the law of *Moses* is abolished, except so far as it is established by the law of nature. And we have already endeavored to prove that suicide is not prohibited by that law. In all cases Christians and Heathens are precisely upon the same footing; *Cato* and *Brutus, Arrea* and *Portia* acted heroically; those who now imitate their example ought to receive the same praises from posterity. The power of committing suicide is regarded by *Pliny* as an advantage which men possess even above the Deity himself. "Deus non sibi potest mortem consciscere si veldt, quod homini dedit optimum in tantis vitae poenis." [*Natural History,* II. 5.]

4

Duties towards the Body in Regard to Life

Immanuel Kant

What are our powers of disposal over our life? Have we any authority of disposal over it in any shape or form? How far is it incumbent upon us to take care of it? These are questions which fall to be considered in connection with our duties towards the body in regard to life. We must, however, by way of introduction, make the following observations. If the body were related to life not as a condition but as an accident or circumstance so that we could at will divest ourselves of it; if we could slip out of it and slip into another just as we leave one country for another, then the body would be subject to our free will and we could rightly have the disposal of it. This, however, would not imply that we could similarly dispose of our life, but only of our circumstances, of the movable goods, the furniture of life. In fact, however, our life is entirely conditioned by our body, so that we cannot conceive of a life not mediated by the body and we cannot make use of our freedom except through the body. It is, therefore, obvious that the body constitutes a part of ourselves. If a man destroys his body, and so his life, he does it by the use of his will, which is itself destroyed in the process. But to use the power of a free will for its own destruction is self-contradictory. If freedom is the condition of life it cannot be employed to abolish life and so to destroy and abolish itself. To use life for its own destruction, to use life for producing lifelessness, is self-contradictory. These preliminary remarks are sufficient to show that man cannot rightly have any power of disposal in regard to himself and his life, but only in regard to his circumstances. His body gives man power over his life; were he a spirit he could not destroy his life; life in the absolute has been invested by nature with indestructibility and is an end in itself; hence it follows that man cannot have the power to dispose of his life.

From *Lectures in Ethics*, trans. Louis Infield (New York: Harper & Row, 1963), pp. 147–57. Reprinted by permission of Methuen & Co.

Suicide

Suicide can be regarded in various lights; it might be held to be reprehensible, or permissible, or even heroic. In the first place we have the specious view that suicide can be allowed and tolerated. Its advocates argue thus. So long as he does not violate the proprietary rights of others, man is a free agent. With regard to his body there are various things he can properly do; he can have a boil lanced or a limb amputated, and disregard a scar; he is, in fact, free to do whatever he may consider useful and advisable. If then he comes to the conclusion that the most useful and advisable thing that he can do is to put an end to his life, why should he not be entitled to do so? Why not, if he sees that he can no longer go on living and that he will be ridding himself of misfortune, torment, and disgrace? To be sure he robs himself of a full life, but he escapes once and for all from calamity and misfortune. The argument sounds most plausible. But let us, leaving aside religious considerations, examine the act itself. We may treat our body as we please, provided our motives are those of self-preservation. If, for instance, his foot is a hindrance to life, a man might have it amputated. To preserve his person he has the right of disposal over his body. But in taking his life he does not preserve his person; he disposes of his person and not of its attendant circumstances; he robs himself of his person. This is contrary to the highest duty we have towards ourselves, for it annuls the condition of all other duties; it goes beyond the limits of the use of free will, for this use is possible only through the existence of the Subject.

There is another set of considerations which make suicide seem plausible. A man might find himself so placed that he can continue living only under circumstances which deprive life of all value; in which he can no longer live conformably to virtue and prudence, so that he must from noble motives put an end to his life. The advocates of this view quote in support of it the example of Cato. Cato knew that the entire Roman nation relied upon him in their resistance to Caesar, but he found that he could not prevent himself from falling into Caesar's hands. What was he to do? If he, the champion of freedom, submitted, everyone would say, "If Cato himself submits, what else can we do?" If, on the other hand, he killed himself, his death might spur on the Romans to fight to the bitter end in defense of their freedom. So he killed himself. He thought that it was necessary for him to die. He thought that if he could not go on living as Cato, he could not go on living at all. It must certainly be admitted that in a case such as this, where suicide is a virtue, appearances are in its favor. But this is the only example which has given the world the opportunity of defending suicide. It is the only example of its kind and there has been no similar case since. Lucretia also killed herself, but on grounds of modesty and in a fury of vengeance. It is obviously our duty to preserve our honor, particularly in relation to the opposite sex, for whom it is a merit; but we must endeavor to save our honor only to this extent, that we ought not to surrender it for selfish and lustful purposes. To do what Lucretia did is to adopt a remedy which is not at our disposal; it would have been better had she defended her honor unto death; that would not have been suicide and would have been right; for it is no suicide to risk one's life against one's enemies, and even to sacrifice it, in order to observe one's duties towards oneself.

No one under the sun can bind me to commit suicide; no sovereign can do so. The sovereign can call upon his subjects to fight to the death for their country, and those who fall on the field of battle are not suicides, but the victims of fate. Not only is this not suicide; but the opposite, a faint heart and fear of the death which threatens by the necessity of fate, is no true self-preservation; for he who runs away to save his own life, and leaves his comrades in the lurch, is a coward; but he who defends himself and his fellows even unto death is no suicide, but noble and high-minded; for life is not to be highly regarded for its own sake. I should endeavor to preserve my own life only so far as I am worthy to live. We must draw a distinction between the suicide and the victim of fate. A man who shortens his life by intemperance is guilty of imprudence and indirectly of his own death; but his guilt is not direct; he did not intend to kill himself; his death was not premeditated. For all our offenses are either *culpa* or *dolus*. There is certainly no *dolus* here, but there is *culpa*; and we can say of such a man that he was guilty of his own death, but we cannot say of him that he is a suicide. What constitutes suicide is the intention to destroy oneself. Intemperance and excess which shorten life ought not, therefore, to be called suicide; for if we raise intemperance to the level of suicide, we lower suicide to the level of intemperance. Imprudence, which does not imply a desire to cease to live, must, therefore, be distinguished from the intention to murder oneself. Serious violations of our duty towards ourselves produce an aversion accompanied either by horror or by disgust; suicide is of the horrible kind, *crimina carnis* of the disgusting. We shrink in horror from suicide because all nature seeks its own preservation; an injured tree, a living body, an animal does so; how then could man make of his freedom, which is the acme of life and constitutes its worth, a principle for his own destruction? Nothing more terrible can be imagined; for if man were on every occasion master of his own life, he would be master of the lives of others; and being ready to sacrifice his life at any and every time rather than be captured, he would perpetrate every conceivable crime and vice. We are, therefore, horrified at the very thought of suicide; by it man sinks lower than the beasts; we look upon a suicide as carrion, whilst our sympathy goes forth to the victim of fate.

Those who advocate suicide seek to give the widest interpretation to freedom. There is something flattering in the thought that we can take our own life if we are so minded; and so we find even right-thinking persons defending suicide in this respect. There are many circumstances under which life ought to be sacrificed. If I cannot preserve my life except by violating my duties towards myself, I am bound to sacrifice my life rather than violate these duties. But suicide is in no circumstances permissible. Humanity in one's own person is something inviolable; it is a holy trust; man is master of all else, but he must not lay hands upon himself. A being who existed of his own necessity could not possibly destroy himself; a being whose existence is not necessary must regard life as the condition of everything else, and in the consciousness that life is a trust reposed in him, such a being recoils at the thought of committing a breach of his holy trust by turning his life against himself. Man can only dispose over things; beasts are things in this sense; but man is not a thing, not a beast. If he disposes over himself, he treats his value as that of a beast. He who so behaves, who has no respect for human nature and makes a thing of himself, becomes for everyone an Object of freewill. We are free to treat him as a beast, as a thing, and to use him for our sport as we do a horse or a dog, for he is no longer a human being, he has made a thing of himself, and, having himself discarded his humanity, he cannot expect that others should respect humanity in him. Yet humanity is worthy of esteem. Even when a man is a bad man, humanity in his person is worthy of esteem. Suicide is not abominable and inadmissible because life should be highly prized; were it so, we could each have our own opinion of how highly we should prize it, and the rule of prudence would often indicate suicide as the best means. But the rule of morality does not admit of it under any condition because it degrades human nature below the level of animal nature and so destroys it. Yet there is much in the world far more important than life. To observe morality is far more important. It is better to sacrifice one's life than one's morality. To live is not a necessity; but to live honorably while life lasts is a necessity. We can at all times go on living and doing our duty towards ourselves without having to do violence to ourselves. But he who is prepared to take his own life is no longer worthy to live at all. The pragmatic ground of impulse to live is happiness. Can I then take my own life because I cannot live happily? No! It is not necessary that whilst I live I should live happily; but it is necessary that so long as I live I should live honorably. Misery gives no right to any man to take his own life, for then we should all be entitled to take our lives for lack of pleasure. All our duties towards ourselves would then be directed towards pleasure; but the fulfillment of those duties may demand that we should even sacrifice our life.

Is suicide heroic or cowardly? Sophistication, even though well meant, is not a good thing. It is not good to defend either virtue or vice by splitting hairs. Even right-thinking people declaim against suicide on wrong lines. They say that it is arrant cowardice. But instances of suicide of great heroism exist. We cannot, for example, regard the suicides of Cato and of Atticus as cowardly. Rage, passion, and insanity are the most frequent causes of suicide, and that is why persons who attempt suicide and are saved from it are so terrified at their own act that they do not dare to repeat the attempt. There was a time in Roman and in Greek history when suicide was regarded as honorable, so much so that the Romans forbade their slaves to commit suicide because they did not belong to themselves but to their masters and so were regarded as things, like all other animals. The Stoics said that suicide is the sage's peaceful death; he leaves the world as he might leave a smoky room for another, because it no longer pleases him; he leaves the world, not because he is no longer happy in it, but because he disdains it. It has already been mentioned that man is greatly flattered by the idea that he is free to remove himself from this world, if he so wishes. He may not make use of this freedom, but the thought of possessing it pleases him. It seems even to have a moral aspect, for if man is capable of removing himself from the world at his own will, he need not submit to anyone; he can retain his independence and tell the rudest truths to the cruelest of tyrants. Torture cannot bring him to heel, because he can leave the world at a moment's notice as a free man can leave the country, if and when he wills it. But this semblance of morality vanishes as soon as we see that man's freedom cannot subsist except on a condition which is immutable. The condition is that man may not use his freedom against himself to his own destruction, but that, on the contrary, he should allow nothing external to limit it. Freedom thus conditioned is noble. No chance or misfortune ought to make us afraid to live; we ought to go on living as long as we can do so as human beings and honorably. To bewail one's fate and misfortune is in itself dishonorable. Had Cato faced any torments which Caesar might have inflicted upon him with a resolute mind and remained steadfast, it would have been noble of him; to violate himself was not so. Those who advocate suicide and teach that there is authority for it necessarily do much harm in a republic of free men. Let us imagine a state in which men held as a general opinion that they were entitled to commit suicide, and that there was even merit and honor in so doing. How dreadful everyone would find them. For he who does not respect his life even in principle cannot be restrained from the most dreadful vices; he recks neither king nor torments.

But as soon as we examine suicide from the standpoint of religion we immediately see it in its true light. We have been placed in this world under certain conditions and for specific purposes. But a suicide opposes the purpose of his Creator, he arrives in the other world as one who has deserted his post; he must be looked upon as a rebel against God. So long as we remember the truth that it is God's intention to preserve life, we are bound to regulate our activities in conformity with it. We have no right to offer violence to our nature's powers of self-preservation and to upset the wisdom of her arrangements. This duty is upon us until the time comes when God expressly commands us to leave this life. Human beings are sentinels on earth and may not leave their posts until relieved by another beneficent hand. God is our owner, we are His property, His providence works for our good. A bondman in the care of a beneficent master deserves punishment if he opposes his master's wishes.

But suicide is not inadmissible and abominable because God has forbidden it; God has forbidden it because it is abominable in that it degrades man's inner worth below that of the animal creation. Moral philosophers must, therefore, first and foremost show that suicide is abominable. We find, as a rule, that those who labor for their happiness are more liable to suicide; having tasted the refinements of pleasure, and being deprived of them, they give way to grief, sorrow, and melancholy.

Care for One's Life

We are in duty bound to take care of our life; but in this connection it must be remarked that life, in and for itself, is not the greatest of the gifts entrusted to our keeping and of which we must take care. There are duties which are far greater than life and which can often be fulfilled only by sacrificing life. Observation and experience show that a worthless man values his life more than his person. He who has no inner worth sets greater store by his life; but he who has a greater inner worth places a lesser value upon his life. The latter would sacrifice his life rather than be guilty of a disgraceful action; he values his person more than his life. But a man of no inner worth would act basely rather than sacrifice his life. He certainly preserves his life, but he is no longer worthy to live; he has, in his person, disgraced human nature and its dignity. But is it consistent that the man who places a lesser value upon his life should command a greater value in his person? There is something obscure about this, though the fact is clear enough. Man looks upon life, which consists in the union of the soul with the body, as a contingent thing, and rightly so. The principle of free action in him is of a kind which insists that life, which consists in the union of soul and body, should be held in low esteem. Let us take an example. Assume that a number of persons are innocently accused of treachery, and that whilst some of them are truly honorable, others, although innocent of the particular accusation leveled against them, are contemptible and of no real worth; assume further that they are all sentenced together, and that each of them has to choose between death and penal servitude for life; it is certain that the honorable amongst them would choose death, and the vile ones the galleys. A man of inner worth does not shrink from death; he would die rather than live as an object of contempt, a member of a gang of scoundrels in the galleys; but the worthless man prefers the galleys, almost as if they were his proper place. Thus there exist duties to which life must be subordinated, and in order to fulfill them we must give no countenance to cowardice and fears for our life. Man's cowardice dishonors humanity. It is cowardly to place a high value upon physical life. The man who on every trifling occasion fears for his life makes a laughingstock of himself. We must await death with resolution. That must be of little importance which it is of great importance to despise.

On the other hand we ought not to risk our life and hazard losing it for interested and private purposes. To do so is not only imprudent but base. It would, for instance, be wrong to wager for a large sum of money that we would swim across some great river. There is no material benefit in life so great that we should regard it as a duty to risk our life for it. But circumstances do exist in which men risk their lives from motives of interest. A soldier does so in the wars; but his motives are not of private interest, but of the general good. But seeing that human beings are so constituted that they war against each other, men are to be found who devote themselves to war merely as a profession. How far we should value our life, and how far we may risk it, is a very subtle question. It turns on the following considerations. Humanity in our own person is an object of the highest esteem and is inviolable in us; rather than dishonor it, or allow it to be dishonored, man ought to sacrifice his life; for can he himself hold his manhood in honor if it is to be dishonored by others? If a man cannot preserve his life except by dishonoring his humanity, he ought rather to sacrifice it; it is true that he endangers his animal life but he can feel that, so long as he lived, he lived honorably. How long he lives is of no account; it is not his life that he loses, but only the prolongation of his years, for nature has already decreed that he must die at some time; what matters is that, so long as he lives, man should live honorably and should not disgrace the dignity of humanity; if he can no longer live honorably, he cannot live at all; his moral life is at an end. The moral life is at an end if it is no longer in keeping with the dignity of humanity. Through all the ills and torments of life the path of morality is determined. No matter what torments I have to suffer, I can live morally. I must suffer them all, including the torments of death, rather than commit a disgraceful action. The moment I can no longer live in honor but become unworthy of life by such an action, I can no longer live at all. Thus it is far better to die honored and respected than to prolong one's life for a few years by a disgraceful act and go on living a rogue. If, for instance, a woman cannot preserve her life any longer except by surrendering her person to the will of another, she is bound to give up her life rather than dishonor humanity in her own person, which is what she would be doing in giving herself up as a thing to the will of another.

The preservation of one's life is, therefore, not the highest duty, and men must often give up their lives merely to secure that they shall have lived honorably. There are many instances of this; and although lawyers may argue that to preserve life is the highest duty and that *in casu necessitatis* a man is bound to stand up for his life, yet this is no matter of jurisprudence. Jurisprudence should concern itself only with man's duties to his neighbor, with what is lawful and unlawful, but not with duties towards oneself; it cannot force a man on any occasion to give up his life; for how could it force him? Only by taking his life from him. Of course, lawyers must regard the presentation of life as the highest duty, because the threat of death is their most powerful weapon in examining a man. In any event, there is no *casus necessitatis* except where morality relieves me of the duty to take care of my life. Misery, danger, and torture are no *casus necessitatis* for preserving my life. Necessity cannot cancel morality. If, then, I cannot preserve my life except by disgraceful conduct, virtue relieves me of this duty because a higher duty here comes into play and commands me to sacrifice my life.

5

Attitudes toward Suicide
Joseph Fletcher

Most of us know that anthropologists have found every imaginable attitude toward suicide in both savage and civilized societies. Anthropologists, however, like psychiatrists and sociologists, are able only to provide us with data; in their scientific capacity they cannot jump the gap between what is and what ought to be. To suppose that tabulating moral sentiments described from observation settles an ethical question is what is called the naturalistic fallacy—confusing what is with what ought to be. Whether we ought to be free to end our lives or not is a question of philosophy, of ethics in particular. If a psychiatrist, for example, asserts or implies that people ought not to choose naughtness or oblivionate themselves (to use Herman Melville's neologisms), that scientist is wearing a philosopher's hat. *Ought* is not in the scientific lexicon.

In spite of the defiant immortalists who look forward to resurrection by cryonics or by outwitting cell death biochemically (such as Alan Harrington, who stated, "Death is an imposition on the human race, and no longer acceptable"), we know perfectly well that aging is a fatal disease and we all are its victims. The ethical question is whether we may ever rightly take any rational human initiative in death and dying or are, instead, obliged in conscience to look upon life and death fatalistically, as something that just has to happen to us willy-nilly.

We have pretty well settled the life-control issue with our contraceptive practices and policies; now we must look just as closely at the death-control problem. If we may initiate life, may we not terminate it? Were Ernest Hemingway and his father before him wrong to shoot themselves? Ethically? Psychologically?

Originally published as "In Defense of Suicide," in *Suizid und Euthanasie*, edited by Albin Eser (Stuttgart: Ferdinand Enke Verlag, 1976), pp. 233–44. Reprinted by permission.

The Ethical Question

Speaking as we are from the vantage point of moral philosophy, we must begin with the postulate that no action is intrinsically right or wrong, that nothing is inherently good or evil. Right and wrong, good and evil, desirable and undesirable—all are ethical terms and all are predicates, not properties. The moral "value" of any human act is always contingent, depending on the shape of the action in the situation—*Sitz im Leben* or *Situationsethik*. The variables and factors in each set of circumstances are the determinants of what ought to be done—not prefabricated generalizations or prescriptive rules. Clinical analysis and flexibility are indispensable. No "law" of conduct is always obliging; what we ought to do is whatever maximizes human well-being.

It is essential to grasp the difference between moral values and behavioral norms. Only in this way will we understand why our values are a priori while our actions should be flexibly selective and not legalistic or rule-bound. We might say that our opinions about what is good are subjective and visceral; our judgments about what we ought to do about what we feel is good are more objective and cerebral.

There simply is no way to "prove" our values by logic; they are established by a mixture of conditioning, choice, and commitment. As Ludwig Wittgenstein saw the problem, "This is a terrible business—just terrible. You can at best stammer when you talk of it."

On the other hand, when acting as moral agents, tailoring our deeds to fit our values and ideals, we have to use logic and critical reason, especially when we have to decide which value gets priority in cases of competing values. For example, if truth telling has a high-order value but conflicts with a therapeutic goal, telling the truth might sometimes be the wrong thing to do.

To suppose that we would always be obliged to follow any rule of conduct is only tenable on a metaphysical basis or because of an alleged revelation of eternal absolutes. Such universals are what the Greeks called the *proton pseudon*, the basic error of conventional (that is, unexamined) moralism. Most Christian and many Jewish moralists use starting points of this kind. Without such a supernatural support, however, any attempt to assign intrinsic moral value to anything—truth, chastity, property, health, or even life itself—is an abysmal ethical mistake.

Stepping for a moment into another context, we can clarify the point at stake by quoting a question-and-answer column in a religious magazine: "*Q.* My wife is sterile but wants her 'marital rights.' I have a contagious venereal disease. May I wear a prophylactic sheath? *A.* No. Even though she could not conceive and you would infect her, contraceptive intercourse is an intrinsically evil act." The situation makes no difference. The end sought makes no difference. The good consequences make no difference. Nothing makes any difference. The act itself is wrong. This is the essence of "intrinsic" morality.

The typical moral theologian, for example, whose ethics prohibit suicide as such, would condemn a captured soldier's committing suicide to avoid betraying his comrades under torture—because suicide is held to be an evil act in itself, like Kant's *Ding-an-sich*, a defiance of the will of God. An empirical or clinical ethic, .

being without that kind of dogmatic sanction, would have to agree that suicide can be right sometimes, wrong sometimes.

A slight variant on saying "suicide is not right" is saying "we have no right" to end our lives by choice. People are always mixing human "rights" and right conduct together. In a humanistic ethics, when suicide helps human beings it is right. That is, we have a right to do it. What makes it right is human need. Human rights are not self-validating, not intrinsically valid. It is need that validates rights, not the other way around. When rights are asserted over or cut across human needs, we are faced with a set of superhuman moral principles that often can be callous and cruel contractions of a humane morality.

Some History

William Shakespeare put the ethical question this way: "Then is it sin / To rush into the secret house of death / Ere death dare come to us?" *Antony and Cleopatra* IV, XV:8–82. Cassio, though a good Catholic, thought Othello's suicide was noble. In *Romeo and Juliet* the priest did not condemn the self-conclusion chosen by the young lovers. Shakespeare never expressed the kind of moralistic horror we find in Dante, who put suicides in the Seventh Circle of Hell, lower than murderers and heretics. As a matter of fact, few cultures or traditions have condemned suicide out of whole cloth, indiscriminately.

Suicide poses an ethical issue that is ultimately a matter of values and how we reason about them. The story of what various people have thought and done about suicide does not settle the problem of what is right and good about it. Even so, the pages of history tell us things that help us to put the ethics of elective death in perspective, and we will look at the record in capsule.

Europe, Asia, Africa, America—all tell much the same story. Suicide is seen as absurd and tragic, noble and mean, brave and cowardly, sane and silly; every way of judging it has been taken. Some of the religious and superstitious have condemned it wholesale; others have even praised it. For example, the Koran holds that suicide interferes with kismet, Allah's control of life and destiny, making it therefore much more to be condemned than homicide. Cardinal Richelieu expressed a similar idea. Some cultures, on the other hand, have honored suicides; the American Indians endured genocide at the hands of the Christian conquistadors Cortez and Pizarro even while their Spanish priests were condemning the Indians' selective suicide.

The Japanese honor the rite of seppuku, or hara-kiri, and the Hindus honor suttee. Buddhist monks who used self-immolation to protest Thieu's dictatorship in South Vietnam are another example.

The Buddhist admiration for kamikaze is more complicated ethically because suicidal practices of that order combine killing oneself with killing others. Something like banzai is to be seen in the suicidal commando tactics of Palestinian guerrillas and in the "living bomb" gestures of Viet Cong terrorists. The supposed difference between committing suicide in banzai and volunteering to fly in the

Luftwaffe or the RAF during the Battle of Britain pose an interesting analysis problem—speaking ethically, not psychiatrically.

More primitive peoples often believed that a suicide's soul or ghost would wander around without a resting place, haunting the living. To prevent this, medieval Christians buried a suicide with a stake through the heart and dug the grave at a crossroads instead of in "hallowed" (blessed) ground to keep it from poisoning the soil. The Baganda people used a similar defense strategy, as the storied missionary Livingstone discovered when he stayed among them. The Alabama Indians threw the bodies of suicides into a river; people in Dahomey threw them where they would become carrion. As often as cultural groups made suicide taboo, however, others respected it or even revered it. In North America the Zuni frowned on it, but the Navajo and the Hopi did not; in the Pacific suicide was condemned in the Andaman Islands, but praised in the Fijis.

The Bible never condemned suicide, although in later times the rabbinical Talmud did and the Christian church followed suit. Samson, Saul, Abimilech, Achitophel—their stories are told without censure. The term *suicide* itself only appeared in the seventeenth century. Not until the sixth century was the act proscribed; until that time, in the absence of biblical authority, condemnation of suicide had to be inferred from the sixth of the Ten Commandments, "Thou shalt not kill."

The Greeks were more judicious and therefore more selectively in favor of suicide than the Jews, and so were the Romans. Both the Stoics and the Epicureans approved it in principle. Zeno approved and so did Cleanthes. Seneca actually committed suicide, to forestall the murderous Nero's fun and games, and his wife Paulina joined him. On the other hand, the Pythagoreans, opponents of Hippocratic medicine, having their special knowledge of the god's decrees, opposed suicide because of what Islam later called kismet. (After all, if one "knows" what a transcendental and ultimate will forbids, one would be prudent not to do it.)

Plato allowed euthanasia, as Aristotle did, but in the manner of suicide, not in the manner of "letting a patient go." Homer and Euripides thought well of Jocasta committing suicide after she learned that her new husband Oedipus was her own son—which was, perhaps, an excessive and irrational reaction, but humanly understandable because of the strength of the incest taboo. The Romans, as we all know, allowed the *libertas mori* for a great many reasons; they denied it only to criminals, soldiers, and slaves—for obvious military and economic reasons. Justinian's *Digest* spelled out the subject judiciously.

Christian Europe started moving from pagan Rome's compassionate regard for the dignity of free persons to the savagery of an indiscriminating condemnation of all suicide in the Middle Ages only after the Greco-Roman civilization had been ended by the Barbarian-Teutonic hordes. Once the classical philosophy was buried, the Catholic-medieval synthesis was able to take over, and one of its first major elements was an absolute taboo on suicide. In the manorial system nearly everybody was enfeoffed to somebody else; hence suicide was, in effect, a soldier's or a slave's unlawful escape from somebody's possession. It was fundamentally "subversive" of property rights.

The Christian moralists never put it that way, of course. Instead, they said that human life is a divine monopoly: "Our lives are God's." To take one's own life, therefore, is to invade Jesus Christ's property rights because he has saved us "and we are therefore his." This mystical theology was the bottom layer of the moral and canonical prohibition. It led some theologians to say that Judas Iscariot's suicide in remorse and despair was even more wicked than his earlier betrayal of Jesus and Jesus' consequent crucifixion.

A False Turning Point

St. Augustine marked the turning point in the hardening process. He was the first to make the prohibition absolute. None of the later antisuicide moralists improved on him; even Aquinas added only "It is unnatural," thus buttressing the theology with a religious metaphysics of "natural law."

We can outline Augustine's objections to any and all suicide in four propositions: (1) If we are innocent, we may not kill the innocent; if we are guilty, we may not take justice into our own hands. (2) The sixth commandment of the Decalogue forbids it, *non occides*; suicide is homicide; it is a felony, *felo de se*. (3) Our duty is to bear suffering with fortitude; to escape is to evade our role as soldiers of Christ. (4) Suicide is the worst sin; it precludes repentance; to do it in a state of grace (after one is saved, or cleansed of sin by Christ's blood) means one dies out of grace (unsaved, eternally lost or rejected). Augustine allowed an occasional exception for martyrs who had God's express directive or "guidance" to kill themselves; they were said to be acting as innocently as those who sin *ex ignorantia inculcata* (in invincible ignorance). This is the argument Augustine used to answer the Donatists, a Christian sect that pointed out that dying baptized in a state of grace, by one's own hand, was better than living long enough to fall back into sin, losing one's chance to have eternal life in heaven.

At the end of the Holy Roman hegemony, people began to reason again. By 1561 Thomas More (the "man for all seasons" who died for conscience's sake) had allowed suicide in his *Utopia,* even though Sir Thomas Browne frowned on it in his *Religio Medici* (1642). Montaigne backed More, and so it went. The great classic *coup de grâce* to the moral prohibition of suicide came with David Hume's essay *On Suicide* (1777), in which he reasoned that if suicide is wrong it must be because it offends God, one's neighbor, or one's self, and then showed how this would not always be true. Hume was joined by Voltaire, Rousseau, Montesquieu, and d'Holbach.

The conventional wisdom after nearly a thousand years of prohibition continued unchanged, as attempted suicides were hanged from the public gibbet. In Christian France, as in animist Dahomey, the bodies of the executed were thrown on garbage dumps. The properties of suicides were confiscated in England until 1870, and prison was the legal penalty for attempts until 1961.

At last, in the Suicide Act of 1961, England stopped making it a crime for a person, whether well or ill, to end his life or attempt to do so. There are only a few places left in the world where the courts are still trying to catch up to that kind of moral "sanity." Courts of law today are seldom as unethical about suicide as the conventional moralists continue to be.

Always and everywhere we find cultural variety and difference all along the spectrum of ethical opinion—from blanket prohibition to selective justification. In a very sane and discriminating fashion most communities, both savage and civilized, have believed that disposing of one's own life is like disposing of one's own property, that is, a personal election.

It is on this last ground that most governments in the West have been opposed to suicide. They have followed Aristotle and Plato, who contended pragmatically that except for grave reasons suicide seriously deprived the community of soldiers to defend it and workers to do its labor of head and hand. How weighty this objection is now, in an age of overpopulation, cybernated warfare, and automated industry, is an open question. In any case, the "right" to die is not right if and when it invades the well-being of others. On the other hand, when it is truly and only a personal choice, it is right. To deny this is to deny the integrity of persons, to reduce them to being only functions or appendages of systems of lords and seigneurs, or church and state.

Types of Suicide

Just as facts cannot tell us which things to value (although they may help) or how to rank them as priorities, neither can typologies. This caution applies, for example, to Émile Durkheim's famous classification of suicides into egoistic and altruistic, which is close to what we have come to mean in more recent days by "inner directed" and "other directed"—in the language of Riesman's *Lonely Crowd*.

Strong self-sustaining personalities are able (have the "ego strength") to defy cultural disapproval when or if a balance of prolife and prodeath factors seems to weigh against going on living. As Albert Camus said, "Judging whether life is or is not worth living amounts to answering the fundamental question of philosophy." To drive home his point that philosophy is not merely impersonal abstraction, he added drily, "I have never seen anyone die for the ontological argument." There are times, although we may hope not often, when people find that the flame is no longer worth the candle. History and literature abound with instances.

Similarly, on the altruistic side, there are times when sacrificial love and loyalty may call on us for a tragic decision, to choose death for the sake of a wider good than self. The decision is made pragmatically, to promote the greater good or the lesser evil. An example is Captain Oates in the Antarctic snafu, who eliminated himself to speed up the escape of his companions; other instances are disabled grandparents pushing off on ice floes to relieve hungry Eskimos and brave men staying on the sinking *Titanic* or dropping off from overloaded lifeboats.

Durkheim had a third type of suicides, the anomie—those who suffer anomie, who have come to despair for either subjective reasons (including psychogenic illness) or objective reasons (maybe unemployability or outright social rejection). They reach a point where they cannot "care less." Demoralized, unnerved, disoriented, they throw in their remaining chips. One recalls Jeb Magruder telling the Senate Watergate committee, by way of self-excuse, that he had lost his "ethical compass." Suicide out of anomie or being normless, just as in cases when it is done out of ego strength or for loyalty reasons, may be rationally well-founded and prudent or may not. Suicides of all kinds, in any typology, can be wise or foolish.

This is perhaps the point at which to challenge directly and flatly the widespread assumption that "suicides are sick people, out of their gourds." This canard has lodged itself deeply even in the mental attitudes of physicians. It has managed to become the "conventional wisdom" of psychiatric medicine, partly, no doubt, because psychiatrists deal so much with false suicides whose verbal or nonverbal threats or "attempts" are signals of emotional or mental distress. Nevertheless, for all its persistence, the idea is basically silly.

Like universalized or absolutized moral norms, this one, too, is undiscriminating—a frequent diagnosis turned into a universalized stereotype. Some suicides are suffering from what Freud first called misplaced aggression and later thought to be diseased superego, but not all are. To say all is to be playing with universalized characterizations, and universals of any kind are fantasies, not empirical realities. (The hypocrisy of the courts has done a lot to encourage the dogma that suicides are unhinged.) The fact is that suicide sometimes can be psychiatrically discredited or sometimes can be ethically approved, depending on the case.

Those suicides who tell us about the fears and doubts that go through their minds are the "attempteds," not the successful and thorough ones, and the result is a marked bias or skew to the speculations and theories of therapists. Even more speculative are the ideas of writers who have lively imaginations (Thomas Mann, Boris Pasternak), especially when imagination is combined with a grasp of psychological jargon. Real suicides rarely leave any record and even more rarely explain themselves in any reflective detail; there are only a few exceptions like Arthur Schopenhauer, who thought suicide through but did not do it, and Sylvia Plath, who did. We only have to read Lael Wertenbaker's *Death of a Man* (1957), the story of her husband's noble and sane decision to cheat Big C, to get a more realistic appreciation of what suicide can be.

Suicide Today

In recent years the ethical issue about human initiatives in death and dying has been posed most poignantly for the common run of those in medical care, in the treatment of the terminally ill. Resuscitative techniques now compel them to decide when to stop presenting and supporting life; people no longer just die. What is called negative euthanasia, letting the patient die without any further struggle against it, is a daily event in hospitals. About 200,000 legally unenforceable "living wills" have been recorded, appealing to doctors, families, pastors, and lawyers to stop treatment at some balance point of prolife, prodeath assessment.

What is called positive euthanasia—doing something to shorten or end life deliberately—is the form in which suicide is the question—as a voluntary, direct choice of death.

For a long time the Christian moralists have distinguished between negative or indirectly willed suicide, like not taking a place in one of the *Titanic*'s lifeboats, and positive or directly willed suicide, like jumping out of a lifeboat to make room for a fellow victim of a shipwreck. The moralists mean that we may choose to allow an evil by acts of omission but not to do an evil by acts of commission. The moralists contend that since all suicide is evil we may only "allow" it; we may not "do" it. The moralists do not mean that death is evil, only that dying is evil if it is done freely and directly by personal choice. Choosing to die is self-murder, just as a physician or friend helping you die at your earnest request would be guilty of murder.

Is it not ridiculous, however, to say that given the desirability of escape from this mortal coil or a tragic "crunch" in which one elects to give one's life for another value, all acts of omission to that end are licit, yet all acts of commission to the same end are wrong? Taboo thinking such as "all suicide is wrong" enlists false reasoning and invites inhumane consequences. The end or goal or purpose in both direct (positive) and indirect (negative) euthanasia is precisely the same—the end of the patient's life, release from pointless misery and dehumanizing loss of functions. The logic here is inexorable.

As Kant said, if we will the end we will the means, and if the means required is inordinate or disproportionate we give up the end. The old maxim of some religious thinkers was *finis sanctificat media*. Human acts of any kind, including suicide, depend for their ethical status on the proportion of good between the end sought and the means needed to accomplish it. Only if the means were inappropriate or too costly would the end have to be foregone. It follows that suicide is probably sometimes a fitting act and well worth doing.

How can it be right for a person to go over the cliff's edge helplessly blindfolded, while we stand by doing nothing to prevent it, but wrong if that person removes the blindfold and steps off with eyes open? It is naïve or obtuse to contend that if we choose to die slowly, forlornly, willy-nilly, by a natural disintegration from something like cancer or starvation, we have no complicity in our death and the death is not suicide; but if we deliberately our "quietus make with a bare bodkin," it is suicide. Every person's fight with death is lost before it begins. What makes the struggle worthwhile, therefore, cannot lie in the outcome. It lies in the dignity with which the fight is waged and the way it finds an end.

The summary principle is limpid clear: Not to do anything is a decision to act every bit as much as deciding to do what we would accomplish by "not" acting.

Consideration of suicide for social reasons (Durkheim's altruistic type) can easily lead to a philosophical debate about ethical egoism or self-interest versus social integration and utilitarian concern for the greatest good of the greatest number. Whether we limit our obligation to others to the parameters of enlightened self-interest or, more altruistically, of social solidarism, it still follows that we may be called to suicide for heroic or for sacrificial reasons. The fact that sometimes suicide subjects are unconsciously wanting to die anyway (Menninger, 1938) is psychiatrically important but ethically irrelevant—unless, of course, we slide into the semantic swamp and assert that all who sacrifice their lives—parents, soldiers, police officers, researchers, explorers, or whoever—are sick.

More problematic and subtle than suicide for medical or social reasons are what we may call the personal cases. The ethical principle here is the integrity of persons and respect for their freedom. Sometimes suicides act for profoundly personal, deeply private reasons. Often enough other people, even those close to the suicides, cannot add things up in the same way to justify the election of death. If there is no clear and countervailing injustice involved, however, surely the values of self-determination and liberty weigh in the suicide's favor. Social, physical, esthetic, and mental deficiencies, when combined, could weigh against the worth of a person's life. And who is to be the accountant or assessor if not the one whose death it is?

Conclusion

It appears that a basic issue is whether quality of life is more valuable than life *qua* life. And defense of suicide has to opt for quality, not quantity. The sacralists, those who invest life with a sacred entelechy of some kind, consequently make all direct control over life taboo. (We see this in the abortion debate as well as in the question of suicide.)

This question, whether we may act on a quality-of-life ethic or must go on with the medieval sanctity-of-life ethic, runs through nearly every problem in the field of biomedical policy—genetics, transplants, the determination of death, allocation of scarce treatment resources, management of the dying patient, human experimentation, fetal research, nearly everything.

Quality concern requires us to reorder values; those who promptly and dogmatically put being alive as the first-order value need to reappraise their ethics. One's life is a value to be perceived in relation to other values. At best it is only *primus inter pares*. Without life other things are of no value to us, but by the same token without other things life may be of no value to us. In *The Tyranny of Survival* Daniel Callahan puts it succinctly: "Unlike other animals, human beings are consciously able to kill themselves by suicide; some people choose to die." They want more than "mere survival," he thinks. "Models which work with ants do not work well when extrapolated to human beings."

The reason for this, we can add, is that human beings, unlike purely instinctual creatures, do not regard life as an end in itself. Life, to be up to human standards, has to integrate a number of other values to make it worth our while. Human beings can choose to die not only for reasons of love and loyalty but just because life happens to be too sour or bare. In Sean O'Casey's words, a time may come when laughter is no longer a weapon against evil.

The ethical problem, how to make value choices, comes down, as we have seen, to whether we reason with or without absolutes of right and wrong. Bayet back in 1922 had his own way of putting it in *Le Suicide et la Morale*. He said there are two kinds of approaches: an ethic of a priori rules and taboos or universal prohibitions or, alternatively, a "*morale nuancée*," an ethic rooted in variables and discrimination, that judges acts by their consequences, a posteriori. This essay is built on moral nuances.

Socrates and Karl Jaspers, 2,300 years apart, thought that the business of philosophy is to prepare us for death. Religionists, in their own way, have taken hold of that task; they have coped by a denial maneuver and a counterassertion of eternal life. Philosophers have ignored the problem for the most part. A good start was made with Epictetus' dictum: "When I am, death is not. When death is, I am not. Therefore we can never have anything to do with death. Why fear it?" Or take, in present-day terms, Camus' opening remark in his absurd essay *The Myth of Sisyphus,* that there is "but one truly serious philosophical problem, and that is suicide."

We have a striking paradigm for the ethics of suicide. In his *Notebooks 1914–16* Wittgenstein says that suicide is the "elementary sin"—blandly assuming, in tyro fashion, that survival is the highest good, even though it is individually impossible and corporately improbable that experience will bear this assumption out. Only on that unacknowledged premise was he able to say that "if anything is not allowed then suicide is not allowed." But then his superb mind forced him to ask, in conclusion, "Or is even suicide in itself neither good nor evil?" There, in a phrase, is the whole point ethically. Nothing in itself is either good or evil, neither life nor death. Quality is always extrinsic and contingent.

The full circle is being drawn. In classical times suicide was a tragic option, for human dignity's sake. Then for centuries it was a sin. Then it became a crime. Then a sickness. Soon it will become a choice again. Suicide is the signature of freedom.

6

Medicide:
The Goodness of Planned Death

An Interview with Dr. Jack Kevorkian

In 1990 Jack Kevorkian, M.D., was cleared of first-degree murder, a charge that was brought after he helped an Alzheimer's patient commit suicide. Recently he discussed with Free Inquiry *editor Paul Kurtz his option for the sick or incapacitated for whom life has become unbearable. His book,* Prescription: Medicide—The Goodness of Planned Death, *was published in 1991 by Prometheus Books*

F | REE INQUIRY: Dr. Kevorkian, you've been involved in a number of battles, particularly in the last year, that have received public attention. What is your main interest? What are you trying to get across to the public?

JACK KEVORKIAN: I suppose my main interest is to reinstitute an *ethical* medical practice, which today is more necessary and more needed than ever, to extract from inevitable human death benefit in the form of life-prolonging maneuvers.

FI: Can you amplify what you mean by "extract benefit from death"?

JK: Death under any circumstances is negative—it's a loss of human life. Today we have death that' mandated: There are prisoners and there are termina 'y ill, crippled, or incap.citated people who, for various reasons, kill themselves. To some degree these may be beneficial acts for the individuals, perhaps to their families, or to society in the case of prisoners. But still, all the benefits put together cannot counterbalance the negativity of the loss of a human life.

FI: Is life cherished in itself?

JK: Yes. This is not a matter of divinity or sanctity, but of empirical existence.

FI: Life is good.

JK: That's beyond argument! Whether any specific individual's life is good or

---

From *Free Inquiry* 11 (Fall 1991): 14–18. © *Free Inquiry* magazine. Reprinted by permission.

bad is a matter of judgment; but life itself is a *prerequisite* for existence, for a meaningful existence.

FI: Life becomes a value.

JK: Yes, it's the highest value because everything else depends on life.

FI: What position do you take regarding terminal patients who are dying?

JK: In my view the highest principle in medical ethics—in any kind of ethics—is personal autonomy, self-determination. What counts is what the patient wants and judges to be a benefit or a value in his or her own life. That's primary.

Now, if a patient is suffering from some kind of debilitating condition and says, "I want to end my life. It's no longer worth going on," value is diminishing. The patient should go to a medical person, as this is primarily a medical problem. If the patient wishes he can go to a theologian or a sociologist, but that won't solve the medical problem. It's the medical problem that's causing this shift in values in the patient's own mind, so the patient goes to a doctor.

Now, let's assume the doctor personifies the medical field. The doctor would then have to judge whether the patient's wishes are medically justified. I break this down into five components, of which the patient has two and the doctor three. The patient's components are wish and need: The wish to terminate his or her life, which stems from a need felt because of the suffering.

FI: Does this have to be a reflective or a rational choice?

JK: It should be, it must be, rational. Emotions certainly play a part. Emotions color life. But emotions cannot be the major basis for a decision. Humanity is characterized by one faculty which so-called lower animals don't have—reason. Reason must predominate.

FI: You're talking here about competent adults, of course?

JK: Yes.

FI: What are the three components for the doctor?

JK: The doctor has three tools. One is basic common sense, which is difficult to define, but I think we all know what it is.

FI: Common sense is a kind of reflective, sensible analysis of the patient's situation.

JK: Almost all of humanity would agree on that. For example, if the stove is red hot, don't touch it. Now, a Hindu guru might think differently, touch it, and say it's not hot. But most of humanity would agree that common sense says not to touch the stove.

The second tool that we are supposed to prize so highly is rationality. *Ratiocination* is actually a better word. That would be defined as "clear thinking."

The third tool is the most important—medical expertise. That's why the patient would go to a doctor instead of a theologian. Almost all doctors have the medical expertise. Unfortunately, fewer have common sense and rationality, and this is a problem.

If the doctor has common sense and uses ratiocination and his medical expertise, he can evaluate every nuance of the medical problem and decide whether the patient's desire to end his or her life is justified. No other professional can do this, and that's what takes this out of the realm of bioethics as espoused by nonphysicians who are medically ignorant and, therefore, ignorant of the foundation of this whole system.

FI: So in your system the patient makes the choice. The doctor merely analyzes the situation and provides the means for the patient to terminate his or her life.

JK: Yes. As an analogy, let's say a patient goes to a doctor-surgeon and says, "Doctor, I want my appendix out." The patient has a desire. The doctor can't affect the desire, but he can determine the need. So the surgeon would say, "Oh really?" and then do a history, a physical, and laboratory tests to determine whether there is a valid need.

FI: The title of your new book is *Prescription: Medicide—The Goodness of Planned Death*. What does "planned death" involve?

JK: Planned death is a rational system that honors self-determination and extracts from a purposeful, unavoidable death the maximum benefit for the subject, the subject's next of kin, and for all of humanity. In other words, planned death is a system for making death, euthanasia, and suicide positive instead of negative.

FI: And one positive benefit is that the patient will not suffer agonizing pain and torment.

JK: That's a minor benefit. That the family will suffer less psychological pain and loss of assets is also minor, as well as that society will be spared the waste of some resources. Three minor benefits do not counter-balance the loss of a human life. But if the patient opts for euthanasia, or if someone is to be executed, and at the same time opts to donate organs, he or she can save anywhere from five to ten lives. Now the death becomes definitely, incalculably positive. The patient may opt to undergo experimentation under anesthesia, from which he or she won't awaken. This could affect millions of lives now and in the future. If the person wants only to donate organs, that's fine. The ultimate value is autonomy.

So the patient would have several choices, which don't exist now, besides just wanting to be put to death. The patient can say, "Fine, I just want to be put to death." That's option one. Or the patient can say: "I want to have organs taken out under anesthesia from which I won't awaken." That's option two. Or the patient can say, "You can experiment on me, under anesthesia from which I won't awaken." That's option three. And there are yet more options under number three, such as the option to choose the experiment.

FI: What kinds of experiments are you talking about?

JK: Any kind. Whatever the patient wants. For example, if the patient is dying of Lou Gehrig's disease, he can stipulate that the experiment must deal with that affliction. The doctor and the researchers would be bound by that wish. Another suboption would be to allow the doctor to do any experiment he or she wants.

FI: Wouldn't there be fear that the patient would suffer pain and torment if experimentation is allowed on his body while he or she is still alive?

JK: Well, the patient would be under anesthesia. Anyone who's had a major operation knows that the patient would be unaware of any pain or discomfort.

FI: What guarantee would the patient have that he or she would not suffer in this situation?

JK: The patient would be under constantly controlled anesthesia. The procedure would not be done privately or secretly. There would be witnesses: the patient's attorney, or the patient's family members if they wish to be there, the patient's minister or priest or rabbi, and one or two other authorities.

FI: Let's talk about execution. Are you opposed to capital punishment?

JK: Publicly I have to say I'm neutral because I don't want to be accused of fostering a pro or con viewpoint. I only say that where capital punishment exists the options of organ donation or experimentation should be granted. That would mean that prisoners would be executed under anesthesia. No hangings, no firing squads, no lethal injections. They would be put under routine general anesthesia in a hospital-like setting.

FI: Do you think this is a more humane method of execution?

JK: Anybody who's had an operation under anesthesia would say that. There's also, of course, the benefit that death would occur in a clean, clinical atmosphere rather than in a prison execution chamber.

FI: What happens if a prisoner does not want to donate any organs?

JK: Fine! That's his wish. He or she would then be executed the way the law stipulates. But I think prisoners sentenced to death should be executed under anesthesia. If they don't opt for experimentation or organ donation, just put them under and don't let them wake up.

FI: In terms of your medical ethics, from the standpoint of the individual there is a reflective choice and therefore there ought to be active euthanasia. But you go beyond that and say there's a possibility to make an ultimate altruistic moral decision. Yes, the patient wants to die to lessen his suffering, but he also wants to help others by donating organs.

JK: The system I'm proposing gives maximum respect for self-determination, by granting the person not only the wish to die in a humane, dignified way, but also by allowing organ transplant or experimentation options. *The person can decide exactly what value his or her death will have.* This has nothing to do with altruism.

FI: It's self-determination as well as a compassionate regard for others by donating organs to be used for the good of humankind. That's altruism.

JK: But altruism may not be the motivation. Many prisoners will say, "I don't want an empty death. It's empty to die for nothing."

FI: That isn't altruistic?

JK: It is implied, but it's an indirect altruism and more a matter of simple egoism. But at least it's ultimate respect for self-determination because, as it is now, none of us—you and I included—has the option of determining exactly what value our deaths will have.

A donor might comfort himself by thinking that a part of himself lives on in others. His heart, his lungs, his liver, they're going on. That make some people feel good. That may not be altruism, but it has value for the person—even if it is also self-serving.

FI: Let us focus on euthanasia. There is passive euthanasia, in which people are not kept alive by the use of extraordinary methods, and . . .

JK: That's not euthanasia. "Passive euthanasia" is a misnomer. "Passive euthanasia" is just natural death. Euthanasia means "good death." "Passive euthanasia" is a brutal death. Allowing someone to starve to death and to die of thirst, the way we do now, is barbaric. Our Supreme Court has validated barbarism. The Nazis did that in the concentration camps.

FI: So, not leaving the respirator on, pulling the plug—that's not a good death?

JK: Gasping, for air? Starving and thirsting to death? Like Nancy Cruzan? It took her a week to die. Try it! You think that just because you're in a coma you don't suffer?

FI: Let's go on to active euthanasia.

JK: Drop the word *active*. Euthanasia by definition has to be active, otherwise it's assisted suicide.

FI: Let's take the case of giving increasing dosages of morphine.

JK: That's euthanasia. When the doctor gives the pills or "shots," he or she's the agent of death.

FI: So euthanasia is the hastening of the process of death.

JK: That's right—but mercifully.

FI: Now, you go beyond that. You advocate assisted suicide and have constructed a "suicide machine."

JK: We call it the "mercitron."

FI: What's the difference between the mercitron and active euthanasia?

JK: It's like giving someone a loaded gun. The patient pulls the trigger, not the doctor.

If the doctor sets up the needle and syringe but lets the patient push the plunger, that's assisted suicide. If the doctor pushed the plunger it would be euthanasia.

FI: In your view assisted suicide is a higher ethical act of self-determination than euthanasia?

JK: Yes. It's more ethical and less vulnerable to censure because the patient himself is more directly involved. The only one actually committing the act is the patient. That's why assisted suicide, where possible, is always preferable to euthanasia. That's the way executions should be carried out, an idea that has been suggested by four condemned prisoners I've had contact with.

FI: What do you mean by the term *medicide*?

JK: Medicide is euthanasia performed by a professional medical person—a doctor, nurse, technician, paramedic, or nurse anesthetist, for example. Euthanasia is humane, merciful death, performed by anybody. When the patient allows organ transplants or experimentation, it's called "obitiatry." Obitiatry is medicide from which the actual medical benefit is extracted for other human beings.

FI: There are people who are worried about abuse. How do you address this possibility?

JK: Anything can be abused. Name something that hasn't been abused. The office of the presidency was abused. Everyone could foresee that it would be. Why was it created? Because there was a need for it. You don't put a halt to a project of immense potential good just because you envision abuse. You try to control it.

FI: There is the slippery slope argument, that once euthanasia is legalized, someone may try to kill Aunt Millie for her estate. How do you prevent that from happening?

JK: Well, you need to have honest, competent people in charge. They could be difficult to find.

FI: Shouldn't two doctors rather than one make the decision?

JK: Yes.

FI: Should a court order be required?

JK: No! Keep the courts out of the decision-making. Medicine should be *absolutely separate* from the law, politics, religion, and the judiciary.

An entirely new medical specialty should be created to deal with this subject. These new medical specialists would consult with each other and with other doctors. There would be a five-member group of these specialists in every locality, each divided into two sections: a decisions section and an implementation section. The members would rotate between these two sections.

Let's say that one year three of the five members are in the decision group, and the other two are in the implementation group. Only the decision group votes, while doctors from the implementation group must carry out the medicide. One of those two group members can veto the decision. The case goes back to the decision group for review of the objections. The next decision must be agreed upon by all members of the group.

In the meantime, the patient fills out a questionnaire, in part to identify his or her religion. Then the patient's minister, priest, or rabbi would be called in to talk to the patient and to fill out a consultation sheet, which would be sent to specialists. The patient would then be confronted with whatever was said concerning religion. Of course, if the patient checks "Atheist," calling in a religious counselor would be out of the question.

Let's say the patient is confronted by a religious counselor who says, "This is against God's law." If the patient then says, "I don't care. I still want to die," and signs a document to that effect, then the medical specialists would be covered pretty well. Different professionals would be called in to address the different implications of the patient's decision.

FI: You want safeguards, not a decision by merely one physician.

JK: The decision should be based not only on medicine, but on extraneous consultations that the physician must evaluate. But the doctors have to make the final decision because this is a *medical problem*.

FI: Isn't there something like medicide in The Netherlands?

JK: Yes, but there, I think, two doctors have to make the decision. Unfortunately, they have to be a little hypocritical because there it is technically illegal.

FI: What about the hospice movement? People choose it because they want to die with dignity and less pain.

JK: If a person in a hospice says, "I don't want to live anymore with all this pain," the doctor who runs that hospice is obligated by ethics to consult a euthanasia specialist. If the person is adamant about dying, then, by all rights, his or her wish should be granted, if it's medically justified.

FI: You're talking about cases of terminal illness?

JK: Not necessarily terminal. The patient could be incapacitated by paralysis, stroke, emphysema, or severe arthritis.

FI: What happens with someone who has been severely handicapped in an accident and doesn't want to live?

JK: It depends on how badly he or she has been handicapped. That has to be evaluated. There has to be discussion with the family members. The decision may be difficult, but the ultimate deciding factor is the person's wish.

If a patient's desire to end his or her life seems medically unjustified, the case can be periodically reviewed.

Contrary to what people think, by doing this the incidence of suicides will drop drastically. Today, as you know, people kill themselves mainly out of panic, especially the elderly who are well but who are afraid of becoming incapacitated.

Assume you're going into a dark, unknown cave. That's what death is, no matter what your religion. You take a little step at a time, always fearful. And what develops the deeper you go in? Panic. Because you see the light disappearing.

But what if I tie a big rope around a rock, give you one end, and say, "Go in there now and explore the cave and just keep hanging onto this rope." You will have much less panic, because you know that if you come to the point where you don't care to explore anymore, you just pull yourself out by the rope. This is the "rope" that will reduce the incidence of suicide.

FI: What about the case of Janet Adkins in Michigan? She requested medicide when she was faced with Alzheimer's disease. Some doctors have said that she could have lived longer, that she could have lived a significant life.

JK: Her doctor, on the phone, told me she could have lived mentally competent another year. But in court he said three years. I interviewed Janet Adkins in person for twelve straight hours. I agreed with the diagnosis of Alzheimer's. I knew she would be mentally incompetent within four to six months, maybe even three months. She was fading fast. Her memory had gone, but she was rational. She was extremely intelligent and very talented, but her talents had disappeared with the loss of her memory. She was a strong-willed woman who made up her mind to commit suicide the day the doctor told her she had Alzheimer's.

FI: Her family supported her?

JK: They respected her wish, but they didn't want to see her die.

FI: Should you have waited longer?

JK: If possible, I would have visited her frequently, at first every month, then every week, then every day, to fine tune the point at which I knew she was going to be irrational. That would have extracted the maximum cognitive life. But irrational laws forced me into a slightly premature action.

She was terribly distraught. She was going to kill herself. She had a gun. She had pills stored up. She was going to jump off a building. She was going to walk into the ocean. My option was the way she wanted to go, and she went 2,000 miles away from home, from Oregon to Michigan, to get it. And there are other patients who feel the same. It's time to legalize this.

FI: How does the mercitron work? She pressed a button?

JK: Yes, I started the intravenous dripper, which released a salt solution through a needle into her vein, and I kept her arm tied down so she wouldn't jerk it. This was difficult as her veins were very fragile. And then once she decided she was ready to go, she just hit the switch and the device cut off the saline drip and through the same needle released a solution of thiopental that put her to sleep in ten to fifteen seconds. A minute later, through the same needle flowed a lethal solution of potassium chloride.

FI: She died without any pain?

JK: Yes.

FI: The family was not there with her?

JK: No, she didn't want her family there, because they were very sensitive people, and she didn't want them to observe her death. On the other hand, I'll say that if this were legal and could have been done in her home, I think her family would have been there. I think part of the reason that she didn't want her family there was because this was illegal in Oregon.

FI: So she came into Michigan where you live, and then, once the courts found out about this, you were prosecuted or charged with a crime?

JK: Not at first. Actually, there was no law in Michigan that I had violated. They charged me about six months after the act, and one rational judge threw it out, saying that I had not violated any law, that this was a case of suicide, plain and simple. They were basing their argument on a Michigan case of 1920. Another judge imposed an injunction on me, hoping to stop me from exercising further actions. I won't be stopped. I consider the injunction invalid, first, because it's immoral, and second, because, according to my attorney, it was illegally imposed. I am appealing it now in a county circuit court.

FI: Do you consider your actions to be within an ethical framework and based upon high, humanistic morality?

JK: Yes. After all, what is morality? It is doing and thinking right. And that changes with time. So in rule ethics versus situation ethics, I go by situation ethics. You try to solve the situation *at that time*. You can't use some idea two thousand years old!

FI: Your ethics is based upon the principle of self-determination. Where a person decides to bequeath his or her organs, or opts for experimentation, this is a concern for the good of others.

JK: And experimentation, sometimes, is the only option available, say if the person is too old to donate organs, or if he or she has AIDS or cancer. Why not grant it? Let him or her choose the value that is going to be put on his or her death.

FI: You say there's no such thing as the right to die? What do you mean by that?

JK: How can there be a right to die? You don't have a right to live or die. You're going to die. It's mandated by nature. It's a natural axiom. All you have is the right to choose when, how, and where. The phrase "right to die" shows how muddy our thinking is. Precision of language measures precision of thought.

FI: Have you studied philosophy?

JK: Not formally. I'm only honest.

FI: Do you find that many people in the medical professions support what you do?

JK: Yes. Judging from the polls, I would guess that almost half the practicing doctors support medicide, but not the authorities or the American Medical Association.

FI: What about the general public?

JK: Overwhelming support. I would estimate three to one persons are in favor of it. In a poll in the June 1991 issue of *Longevity* magazine the result was 86 to 11 percent in support.

There were five questions asked in the survey, and the first three are relevant: The first one: "Do you think it's correct to allow a terminally ill or suffering patient to be assisted in suicide?" Eighty-six percent said yes. The second question was, "Do you think that this should be allowed even if the patient has a long time to live yet and is not in pain?" Fifty-six percent were in favor. That describes the Adkins case. The third question concerned whether I should be prosecuted for the Adkins case. I think nearly 92 percent said no.

There is a wild adventure ahead of us. We consider ourselves to be the leading nation in the world. Philosophically we're rather benighted.

FI: Do you think there ought to be a law legalizing euthanasia and assisted suicide?

JK: There should simply be a law stating that these are *medical problems.* The laws don't say how we should perform a gallbladder operation. A doctor has to act competently and honestly, and if he doesn't, he is prosecuted. In cases of medicide and assisted suicide, the doctors should call upon consultants and together with them cover every aspect of each case.

But it is the doctors in consultation with the patient who should make the final decisions concerning medicide and assisted suicide. This should be the case, as it is with every medical specialty.

7

Love and Death
Celeste Fremon

In his final interview, just months before his suicide,
Bruno Bettelheim explained why he wanted to die

"T he problem is finding a reason to live."

The man talking was Bruno Bettelheim, legendary psychoanalyst and child psychologist. He was seated in his favorite chair, a 1960s vintage Danish Modern, in the living room of his fifth-floor Santa Monica condominium. The Pacific Ocean glittered blue and white through the floor-to-ceiling glass doors behind him. He was eighty-six years old, and although his mind was quicker than that of most thirty-year-olds, his body was failing. When he conducted his guest to a chair, his gait was shuffling and labored, his shoulders permanently hunched. As he talked, the movements of his right hand—his writing hand—were jerky, inaccurate and obviously not completely within his conscious control.

Although the calendar read late October, it was one of those flawless, forever-summer Southern California days—a disturbing contrast to the conversation at hand: Bruno Bettelheim was talking about whether or not he would kill himself.

For a moment his gaze traveled around the room, which was filled with a life-time's treasures: Greek and pre-Columbian artifacts from various trips abroad, a wall full of art books and operatic recordings, Rembrandt etchings and, centered over the couch, an eerily beautiful painting of a woman walking down the side of a building, titled "The Dreamer."

"Things I enjoyed are no longer available to me, you know," he said. "I like to walk. I like to hike. Now when I read, I get tired. Dickens wrote: 'It was the best of all times. It was the worst of all times.' It all depends on how you look at it. At my age you can no longer look at it and say, 'It is the best of all times.' At least, I find it impossible."

He paused. "However, if I could be sure that I would not be in pain or be a

From the *Los Angeles Times Magazine*, January 27, 1991, pp. 17–21, 35. Copyright 1991, *Los Angeles Times*. Reprinted by permission.

vegetable, then, like most everyone, I believe I would prefer to live." And then he smiled. "But, of course," he said, "there is no such guarantee. This is why the decision is so problematic."

That was October 1989. On March 13, 1990, Bruno Bettelheim was found dead on the floor of his new apartment in a Maryland nursing home, a plastic bag over his head and barbiturates in his bloodstream.

The news of his death stunned the psychological community. For fifty years, Bruno Bettelheim had been acknowledged as one of the most important thinkers and practitioners in the field of psychology and child development. If he had a genius, it was his uncanny ability to find healing and hope in circumstances in which others could see only despair. He used his own horrific experiences as a prisoner of the Nazis in Dachau and Buchenwald to draw conclusions about the nature of human suffering that would help him heal the psychic wounds of others. As director of the Orthogenic School in Chicago, he successfully treated children who were so emotionally withdrawn they had been written off as incurable. He wrote dozens of influential essays and books, among them the 1976 National Book Award winner *The Uses of Enchantment,* which explored how fairy tales help children wrestle with their most troublesome problems and fears.

"Bettelheim would often use what he called 'The Man in the White Coat Theory,'" says Roger Pittman, a Los Angeles therapist who worked with Bettelheim in a case-study group as late as January, 1989. "He said that in addition to honesty there has to be a quality of 'The Man in the White Coat' in your professional presentation—the image of the magical ability to heal. Well, certainly 'The Man in the White Coat' doesn't kill himself.

"In the therapeutic profession, when a client kills himself, it's the most conspicuous failure you can have. When Bettelheim killed himself it was as if the profession itself had failed."

"It's devastating when anyone who is in a therapeutic role takes an action that is on the surface so despairing," says an editor who worked with Bettelheim. "But it was 100 times worse because he was someone who saved so many people from despair."

Why had Bruno Bettelheim, of all people, engineered his own death?

I discovered at least part of the answer by accident. Early in the fall of 1989, Bettelheim agreed to be interviewed on aspects of his life story that had never made their way into his published work: his marriage, his own analysis, his friendships with Wilhelm Reich and other notables of the century.

From the first interview, though Bettelheim was his usual articulate self on subjects from Reich ("Few people were as stubborn as he was") to his favorite fairy tale ("Hansel and Gretel," "because the boy and the girl needed each other"), he seemed preoccupied. It was as if asking him to talk about his life and ideas was equivalent to asking him to look through a scrapbook from a now-inconsequential journey. Finally frustrated by his disinterest, I asked him abruptly: "Are you afraid of dying?"

Suddenly I had his attention.

"No," he said. "I fear suffering. The older one gets, the greater the likelihood that one will be kept alive without purpose."

I asked him to elaborate, and he dodged the question. Seeing that he was growing tired, I turned off the tape recorder and prepared to leave, when Bettelheim unexpectedly turned to me. "There is something you should know," he said. "I am planning to take a trip to Europe from which I may or may not come back." His intention, he said, was to meet with a doctor in Holland, an old friend of his, who was willing to give him a lethal, and in Holland a perfectly legal, injection.

In all, Bettelheim sat for some six hours of interviews on three separate occasions; at least half the time he spoke of death and dying. At times, he seemed to be explaining a decision he had already made; at other times it was clear he was still considering the pros and cons of choosing to die. But he came back, again and again, to certain inalterable facts—what he called the "ravages of age"—the death of his wife and the very fearful prospects of extreme disability and incapacity.

"If I can make it until my friend can see me in Holland," he told me that first afternoon, "I will be safe."

He could see the dismay in my face.

"The thing that is so frightening," he continued patiently, "is that I could have a stroke the next minute. I've had two strokes already. Most of the arteries to my brain are blocked. Right now, I'm living on borrowed time."

When the news of Bettelheim's suicide became public, there was a general attempt to quickly wrap up the reasons for his action in a tidy little package. Friends and colleagues were quoted in the media speaking about Bettelheim's depression and his recent estrangement from his eldest daughter. There was talk of diminished mental capacity. The implication was the one easiest for everyone to accept when the taboo of suicide is broken: Bettelheim had apparently gone a bit round the bend

But I think that nothing could have been further from the truth. That October, it was clear that he had squarely faced the multiplicity of issues brought on by old age and confronted the question: To be or not to be? Rationally, analytically, he was considering how to answer. He defined, it seems to me now, exactly what is meant by the phrase "sound mind."

In the two weeks after we first met, Bettelheim's dilemma was constantly in my thoughts. I had to fight the illogical and unjournalistic urge to bring him a dozen brightly colored balloons in the childish hope of cheering him up. When we sat down for our second interview, I asked him if he was still planning a trip to Holland, hoping that he had reconsidered.

"Let me answer," he said, "by telling you a story of a really close friend of mine who was fifteen years older than I and a cavalry officer in the Austrian army. A very elegant man, he was engaged to an heiress. Then came the collapse of the Austrian monarchy. This dashing imperial officer became an average private citizen, and the heiress lost interest in him. He was heartbroken. But, being an officer, he knew what to do. He dressed himself up in civilian clothing, rented a room in the best hotel in Vienna and put a bullet into his heart.

"The noise of the shot reverberated in the hotel and the maid rushed in. When she saw what had happened, she said, 'Oh, my God! Your beautiful shirt all ruined!' then he lost consciousness. When he came to again, he thought, 'If my effort to kill myself has this kind of a reaction, then I might as well live.'"

Bettelheim smiled. "And he continued to live with a bullet in his heart for another twenty-five or thirty years. He made his peace. He became a director of an iron foundry, then one day dropped dead of a heart attack.

"So, there you are. One might find life unbearable at a certain moment and, in an act of desperation, try to end it. Then it actually turns out that one is quite successful at continuing to live and enjoying life for many more years. As long as one has the energy and the strength, one should go on living.

"But," he added, "my friend was a young man. I am not." He took a sip of water and said, "Sidney Hook wrote about the problem of old men who are thoughtful and sensitive, and their difficulty in finding reasons to go on living. For many people their reason to live is watching their grandchildren grow up. For me this is not the case. I have watched so many children grow up, that is not so much of an issue."

Bettelheim said he looked at death and suicide from the point of view of an "intellectual rationalist." He was not, he said, a religious person, so those issues did not affect his thinking. "For me, death is the end of the road," he said. "That's it."

He mentioned, almost in passing, that the German language afforded a distinction between two kinds of suicide. "It is interesting," he said, "that in English you have no other word than *suicide*. But in German there's another word, *freitod*, which means a free, willed death. And there are tribal societies in which at a certain moment one goes up in the mountains and lies down and dies. Theirs is certainly a more civilized way."

If Bettelheim had any hero, it was Sigmund Freud. I wondered if the fact that Freud, during the latter stages of cancer, chose to have a lethal injection administered to him had influenced his thinking.

"Well," Bettelheim said, "it's obvious he felt that he really couldn't go on with his life and still write and be productive and so on. He wanted to die with his boots on, with his mind unimpaired by his sickness and old age. I think that it was a rational decision. And well-taken."

"What keeps you from choosing your death now?" I asked.

"Nothing."

"But here you are, still alive, still vibrant, still able to enlighten others, still full of ideas."

There was a long pause. "Yes," he said. "At great risk to myself."

Bruno Bettelheim was born in Vienna in 1903 to wealthy Jewish parents. As a teenager he became fascinated with the radical new field of psychoanalysis and its founder, Sigmund Freud; while earning his doctorate in psychology at the University of Vienna, he studied under his idol. It was Freud's daughter, Anna, who encouraged Bettelheim to work with autistic children, suggesting in the early 1930s that he bring a supposedly incurable autistic girl into his home, where the child improved.

His work was interrupted in March 1938, when Hitler invaded Austria. The Nazis confiscated Bettelheim's writings, and he and other Jews were loaded onto a train for Dachau. Months later he was transferred to Buchenwald. Only the intervention of Eleanor Roosevelt saved him; having heard of his work with disturbed children, she had him plucked out of the camps in April 1939, and brought, with his wife, Gertrud, to the United States.

Penniless on his arrival, Bettelheim was asked to resume his work at the University of Chicago. He accepted, and he and Gertrud moved to the city where they would raise their two daughters and son.

In 1944, he was appointed director of the university's Sonia Shankman Orthogenic School for emotionally disturbed children. Bettelheim had by then fashioned a theory of healing based on his experiences in the camps. If the dehumanizing treatment that the prisoners were subjected to resulted in personality disintegration, he reasoned, shouldn't the reverse be true? He transformed the traditional mental institution: Locks were taken off the outside of doors and reinstalled on the inside, meaning that visitors needed permission to enter but the children could leave at will. Plastic dishes and knifeless place settings were replaced by bone china and full sets of silver. Bars were removed from the windows. Art was commissioned for the walls.

The strategy was successful. According to Bettelheim and his counselors, in Bettelheim's thirty years at the Orthogenic School, more than 85 percent of the "hopeless" patients treated returned to active participation in the outside world.

In 1973, at age 70, Bettelheim retired from the Orthogenic School and moved with Gertrud to Palo Alto. He continued to lecture and write. Through *The Uses of Enchantment* and another bestseller, *A Good Enough Parent*, he gained a widely popular following and even wrote a parenting column in *Ladies' Home Journal*.

"He was that very rare animal, a public intellectual," says Los Angeles psychoanalyst David James Fisher. "His writing could be read by both the literate public and by specialists."

Often, however, Bettelheim was as controversial as he was influential. His essays on subjects ranging from the American educational system (counterproductive, he said) to the antiwar movement of the 1960s (a "destructive" attempt by youth to express its feelings of uselessness) were hardly greeted with open arms in all quarters. His main critics often came from the psychoanalytic community itself. His assertion that autism was primarily environmentally produced has since been disproved. Even as late as 1983, Bettelheim unleashed a storm of criticism when he published *Freud and Man's Soul*, in which he stated that central aspects of the English translations of Freud's theories are incorrect, implying that the tenets on which the American psychoanalytic community is founded are deeply flawed. And even after his death, controversy arose about his use of corporal punishment to discipline patients at the Orthogenic School.

"His audience seemed to separate into fans and people who couldn't stand him," says Theran Raines, Bettelheim's long-time literary agent.

Into his eighties, Bettelheim could fill lecture halls across the country. However, the death of his wife of forty-three years in 1984 slowed him considerably. Bettelheim tried to live with Ruth, his eldest daughter, in a house they purchased together. The arrangement ended acrimoniously, and he moved to the seaside condominium.

"Once my mother died," says Naomi, his younger daughter, "my father couldn't really find a way to live at peace. I think he wanted Ruth to be in my mother's place, but that was impossible."

In 1987, Bettelheim had a stroke, partially paralyzing the right side of his body. For several months, his work ground to a halt

"The stroke impaired his ability to do everything," says Jacquelyn Sanders, current director of the Orthogenic School. "I remember when we went to lunch, it took him forever to get the money out to pay the bill. That was very difficult for a man like him."

It was during our second interview that Bettelheim began to talk concretely about old age.

"Part of the problem," he said, "is that our society doesn't know what to do with old people. We want to put them away. There are societies where the old are venerated, like in China. The Israeli kibbutzim make very special arrangements so that their old people remain active according to their abilities. They are not relegated to some old people's home or some retirement home, as is done here. It is very hard to go on living if you no longer feel useful or very important."

"But," I said, "many people seek you out for advice."

"People do seek me out," he admitted. "Perhaps not as much as I would like. But there are some to whom I am important and to whom I feel I make a contribution. That certainly is what is attractive about life."

It sounded as though he was leaning toward letting his life take its natural course.

"I'm ambivalent," he replied quickly. "I'm ambivalent."

"What pulls you in the direction of life now?" I asked.

"That I might still be of use to somebody—the hope that some things might still be enjoyable. There are some old people that are full of this *joie de vivre.* I am not. That is my misfortune, if you want to call it that. I've had some disappointments in my private life. There was the death of my wife, to whom I was deeply attached and whom I miss very much. While my wife lived I was well contented with my life and managed it very well. But since her death I find it more and more difficult to manage. I envy those people who believe that in an afterlife you will be reunited with your loved ones. That's a very comfortable thought, but I can't believe it."

I wondered if his yearlong estrangement from Ruth was another of those disappointments. When I began to ask him about that, he listed instead his physical disappointments. "I have only so much energy left. I have, I think, accepted that I have to slow down a great deal, that I can do relatively little, and that things I used to do without thinking are problematic"

For instance, he said, "because of my stroke, I can no longer write. I always found that I understood a problem much better after I began to write about it. I can no longer do that. This is one of the things one has to accept about old age."

Bettelheim sighed deeply. "I think I have made my peace with that aspect of old age—not that it is a happy peace."

✳ ✳ ✳

For all his physical difficulties after the 1987 stroke, Bettelheim maintained a moderately active schedule. He spoke in September 1989, before an appreciative crowd at the Phoenix Bookstore in Santa Monica. He found the energy to collaborate on a book—*In the Shoes of a Stranger*. And every Thursday night for his last two and a half years he supervised six local therapists in a case-study group.

"Despite the condition of his body, his outlook was always vibrant," says the group's organizer, therapist Barbara Waldman. "No matter how he was feeling, when he worked, he would come alive. The work was always from the gut with him."

But by 1989, it was evident to many that Bettelheim's energy was dwindling. In May, he was made an honorary member of the Los Angeles Psychoanalytic Society. At the gathering in his honor, he accepted the membership with a long and entertaining speech recounting stories about friends ranging from Wilhelm Reich to Woody Allen (Bettelheim played himself in Allen's film *Zelig*). It was a bravura performance and convinced most of those assembled that, despite his age, Bettelheim was in decent shape. But afterward, as he was being helped to his car, he looked spent, dazed. He failed to recognize a member of his case-study group who had come up to congratulate him. It was clear Bettelheim could still rise to the occasion, but it cost him dearly.

"I noticed there was a certain point where even his interest in the group started to wane," says Walden. "Looking back I think he was becoming more and more preoccupied with how he was going to end his life."

When I met with Bettelheim for the final time, his mood was vastly improved. Even in the midst of the most somber parts of our discussions he was never above a joke. He particularly enjoyed California jokes. "It seems in California, among the middle class, everyone is either a patient or a therapist," he said, with a barking laugh and a sidelong glance.

That day he seemed full of such humor. He laughed when I said so. "Maybe it's some new drug I'm taking," he said. "But let's not talk about depression. It's depressing." He laughed again.

We talked instead about his writings and ideas. The conversation came around to the Holocaust and, like so many of our conversations, back to questions of living and dying.

"How did you get past the sorrow of such an experience?" I asked.

"I don't think that one ever really fully masters this experience of having been a prisoner in a German concentration camp," he said. "It's very damaging. I think this is the reason why some who tried to understand their own experience in the concentration camp have committed suicide. The ones who come first to mind are Primo Levi and Paul Celan, the German poet.

"The damage is obviously done also in the second generation. My son told me just a few years ago that he felt that there was always a high level of anxiety in his home because of his parents' experience under the Nazis. I think there are experiences so damaging, so traumatic, that one never fully recovers."

"So, how does one live with them?"

"The best one can," Bettelheim said. "Now, I will not say that psychoanalysis doesn't help in many ways. After all, if I didn't believe that, I wouldn't be a psychoanalyst. But it doesn't solve all the problems of life. And what is more unbearable to one person can be less unbearable to another. But in general I believe that the concentration camp experience, particularly to sensitive people, is a very difficult experience to be mastered."

"At what point are you now in the mastery of this experience?"

There was a long pause.

"I don't know," he replied. "At certain periods of one's life one finds it easier to cope than at others. I now have to cope not only with this past experience, I have to cope with the ravages of old age. And anyway, I think all my life I have not been a great optimist. And considering the state of human affairs it is very difficult to be optimistic—unless one is born in California," he added with another sidelong glance.

"But I am still puzzling about what it is that makes this an experience that is so difficult to live with—even in my own case. Because there are other miserable experiences, and we manage to live with them quite well—or relatively well. As far as I can figure out, it is an experience that makes one lose one's belief in mankind. When I think of those individuals who committed suicide in the camps—of which there were quite a few—I would say that they not only had lost their belief in meaning in life, they had also detached themselves from their libidinal objects—from their love objects. Why they detached themselves I do not know. But as long as we are in love with somebody, we try to stay alive to be reunited with them. It is as simple as that."

Bettelheim spoke repeatedly of the necessity of believing that there is meaning in one's life, but he also maintained that that belief was a fiction. Hoping to get him to clarify that contradiction, I read to him from the introduction to *The Uses of Enchantment*: "If we hope to live not just from moment to moment, but in true consciousness of our existence, then our greatest need and most difficult achievement is to find meaning in our lives. It is well-known how many have lost the will to live, and have stopped trying because such meaning has evaded them. ... The most important and also the most difficult task in raising a child is helping him find meaning in life."

"It is a paradox," he responded. "In order to live one has to believe that there is some meaning to life. On the other hand, science tells us that we are the chance product of evolution and there is no purpose to life. With this idea one cannot manage to live well.

"Let me put it another way. I believe that Freud is right that we have both a life drive [Eros] and also a death drive [Thanatos]. As long as the life drive, or the libido, is in ascendancy—certainly as long as we are sexually active and we want to procreate—we are going to live. But it can also reach a point in old age where one must accept that one withdraws the libido from the world because otherwise one couldn't face death. So for me it's a case of the balance between Thanatos and libido, or Eros. As long as Eros is winning the battle, we are happy in living."

The words he used—Eros, libido, and Thanatos—are formal, psychoanalytic terms, but I came to see that Bettelheim experienced Eros and Thanatos not as metaphorical jargon but rather as genuine internal forces.

"In your opinion, love is an important key to the question of living or dying," I said.

"Yes," he replied. "Yes. Most important. We called it libido. Call it love. Call it sex. Libido is, after all, to a large degree sex. But in old age one doesn't have sex any more."

"I hear there are those who do."

"At my age? I'll tell you a story about that. There's a man who goes to his doctor and says, 'I can't have intercourse any more.' And his doctor says, 'Well, you know, you're in your seventies. What do you expect?' And the man says, 'Yes, but my friend Sammy, who is a year older, says he has it every week.' And the doctor says, 'You can say it, too.'" Bettelheim laughed raucously.

"Some people manage to fall in love at all ages," he added, more seriously. "I think they're the happy ones. I have watched in myself the withdrawal of my libido from those things in which it was vested in the past."

"Then is the waning of the libido, the waning of life, a consequence of the loss of love?"

"Loving and being loved," Bettelheim said. "The two work together." Emotion suddenly flooded his face. "Maybe," he said, turning his gaze away, "we could talk about some other topic."

As significant as Bettelheim's death was for those who knew him or his work, he was also just another statistic in the growing number of elder suicides. Suicide rates for those over sixty-five have risen 25 percent since 1980; while this group makes up only 11 percent of the population, it accounts for 25 percent of reported suicides.

The question, of course, is why?

"Part of it is economic," answers Nancy Osgood, an associate professor of gerontology at the Medical College of Virginia and author of *Suicide in the Elderly*. "Another thing we have to consider is the social isolation of the elderly in this society. And our medical technology is a two-edged sword. Too often it extends the *quantity* of life but not the quality."

"There are certain intense losses that lead elderly people to suicide," concurs John McIntosh, associate professor of psychology at Indiana University and the author of several studies on elder suicide. "The threat of losing more physical or mental functions, the death of a spouse, institutionalization, loss of ability to work."

Paul Torrance, famous for his research on creativity, believes that his colleague's decision fit those parameters. "Bettelheim was a creative person with a lot of ideas," says Torrance, author of the Torrance Test for Creative Thinking. "When a creative person can no longer produce, he feels like he is spiritually dead. The body is there, but the spirit seems to leave."

"He didn't commit suicide after the camps," says Alvin Rosenfeld, a psychiatrist and one-time head of child psychiatry at Stanford University. "He didn't commit suicide when he came to this country without a penny. He didn't commit suicide after his wife's death or even after two strokes. So the question you have to ask is, what's the proper way for a man to end his existence? Do you believe that God or fate has to choose your day, or can you choose that day yourself?"

Bettelheim's three children—Ruth, a psychotherapist; Naomi, a regional planner; and Eric, an international lawyer—were all crushed by his suicide. But all of them expected it. "I tried to talk him out of it," Naomi says. "But I was not in my father's shoes. So it's not for me to judge or criticize what he did in any way." She sighs. "There are many, many factors why my father did choose this route, going as far back as his upbringing in Vienna. There was quite a preoccupation with suicide in Austria when he was young. [It is well-documented that for decades suicide was nearly epidemic in Austria.] Another factor was that as a young man my father watched his own father become incapacitated. Then he watched the same thing happen with many of his close friends. Then finally there was my mother's death. He had always hoped to predecease her. I can't say that he wouldn't have killed himself if my mother had been alive. But I seriously doubt it."

Toward the end of our last meeting, I read to Bettelheim from Peter Gay's biography of Freud, and we came to the passage in which Freud's doctor described how Freud "faced death with dignity and without self-pity." "What preparation can one make," I asked, "to face death consciously, with dignity and without self-pity?"

He laughed.

"I think that you have to be satisfied with your own life," he said. "To feel that you more or less did what you wanted to do. And I think also that you must have the conviction that you won't miss very much. It's a personal decision. There is no certainty about it. There's never any certainty about anything in life. If I should die today or tomorrow, I don't think I would miss much."

"Do you feel you have accomplished what you set out to accomplish?"

"Yes, I think that I have," he replied. "When I was young, I was politically active. But over the years I shifted from believing that one has to change society to create a better world to a feeling that one has to create better people to create a better world. That is what I tried to do."

"What have you left undone?"

He smiled. "I guess many things. My German publisher wants me to bring out another book about my talks with mothers. But that will have to wait for another life. Probably there are many books that I wanted to have read. Why don't I read them now? Obviously, it's not important enough to me. It would be nice to study classical Greek; then I'd be able to read some of the Greek writers in the original. Well, obviously, it wasn't important enough to me either.

"There's so much to know. And so little time, really. And particularly so little time for me left. My goal was to say what I wanted to say as well as I could. And make it relatively easy to understand. I tried to write clearly. I don't know if I succeeded, but I tried."

"But is there anything else left undone?" I pushed. "Anything?"
"A good death," he said softly. "That's what is left undone."

Bettelheim never made it to Holland. "He didn't want to go alone," explains
Naomi. And it seems he had to go alone or not at all; none of his children felt that
they could in good conscience participate in his plan. So instead of going to
Europe, shortly before Christmas, Bettelheim moved to a Silver Spring, Maryland,
retirement home to be closer to Naomi.

It was on the evening of March 13 that I got a call from Barbara Waldman,
one of the case-study group members. She had heard on the radio that Bettelheim
had died. The word *suicide* was not mentioned. I sat down, possessed of wildly disparate emotions. On one hand, there was the realization that the thoughts of a
unique mind had been silenced forever. And yet it looked like Bettelheim had
gotten the "good death" that he had wished for.

Then I read the morning newspapers. *A plastic bag.* Holding the newspaper, I
burst into tears in my driveway. It seemed so desperate.

"He committed suicide when the weather changed," Naomi says. "It had been
winter, and suddenly there was a warm spell. And the people at the retirement
home told me that the very beginning of spring, when the weather changes, is the
most common time for older people to kill themselves. They don't know why."

A few days later, in rereading some of his work, a passage from *Freud's Vienna
& Other Essays* caught my eye. " 'Precious in the sight of the Lord is the death of
his righteous ones,' says the Psalmist," Bettelheim wrote. "If one might ask why
the deaths of the righteous ones rather than their lives are precious to the Lord,
the answer is this: While the Lord is pleased with the righteous ones as long as they
are living righteous lives, only at their deaths can there be certainty that they never
deviated from the path of righteousness."

Bettelheim was referring to the Polish martyr Janusz Korczak, but somehow
the words seemed to have a hauntingly autobiographical echo. "Whosoever the
righteous ones may have been in our lifetimes," he continued, "it was their freely
chosen death which finally made the utter righteousness of their lives apparent."

8

Selling Death and Dignity
Herbert Hendin

Advocates use case descriptions to show that euthanasia or assisted suicide is sometimes justifiable. Yet even the seemingly clearest cases can prove deeply troubling.

Dying is hard to market. Voters, many repelled by the image of doctors giving their patients lethal injections, rejected euthanasia initiatives in Washington and California. Learning from these defeats, Oregon sponsors of a similar measure limited it to assisted suicide, while still casting the patient in the role familiar from euthanasia advertising: the noble individualist fighting to exercise the right to die.

Although both assisted suicide and euthanasia have been presented as empowering patients by giving them control over their death, assisted suicide has been seen as protecting against potential medical abuse since the final act is in the patient's hands. Yet opponents see little protection in assisted suicide: people who are helpless or seriously ill are vulnerable to influence or coercion by physicians or relatives who can achieve the same ends with or without direct action.[1] How could advocates counteract not only images of lethal physicians but images of grasping relatives, eager to be rid of a burden or to gain an inheritance by coercing death?

Supporters of assisted suicide and euthanasia have found the ultimate marketing technique to promote the normalization of assisted suicide and euthanasia: the presentation of a case history designed to show how necessary assisted suicide or euthanasia was in that particular instance. Such cases may rely either on nightmarish images of unnecessarily prolonged dying or on predictions of severe disability. The instance in which it is felt that most would agree it was desirable to end life is represented as typical. Those who participate in the death (the relatives, the euthanasia advocates, the physician) are celebrated as enhancing the dignity of the patient, who is usually presented as a heroic, fully independent figure.

From the *Hastings Center Report* 25, no. 3 (1995): 19–23. © Herbert Hendin. Reprinted by permission. Reprint by permission of the Hastings Center and Herbert Hendin, M.D., Director of the American Foundation for Suicide Prevention and Professor of Psychiatry at New York Medical College.

How much truth is there in this advertising? Does this accurately describe what happens? Even in cases advocates believe best illustrate the desirability of legalizing assisted suicide or euthanasia, there is ample room to question whether the death administered in fact realizes the patient's wishes and meets his or her needs. Advocates' desire to dramatize these model cases, moreover, requires that they be presented in some detail—and this creates the opportunity to see the discrepancy between theory and practice with regard to assisted suicide and euthanasia.

Death on Request

The ultimate attempt to normalize euthanasia in the Netherlands and make it seem an ordinary part of everyday life was the showing in the fall of 1994 on Dutch television of *Death on Request*,[2] a film of a patient being put to death by euthanasia. Maarten Nederhurst, who created the film, found an agreeable patient and doctor by contacting the Dutch Voluntary Euthanasia Society.

The patient, Cees van Wendel, had been diagnosed as having amyotrophic lateral sclerosis in June 1993; he expressed his wish for euthanasia a month later. Severe muscular weakness confined him to a wheel chair; his speech was barely audible.

Almost 700,000 people saw the first showing of the film in the Netherlands. Subsequently, the right to show the film has been acquired by countries throughout the world. "PrimeTime Live" excerpted and showed a representative segment to American viewers with a voiceover in English. Sam Donaldson introduced the program saying that it took no sides on the issue but added, "It is a story of courage and love."[3] Only for the most gullible viewer.

In point of fact, the doctor, Wilfred van Oijen, is the film's most significant person. He is the manager who can make "everything"—even death—happen. He is presented as someone who has accepted the burden of all phases of experience. The patient is nearly invisible.

The film opens with a chilly scene in winter—trees are bare of leaves, it is cold, wet, inhospitable—not a bad time to die. In an undershirt in his bathroom, the doctor combs his hair getting ready for just another day. His encounters will include treating a child of about ten months, a pregnant woman and a baby, and bringing death to Cees. The purpose of the film is to include euthanasia both as part of his daily burden as a doctor and as the natural course of events.

In the two house calls van Oijen makes to Cees, of most interest is the tension between the film's professed message—that all want release from illness, the patient most of all—and the message conveyed by what is actually filmed. The relationship depicted is between van Oijen and Antoinette, the patient's wife, who has called the doctor and clearly wants her husband to die.

The wife appears repulsed by her husband's illness, never touching him during their conversation and never permitting Cees to answer any question the doctor asks directly. She "translates" for him, although Cees is at this point in his illness intelligible, able to communicate verbally, but slowly, and able to type out messages on his computer. The doctor asks him if he wants euthanasia, but his wife replies. When Cees begins to cry, the doctor moves sympathetically toward him to touch his arm, but his wife tells the doctor to move away and says it is better to let him cry alone. During his weeping she continues to talk to the doctor. The doctor at no time asks to speak to Cees alone; neither does he ask if anything would make it easier for him to communicate or if additional help in his care would make him want to live.

Virtually the entire film is set up to avoid confronting any of the patient's feelings or how the relationship with his wife affects his agreeing to die. Cees is never seen alone. Van Oijen is obliged to obtain a second opinion from a consultant. The consultant, who appears well known to the doctor, also makes no attempt to communicate with Cees alone, and he too permits the wife to answer all the questions put to Cees. When the consultant asks the pro forma question if Cees is sure he wants to go ahead, Antoinette answers for him. The consultant seems uncomfortable, asks a few more questions, and leaves. The consultation takes practically no time at all. The pharmacist who supplies the lethal medication—one shot to put Cees to sleep and another to help him die—seems only another player in this carefully orchestrated event.

Antoinette visits the doctor to ask where "we stand." She wants the euthanasia over with. Cees has set several dates, but keeps moving them back. Now he has settled on his birthday, and they arrange for van Oijen to do it at eight o'clock after Cees celebrates by drinking a glass of port. Cees makes a joke that sleeping is a little death but this time his sleep will be a lot of death. Van Oijen tries to laugh warmly. Antoinette keeps her distance from the two and remarks that the day has gone slowly and it seemed eight o'clock would never come.

Antoinette helps Cees into bed in preparation for van Oijen to administer the first shot. Van Oijen smiles, gives the injection, and explains the medication will take a while to put Cees into a deep sleep. No one says goodbye. Only after the shot has put Cees to sleep does Antoinette murmur something to her husband. She then moves into the other room with the doctor to permit Cees to sink into a deeper sleep. After a few minutes, they return. When the doctor wants to place Cees in a more comfortable position, she withdraws again. After the second shot is administered, Antoinette and van Oijen sit next to the bed, both holding the arm that has received the injections. Antoinette asks if this was good, presumably wanting to know if it was "good" to kill Cees. Van Oijen reassures her. They leave Cees alone very quickly. On the way into the next room, Antoinette takes a note Cees wrote to her about their relationship and what it meant to him and reads it to the doctor. She seems to want to convey to him that they in fact once had a relationship.

From the beginning, the loneliness and isolation of the husband haunts the film. Only because he is treated from the start as an object does his death seem inevitable. One leaves the film feeling that death with dignity requires more than effective management; it requires being accorded personhood even though one's speech is slurred or one needs to point to letters on a board or communicate through writing on one's computer. Throughout the film, Cees's wife denies him such personhood, as does the doctor, who never questions her control over all of the patient's communication and even the doctor's communication with Cees. The doctor and wife took away Cees's personhood before ALS had claimed it.

A Good Death for Louise

An article featured on the cover of the *New York Times Magazine* in the fall of 1993 also used a case description to try to prove the value of assisted suicide to an American audience.[4] The article described the assisted suicide of Louise, a Seattle woman whose death was arranged by her doctor and the Reverend Ralph Mero, head of Compassion in Dying, a group that champions legalizing assisted suicide. Members of the group counsel the terminally ill, offer advice on lethal doses, convince cautious doctors to become involved, and are present during the death. Mero and his followers do not provide the means for suicide (the patients obtain such help from their doctors) and claim not to encourage the patients to seek suicide.

Mero arranged for a *Times* reporter to interview Louise in the last weeks of her life, offering Louise's death as an illustration of the beneficial effects of the organization's work. Yet the account serves equally to illustrate how assisted suicide made both life and death miserable for Louise.

Louise, who was referred to Mero by her doctor, had been ill with an unnamed, degenerative neurological disease. The reporter tells us that "Louise had mentioned suicide periodically during her six years of illness, but the subject came into sudden focus in May during a somber visit to her doctor's office." As Louise recounted it, "I really wasn't having any different symptoms, I just knew something had changed. I looked the doctor right in the eye and said, 'I'm starting to die.' And she said, 'I've had the same impression for a couple of days.'" An MRI scan confirmed that the frontal lobes of Louise's brain had begun to deteriorate, a sign that led her doctor to warn Louise that her life would most likely be measured in months, perhaps weeks. Louise said her doctor explained that "she didn't want to scare me . . . she just wanted to be honest. She told me that once the disease becomes active, it progresses very fast, that I would become mentally incapacitated and wouldn't be myself, couldn't care for myself anymore. She would have to look into hospice care, or the hospital, or some other facility where I would stay until I died."

We are told that Louise did not hesitate with her answer. "I can't do that. . . . I don't want that." The reporter continues, "Her doctor, Louise thought, looked both sad and relieved. 'I know, I know,' the doctor said. 'But it has to come from you.'" Louise makes sure that they are both talking about suicide and says, "That's what I'd like to do, go for as long as I can and then end it."

What has happened between Louise and her doctor? The doctor's quick affirmation that Louise is starting to die, even before the MRI scan confirms her decline, is disturbing. She prefaces a grim description of Louise's prognosis with assurance that she does not want to scare her. The doctor's relief when Louise indicates that she is choosing suicide gives us some feeling about her attitudes toward patients in Louise's condition.

As the account continues, the doctor indicates that she would be willing to help, had recently helped another patient whom Louise knew, and said she would prescribe enough barbiturates to kill Louise. To avoid legal trouble, she would not be there when Louise committed suicide. They exchanged several hugs and Louise went home. The doctor called Compassion in Dying for advice. The reporter quotes the doctor as saying about contacting Mero, "I was ecstatic to find someone who's doing what he's doing . . . I loved the fact that there were guidelines."

On the phone, Mero advises the doctor on the medication to prescribe and then visits Louise, suggesting that he is prepared to help Louise die before knowing or even meeting her or in any way determining whether she meets any guidelines. When he does meet Louise, she asks him at once if he will help her with her suicide and be there when she does it, and she is almost tearfully grateful when he says yes. He repeats many times that it has to be her choice. Louise affirms that it is, saying that all she wants "these next few weeks is to live as peacefully as possible." Louise seems concerned with being close to others during her final time and with spending what is left of her life in an environment of loving leave-taking.

The doctor is concerned that Louise's judgment might soon become impaired: "The question is, at what point is her will going to be affected, and, if suicide is what she wants, does she have the right to do it when she still has the will?" The doctor, like Mero, says she does not want to influence the patient, but worries that Louise might not act in time. "If she loses her mind and doesn't do this, she's going into the hospital. But the last thing I want to do is pressure her to do this."

Yet the closeness before dying that Louise seemed to want is lost in the flurry of activity and planning for her death as each of those involved with her dying pursues his or her own requirements. At a subsequent meeting of Mero and Louise, with Louise's mother and her doctor also present, Mero gives Louise a checklist in which he reviews steps to be taken during the suicide, from the food to be eaten to how the doctor would call the medical examiner.

The doctor indicates she will be out of town for the next week, but that she has told her partner of Louise's plans. "You don't have to wait for me to get back," she tells Louise, hinting, the reporter tells us, that it might be a good idea not to wait. The doctor was more direct when alone with Louise's mother, telling her that she was afraid Louise might not be coherent enough to act if she waited past the coming weekend.

The doctor and Mero discuss how pointed they can be with Louise, wanting her to make an informed decision without frightening her into acting sooner than she was ready. They hoped "she would read between the lines." Mero assures the reporter that he always wants to err on the side of caution. Nonetheless, a few days after the meeting, Mero called the reporter in New York, asking her to come to Seattle as soon as possible. He knew she was planning to come the following week, but he warned her not to wait that long.

The reporter leaves immediately for Seattle and finds Louise in a debilitated condition. She is in pain, getting weaker, and speaks of wanting to end her life while she can still be in control. She says she is almost ready, but not quite. She needs about a week, mainly to relax and be with her mother.

The reporter blurted out, "Your doctor feels that if you don't act by this weekend you may not be able to." Her words are met with a "wrenching silence" and Louise, looking sharply at her mother, indicates that she hadn't been told that. Her mother says gently that is what the doctor had told her. Louise looks terrified and her mother tells her it's OK to be afraid. "I'm not afraid. I just feel as if everyone is ganging up on me, pressuring me," Louise said. "I just want some time."

Louise's mother was growing less certain that Louise would actually take her own life. When she tried to ask her directly, Louise replied, "I feel like it's all we ever talk about." A friend who had agreed to be with Louise during the suicide is also uncomfortable with Louise's ambivalence but is inclined to attribute her irritability and uncertainty to her mental decline. When Louise indicates that she would wait for Mero to return from a trip and ask his opinion on her holding on for a few days, the friend indicates that this was a bad idea since the change in her mood might be missed by someone like Mero who did not know her well.

Like many people in extreme situations, Louise has expressed two conflicting wishes—to live and to die—and found support only for the latter. The anxiety of her doctor, Mero, her mother, and her friend that Louise might change her mind or lose her "will" may originate in their desire to honor Louise's wishes, or even in their own view of what kind of life is worth living, but eventually overrides the emotions Louise is clearly feeling and comes to affect what happens more than Louise's will. Although those around her act in the name of supporting Louise's autonomy, Louise begins to lose her own death.

Despite predictions, Louise makes it through the weekend. Over the next days she speaks with Mero by phone, but he tells the reporter he kept the conversations short because he was uncomfortable with her growing dependence on his opinion. Nevertheless, after a few such conversations, the contents of which are not revealed, Louise indicated she was ready; that evening Mero came and the assisted suicide was performed. A detailed description of the death scene provides the beginning, the end, and the drama of the published story. Louise did not die immediately but lingered for seven hours. Had she not died from the pills, Mero subsequently implied to the reporter, he would have used a plastic bag to suffocate her, although this violates the Compassion in Dying guidelines.

Everyone—Mero, the friend, the mother, the doctor, and the reporter—all became part of a network pressuring Louise to stick to her decision and to do so in a timely manner. The death was virtually clocked by their anxiety that she might want to live. Mero and the doctor influence the feelings of the mother and the friend so that the issue is not their warm leave-taking and the affection they have had for Louise, but whether they can get her to die according to the time requirements of Mero, the doctor (who probably cannot stay away indefinitely), the reporter (who has her own deadlines), and the disease, which turns out to be on a more flexible schedule than previously thought. Louise is explicit that the doctor, mother, friend, and reporter have become instruments of pressure in moving her along. Mero appears to act more subtly and indirectly through his effect on the others involved with Louise.

Without a death there is, of course, no story, and Mero and the reporter have a stake in the story, although Mero has criticized Jack Kevorkian to the reporter for wanting publicity. The doctor develops a time frame for Louise; her own past troubling experience with a patient who was a friend seems to color the doctor's need to have things over with quickly and in her absence if possible. Louise is clearly frustrated by not having someone to talk to who has no stake in persuading her.

Individually and collectively those involved engender a terror in Louise with which she must struggle alone, while they reassure each other that they are gratifying her last wishes. The end of her life does not seem like death with dignity; nor is there much compassion conveyed in the way Louise was helped to die. Compassion is not an easy emotion to express in the context of an imminent loss. It requires that we look beyond our own pain to convey the power and meaning of all that has gone before in our life with another. Although the mother, friend, and physician may have acted out of good intentions in assisting the suicide, none appears to have honored Louise's need for a "peaceful" parting. None seems to have been able to accept the difficult emotions involved in loving someone who is dying and knowing there is little one can do but convey love and respect for the life that has been lived. The effort to deal with the discomfort of Louise's situation seems to drive the others to "do something" to eliminate the situation.

Watching someone die can be intolerably painful for those who care for the patient. Their wish to have it over with quickly is understandable. Their feeling can become a form of pressure on the patient and must be separated from what the patient actually wants. The patient who wants to live until the end but senses his family cannot tolerate watching him die is familiar to those who care for the terminally ill. Once those close to the patient decide to assist in the suicide, their desire to have it over with can make the pressure put on the patient many times greater. The mood of those assisting is reflected in Macbeth's famous line, "If it were done when 'tis done, then 'twere well it were done quickly."

Certainly assisted *suicide*—the fact that she took the lethal medication herself—offered no protection to Louise. Short of actually murdering her, it is hard to see how her doctor, Mero, her mother, her friend, and the reporter could have done more to rush her toward death. Case vignettes limited to one or two paragraphs describing the patient's medical symptoms, and leaving out the social context in which euthanasia is being considered, obscure such complex—and often subtle—pressures on patients' "autonomous" decisions to seek death.

Empowerment for Whom?

Our culture supports the feeling that we should not tolerate situations we cannot control. "Death," Arnold Toynbee has said, "is un-American." The physician who feels a sense of failure and helplessness in the face of incurable disease, or the relative who cannot bear the emotions of loss and separation, finds in assisted suicide and euthanasia an illusion of mastery over the disease and the accompanying feelings of helplessness. Determining when death will occur becomes a way of dealing with frustration.

In the selling of assisted suicide and euthanasia words like "empowerment" and "dignity" are associated only with the choice for dying. But who is being empowered? The more one knows about individual cases, the more apparent it becomes that needs other than those of the patient often prevail. "Empowerment" flows toward the relatives, the doctor who offers a speedy way out if he cannot offer a cure, or the activists who have found in death a cause that gives meaning to their lives. The patient, who may have said she wants to die in the hope of receiving emotional reassurance that all around her want her to live, may find that like Louise she has set in motion a process whose momentum she cannot control. If death with dignity is to be a fact and not a selling slogan, surely what is required is a loving parting that acknowledges the value of the life lived and affirms its continuing meaning.

Euthanasia advocates try to use the individual case to demonstrate that there are some cases of rational or justifiable assisted suicide or euthanasia. If they can demonstrate that there are some such cases, they believe that would justify legalizing euthanasia.

Their argument recalls Abraham's approach in persuading God not to go ahead with his intention to destroy everyone in Sodom. Abraham asks if it would be right for God to destroy Sodom if there were fifty who were righteous within the city. When God agrees to spare Sodom if there were fifty who were righteous, Abraham asks what about forty-five, gradually reduces the number to ten, and gets God to spare the city for the time being for the sake of the ten.

Abraham, however, is arguing in favor of saving life; we want him to succeed and are relieved that he does. Euthanasia advocates are arguing that if there are ten cases where euthanasia might be appropriate, we should legalize a practice that is likely to kill thousands inappropriately.

The appeal of assisted suicide and euthanasia is a symptom of our failure to develop a better response to death and the fear of intolerable pain or artificial prolongation of life. The United States needs a national commission to explore and develop a consensus on the care and treatment of the seriously or terminally ill—a scientific commission similar to the President's Commission that in 1983 gave us guidelines about forgoing life-sustaining treatment with dying patients. Work of a wider scope needs to be done now. There is a great deal of evidence that doctors are not sufficiently trained in relieving pain and other symptoms in the terminally ill.

Hospice care is in its infancy. We have not yet educated the public as to the choices they have in refusing or terminating treatment, nor has the medical profession learned how best to avoid setting in motion the technology that only prolongs a painful process of dying. And we have not devoted enough time in our medical schools or hospitals to educating future physicians about coming to terms with the painful truth that there will be patients they will not be able to save but whose needs they must address.

How we deal with illness, age, and decline says a great deal about who and what we are, both as individuals and as a society. We should not buy into the view of those who are engulfed by fear of death or by suicidal despair that death is the preferred solution to the problems of illness, age, and depression. We would be encouraging the worst tendencies of depressed patients, most of whom can be helped to overcome their condition. By rushing to "normalize" euthanasia as a medical option along with accepting or refusing treatment, we are inevitably laying the groundwork for a culture that will not only turn euthanasia into a "cure" for depression but may prove to exert a coercion to die on patients when they are most vulnerable. Death ought to be hard to sell.

References

1. Yale Kamisar, "Physician-Assisted Suicide: The Last Bridge to Active Voluntary Euthanasia," in *Euthanasia Examined*, ed. John Keown (Cambridge: Cambridge University Press, 1995); Yale Kamisar, "Are Laws against Assisted Suicide Unconstitutional?" *Hastings Center Report* 23, no. 3 (1993): 33–41; Herbert Hendin, "Seduced by Death: Doctors, Patients and the Dutch Cure," *Issues in Law and Medicine* 10, no. 2 (1994): 123–68; Carlos Gomez, *Regulating Death: Euthanasia and the Case of the Netherlands* (New York: Free Press, 1991).

2. "Death on Request," Ikon Television Network, 1994.

3. "Death on Request," "PrimeTime Live," 8 December 1994.

4. Lisa Belken, "There's No Simple Suicide," *New York Times Magazine,* 14 November 1993.

9

Report of the Council on Ethical and Judicial Affairs of the AMA

Subject: Physician-Assisted Suicide (Resolution 3, A-93)

Presented by: John Glasson, M.D., Chair

Referred to: Reference Committee on Amendments to Constitution and Bylaws (Louis R. Zako, M.D., Chair)

Introduction*

Physician-assisted suicide presents one of the greatest contemporary challenges to the medical profession's ethical responsibilities. Proposed as a means toward more humane care of the dying, assisted suicide threatens the very core of the medical profession's ethical integrity.

While the Council on Ethical and Judicial Affairs has long-standing policy opposing euthanasia, it did not expressly address the issue of assisted suicide until its June 1991 report, "Decisions Near the End of Life." In that report, the Council concluded that physician-assisted suicide is contrary to the professional role of physicians and that therefore physicians "must not . . . participate in assisted suicide." Previously, the Council had issued reports rejecting the use of euthanasia. In June 1977, the Council stated that "mercy killing or euthanasia—is contrary to public policy, medical tradition, and the most fundamental measures of human value and worth." Similarly, in June 1988, the Council reaffirmed "its strong opposition to 'mercy killing.'"

From *Issues in Law and Medicine* 10 (1994): 91–97. Copyright © 1995 American Medical Association.
    *In accordance with the Joint Report of the Council on Ethical and Judicial Affairs and the Council on Constitution and Bylaws (1-91), this report may be adopted, not adopted, or referred. It may only be amended, with the concurrence of the Council, to clarify its meaning.

Broad public debate of assisted suicide was sparked in June 1990, when Dr. Jack Kevorkian assisted in the suicide of Janet Adkins. The debate was advanced in March 1991 when Dr. Timothy Quill disclosed his assistance in the suicide of Diane Trumbull. Other public events quickly followed. Physician-assisted suicide, together with euthanasia, was placed on the public ballot in Washington state, in November 1991, and in California, in November 1992. Both times, voters turned down proposals to legalize physician-assisted dying. In September 1993, by a vote of 5-4, Canada's Supreme Court denied a woman's request to end her life by assisted suicide. In 1994, voters in Oregon will decide whether to legalize assisted suicide in their state.

Resolution 3, introduced at the 1993 Annual Meeting by the Medical Student Section and referred to the Board of Trustees by the House of Delegates, requested an ethical study of assisted suicide. In this report, the Council revisits the issue of physician-assisted suicide.

Definitions

Assisted suicide occurs when a physician provides a patient with the medical means and/or the medical knowledge to commit suicide. For example, the physician could provide sleeping pills and information about the lethal dose, while aware that the patient is contemplating suicide. In physician-assisted suicide, the patient performs the life-ending act, whereas in euthanasia the physician administers the death-causing drug or other agent.

Assisted suicide and euthanasia should not be confused with the provision of a palliative treatment that may hasten the patient's death ("double effect"). The intent of the palliative treatment is to relieve pain and suffering, not to end the patient's life, but the patient's death is a possible side effect of the treatment. It is ethically acceptable for a physician to gradually increase the appropriate medication for a patient, realizing that the medication may depress respiration and cause death.

Assisted suicide also must be distinguished from withholding or withdrawing life-sustaining treatment, in which the patient's death occurs because the patient or the patient's proxy, in consultation with the treating physician, decides that the disadvantages of treatment outweigh its advantages and therefore that treatment is refused.

Ethical Considerations

Inappropriate Extension of the Right to Refuse Treatment

In granting patients the right to refuse life-sustaining medical treatment, society has acknowledged the right of patients to self-determination on matters of their medical care even if the exercise of that self-determination results in the patient's death. Because any medical treatment offers both benefits and detriments, and people attach different values to those benefits and detriments, only the patient can determine whether the advantages of treatment outweigh the disadvantages. As the Council has previously concluded, "[t]he principle of patient autonomy requires that physicians must respect the decision to forgo life-sustaining treatment of a patient who possesses decision-making capacity."

Although a patient's choice of suicide also represents an expression of self-determination, there is a fundamental difference between refusing life-sustaining treatment and demanding a life-ending treatment. The right of self-determination is a right to accept or refuse offered interventions, but not to decide what should be offered. The right to refuse life-sustaining treatment does not automatically entail a right to insist that others take action to bring on death.

When a life-sustaining treatment is declined, the patient dies primarily because of an underlying disease. The illness is simply allowed to take its natural course. With assisted suicide, however, death is hastened by the taking of a lethal drug or other agent. Although a physician cannot force a patient to accept a treatment against the patient's will, even if the treatment is life-sustaining, it does not follow that a physician ought to provide a lethal agent to the patient. The inability of physicians to prevent death does not imply that physicians are free to help cause death.

For a number of reasons, the medical profession has rejected assisted suicide as fundamentally inconsistent with the professional role of physicians as healers. Indeed, according to the Hippocratic Oath, physicians shall "give no deadly drug to any, though it be asked of [them], nor will [they] counsel such." Physicians serve patients not because patients exercise self-determination but because patients are in need. Therefore, a patient may not insist on treatments that are inconsistent with sound medical practices. Rather, physicians provide treatments that are designed to make patients well, or as well as possible. The physician's role is to affirm life, not to hasten its demise.

Permitting assisted suicide would compromise the physician's professional role also because it would involve physicians in making inappropriate value judgments about the quality of life. Indeed, with the refusal of life-sustaining treatment, society does not limit the right to refuse treatment only to patients who meet a specific standard of suffering. With refusal of treatment, the state recognizes that the patient (or the patient's proxy) alone can decide that there no longer is a meaningful quality of life.

Objections to causing death also underlie religious views on assisted suicide. Most of the world's major religions oppose suicide in all forms and do not condone physician-assisted suicide even in cases of suffering or imminent death. In justification of their position, religions generally espouse common beliefs about the sanctity of human life, the appropriate interpretation of suffering, and the subordination of individual autonomy to a belief in God's will or sovereignty.

The Physician's Role

The relief of suffering is an essential part of the physician's role as healer, and some patients seek assisted suicide because they are suffering greatly. Suffering is a complex process that may exist in one or several forms, including pain, loss of self-control and independence, a sense of futility, loss of dignity, and fear of dying. It is incumbent upon physicians to discuss and identify the elements contributing to the patient's suffering and address each appropriately. The patient, and family members as well, should participate with the physician to ensure that measures to provide comfort will be given the patient in a timely fashion.

One of the greatest concerns reported by patients facing a terminal illness or chronic debilitation is the fear that they will be unable to receive adequate relief for their pain. Though there is some basis for this fear in a small number of cases, for most patients pain can be adequately controlled. Inadequate pain relief is only rarely due to the unavailability of effective pain control medications; more often, it may be caused by reluctance on the part of physicians to use these medications aggressively enough to sufficiently alleviate the patient's pain. Further efforts to educate physicians about advanced pain management techniques, both at the undergraduate and graduate levels, are necessary to overcome any shortcomings in this area.

Pain control medications should be employed in whatever dose necessary, and by whatever route necessary, to fully relieve the patient's pain. The patient's treatment plan should be tailored to meet the particular patient's needs. Some patients will request less pain control in order to remain mentally lucid; others may need to be sedated to the point of unconsciousness. Ongoing discussions with the patient, if possible, or with the patient's family or surrogate decisionmaker will be helpful in identifying the level of pain control necessary to relieve the patient's suffering in accordance with the patient's treatment goals. Techniques of patient controlled analgesia (PCA) enhance the sense of control of terminally ill patients and, for this reason, are particularly effective. Often, it is the loss of control, rather than physical pain, that causes the most suffering for dying patients.

The first priority for the care of patients facing severe pain as a result of a terminal illness or chronic condition should be the relief of their pain. Fear of addiction to pain medications should not be a barrier to the adequate relief of pain. Nor should physicians be concerned about legal repercussions or sanctions by licensing boards. The courts and regulatory bodies readily distinguish between use of narcotic drugs to relieve pain in dying patients and use in other situations. Indeed, it is well accepted both ethically and legally that pain medications may be administered in whatever dose necessary to relieve the patient's suffering, even if the medication has the side effect of causing addiction or of causing death through respiratory depression.

Relieving the patient's psychosocial and other suffering is as important as relieving the patient's pain. When the treatment goals for a patient in the end stages of a terminal illness shift from curative efforts to comfort care, the level of physician involvement in the patient's care should in no way decrease. Patients in these circumstances must be managed "in a setting of [the patient's] own choosing, as free as possible from pain and other burdensome symptoms, and with the optimal psychological and spiritual support of family and friends." Because the loss of control may be the greatest fear of dying patients, all efforts should be made to maximize the patient's sense of control.

Accomplishing these goals requires renewed efforts from physicians, nurses, family members, and other sources of psychological and spiritual support. Often, the patient's despair with his or her quality of life can be relieved by psychiatric intervention. Seriously ill patients contemplating suicide may develop a renewed desire to live as a result of counseling and/or antidepressant medications. When requests for assisted suicide occur, it is important to provide the patient with an evaluation by a health professional with expertise in psychiatric aspects of terminal illness.

The hospice movement has made great strides in providing comfort care to patients at the end of life. In hospice care, the patient's symptoms, including pain, are aggressively treated to make the patient as comfortable as possible, but efforts to extend the patient's life are usually not pursued. Hospice patients are often cared for at home, or, if their condition requires care to be delivered in an institutional setting, intrusive medical technology is kept to a minimum. The provision of a humane, low technology environment in which to spend their final days can go far in alleviating patients' fears of an undignified, lonely, technologically dependent death.

Physicians must not abandon or neglect the needs of their terminally ill patients. Indeed, the desire for suicide is a signal to the physician that more intensive efforts to comfort and care for the patient are needed. Physicians, family, and friends can help patients near the end of life by their presence and by their loving support. Patients may feel obligated to die in order to spare their families the emotional and financial burden of their care or to spare limited societal resources for other health care needs. While patients may rationally and reasonably be concerned about the burden on others, physicians and family members must reassure patients that they are under no obligation to end their lives prematurely because of such concerns.

In some cases, terminally ill patients voluntarily refuse food or oral fluids. In such cases, patient autonomy must be respected, and forced feeding or aggressive parenteral rehydration should not be employed. Emphasis should be placed on renewed efforts at pain control, sedation, and other comfort care for the associated discomfort.

"Slippery Slope" Concerns

Permitting assisted suicide opens the door to policies that carry far greater risks. For example, if assisted suicide is permitted, then there is a strong argument for allowing euthanasia. It would be arbitrary to permit patients who have the physical ability to take a pill to end their lives but not let similarly suffering patients die if they require the lethal drug to be administered by another person. Once euthanasia is permitted, however, there is a serious risk of involuntary deaths. Given the acceptance of withdrawal of life-sustaining treatment by proxies for incompetent patients, it would be easy for society to permit euthanasia for incompetent patients by proxy.

The Dutch experience with euthanasia demonstrates the risks of sanctioning physician-assisted suicide. In the Netherlands, there are strict criteria for the use of euthanasia that are similar to the criteria proposed for assisted suicide in the United States. In the leading study of euthanasia in the Netherlands, however, researchers found that, in about 28 percent of cases of euthanasia or physician-assisted suicide, the strict criteria were not fulfilled, suggesting that some patients' lives were ended prematurely or involuntarily. In a number of cases, the decision to end the patient's life was made by a surrogate decisionmaker, since the patient had lost decisionmaking capacity by the time the decision to employ euthanasia was made.

Recommendations

In lieu of Resolution 3, A-93, the Council on Ethical and Judicial Affairs recommends that the following statements be adopted and the remainder of this report be filed:

1. Physician-assisted suicide is fundamentally inconsistent with the physician's professional role.
2. It is critical that the medical profession redouble its efforts to ensure that dying patients are provided optimal treatment for their pain and other discomfort. The use of more aggressive comfort care measures, including greater reliance on hospice care, can alleviate the physical and emotional suffering that dying patients experience. Evaluation and treatment by a health professional with expertise in the psychiatric aspects of terminal illness can often alleviate the suffering that leads a patient to desire assisted suicide.
3. Physicians must resist the natural tendency to withdraw physically and emotionally from their terminally ill patients. When the treatment goals for a patient in the end stages of a terminal illness shift from curative efforts to comfort care, the level of physician involvement in the patient's care should in no way decrease.
4. Requests for physician-assisted suicide should be a signal to the physician that the patient's needs are unmet and further evaluation to identify the elements contributing to the patient's suffering is necessary. Multidisciplinary intervention, including specialty consultation, pastoral care, family counseling, and other modalities, should be sought as clinically indicated.
5. Further efforts to educate physicians about advanced pain management techniques, both at the undergraduate and graduate levels, are necessary to overcome any shortcomings in this area. Physicians should recognize that courts and regulatory bodies readily distinguish between use of narcotic drugs to relieve pain in dying patients and use in other situations.

[A complete list of references can be obtained from the Office of General Counsel of the American Medical Association.]

PART TWO

When Do We Call It Suicide?

10

Suicide, Self-Sacrifice, and Coercion
William E. Tolhurst

T hat not all self-caused deaths are suicides is obvious, but what is not so clear is how the line should be drawn to distinguish those which are from those which are not. In many cases the difficulty in determining whether a self-caused death is suicide does not stem from a lack of empirical evidence but rather from the lack of a clear account of what makes a particular self-caused death a case of suicide. It is the aim of this paper to provide and defend a definition of suicide which will clarify what is at issue in these cases. In the process I shall consider the relevance of altruistic motivation and of coercion to the determination of whether a person has committed suicide.

After a brief discussion of the relevance of particular cases to the assessment of possible definitions, I shall begin by showing that any definition, such as Durkheim's or Brandt's, which implies that the mere foreknowledge that one's death will result from one's actions is a sufficient condition for suicide must be rejected. Then I shall go on to consider what, in addition to this foreknowledge, is required if a self-caused death is to be properly classed as a suicide. The definitions offered by Margolis and Beauchamp will be examined, and it will be argued that they are inadequate and that the absence of altruistic motivation and coercion are not necessary conditions for a person's death to be a suicide. Having shown that these alternatives should be rejected, I shall defend the view that suicide is a matter of successfully implementing a course of action in order to bring about one's death.

Any attempt to provide a definition for a term in a natural language must take as its basis the linguistic intuitions of native speakers about the proper application of this term to particular cases, both actual and possible. With respect to the con-

From *The Southern Journal of Philosophy* 21 (1983): 109–21. Reprinted by permission of the publisher.

cept of suicide, there are three relevant categories of cases: (1) clear cases of suicide, (2) clear cases of self-caused deaths which are not suicides, and (3) cases of self-caused deaths where our pretheoretical dispositions to apply or withhold the label do not provide us with a clear verdict. Of course, the boundaries of these categories will inevitably be imprecise. The most one can hope for is a definition which yields the correct results in those cases on which all or most native speakers agree and plausible results in all the others. In what follows, I shall argue that the definition of suicide as successfully implementing a course of action in order to bring about one's death meets this criterion better than any of the alternative definitions defended in the literature thus far.

One further working assumption should be noted at this point. I shall assume that the concept of suicide is not morally loaded in the way that the concept of murder is, that it is not part of the meaning of the term "suicide" that suicide is morally objectionable. I take it that the concept of murder is such that a homicide could not properly be termed a murder unless it was, in some sense, wrong (either legally or morally). The case is different with the concept of suicide. One can sensibly ask whether suicide is ever morally permissible and while those who would answer in the affirmative might turn out to be in error, they do not contradict themselves. Thus the question of which self-caused deaths are morally objectionable is distinct from the question of which self-caused deaths are suicide.

I. Suicide and Foreknowledge

Clearly those who cause their own deaths while ignorant of the likelihood that their actions will have this result should not be considered suicides. Thus the foreknowledge that a course of action upon which one has embarked is likely to bring about one's death is at least a necessary condition for a self-caused death to be a suicide. Some proposed definitions of suicide, most notably those of Durkheim[1] and Brandt,[2] take this condition to be not only necessary but also sufficient. Durkheim held that "the term suicide is applied to all cases of death resulting directly or indirectly from a positive or negative act of the victim himself which he knows will produce this result."[3] Brandt's definition though worded differently also implies that the foreknowledge that a person's death will result from his action is sufficient to make that person's death a suicide.

> "Suicide" is conveniently defined, for our purposes, as doing something which results in one's death, either from the intention of ending one's life or the intention to bring about some other state of affairs (such as relief from pain) which one thinks it certain or highly probable can be achieved only by means of death or will produce death.[4]

That these views are mistaken can be demonstrated by the following hypothetical example which I take to be a clear case of a self-caused death which is not a suicide (i.e., a case of type [2]). Imagine the following. A doctor with a defective heart knows that she will die soon unless she has a transplant. Let us suppose further that she has a patient whose heart would be an ideal candidate for a transplant and that she can kill her patient while making it appear that the patient died of natural causes. If our imaginary doctor were to reject this option because it would require her to murder her patient, and if this condition were sufficient, then we would have to say that in so deciding the doctor has committed suicide (on the assumption that her death results from the decision). But clearly our imaginary doctor would not, in any ordinary sense of the term, be committing suicide in refusing to murder her patient. Thus Durkheim's and Brandt's definitions must be rejected.

Since this condition is necessary but not sufficient, the question that remains is what additional restrictions must be added to rule out cases of the sort described above. Two prominent features of our imaginary case present themselves as bases for possible restrictions. One is that our imaginary doctor's death is the result of what Durkheim would call a negative act of the victim, i.e., it results from her decision not to do something. The other is that the doctor does not choose the option which results in her death for selfish reasons. Presumably it is her concern for the welfare of her patient which motivates her decision. A brief argument is sufficient to show the irrelevance of the first consideration, but the second will be considered at some length in the next section.

One might argue for the first condition on the grounds that suicide is essentially a matter of killing oneself and that one whose death results from a negative act or an omission to do something has not killed himself and hence cannot have committed suicide. That this consideration, although initially plausible, is ultimately irrelevant can be shown by the fact that it is clearly possible for a person to commit suicide by willfully deciding not to perform an action which is necessary to sustain his life. For example, imagine a man who finds himself in need of a routine (relatively safe and painless) operation which is necessary to save his life. Suppose further that this man has no abnormal fear of operations, but rather that he finds his present and foreseeable future life not worth living; it is characterized by a high level of psychic and/or physical suffering which is unrelated to the condition which necessitates the operation. If this person were to refuse to have the operation because he wanted to end it all, his subsequent demise would properly be classed as suicide. I take it that this case falls into category (1) as a clear case of suicide. Thus I conclude that it is, in principle, possible for the category of suicide to include what we might call cases of passive suicide[5] where a person intentionally allows himself to die.

2. Suicide and Self-Sacrifice

Margolis has argued[6] that altruistically motivated suicides are not possible. His reasons for this are both clear and mistaken. Margolis takes suicide to be essentially a matter of choosing death for its own sake. In the case of genuine suicide, according to Margolis, the victim's "overriding concern is to end his own life...."

Those who bring about their own deaths in order to benefit others are not willing their deaths as an ultimate goal of their actions; therefore, they fail to meet his definition of suicide. However, Margolis's definition of suicide is clearly mistaken; almost no one who commits suicide (in the ordinary sense of the term) could meet the conditions of his definition. A great many suicides are the result of the victim's desire to end his suffering (psychic or physical) and in none of these cases is death chosen for its own sake.

But even if Margolis's definition is mistaken, it might still be the case that altruistic motivation is incompatible with suicide. Certainly, it is possible to imagine a great many altruistically motivated self-caused deaths which are not suicides. The following are representative examples.

> Case A: The pilot of a disabled plane decides not to use her parachute and to remain in the plane in order to prevent it from crashing in a populated area
>
> Case B: One of the occupants of an overloaded lifeboat decides to go overboard in order to prevent the boat from sinking.
>
> Case C: A soldier covers a live hand grenade with his body in order to protect his comrades.

Such cases are quite often discussed in the literature and do pose a difficult problem for anyone who would seek to provide a plausible definition of suicide. I take it that these are clear cases of nonsuicidal self-caused death and that an adequate definition should exclude them. But from this it does not follow that all altruistically motivated self-caused deaths should be excluded. That is, the feature of these cases which is responsible for their not being cases of suicide might turn out to have nothing to do with the fact that they are cases of self-sacrifice.

That this is so is supported by the existence of other cases of sacrificial self-caused deaths which do seem to be suicides. One such case (which Margolis discusses) is that of the Buddhist monk who burns himself to death to express his opposition to a war. This seems to me to be a reasonably clear case of suicide, but since Margolis disagrees I shall appeal to another in support of my contention that altruistic motivation is compatible with suicide. Imagine a person who has discovered that he is terminally ill. Since his family is in dire need of money and his life insurance policy contains a double-indemnity clause he arranges a fatal "accident" to benefit his family. I take it that one does not have to be an insurance investigator to see that this is a clear case of suicide. Thus I conclude that altruistically motivated suicides are, in principle, possible and that while an adequate definition should exclude cases A-C, it should not imply that an absence of altruistic motivation is a necessary condition for suicide. The failure of this criterion leaves the question as to why our conscientious doctor is not a suicide unanswered. In the next section I shall consider Beauchamp's attempt to answer this question and with it his contention that coercion is incompatible with suicide.

3. Suicide and Coercion

If the reason our imaginary doctor does not commit suicide in refusing to murder her patient is not because she merely lets her death happen nor because she acts out of concern for others, one might well wonder what it is about this case that makes it a nonsuicide. To this question Beauchamp gives the following answer. The doctor is not a suicide because "the condition causing death is not brought about by the regent for the purpose of ending his or her life."[7] However, Beauchamp does not hold that this condition is the only one which must be added to come up with a plausible definition since he holds that a self-caused death may fail to be a suicide if the agent acted under coercion. His candidate for a definition is as follows:

> An act is a suicide if a person intentionally brings about his or her own death in circumstances where others do not coerce him or her to the action, except in those cases where death is caused by conditions not specifically arranged by the agent for the purpose of bringing about his or her own death.[8]

Although this might seem to be a preferable alternative, it, too, must be rejected. The reason is that neither the absence of coercion nor the condition that the agent's death not be caused by conditions not arranged by him in order to cause his death are necessary conditions for committing suicide.

That the latter condition is not necessary can be shown by the following case. A man has decided that his life is no longer worth living and proposes to end it all by jumping into a nearby ravine. However, on the way to the ravine he finds himself about to be engulfed by an avalanche which he could avoid without much difficulty. Nonetheless he allows himself to be killed by the avalanche and thus saves the trouble of walking to the ravine. Surely this man has committed suicide even though he was killed by conditions which he did not arrange in order to bring about his death. Thus this requirement must be rejected as too strong. However, if we merely delete it from Beauchamp's definition, then it will succumb to the case of our conscientious doctor.

Although Beauchamp does not offer any arguments for his contention that coercion is incompatible with suicide (he seems to think that it is too obvious to need support), he does provide two illustrative cases.

> Consider ... a captured soldier who, given the "choice" of being executed or of executing himself, chooses self-execution. Since coercion is heavily involved in this intentional self-killing, we do not classify it as a suicide, just as we do not think that Socrates committed suicide by intentionally drinking the hemlock, thereby causing his death.[9]

Both the contention and the cases are problematic. It is by no means clear that these are not cases of suicide; at best they seem to fall into category (3) as cases where the pre-theoretical dispositions of native speakers to apply the term do not provide a clear verdict. Indeed, R. G. Frey has recently argued that Socrates did commit suicide.[10] While his argument may be mistaken, the fact that he is prepared to offer one for this conclusion is some indication that the issue is open to doubt and that this case should not be cited without argument as a clear example of non-suicide. Furthermore, even if one were to agree that Socrates' self-caused death is not a suicide, one might well wonder whether it is the presence of coercion which accounts for this fact, if it be a fact. This is because one might well hold that Socrates drank the hemlock freely. Certainly Socrates had ample opportunity to escape execution, but he freely chose to stay.

In the absence of any clear reasons for thinking that suicide is incompatible with coercion, let us consider some reasons for thinking that it is not. Japanese literature abounds with stories of samurai who are pressured into committing *seppuku*, ritual disembowelment. For example, the historical events upon which the play *Chushingura* is based involve a vendetta which was instigated by the forced *seppuku* of Lord Asano Naganori of Akō and whose perpetrators (forty-six *rōnin*) were punished by being condemned to commit *seppuku*. It seems plausible to suppose that anyone who commits *seppuku* commits suicide. Since people can be (and have been) forced to commit *seppuku*, it is reasonable to conclude that coerced suicide is possible. Thus Donald Keene describes one of the events which set off the vendetta mentioned above as follows: "... Tsunayoshi, the shogun, was so outraged by this unseemly breach of decorum in the palace that he commanded Asano to commit suicide."[11]

The view that coercion is compatible with suicide is further supported by a consideration of the following hypothetical cases.

> Case D: Smith has discovered that he has terminal cancer. In order to avoid a long and painful death, he shoots himself.
>
> Case E: Jones is a soldier and is about to be captured by the enemy. He knows if he is captured, he will be tortured to death. In order to avoid a long and painful death, he shoots himself.
>
> Case F: Brown is a prisoner of a sadistic tyrant who informs him that he can either kill himself or be tortured to death. (The tyrant would marginally prefer the latter option, but for reasons unknown to me is willing to allow Brown a choice.) In order to avoid a long and painful death, he shoots himself.
>
> Case G: Robinson is a prisoner of a tyrant who wants him to kill himself and who informs Robinson that unless he does so he will be tortured to death. In order to avoid a long and painful death, he shoots himself.

Although the circumstances surrounding the actions of Smith, Jones, Brown, and Robinson are markedly different, each is faced with substantially the same choice. Furthermore, each is equally free (or unfree) to choose between the options available to him even though these are, given the circumstances, severely limited. However, only case G clearly involves a person who has been coerced into killing himself.[12] I take it that Smith and Jones have clearly committed suicide and since Brown and Robinson have the same options as Smith and Jones and acted for the same reasons, I conclude that it is reasonable to suppose that Brown and Robinson have committed suicide as well. Thus I conclude that suicide is compatible with coercion.

At this point some discussion of why people might be misled into thinking that altruistic motivation and coercion are incompatible with suicide may well be in order. One explanation may be the simple fact that the most common cases of suicide do not involve these factors and hence these sorts of cases are easily overlooked. In addition to this, the presence of altruistic motivation and of coercion in a case of self-killing has a marked affect on its moral status. Altruistic acts tend to be morally admirable and those who act under coercion are less blameworthy for their actions than they would have been had coercion not been present. Many people are inclined to view suicide as selfish and blameworthy and when confronted with self-killings that are neither may be tempted to deny that these self-killings are suicide. However, in my view the proper response to these cases should be to reconsider the moral status of suicide. It seems clear that suicide is not selfish and blameworthy by definition and hence these essentially moral considerations ought not to distort the classification of self-caused deaths as suicides and nonsuicides.

4. Suicide Defined

In this section I propose to defend the view that a person has committed suicide if and only if that person has brought about his death intentionally.[13] In defending this answer it will be necessary to consider in some detail the question of what makes an action intentional. It will also be necessary to distinguish two senses in which an action might be said to be intentional, a strong and a weak sense. The analysis of suicide will require a self-caused death to be intentional in the strong sense. In explicating this sense of intentional action I shall assume the basic correctness of the causal account of intentional action advocated by Goldman and others.[14] The main idea of this account is that an intentional action is one which has the right sort of causal history, roughly one which is caused by the agent's beliefs and desires in the right way.

In order to distinguish the weak from the strong sense of intentional action it is useful to begin with an imaginary example. A person, let's call her Mary, has decided to buy a Coke in order to quench her thirst and has proceeded to put the requisite amount of money in the nearest Coke machine. In the process she has (a) moved her arm, (b) put the money in the machine, (c) obtained a Coke, (d) increased the profits of the owners of the machine, and (e) emptied the machine of Coca-Cola.[15] Let us suppose further Mary knew that (b) would result in the increase in profits but not that it would empty the machine. We may also suppose that Mary had no desire to bring about the increase in profits but that she was willing to accept this consequence as a necessary concomitant of the optimal way of getting a Coke. In this case (a), (b), and (c) are both strongly and weakly intentional; (e) is neither; and (d) is weakly but not strongly intentional.

In explaining the difference between strongly and weakly intentional action it will be convenient to use Goldman's notion of act-generation. Sometimes two actions are related in such a way that it is appropriate to say that the agent performed one by performing the other. With regard to the above example, one can say that by putting the money in the machine Mary performed (c), (d), and (e). To say that one act, a, has generated another act, a*, is just to say that the agent performed a* by performing a.[16]

It is clear why one would want to hold that (c) is intentional; (c) is an action which Mary wanted to perform and (we may suppose) her successful performance of it resulted from her desire to perform it and her beliefs about how she might perform it by means of an appropriate causal chain. It is also apparent why (a) and (b) are intentional as well since both resulted in the proper way from Mary's desire to perform (c) together with her belief that (b) would generate (c) and that (a) would generate (b). This suggests the following (strong) sense of intentional action:

> An act, a, is strongly intentional iff [if and only if] (1) there is an act, b, which the agent wanted to perform and a either is or generates b and (2) the agent's performance of a is caused in an appropriate manner by the agent's desire to perform b together with his beliefs about how b might be generated.[17]

Clearly, (a), (b), and (c) are strongly intentional while (d) and (e) are not because Mary had no desire to perform (d) or (e) and neither generated any action which she wanted to perform.

But despite the fact that neither (d) nor (e) is strongly intentional there is an important difference between them. For one thing, Mary could be held responsible for performing (d) but not for performing (e). Mary's performance of (d) as a result of performing (b) was foreseen and hence it was not accidental in the way that (e) was. Thus one might hold (d) but not (e) to be intentional because Mary knew that it would be generated by an act which would generate the action which she wanted to perform. The weaker sense of intentional action can be expressed as follows:

> An act, a, is weakly intentional if and only if (1) there is an act, b, which the agent wanted to perform and a is generated in the process of performing b; (2) the agent believed that a would be generated in the process of performing b; and (3) the agent's performance of a results in an appropriate manner from his desire to perform b together with his beliefs about how b might be generated.

Being weakly intentional is thus necessary but not sufficient for being strongly intentional. Actions which are weakly but not strongly intentional usually involve the causation of effects which are, to use the scholastic terminology, foreseen but unintended. Thus something like the above distinction seems to be presupposed by the doctrine of double effect. One advantage of this analysis is that it provides a clear explanation of why those who hold that it is always wrong to perform an action which has the death of an innocent person as a foreseen and intended consequence would judge suicide to be morally impermissible. This is because an agent's self-caused death will be strongly intentional only if the agent directly intended his death.

In defending the contention that suicide consists in an agent's bringing about his own death in such a way that this action is strongly intentional, it will be useful to reconsider some of the problem cases discussed above. The first of these concerned the relationship between foreknowledge and suicide. The case of the conscientious doctor demonstrates that the foreknowledge that an agent's death will result from his action is not sufficient to render that agent's death a suicide. When an agent performs an action, *a*, which has a consequence, *c*, the agent has performed the action of bringing about *c* by performing *a*. If, furthermore, the agent realized that *c* would result from *a* (and *c* did result from *a* in an appropriate way), then the agent's action of bringing it about that *c* is weakly intentional. This being so, it seems clear that since our imaginary doctor knew that her death would result from her act of refusing to murder her patient, her death is weakly intentional. However, from this it does not follow that it is strongly intentional. If we assume that the doctor did not want to die, then her action of bringing about her death, which is generated by her refusal to murder her patient, is strongly intentional only if there is some other action which she wanted to perform and which is generated by her action of bringing about her death. Since we may assume that there is no such action her action of bringing about her death is not strongly intentional and the definition implies, rightly, that her death is not a suicide.

The second problem considered above concerned the relationship between suicide and self-sacrifice. In most cases altruistically motivated self-caused deaths are not strongly intended. This is true not only of the conscientious doctor but also of cases A, B, and C described above. In all of these cases the agent did not want to die and there is no action generated by the agent's action of bringing about his death which the agent wanted to perform. Thus these deaths are not strongly intended and the definition implies that they are not suicides. Nonetheless the person who arranges a fatal "accident" so that his family can collect more insurance money is correctly classed as a suicide by this definition. In this case there is an action which the agent wanted to perform, i.e., bringing it about that his family collects twice as much money, which is generated by the action of causing his death. This being so, his death is strongly intended and the definition implies that it is a suicide.

The third problem concerned cases of passive suicide where a person refuses to avoid life-threatening conditions in order to end his life. In these cases the agent wants to die and brings about his death by his refusal. Since the action of bringing about his death is an action the agent wants to perform, it is strongly intentional in these cases, and the definition implies that these deaths are suicides as well. Thus I conclude that the analysis has plausible implications for the problem cases discussed above. Having disposed of these cases, I will now consider the somewhat more difficult question of whether or not Socrates' self-caused death is a case of suicide.

It is clear that if this definition is correct, then our ability to decide in any given case whether a self-caused death is a suicide will depend on our ability to ascertain the agent's beliefs and desires. With regard to Socrates we may assume that Socrates wanted to comply with Athenian law and that he believed that his action of drinking the hemlock would generate the action of complying with Athenian law. We may also suppose that Socrates knew that his action of drinking the hemlock would cause his death. However, these assumptions by themselves do not enable us to determine whether Socrates committed suicide. In order to do this we need to know what Socrates believed about the relations between the following actions: (a) drinking the hemlock, (b) causing Socrates' death, and (c) complying with Athenian law. We are assuming that Socrates believed that (a) would generate (b) and (c) and that Socrates wanted to perform (c). From this it follows that (a) and (c) are strongly intentional and that (b) is (at least) weakly intentional. The crucial question is whether Socrates believed that the law required him merely to drink the hemlock or whether he believed that the law required him to bring about his death. If Socrates believed the former then he believed that (a) would generate (c) directly and that (c) would not be generated by (b). If this was the case then Socrates' death was weakly but not strongly intentional and he did not commit suicide. However, if Socrates believed that the performance of (b) was necessary to generate (c), that (a) would generate (c) by means of generating (b), then (b) was strongly intentional and Socrates' death was a suicide. Given the difficulty in determining Socrates' act-generational beliefs, i.e., in determining his action-plan, in such fine detail, it is clear why the question of whether his death was a suicide is controversial. Since the aim of this discussion is merely to illustrate how the proposed analysis applies to problem cases of this sort, I shall not speculate on which of the two hypotheses concerning Socrates' act-generational beliefs is the more plausible. Although this and other cases are problematic because of our difficulties in ascertaining the agent's beliefs, there is another class of intractable cases to be considered whose problematic character arises from a very different source which will provide the subject for the following section. These arise out of the difficulties involved in specifying the sort of causal connection which must obtain between an agent's beliefs and desires and his actions if these are to be intentional (in either sense).

5. The Problem of Deviant Causal Chains

In sketching out the definitions of both strongly and weakly intentional action it was necessary to use the vague requirements that the causal link between the agent's beliefs and desires be of the right sort. Although the vagueness of this requirement is not a barrier to understanding the difference between these two different types of intentional action, it is clear that a fully adequate account of intentional action must replace it with a more informative description of the appropriate sort of causal chain. This project is one which has proved troublesome not only for the causal theory of action but also for causal theories of reference, knowledge, and perception. Although the resolution of this difficulty is clearly beyond the scope of this paper, it merits some discussion in this context. In particular, a discussion of it will show both how and why the determination of whether certain kinds of self-caused deaths are suicides depends upon a more detailed account of intentional action.

It will be useful to begin with a clear example of a self-caused death in which the agent has failed to commit suicide not because he failed to have the right beliefs and desires but because the causal link between his beliefs and desires was not of the right sort. Suppose that a person has decided to commit suicide by throwing himself in front of a truck, but that just after he throws himself in front of the nearest one (and before he is hit by it) he is killed by a stray bullet from a shootout between two street gangs which just happens to be in progress nearby. Thus he is already dead by the time he is hit by the truck. Although this person has tried to commit suicide, his premature death prevented him from succeeding. It is clear in this case that despite the person's intention to commit suicide and the fact that his beliefs and desires led to his performing an action which caused his death, the person's death is an accident and hence not suicide, because his death did not result from his action in the right way. One condition which would exclude this sort of case is the requirement that the action be generated in the way that the agent believed it would be generated if it is to be intentional (in either sense). If, following Goldman, we call the agent's act-generational beliefs his action-plan, then this is just Goldman's requirement that the actual causal chain conform to the agent's action-plan.

Though this requirement seems to provide a plausible account of why the above self-caused death is not intentional, and hence why it is not a suicide, it seems to be too strong. It is not plausible to suppose that any deviation, however slight, between the actual course of events and the agent's action-plan is sufficient to render an action nonintentional.

Suppose a person has decided to commit suicide by shooting himself in the head but that when the occasion arises his hand shakes so severely that he shoots himself in the heart. Clearly this person has committed suicide even though the way he intended his death to come about does not exactly coincide with the way his death did come about.[18] Some level of conformity between an agent's action-plan and the actual course of events seems to be required even though an exact fit between the two is not. Thus we are still left with the problem of explaining just what makes a particular causal chain a deviant causal chain.[19] Until this problem in the theory of action is satisfactorily resolved, we will not be in a position to say whether particular self-caused deaths which result from causal chains which do not exactly coincide with the agent's action-plan are suicides or not.

This analysis of suicide is clearly preferable to the alternatives discussed above; it provides a reasonably clear account of what makes a self-caused death a suicide. Since the definition is framed in terms of the concept of intentional action, it is to be expected that our lack of a complete analysis of this concept will give rise to problem cases. But this fact is no reason for objecting to the analysis. In the first place, the respect in which the analysis of intentional action is incomplete does not affect our ability to draw a clear distinction between strongly and weakly intentional action. Second, the definition, by showing how the concept of suicide can be understood in terms of the concept of intentional action, has reduced two problems to one; the problem of determining whether these problem cases are genuine cases of suicide is seen to be nothing other than the problem of determining whether the self-caused death is intentional. Finally, the problem which remains, that of distinguishing deviant from nondeviant causal chains, is a general problem which faces a number of otherwise plausible theories. Thus we may hope that a solution to it in any of the contexts in which it has arisen will prove applicable in other contexts as well.

Notes

1. Émile Durkheim, *Suicide,* trans. Spaulding and Simpson (Glencoe, Ill.: The Free Press, 1951).

2. R. B. Brandt, "The Morality and Rationality of Suicide," *A Handbook for the Study of Suicide,* ed. Seymour Perlin (Oxford, 1975), reprinted in Battin and Mayo, eds., *Suicide: The Philosophical Issues* (New York, 1980), pp. 117–32, [see chapter 21 in this volume].

3. Durkheim, p. 44.

4. Brandt (1975), p. 117.

5. The distinction between active and passive suicide is analogous to the distinction between active and passive euthanasia and is equally problematic since it is based on the killing/letting die distinction.

6. Joseph Margolis, *Negativities: The Limits of Life* (Columbus, 1975), pp. 23-36.

7. Tom L. Beauchamp, "Suicide," *Matters of Life and Death,* ed. Tom Regan (New York, 1980), p. 76.

8. Ibid., p. 77.

9. Ibid., p. 72.

10. "Did Socrates Commit Suicide?" *Philosophy* 53 (1978): 106–108.

11. Izuma, Takedo, et al., *Chushingura,* trans. Donald Keene (New York, 1971–72).

12. Case F is tricky. I would contend that although the sadist has coerced Brown into choosing between these options, he has not coerced him into killing himself. However, whether I am right about this is irrelevant to the point at issue.

13. It is true that Beauchamp's definition requires the agent to bring about his death intentionally. But he does not explain what he takes this requirement to involve. So far as I can tell, he seems to be using the term in the weak sense discussed below.

14. See, for example, Alvin I. Goldman, *A Theory of Human Action* (Englewood Cliffs, N.J.: Prentice-Hall, 1970), (hereafter referred to as *THA*).

15. Some controversy surrounds the question of whether actions (a)–(e) are distinct. I shall assume, contra Anscombe and Davidson, that Goldman's arguments for an affirmative answer are sound. Those who disagree may well be able to restate the views expressed in this section so as to avoid this assumption.

16. For a more detailed account of act-generation see *THA,* pp. 20–48.

17. This definition is modeled on Goldman's definition of intentional action (*THA,* p. 57).

18. I am indebted to Michael Tye for this example. A similar case is discussed by Castañeda, "Intensionality and Contingent Identity in Human Action," *Nous* 13 (May 1979): 25–55.

19. For promising attempts to resolve this problem see Christopher Peacocke's

"Deviant Causal Chains," *Midwest Studies in Philosophy* 4 (1979): 123–53; and Michael H. Robins, "Deviant Causal Chains and Non-Basic Action," unpublished. A version of this article was read at the Eastern Division meetings of the American Philosophical Association, Boston, Mass., December 27, 1980.

11

The Rhetoric of Suicide
Suzanne Stern-Gillet

I n this paper I intend to draw attention to one aspect of the concept of suicide, namely, what I shall call its "responsibility-ascribing" function. In view of the lively controversy generated by R. G. Frey's contention that Socrates committed suicide,[1] I shall use the case of Socrates as a convenient thread to run through my argument. Though I hope, in the process, to shed some light on the way we view the death of Socrates, it is not my main purpose in this paper to solve the problem of describing correctly his manner of death.

True enough, Socrates died, literally, "by his own hand": he knew what he was doing when he lifted the hemlock to his lips and he could (in one sense of "could," at any rate) have escaped into exile. Nevertheless I want to deny that most of us should want to call him a suicide. My ground is that any definition of suicide (such as Durkheim's or Frey's) which allows for Socrates' inclusion in this class is incomplete insofar as it blurs important distinctions between what are, in fact, different *manners of viewing* a person's death. To claim, as Frey does, that Socrates committed suicide amounts to a disregard of the practical function and, therewith, the rhetorical connotation(s) of the concept of "suicide."

Durkheim, Frey, and Holland

In Durkheim's words: "The term *suicide is applied to all cases* of death resulting directly or indirectly from a positive or negative act of the victim himself, which he knows will produce this result."[2] This definition, by doing away with motives and intentions, led Durkheim to term suicides acts which are not normally so clas-

From *Philosophy and Rhetoric* 20, no. 3 (1987): 160–70. Copyright 1987 by The Pennsylvania State University. Reproduced by permission of The Pennsylvania State University Press.

sified. As he wrote: "...if the intention of self-destruction alone constituted suicide, the name 'suicide' could not be given to acts which, despite apparent differences, are fundamentally identical with those always called suicide and which could not be otherwise described without discarding the term. The soldier facing certain death to save his regiment does not wish to die, and yet is he not as much the author of his own death as the manufacturer or merchant who kills himself to avoid bankruptcy? This holds true for the martyr dying for his faith, the mother sacrificing herself for her child, etc. Whether death is accepted merely as an unfortunate consequence, but inevitable given the purpose, or is actually itself sought and desired, in either case the person renounces existence, and the various methods of doing so can only be varieties of a single class.... Thus, when resolution entails certain sacrifice of life, scientifically this is a suicide...."[3] Though he expresses concern not to go "counter" to ordinary usage,[4] Durkheim is resolved not to be deterred if the resulting class "fails to include all cases ordinarily included under the name or includes others usually otherwise classified."[5] Thus he presents martyrdom as a mere species of the genus "suicide."

R. G. Frey defines suicide as the act of "killing oneself intentionally, or self-murder."[6] He follows this up by asserting that: "...Socrates did plainly commit suicide. For he drank the hemlock knowingly, not unknowingly, or in ignorance of what its effect on him would be, and intentionally, not accidentally or mistakenly; and he died as a result of his act of drinking the hemlock."[7] The main difference between Durkheim's and Frey's definitions is that, unlike Durkheim, Frey has the concept of intention play a central role. As to calling Socrates' death a suicide, there is, however, no difference between the two authors, though the case is not explicitly mentioned by Durkheim. Indeed, since he allows the death of one who "accepts death merely as an unfortunate consequence" to be classified as a suicide, Durkheim clearly would have agreed with Frey's contention.

R. F. Holland, who reproaches Durkheim with not having "understood what suicide is,"[8] specifically raises the following objection: "On this account of the matter it looks as if we have to say that a man who exposes himself to mortal danger, for whatever reason and whatever the circumstances, is exposing himself to suicide."[9] Thus extended, the class of suicide, claims Holland, would include not only Captain Oates and Socrates but also, in general, all cases usually understood as "altruistic suicides" (though not in Durkheim's sense of this expression).[10] This seems to constitute a cause of worry for Holland, whose purpose it is to examine the "ethicoreligious status of self-slaughter."[11] Indeed, insofar as he is reluctant to allow that suicide can be morally commendable Holland has an axe to grind. This becomes clear when he deals with the hypothetical example of a spy who, on his impending capture, kills himself to avoid betraying his comrades: "... the spy ... is concerned solely with the good of others. *Because of this* one would like to deny that his is the spirit of suicide."[12] Further on, discussing the case of Captain Oates, Holland writes: "The sentiment that he was entitled to quit, or that anyway he was going to quit, never entered into it. Accordingly, I want to deny that he was a suicide."[13] Later in the same paragraph, Holland startlingly asserts that Oates didn't kill himself but that "the blizzard killed him."[14]

Difficulties in the Above Definitions

While Durkheim is, in my view, correct in claiming that a suicide rightly so called need not have taken an active part in his or her own death, the definition he proposes leads to a questionable broadening of the concept of suicide. It would include not only clear cases of self-sacrifice and martyrdom but also more borderline cases such as those of Socrates, Jesus, and, probably, Bobby Sands.[15] Furthermore, as I hope to show presently, it seems doubtful whether the existence of the class of suicide can be determined "scientifically."

Though Frey mentions Socrates' wish to die, he centers his argument on the surely trifling fact that Socrates "did not drink the hemlock against his will"[16] and, therefore, took an *active* part in his own death. Frey has been criticized for this justificatory move. As Michael Smith convincingly argued, drinking the hemlock intentionally does not entail killing oneself intentionally.[17] Besides, if a person's *active participation* in bringing about his own death be needed for calling him a suicide then a mention of Socrates' second address to the court[18] would surely have been more to the point.

As to Holland's objection to the extension of the class of suicide, I agree with the substance of it though not with its grounds. Almost without exception Holland considers suicide to be morally wrong; however, this alleged moral wrongness is hardly the reason why we are reluctant to accept the view that Socrates, the patron saint of philosophers, committed suicide. Or should we not be so reluctant? Anyway, why should the possibility of "altruistic suicides" be almost ruled out? Surely Holland would not deny that Oates deserves praise for walking into the blizzard. If Oates didn't deliberately go to his death and if it was the blizzard that "killed him," what do we praise him for? Should we rather praise the blizzard?

The Death of Jesus

Is it only "piety" that prevents us from viewing Jesus' death as a suicide? Indeed, if we read the Gospels with the question, "Did Jesus intend his own death?" a positive answer appears almost inevitable. Early on in his public life Jesus told the assembled disciples that "...the son of man must suffer many things, and be rejected by the elders and the chief priests and the scribes, and be killed, and after three days rise again."[19] Later on, in the narrative of the Passion, Matthew reports the episode of Jesus being taken captive by the soldiers of the chief priests and rebuking one of them who had drawn his sword: "Put your sword back into its place; for all who take the sword will perish by the sword. Do you think that I cannot appeal to my Father, and he will at once send me more than twelve legions of angels? But how then should the scriptures be fulfilled, that it must be so?"[20]

Prophecies such as Isaiah's,[21] to which the passage in Matthew is an allusion, were well known to the Jews. We can take the view either that Jesus was indeed the son of God or that he was but a historical figure well-known at the time for various claims he made. In the first case His deliberate refraining from seeking help from the "legions of angels" appears like an acceptance of death, albeit for the sake of His redeeming mission. This would make Him a suicide, sub-class martyrdom, in Durkheim's classification. Though for reasons that have nothing to do with "piety," I shall argue that such a description of Jesus' death is rather misleading.

On the other hand, if we view Jesus' death from outside the Christian perspective, what we have is a man who seeks to convince others that he is more than he might appear, in fact that he is the Messiah of whom the prophets spoke. How better can he prove this than by making the prophecies come true? His death becomes the supreme argument: he proves himself to be what he claims to be *only* if he dies. After all the claims he had made in the course of his public life, Jesus had no option but to make sure that he was condemned to death. Should we call this partly self-engineered martyrdom a suicide?

There are interesting parallels between the death of Jesus and that of Socrates. In the course of their trial both defiantly stood by what they had formerly taught, while being fully aware that a condemnation to death would ensue. In neither case does it seem far-fetched to say that they provoked the Court into condemning them to death. It is true that, unlike Socrates, Jesus didn't die by his own hand. However, as was pointed out earlier against Frey, this difference isn't really significant. It would seem, therefore, that the claims that Socrates as well as Jesus committed suicide are either to stand or to fall together.

The fact that many would balk at the idea that Jesus committed suicide no doubt shows that this is still in some sense a Christian society and that the concept of suicide has, therefore, retained a derogatory connotation. However, there is another, more fundamental and, I should contend, perfectly legitimate reason for our reluctance to place either figure in the class of "suicides." Such a reason stems from a proper appreciation of the rhetoric of the term "suicide."

The Death of Bobby Sands

The rhetoric of suicide can perhaps best be illustrated by the death, in May 1981, of Bobby Sands, the IRA [Irish Republican Army] Provisional who went on a hunger strike in protest against the government's refusal to grant political prisoners' status to himself and his fellow IRA Provisionals in prison. It will be recalled that, in 1972, after an earlier hunger strike, the government had agreed that convicted prisoners claiming a political motive for their "crimes" should be granted "special category" status. That ruling had been rescinded in 1976.

In the course of his long fast Sands had rejected several appeals to call off his hunger strike on the grounds that he had no reason "to suit the people who oppress, torture, and imprison me, and who wish to dehumanize me. While I remain alive, I remain what I am, a political prisoner of war."[22] In the same vein Sands's mother was quoted as saying that her son was "offering his life" for a set of conditions in prison.[23]

In the course of the debate in the House of Commons, subsequent to the announcement of Sands's death, the Prime Minister said: "He chose to take his own life, a choice his organization did not allow to any of its victims."[24] The British establishment mostly took the view that Sands was a suicide. This view and its implications are most clearly and explicitly spelled out in the *Times* editorial of 6th May 1981: "By refusing to submit to Mr. Sands' blackmail, the British Government bears no responsibility whatever for his death. He committed suicide, in full knowledge of what he was doing and determined to reject all initiatives to save his life. He was not hounded into death.... Every discomfort he endured leading up to and including his death was self-inflicted.... There is only one killer of Bobby Sands and that is Sands himself." It is interesting to contrast the tone of this editorial with a pronouncement made by Mr. Carey, then Governor of the State of New York: "I deeply regret that the British Government has let Bobby Sands bring his hunger strike to its bitter conclusion."[25] This remark was taken as an indication that Her Majesty's government had alienated sections of public opinion abroad.

One major difference between the establishment's various pronouncements, on the one hand, and those of Sands's supporters or, e.g., Governor Carey, on the other hand, is immediately apparent: in the first case Sands is presented as having the initiative and thus deciding his fate while in the second case it is the government which is taken to have the initiative while Sands is at its mercy. In such a case, whoever had the initiative both bears the responsibility and incurs praise or blame for what happens. It is thus quite clear why the establishment insisted on putting the label "suicide" on Sands; to do so amounts to denying a direct causal link between their actions and the event and thus denying responsibility. To say that Sands committed suicide is to say that he brought about his own death and, therefore, bears responsibility for it. Equally clearly, Sands's supporters view his death as directly caused by the government's actions or lack of action and so they staunchly deny that he was a suicide. They view him as a martyr.

According to the common conception of martyrdom a death has a claim to come under the heading of martyrdom when it is deliberately or intentionally undergone for the sake of one's principles or cause. That this concept and that of suicide often function as instruments of persuasion comes out clearly in the case of Sands; whether we call him a martyr or a suicide largely depends on how we view, and the role we attribute to, the principles or cause in question. It appears clearly, therefore, that the word "suicide" has rhetorical associations since, at any rate in cases such as Sands's, to say that a person committed or didn't commit suicide amounts to taking a political stand.

Socrates Again

The case of Socrates, obviously, no longer excites the same amount of partisan passions as it did in the fourth century B.C.E. or as the case of Sands did a few years ago. However, the cases are sufficiently similar for the case of Sands to throw light on the case of Socrates. I want to claim that when Frey calls Socrates a suicide he is, in effect, playing Margaret Thatcher to Bobby Sands's Socrates. He is alleviating the responsibility (and thus the blame) incurred by the Athenian court over the death of Socrates while, correspondingly, stressing Socrates' own responsibility. Polemically, he is on the side of the Athenians since he is, more or less, telling them: "Don't be shamed into believing that you have killed Socrates; in fact, he committed suicide."

In Plato's *Apology* Socrates is rejecting in advance such whitewashing of the authorities when, alluding to his advanced age, he warns the Court that: "It is for the sake of a short time, gentlemen of the jury, that you will acquire the reputation and *the guilt, in the eyes of those who want to denigrate the city,* of having killed Socrates. . . ."[26] Those words, not those of a man bent on self-destruction, are Socrates' way of pointing out to the Court the risks involved in their condemning him to death: he will be viewed as a martyr and the Athenians will be taken to bear responsibility for his death.

The Rhetoric of Suicide

We are now in a position to spell out one of the differences between martyrdom and suicide. *To call X a suicide amounts, amongst other things, to ascribing to X the moral responsibility (and sometimes, but not always, the blame) for X's death. To call X a martyr amounts, amongst other things, to ascribing the moral responsibility (and, usually, the blame) for X's death to someone else (usually a government, an institution, or an organization).* Of course, as long as, in the manner of Durkheim, one uses purely behavioral criteria there is no way of distinguishing between martyrs and suicides. Recent work on suicide[27] has tended to concentrate on the concept of intention. However, unless they are accompanied by some kind of double effect type of argument, such analyses will be no help in solving the problem raised by Socrates' or any martyr's death. Had it been noticed that the concept of suicide denotes not only a manner of dying but also a way of viewing the broader circumstances of a death, the problem would not have arisen in the first place. The case of Socrates, as the amount of interest generated by Mr. Frey's article testifies, shows quite plainly that the concept of suicide has a very powerful rhetoric of its own.

That the concept of "suicide" has such a "responsibility-ascribing" function appears also from the fact that in most penal systems great care is taken that a prisoner condemned to death shouldn't kill himself in his cell. In fact, should he fall ill, he will first be nursed back to health before being executed. For several reasons it is considered important that the prisoner should be executed and not come under the heading of "suicide" or "natural death." What light this observation throws on the penal systems in question is not a problem that need concern us here.

The foregoing remarks on responsibility should not be taken as ruling out of court the possibility of "induced suicides." In the case of an "induced suicide" the responsibility (and, most likely, the blame) for X's death falls mainly on whoever induced X to bring about his or her own death. The existence of induced suicides, however, does not invalidate my general claim; in such cases it is usually made clear that the "suicide" was "driven to it" or, indeed, that he or she was a suicide between quotation marks. Besides, such was obviously not in the case of Socrates or, for that matter, of Jesus.

I do not want to suggest either that it is conceptually impossible that one and the same death could be both a suicide and a condemnation to death though it would be a case of over-determination. Might Seneca be an example in point? It would seem so, at any rate, from the account of J. R. G. Wright: "In 65 he was accused of participation in a conspiracy to depose Nero (some said he was to succeed to the throne) and, on imperial *command, embraced* the suicide which his philosophy *permitted* him as a final release from the ills of this world."[28] In view of the fact that he was ordered to commit suicide but was left the choice of means, and anyway belonged to a philosophical persuasion not inimical to suicide, Seneca falls somewhat uneasily between the case of the prisoner condemned to death and the case of the suicide. Though he wasn't a prisoner and hadn't, strictly speaking, been condemned to death, the political circumstances in Rome at that time made Nero's order amount to condemnation to death. Though Seneca's stoicism meant that he didn't have any objection in principle to dying by his own hand, he was in fact given the choice between killing himself and being killed by soldiers of the Pretorian Guard.

Clearly, in the absence of any qualifications, the epithet "suicide" does not fit the death of Seneca. Intuitively, we recognize this when we say, e.g., that Seneca was "*forced* to commit suicide"; we resort to paradox to lessen the inadequacy of the description. In fact, we do want to make the point that responsibility for Seneca's death is to be laid wholly at Nero's door, though it was not contrary to Seneca's principles to die as he did, he died when he did because Nero had decreed that he should. Seneca didn't open his veins either from philosophical conviction or because he was tired of life: he had, in effect, been condemned to death but was allowed to choose how to die.

In conclusion I should want to claim that: (1) the notion of suicide has a practical function or meaning, namely, that of ascribing moral responsibility, and (2) this practical function is not an adventitious adjunct to the so-called descriptive meaning of the concept of suicide but is an integral part of it. In fact, the two aspects, i.e., the descriptive and the practical, are, in this case, inextricably intermingled. What I have called throughout this paper the "rhetoric of suicide" stems from this practical function: if it is, indeed, the case that to call X a suicide is to locate in X him/herself the main responsibility for his or her death, then the question as to whether any particular X was or was not a suicide can become a matter of bitter debate and protracted argument, with no "objective" decision at the end of it. Durkheim hoped that his definition of suicide, by doing away with mental concepts, would allow individual cases to be settled "scientifically" and unambiguously. Besides the difficulties raised by Holland, it should be stressed that the concept of suicide, *de facto*, reflects the views and attitudes of the society or group who apply it to individual instances. As such both "suicide" and "martyrdom" are incapable of being "scientifically" determined.

This *practical* or responsibility-ascribing function of the concept is not to be confused with what Stevenson called the "emotional meaning." Clearly the word "suicide" has, from certain religious points of view and in many people's minds, a derogatory emotive connotation. Since they take suicide to be morally wrong they feel a corresponding reluctance to make conceptual room for "altruistic suicide." The curious reluctance shown by several philosophers to describe Captain Oates's death as a suicide shows this. In fact, Frey's claim might arguably be viewed, Stevenson fashion, as an attempt at a persuasive definition. By extending the denotation of the concept of "suicide" so that it now includes Socrates, Frey is making an attempt at altering its emotive meaning. Frey's concluding remark lends weight to this interpretation: "... the fact that Socrates died a noble and dignified death does not show that he did not commit suicide, but rather that suicide need not be ignoble and undignified."[29] Quite so. But it doesn't show, either, of course, that Socrates did commit suicide. Where Mr. Frey's argument seems to me to misfire is due to his neglect of the responsibility-locating aspect of the concept of suicide.

If my contention concerning the practical function of the concept of suicide is accepted, it will clear suicide of its present negative emotive coloring, while at the same time retaining the important insight that the concept of "suicide" is not purely descriptive. Indeed, since the concept has the practical function of ascribing moral responsibility, such responsibility will be ascribed for moral deeds as well as for immoral ones. We need feel no compunction in describing Captain Oates as a suicide. Suicide can, indeed, be noble and dignified. In order to make this point, however, there is no need to include Socrates in the class of suicides.

Notes

1. R. G. Frey, "Did Socrates Commit Suicide?" *Philosophy* 53 (1978): 106–108.
2. E. Durkheim, *Suicide,* trans. Spaulding and Simpson (Glencoe, Ill.: The Free Press, 1951), p. 44; 1st ed. 1897.
3. Ibid., pp. 43–44.
4. Ibid., p. 42.
5. Ibid.
6. Frey, p. 106.
7. Ibid.
8. R. F. Holland, "Suicide," repr. in *Against Empiricism* (Totowa, N.J.: Barnes and Noble Books, 1980), pp. 143–57.
9. Ibid., p. 144.
10. Holland, p. 221. Durkheim calls "altruistic suicides" or, more specifically, "obligatory altruistic suicides," those that are committed, under compelling reasons imposed by their societies, on (1) men on the threshold of old age or stricken with disease, (2) women on their husband's death, and (3) followers or servants on the death of their chief or master. These cases Durkheim considers to exhibit the essential characteristics of altruistic suicide, while "other varieties are only derivative forms" (Holland, p. 240).
11. Ibid., p. 146.
12. Ibid., p. 149.
13. Ibid.
14. Ibid., p. 151.

15. I say "probably" because it could be argued that Sands couldn't "know" that his hunger strike would result in his own death since he must have hoped, at the very least initially, that the government would accede to his request.

16. Frey, p. 106.

17. Michael Smith, "Did Socrates Kill Himself Intentionally?" *Philosophy* 55 (1980): 253–54; Holland, p. 146, had earlier made a similar point when he had remarked that "Taking hemlock,... in the context of an Athenian judicial execution,... is no more an act of suicide than the condemned man's walk to the scaffold."

18. Plato, *Apology*, 36d–38b.

19. Mark 8:31.

20. Matthew 26:52–53.

21. Chs. 42 and 49.

22. Quoted in *Time* magazine, 4th May, 1981.

23. Quoted in *The Times*, 4th May, 1981.

24. Quoted in *The Times*, 6th May, 1981.

25. Quoted in *New York Times* of 5th May, 1981.

26. Plato, *Apology*, 38c (my italics).

27. Cf., for instance, R. A. Duff, "Socratic Suicide?" *Proceedings of the Aristotelian Society*, 1982–83.

28. J. R. G. Wright, "Seneca," in P. Edwards, ea., *The Encyclopaedia of Philosophy* (New York: The Macmillan Company and The Free Press, 1967). My italics.

29. Frey, p. 108.

12

Suicide and
Self-Inflicted Death
R. G. Frey

T he most common view of suicide today is that it is intentional self-killing.[1] Because of the self-killing component, suicide is often described as self-inflicted death or as dying by one's own hand, and the victim is in turn often described as having done himself to death or as having taken his own life. But must one's death be self-inflicted in order to be suicide? The answer, I want to suggest, is arguably no.

I

In many cases of suicide, death is obviously self-inflicted; I refer, of course, to cases where the individual shoots himself or cuts his wrists or commits hara-kiri. It is equally obvious, however, that there are dozens of cases of what we take to be suicide where death is not self-inflicted in this narrow sense. If Jones wants to die and throws himself under a train, I take it that all of us want to regard him as a suicide, even though it is the train which actually kills him. How, then, do we do this? The answer, of course, is that we distinguish this narrow sense of "self-inflicted" from a broad sense, according to which one's death is self-inflicted if one wants to die, knowingly and willingly places oneself in perilous circumstances, and dies as a result.[2] Thus, Jones, who wants to die, knowingly and willingly places himself in circumstances where his death, if not actually inevitable, at least is exceedingly likely, and he dies as a result; he commits suicide, therefore, even though his death is not self-inflicted in the narrow sense.

I shall not bother with the secondary issue of how perilous the circumstances

From *Philosophy* 56 (1981): 193–202. Copyright © Royal Institute of Philosophy. Reprinted with the permission of Cambridge University Press.

must be before one is deemed a suicide. There is almost certainly, however, a lower limit to perilousness. If instead of throwing himself under a train Jones takes a scheduled flight from London to New York, and if the plane goes down, I should still not want to say that Jones committed suicide. For apart from anything else, though he knowingly and willingly takes this flight, flying the Atlantic on a scheduled flight is not sufficiently perilous—the odds on any single such plane going down are simply too low—to make Jones a suicide.

Merely placing oneself in perilous circumstances and dying as a result, however, does not make one a suicide; one must also want to die. Soldiers who volunteer for hazardous war-time missions knowingly and willingly place themselves in perilous circumstances; but their deaths do not amount to suicide, any more than do those of traffic wardens in Rome, who go into the midst of and vainly try to direct rush-hour traffic. (There is a use of "suicide" in which engaging or persisting in a course of action in perilous circumstances is likened to suicide, even though there is no question of the agent actually wanting to die. A soldier in the trenches who says "To go over the top now is suicide" or who, upon returning from the front, says "It's suicide up there," in fact means that the likelihood of death is very considerably increased by going over the top or to the front, not that all soldiers who so act when ordered commit suicide, if they are killed.)

II

The broad sense of "self-inflicted" death helps in some cases with the vexing problem of whether sacrificial deaths are suicides.[3] R. F. Holland has maintained that Captain Oates, who walked away from Scott's camp in the Antarctic rather than continue through illness to be a burden on the expedition, did not commit suicide, since he did not shoot or eviscerate himself but simply walked off into the freezing cold, which eventually killed him.[4] On the broad sense of "self-inflicted" death, however, Oates certainly did commit suicide, however noble his motive for doing what he did; indeed, on this sense, his motive is irrelevant to whether he committed suicide. For he knowingly and willingly placed himself in circumstances where he would die, and he died as a result; and though it is the freezing cold which actually killed him, he put himself in precisely those circumstances where it would kill him. The only question, then, is whether Oates wanted to die, and we can reasonably infer from his intentionally (not accidentally or mistakenly) walking off, together with his knowledge of what the effect of this on him would be, that he did indeed want to die, if not as an end, at least as a means to the end of allowing Scott to carry on unencumbered. One might argue, I suppose, that though Captain Oates foresaw as a consequence of walking off that he would die, what he wanted was not to die but to allow Scott to carry on unencumbered; but it is equally reasonable to argue that, having taken stock of his situation and Scott's, Oates wanted to die *in order to* allow Scott to carry on.[5]

(Doubtless Oates considered his options carefully and came to the decision to walk off; but deliberation and explicit decision are not necessary in order that one knowingly and willingly do something. I knowingly and willingly come into work each morning, but I certainly do not normally deliberate doing so and decide accordingly, just as I can knowingly and willingly go to the cinema without deliberating the merits of possible alternatives and explicitly deciding on this alternative as opposed to some other.)

Cases of sacrificial death, however, come in all shapes and sizes, and though the broad sense of "self-inflicted" death helps with some, it cannot be seen as the solution to all such cases. A soldier who throws himself on a live grenade, in order to save his comrades, commits suicide, if we can agree that (i) he knowingly and willingly acts as he does, and (ii) he wants to die, if not as an end, at least as a means. The fly in the ointment, of course, is our agreeing upon (i) and (ii). In some cases, (i) and (ii) may be reasonably clear. A father who gives his sole remaining kidney in order to save the life of his young son and who dies as a result, pretty clearly satisfies (i) and (ii). Our initial hesitation, such as it is, over (ii) stems from the fact that, were his son not ill, the father would not contemplate giving up his life; but his son is ill, and if the son can only live with the kidney and the father cannot live without the kidney, then in giving up his kidney to save his son the father consents to his own death as the means to that end. This does not mean that he welcomes death, but it does mean that he not merely foresees his death but also takes steps to bring it about and approves the result it achieves. In the case of the soldier, on the other hand, there are complicating factors, not the least serious of which is time. In respect of (i), knowingly and willingly acting as he does, the whole incident may occur so quickly that the soldier behaves spontaneously and unthinkingly; and though we may be reluctant to say that he acts accidentally or mistakenly, we may be equally reluctant to maintain that, in acting spontaneously and unthinkingly, he acts knowingly and willingly. In respect to (ii), wanting to die, if the whole incident is over and done with in a few seconds, we may be reluctant to say of the soldier that he wanted anything, at least in any occurrent sense of that term. Certainly we should be reluctant to speak of his "deciding" to act as he does and so as a result coming to want to die.

So far as the time-factor is concerned, then, I suspect that the more spontaneous the act can be made to appear, as in the case of the soldier, the less likely we shall be to consider the victim a suicide, whereas the less spontaneous the act appears, as in the case of the father, the more likely we shall be to construe sacrificial deaths as suicides. In the light of this, it is no accident that those cases of sacrificial death most seized upon in the literature and held not to be suicide are precisely those in which the agent at once falls upon a grenade or dashes into a blazing house or dives into a raging sea. Just because of the time-factor, these cases appear to put maximum stress on the broad sense of "self-inflicted" death, as an aid to sorting out sacrificial deaths.

Yet, even these spontaneous cases are open to a difficulty of sorts, in their use against the broad view of "self-inflicted" death. The problem is not that spontaneous (and unthinking) acts cannot be meritorious; on the contrary, I can well imagine someone arguing that the good man is one who, in certain circumstances, does not think and calculate but acts out of ingrained good habits and/or principles. So to speak, the man of good character just does the right thing in these cases, spontaneously and uncalculatedly.[6] No, the problem with such cases is that, the more spontaneous they are made to appear, in order to avoid their succumbing to the broad sense of "self-inflicted" death, the more like reflex actions they become; and the more like reflex actions they become, the less likely we shall be to say of the agents that they acted at all. A reflex kneejerk is not an act in the operative sense, and if falling upon the grenade or dashing into the blazing building or diving into the raging sea is made out to be so spontaneous as to approximate to a knee-jerk, then it is arguable that the agent has not acted at all, in the operative sense. In short, then, in order to avoid being instances of suicide on the broad sense of "self-inflicted" death, these cases of sacrificial death must appear to include a considerable degree of spontaneity in the act of the agent; but in order to avoid their appearing as instances of reflex action and so of not amounting to acts in the operative sense, the degree of spontaneity in the act of the agent must be restricted. I am not suggesting that these two demands are altogether and always incompatible, only that they impose limits on the types of cases of sacrificial death that can be used to evade the broad sense of "self-inflicted" death.

III

If suicide, then, is killing oneself intentionally, one must not interpret this expression so narrowly as to preclude self-inflicted deaths in the broad sense from being suicides. This is why the tendency to use the expressions "dying by one's own hand" and "self-inflicted death" interchangeably of suicide is so very unfortunate; for if all those cases of dying by one's own hand are cases of self-inflicted death (in the narrow sense), not all cases of self-inflicted death (i.e., those in the broad sense) are cases of dying by one's own hand. In the broad sense of self-inflicted death, something in the circumstances kills one, such as a train; and being run over by a train is not dying by one's own hand, a phrase which is typically used to single out an individual's own act of swallowing poison or cutting his wrists.

Now the cases we have in mind to cover by means of the broad sense of self-inflicted death are just those, like the cases of Jones and Captain Oates, where what it is in the circumstances which actually produces death is something like a train or a car or the weather or a fire. But what if the circumstances into which one places oneself, with death as a practically certain outcome, involve fundamentally an explicit and overt act on the part of another human being? If the victim dies as a result of this other person's act, can he be a suicide? The broad sense of "self-inflicted" death was not intended to and does not obviously cover such cases, and it seems reasonable to maintain that, if one dies as the result of another party's act, one's death is not self-inflicted in any sense. Therefore, if we are prepared to allow that the individual in question nevertheless commits suicide, it follows that suicide does not require self-inflicted death.

But *are* we prepared to allow that such an individual commits suicide? I think there are cases where we *will* allow this, unless we go on to regard them as cases of both suicide *and* murder or manslaughter by another party; for there are features to these cases which make it highly doubtful that we shall regard them as cases of murder or manslaughter pure and simple.

The limits within which such cases must fall can be garnered from a more straightforward case in which the victim is killed by another person. In a detective story I read not long ago, Bill and Bob are performing in a play one scene of which calls for Bill to take a pistol from a drawer and shoot Bob. The pistol has always been loaded with blanks, of course, but on the evening in question, when Bill once again takes up the gun and shoots Bob, Bob really is killed. The novelist heightens the tension surrounding the ensuing investigation, first, by presenting evidence that Bob was depressed and under considerable strain, and second, by presenting evidence that he was hated by a number of his fellow players, including Bill.

Three features of this case are important here. First, there is no doubt whatever that Bob has been shot and killed by Bill. It does not follow, however, that Bob did not commit suicide. For he knew that the pistol would be fired by Bill directly at him; and if Bob was the one who loaded the pistol with live bullets, then the police will conclude that Bob committed suicide, even though Bill killed him. If, however, Bill or a third party loaded the pistol then the police will conclude that Bob was murdered. Thus, the determination of whether Bob committed suicide is made to depend, not upon who actually shot and killed Bob, but upon who loaded the pistol. Second, if Bob loaded the pistol, he has contrived his death in such a way that he ends up dead at the hands of another person. For merely loading the pistol with live bullets does not issue in the death of Bob; Bill must also pull the trigger of the pistol. Third, though Bob's death is obviously not self-inflicted in the narrow sense, it is arguable that, if he loaded the pistol this fact suffices to render his death self-inflicted in the broad sense. At the very least, he takes a hand in his own death, not in some indirect or remote sense, but in the wholly direct and immediate sense of knowingly and willingly loading the gun which, given the scene in the play, in all likelihood will kill him.

What this case teaches us is that, if we are to find a case of other-inflicted death which is nevertheless arguably a case of suicide, what we must come up with is a case not only where the victim, who contrives his death, is killed by someone else, but also where he does not perform an act comparable to that of loading the pistol, such as switching the capsules or disguising the poison which kills him. For acts of this sort appear compatible with the broad sense of self-inflicted death. (I shall not consider cases of begging and pleading with someone to kill one, since acts of this kind, by a person who is seriously and painfully ill, raise questions beyond the scope of this paper.) Are there any cases, therefore, which satisfy these requirements? I believe that there are.

IV

In a film I saw as a young boy, Ted, an aging cowboy who is down on his luck, decides to end it all. He does not suffer from any disease and is not otherwise approaching a "vegetable" condition; he is simply miserable and unhappy. In one scene, he puts a loaded pistol to his head but cannot bring himself to pull the trigger. Therefore, he devises a plan: he will challenge his worst enemy, a well-known outlaw, to meet him at high noon, in the knowledge that the outlaw cannot refuse without serious loss of face (quite apart from the fact that refusal exposes *him* to possible death from *his* enemies) and that the outlaw is both fast and accurate with a gun. Ted further plans, if he does manage to draw his gun, not to fire it. The plan is put into effect, the two meet, and Ted is killed. Does Ted commit suicide? Or does the outlaw murder him?

The case for suicide is readily apparent: Ted wants to die and carefully plans his death; he puts this plan into operation and thereby knowingly and willingly places himself in a situation where death is a practical certainty; and he dies as a result. The outcome, in other words, is precisely what he hopes, wants, and plans it to be. The case for murder is equally apparent: the outlaw does not have to accept Ted's challenge or meet him in the street or draw his gun or shoot or kill Ted; and it would be false to think that Ted's death is an accident.

To someone who wanted to regard the case as *obviously* one of murder, what is one to make of Ted's carefully conceived plan and the steps he takes to implement it? One might say, I suppose, that Ted's plan is to bring about or force his own murder, but there are two difficulties with this. First, it suggests that it is a part of Ted's plan that the outlaw come to will Ted's death; but this is not the case. All that matters to Ted is that he end up dead at the hands of the outlaw; and if this can be achieved without the outlaw willing his death then, from Ted's point of view, so be it. Second, therefore, if what Ted is doing is planning his own death, as it certainly is, then the essence of this plan consists in manipulating another human being into circumstances where he will kill Ted. Ted does this because he wants to die. Why, then, if death ensues, is Ted not a suicide? He wants to die, plans his death, carefully puts his plan into operation, and dies. If the only reason why he is not a suicide is that he does not actually kill himself, then neither do Jones or Captain Oates actually kill themselves; and if one can be a suicide and be killed by a train or the weather, why can one not be a suicide and be killed by another person?

Our central worry on this score, I think, is that the other person may have come to will the victim's death. But what if the other person does not will the victim's death? Is there then any reason for denying that it is a case of suicide? For example, though it is possible simply to lay down that anyone in the outlaw's position who becomes embroiled in Ted's plan comes to will Ted's death, there is something artificial about such a stipulation. In *Imputed Criminal Intent, D. P. P. v. Smith* (London: Her Majesty's Stationery Office, 1967), the Law Commission came out against an objective, hypothetical test of intention, which turns upon what a reasonable man would or would not have foreseen as a consequence of his act, and in favor of a subjective test, which concerns itself with the actual state of mind of the agent, not the hypothetical state of mind of some hypothetical individual. If we adopt some sort of distinction like this for willing another's death, if we then concern ourselves with the other person's actual state of mind, and if that person does not come to will the victim's death, then the major impediment of allowing

Ted's case to be suicide is removed. I am not, of course, asserting that the outlaw did not will Ted's death, only that, if he did not, then there appears no reason not to concede this case of other-inflicted death to be suicide.

Consider this case: Tom, who is simply miserable and unhappy, seriously wants to end it all. He has already tried twice to kill himself with a revolver but failed. To ensure success, therefore, he devises a plan: he begins to goad and taunt, to ridicule and humiliate his wife, whom he knows to be of an exceedingly nervous, fragile temperament; and over many weeks his goading, etc., supplemented by beatings, reach fever pitch. His wife is unable to escape the barrage, and, as it grows ever more intense, she reaches the end of her endurance. In a passion, she kills Tom, though she certainly knows what she is doing and realizes full well that a bullet through the heart will kill someone.

In this case, Tom has exploited his wife's temperament in order to bring about his own demise. It is just this exploitation, just this passion which issues in her killing him, and just this outcome which Tom has carefully planned and in the event successfully achieved.

True, the whole episode takes weeks, and it may be suggested, therefore, that Tom's wife has the opportunity to contemplate and plan Tom's death. But what if she does not seize this opportunity? Is there then any reason for denying the case is one of suicide? One can here, too, simply stipulate that anyone in Tom's wife's situation must at least contemplate, if not deliberate, her husband's death; but a stipulation of this sort rings hollow, just because there is no reason, either in logic or in fact, why it must be the case that she contemplates or deliberates or plans Tom's death. Surely, therefore, we must examine her case very closely in order to determine whether she did any of these things. And if she did not, why should we not allow the case to be one of suicide?

Finally, what about planning one's death so that one is killed by what amounts to a reflex action? Consider this case: Tex seriously wants to end it all. He cannot face shooting himself or cutting his wrists, however, so he devises a plan by which someone else kills him. He purchases a gun and blanks and then threatens to kill his small son. When the police arrive, he releases his son and then dashes into a neighboring warehouse, firing his gun as he runs. Once inside the warehouse, he hides behind a large crate, waiting for one of the policemen to come in after him and to get in front of him. When this happens, Tex jumps out from behind the crate, yells an obscenity, waits for the policeman to turn, and then fires one of his blanks. The policeman whirls round, comes face to face with Tex's gun, and instinctively squeezes off his own, only a split second after Tex has fired. Tex is killed.

One might claim that the policeman's initial drawing of his gun indicates a readiness to use it; but to any witness of the above events, his use of the gun was instinctual, a reflex action, in the actual killing of Tex. It is very important to realize, moreover, that the success of Tex's plan *depends upon* a certain readiness by the policeman to use his gun; for he knows that, if policemen were prepared to allow guns repeatedly to be fired at them from point-blank range without defending themselves, his plan would stand no chance whatever of success. Just as Ted exploits the outlaw's reluctance to lose face and to appear in his enemies' eyes as no longer prepared to fight, and just as Tom exploits his wife's fragile temperament, so Tex exploits the policeman's readiness to defend himself.

V

Can one, therefore, commit suicide by planning one's death in such a way that another person kills one? The cases of Ted, Tom, and Tex suggest to me that one can. What, I think, makes them cases of suicide, in spite of the fact that the relevant deaths are not self-inflicted in any sense, is a set of features they all share. Each victim wants to die, and each takes steps to bring this about; each draws up a plan with his death as the outcome; each puts his plan into operation and so knowingly and willingly places himself in circumstances where another person is exceedingly likely to kill him; each exploits and actively manipulates both the circumstances and the other person to this end; each is killed. To leave out these common features in considering these cases is impossible, since they are integral features of them; but to include such features in our consideration of them makes it difficult to conclude that they are cases of murder/manslaughter pure and simple. What this indicates, I think, is that, if the perilous circumstances into which the victim knowingly and willingly places himself involve another person's act, as the result of which the victim dies, then the mere fact that he is killed by someone else *does not preclude* the possibility of his being a suicide, provided it can be shown that he wanted and planned his death and exploited and manipulated the circumstances and the other person to achieve this end as a part of his plan.

More simply, the above cases are all cases of engineering one's death and in this sense describe different ways of doing away with oneself. True, they are not particularly nice ways of doing away with oneself, since they not merely involve but actively exploit and make use of another person in order to accomplish the deed. As such, they are only likely to appeal to those people, for example, who are squeamish and cannot face the thought of blowing off the tops of their heads or cutting out their entrails. These individuals, therefore, are led to plan and contrive their deaths differently, so that they are killed by someone else; and the plans devised in each case have a high probability of producing the desired result.

Of course, there is another and, perhaps, to some, more tempting way of regarding the cases of Ted, Tom, and Tex. I have raised the question of whether they are cases of suicide or murder/manslaughter by another party; but they may be thought by some *to be both*, that is, to be cases of suicide if looked at from the victim's position and cases of murder/manslaughter if looked at from the other party's position. Regarding them as both, moreover, may seem to fit some people's indecision about them: what makes such people hesitate to conclude that they are cases of murder/manslaughter is the set of common features cited above; but what makes them hesitate to conclude that they are cases of suicide is the fear that the other party may have come to will the victim's death. By regarding these cases as both suicide and murder/manslaughter, they try to take into account and so not lose sight of these disparate elements which are the bases of their indecision.

This way of regarding these cases, obviously, runs up against the assumption that one and the same death cannot be both suicide and murder/manslaughter (by another party). This assumption itself, however, depends upon a presumed contrast between suicide as self-inflicted death and murder/manslaughter as other-inflicted death. But if these examples of mine succeed, they either undermine this assumption or at least make plain that it is an assumption, with limitations and exceptions, since there arguably are cases of suicide where the victim's death is not self-inflicted in any sense but other-inflicted. In a word, the presumed contrast breaks down,[7] with the result that the claim of these cases to be both suicide and murder/manslaughter, if it is to be defeated, cannot be defeated simply by relying upon some contrast between self-inflicted and other-inflicted death as the core difference between suicide and murder/manslaughter.

Notes

1. See my "Did Socrates Commit Suicide?" *Philosophy* 53 (1978): 106–108, reprinted in *Suicide: Contemporary Philosophical Issues,* M. Pabst Battin and David Mayo, eds. (New York: St. Martin's Press, 1980).

2. For a very helpful discussion of this broad sense, to which I am indebted, see T. L. Beauchamp, "What Is Suicide?" in *Ethical Issues in Death and Dying,* T. L. Beauchamp and S. Perlin, eds. (Englewood Cliffs, N.J.: Prentice-Hall, 1978), pp. 97–102.

3. See Beauchamp, pp. 99–101, for his discussion of such cases and the case of Captain Oates.

4. "Suicide," in *Moral Problems,* J. Rachels, ed. (New York: Harper & Row, 1971), pp. 352–54.

5. I am grateful to Margaret Battin for assistance on this point, though in another context.

6. For a discussion of one such view of the good man, see my "What a Good Man Can Bring Himself to Do," *Journal of Value Inquiry* 12 (1978): 134–41.

7. My point here is a theoretical one. I do not deny that there may be good reasons in practice for using some distinction between self-inflicted and other-inflicted death as a rough and ready difference between suicide and murder.

13

Suicide and Self-Starvation
Terence M. O'Keeffe

A puzzle has been presented in the recent past in Northern Ireland: what is the correct description of the person who dies as a result of a hunger-strike? For many the simple answer is that such a person commits suicide, in that his is surely a case of "self-inflicted death." Where then is the puzzle? It is that a number of people do not see such deaths as suicides. I am not here referring to political propagandists or paramilitaries, for whom the correct description of such deaths is "murder by Mrs. Thatcher" or "killed by British intransigence" (to quote advertisements in the Belfast nationalist press at the time of Bobby Sands's death). I am rather thinking of some theologians who, despite being opposed to the hunger-strike and indeed publicly condemning the whole campaign, refused to describe what the hunger-strikers did as suicide.

Trying to understand the reasoning involved in this judgment will force us to clarify our notion of what is to count as suicide, the role of the intention of the person acting in such a way as to bring about his own death, and through this notion, something about the principle of "double effect" which seems to be invoked by theologians in cases like this. The following reflections however exclude any consideration of the *politics* of hunger-striking in Northern Ireland, which would require a very different treatment. (Whether it will be possible to exclude entirely any political judgment from a description of the deaths of hunger-strikers will perhaps be clearer by the end of the discussion.)

I have pointed out that there are some people who wish to deny the suicide verdict on the deaths of hunger-strikers. It is clear why they wish to do so. They hold the view that suicide or self-killing is always an extremely grave sin, and if this were the correct description of the hunger-striker, many difficulties would be

From *Philosophy* 56 (1981): 349–63. Copyright © Royal Institute of Philosophy. Reprinted with the permission of Cambridge University Press.

raised for the pastoral care of such persons, especially their right to be admitted to the sacraments and to the last rites.

Perhaps I should indicate the source of their moral disapproval of suicide, for clearly it is not a verdict shared by all. For some people, there is no more difficulty about the suicide verdict on hunger-strikers than there is about a similar verdict on Socrates, the Christian martyrs, the death of Christ himself, Captain Oates, deaths of heroic self-sacrifice such as the soldier who throws himself on a live grenade in order to shield his comrades, etc. There will be no difficulty about accepting a suicide verdict in these sorts of cases because there is in their minds no *moral* disapproval implied by the term "suicide." Disapproval will only arise in cases where it could be suggested that it is not *rational* to end one's life. The officer who chooses "death rather than dishonor" when exposed as an embezzler of the mess funds and shoots himself, could be said to be acting irrationally in supposing that "dishonor"—i.e., living on after quitting the army in disgrace, with one's reputation destroyed, etc.—is somehow necessarily worse or necessarily less desirable than no life at all. David Hume, in "On Suicide," suggests that it is a proper course of action for those leading a life "loaded with pain and sickness, with shame and poverty." Whatever the propriety of escaping through suicide from intolerable pain and suffering, it is not immediately obvious why a life of shame and poverty is not rationally to be preferred to no life at all.

This form of rational calculation of the merits or demerits of suicide depends on a thesis, which I will call the *humanist* thesis, which is roughly this: that I am the judge of my best interests and that I am in charge of my life. It is a thesis about the moral autonomy of the rational individual. Thus, the decision to end my own life, provided it is taken as a fully human decision, on rational grounds, unclouded by irrational fears and motives, is for me and for me alone to make. Richard Brandt provides a good account of the sort of reasoning one might expect:

> [It is] a choice between future world-courses: the world-course that includes [my] demise, say, an hour from now, and several possible ones that contain [my] demise at a later point.... The problem, I take it, is to decide whether the expected utility to me of some possible world-course in which I go on for another twenty years is greater than or less than the expectable utility to me of the one in which my life stops in an hour.... We compare the suicide world-course with the continued-life world-course (or several of them) and note the features with respect to which they differ. We then assign numbers to these features, representing their utility to us if they happen, and then multiplying this utility by a number which represents the probability that this feature will occur. ... The world-course with the highest sum is the one that is rationally chosen.[2]

Brandt goes on to argue that "there is a close analogy between the analysis of the rationality of suicide and a firm's analysis of the rationality of declaring bankruptcy and going out of business."[3]

Such reasoning about suicide, based on the humanist thesis, is very different from the moral reasoning of those who wish to condemn suicide as an extremely evil act. The essential difference is to be found in their contention that one's life is *not* one's own to end or take away. Roy Holland is surely right in calling this standpoint "religious" and in seeing it as based on some thesis about life as a *gift*. The thesis can be expressed in different ways. Aquinas expresses it as follows: "Life is God's gift to man and is subject to his power.... Whosoever takes his own life sins against God even as he who kills another's slave sins against that slave's master. It belongs to God alone to pronounce sentence of life and death" (*Summa Theologica* IIa IIae, q.64, a.5). This echoes Socrates' verdict in the Phaedo: "Mortals are the chattels of the gods.... Wouldn't you be angry if one of your chattels should kill itself when you had not indicated that you wanted it to die?" (62B). The "slaves and chattels" imagery can give way to more "martial" allusions. So Locke argues in the *Second Treatise on Civil Government* that "everyone is bound to preserve himself and not to quit his station willfully" (ch. 2). And Kant argues in similar vein in the *Lectures on Ethics*: "A suicide . . . arrives in the other world as one who has deserted his post... as a rebel against God.... Human beings are sentinels on earth and may not leave their posts unless relieved by another beneficent hand."

It is true that other reasons are advanced in this tradition to establish the sinfulness of suicide. Aquinas gives two others. Suicide is a sin against oneself, thus violating a "natural law" of self-love. And it is a sin against the community and hence a form of injustice, appealing here to a principle that "every part as such belongs to the whole." But neither of these arguments carries the same weight as the "life as a gift" thesis. It is on this that the religious condemnation of suicide rests most strongly.

This condemnation of suicide does not appear to have been central to Christian teaching from the beginning. It is only with Augustine that Christian thinkers begin to specify suicide as the most evil of sins. There are a number of suicides in the Old Testament: Samson, who brought the temple crashing down upon himself with the cry, "May I die with the Philistines" (Judg. 16, 30); Abimelech, who ordered his sword-bearer to kill him when he was mortally wounded by a stone dropped by a woman "So that no one may say of me: a woman killed him" (Judg. 9, 53); Saul, who said "Draw your sword. I do not want uncircumcised men to gloat over me" and, when his sword-bearer refused, fell upon his own sword (2 Sam. 31, 4); and Ahithophel, who is perhaps the clearest case of suicide in the Old Testament: on having his advice rejected by Absalom, he retired to his home village and "having set his house in order, strangled himself and so died" (2 Sam. 17, 23). Yet these acts were not commented on particularly adversely by early writers. The suicide of the "archcriminal" Judas Iscariot is recorded in the Gospel of Saint Matthew without comment—almost, indeed, as a measure of his repentance. It is only later writers who see in Judas's suicide the real reason for his damnation. Tertullian appears to have had no difficulty in describing the death of Jesus as suicide (because he voluntarily gave up his life). What spurred Augustine and others to condemn suicide was the suicidal mania of many of the early Christian martyrs, and in particular the sect of the Donatists, for whom, taking the high valuation of martyrdom seriously, the most sensible course after baptism was to preserve the state of grace thus gained by instant death, by martyrdom if possible but by suicide if necessary. It was in opposition to this that Augustine stressed the condemnation of suicide as a frustration of God's plan and a rejection of God in rejecting his gift of life. Only in the sixth century did Church law incorporate a ban on suicide. Until that time, the promise of escape from temptation and the guarantee of posthumous glory were powerful inducements to martyrdom *and* to suicide.

Despite these caveats, it is clear that after this time a universal condemnation of suicide forms part of the Christian tradition, basing itself on several arguments. Suicide is a type of murder—self-murder—and thus shares the general condemnation of homicide. It is this that gives Aquinas his first argument against suicide, that it is a sin against oneself. It is also seen as an act which in a certain sense forestalls God's will for us. If death is the final evil and the last crucial test for the believer, it is because it signifies our ultimate helplessness before God. Suicide expresses a fundamental refusal of trust in God. It is a quitting of our station before we have been relieved, a desertion to the enemy. Most centrally, however, the thesis about life as a gift brings out clearly something about the religious person's vision of the human relationship with God. It is seen as one of dependence on a divine order of things and thus as a rejection of the total autonomy of the human individual. This sense of dependence is comparable to that sense of *contingency* about the world, that feeling of creaturehood and dependence, that provides the context for causal arguments for the existence of God. Just as, in its absence, some philosophers cannot see the point of such argumentation and, like Hume, find it senseless to "go one step beyond this mundane system" to seek a cause and explanation of the world's existence, so without the essentially religious context of "life as a gift," suicide can appear as a rational option. The humanist outlook is guided by some such principle as that in general life is to be preferred to nonlife. But this can yield to prudential considerations in favor of suicide (and of other cases of killing—euthanasia, abortion, infanticide for grossly handicapped infants, etc.). The other view, which insists on transcending the notion of human autonomy and on seeing a meaning in life beyond this world, insists that life is not one's own. One who ends his own life is thus guilty of denying the religious meaning of life itself. It is in this way that it can be seen as one of the very worst of sins. Holland quotes G. K. Chesterton's *Orthodoxy:* "The man who kills a man, kills a man. The man who kills himself, kills all men; as far as he is concerned he wipes out the whole world."[4] Suicide is thus seen as a turning of one's back on God, a deliberate spurning of God's gift, and ultimately a spurning of God himself. For Chesterton, it is "the refusal to take an interest in existence, the refusal to take the oath of loyalty to life."[5] Thus it is not just a narrowly religious sin; it is also a metaphysical sin. For Schopenhauer, suicide is not to be seen as an escape from the will or from the world, though it might appear so. It is in fact a strong *assertion* of the will: "Just because the suicide cannot cease to will, he ceases to live; and the will affirms itself here even through the abolition of one of its own phenomena because it can no more affirm itself otherwise."[6] Even where life is regarded as painful, the metaphysical duty is to endure, to retain that "first loyalty to things" (to quote Chesterton again).[7] Life as a gift is not necessarily to be understood as meaning that life is always something pleasant or desirable. Within this "religious" tradition, it can also appear as a trial and a burden. The notion of gift underlines that it is given to us and that we hold it in trust, whether to enjoy or not. A. Phillips Griffiths pinpoints the meaning of the act of suicide as it is seen within the "life as a gift" thesis:

> Suicide is the paradigm of evil, the "elementary" sin. To seek death is to reject life (or if it is not, is it really suicide?) and this is fundamentally different from other futile bad strivings of a particular will. . . . In all other sinning we fail to accept the world whatever it is—we would not have it as it is. In suicide we would not have it at all. We desire not merely a different meaning but no meaning: no God.[8]

If I wish to comment on the debate concerning the moral judgment on the hunger-striker—whether he commits suicide or not—I must take for granted this religious perspective. Otherwise the judgment could only be based on the question whether it is ever a rational thing to do to give up your life for a cause. In the eyes of many people it is a rational choice in certain circumstances. And if one asks whether on pragmatic grounds it is justifiable, then clearly it has been a useful tool in political struggles in the past in Ireland and elsewhere. (One can think not only of the death by hunger-strike of Terence McSweeny in the 20s, which had an enormous political impact, but even more recently in the early 70s a determined hunger-strike by prisoners like Billy McKee achieved political status for I.R.A. and loyalist prisoners.)

So I wish to pose the question of the suicide verdict on hunger-striking against the religious view which sees suicide as always a gravely evil act. What is to count within this tradition as an act of suicide? With the "life as a gift" thesis, *any* taking of life is problematic (including war, capital punishment, killing in self-defense, etc.). In the case of suicide, it is self-killing that is evil. There are many clear candidates for acts which could be described as self-killings—cutting one's own throat, poisoning oneself, throwing oneself in front of a train. But there are examples (one is given by Roger Frey)[9] where, though the killing is done by another person, it was so arranged by the person who dies that it seems more natural to call it an act of suicide than homicide. To commit a "self-killing" then, it is not necessary that one kills oneself or that one dies by one's own hand. Whether one shoots oneself or so arranges things that one is shot by someone else, it would still count as suicide. Again, in certain cases, refusing to act or refraining from acting would seem to count more as suicide than anything else. The person who has swallowed poison, however unwittingly, but who refuses to save his life by taking a simple antidote—would we not count him as much a suicide as the person who swallows poison to kill himself?

Can we then say that to commit suicide is by a negative or positive action or by so arranging the circumstances to put one's life in danger and die as a result? I hardly think that this would do. The person who attempts to cross the Place de la Concorde on foot would commit suicide not only in the humorous sense but in the morally blameworthy sense. Many accidental actions which cause our deaths would then have to be counted as suicides. We have to add something to the effect that the agent is aware of the possible results of his action. With the addition of this "subjective" factor—knowing the likely results of one's action—we have an account of suicide that we can call the *objective* account—in fact we have Durkheim's description: "The term suicide is applied to all cases of death resulting directly or indirectly from a positive or negative action of the victim himself which he knows will produce this result."[10]

This account specifically excludes from the definition of suicide any reference to motives, intentions, or reasons for taking the action. Durkheim wishes to exclude these in order to give a sociological account of suicide. His definition then will include a number of actions which have commonly, in the religious tradition we are talking about, been excluded as examples of suicide: martyrs going knowingly to their deaths, soldiers acting heroically and dying to save others, self-sacrifices, etc. Now this is of no significance for Durkheim since he did not wish the description of an action as suicide to have any moral connotation whatever. But for the religious tradition, suicide is always a gravely evil action. So some way has to be found of distinguishing such evil acts from acts in which a person knowingly goes to his death, is capable of avoiding it, does not act to save his own life, and yet is not to be counted a suicide and morally condemned. I am not so much thinking of examples like those given by Saint Jerome who, though asserting that it was never permissible to kill oneself to avoid persecution and torture, nevertheless conceded that it was permissible for a virgin to take her own life when her chastity was threatened; rather more of straightforward cases of martyrdom and those deaths commonly called sacrificial deaths.

Consider the case of Fr. Maximilian Kolbe who, during [World War II], substituted himself in the condemned cell for a fellow prisoner (a Jewish father of a family) and was executed. Did Kolbe commit suicide? If not, on what grounds do we rule out such deaths as suicides? Would we not be inclined to say that, in order to commit suicide, one must not only knowingly and willingly go to one's death, not act to save oneself, be capable of avoiding it—above all, one must *want* to die? The case of Fr. Kolbe, and the much discussed case of Captain Oates, are not suicides because they did not *intend* their deaths but rather some other state of affairs—the saving of the Jewish father, the lives of the other members of Scott's expedition.

In other words, the intention to die is the crucial factor in distinguishing suicides from those cases of deaths. To intend to terminate one's own life—this is the distinguishing mark of the act of suicide. To bring about the termination of one's life by so arranging the circumstances that one dies but with the intention of bringing about some other state of affairs, is not suicide. So the person who leaps from the boat, intending to kill himself and succeeding, commits suicide. The person who leaps from the boat, which is hopelessly overcrowded and in danger of sinking with the children, into a shark-infested sea does not commit suicide because he does not intend to die but rather to lighten the boat. The notion of the agent's intention seems neatly to distinguish the two cases and to enable us to withhold the moral condemnation in the description of the latter act—not suicide but self-sacrifice, a clear case of "laying down one's life for one's friends" which demands our moral approval.

Another way of discriminating between these types of cases is offered by Roy Holland.[11] Holland, too, wishes to condemn suicide for roughly the reasons I have picked out as the religious view. Equally he approves of the sort of action taken by Captain Oates and refuses the description of it as a suicide. He draws a number of distinctions between what Oates did—walking out of the tent into a blizzard and finally dying—and what he might have done but did not do—kill himself. Had Oates stepped outside the tent and shot himself, then according to Holland he would have committed suicide. But it is not what he did but what he *allowed to happen* to him that counts. Oates did not do anything, he let it be done to him, a difference then between *doing* and *suffering*. His action (walking from the tent) only indirectly led to his death, whereas had he cut his throat, that would have directly led to his death. The "temporal lapse" between his action of walking from the tent and his death seems significant to Holland. And so, too, does Oates's use of "natural phenomena" (the blizzard, the intense cold, etc.) rather than a gun or a knife. And in general Holland appeals to what he calls "the context and spirit" of Oates's action which makes it possible to say that Oates was no suicide but a self-sacrificing and heroic individual.

Can we use these three accounts of suicide to comment on the deaths by hunger-strike? Under the "objective" or nonintentional label, the only factor which becomes significant is whether the hunger-striker can be said to know that his action will lead to his death. If he does, then he is a suicide. A lot will depend on what one wants to put into the term "know" here. Obviously in one sense, a person embarking on a hunger strike knows that he will die after a (variable) period without taking food (normally somewhere between 40 and 75 days). It would, however, be argued that, since his decision is to continue on the hunger-strike until the government yields to his demands and since he does not know whether or when the government will give in, then in *some* sense he does not know whether he will die or not. But of course in this sense almost every suicide does not know that the act will be successful—he may be rescued and revived in time, he may only wound and not kill himself, etc. The point seems too slender to serve as an exoneration of the hunger-striker from the suicide verdict. (We must remember that the point of this account was to remove any moral condemnation from the description anyway.) And finally, since this account included both positive and negative actions, there seems little to be gained by attempting to say that the hunger-striker does not *do* anything to kill himself (such as cutting his throat) but simply does nothing in refusing food.

Holland's account at first sight looks a more promising candidate for those who wish to deny the suicide description to the hunger-striker. After all, a number of the features of the Oates case are directly paralleled in the case of the hunger-striker. Hunger-striking is arguably a "suffering" rather than a "doing." The prisoner does nothing, he "allows" the lack of food to kill him, he "suffers" death rather than inflicts it upon himself. His death is thus not the direct result of his action but indirect, just as Oates's was. There is a temporal lapse between the decision to undertake the hunger-strike and death itself. The hunger-striker uses a "natural phenomenon" of hunger like Oates. And finally it is surely plausible that the "context and spirit" of the hunger-strike, which has to be seen within the political struggle in Northern Ireland, is a context quite different from our ordinary understanding of suicides.

Now here, unlike the case of the "objective" account, there is something at stake. Holland wants to use his analysis of suicide to *acquit* Oates of the charge of suicide, which is morally blameworthy. Could we similarly acquit the hunger-striker? The trouble is, I think, that examined individually, the various discriminating features suggested by Holland may not do their job. Take the doing-suffering distinction. In the sense that Oates places himself in a position where he will surely die, he encompasses his own death, he so arranges it that he dies. I cannot see that this is not a case of "doing." Holland will not allow that the man who places his head on the railway line could be said simply to allow the train to crush him, thus suffering death rather than doing something like cutting his throat. Nor that the man who drowns himself could equally claim that he was merely "letting the water kill him." But why not? In the latter case, we have *all* Holland's features—indirectness, lapse of time, natural phenomenon. And the appeal to the "spirit and context" of the event looks like no more than a decision that we are not going to count certain cases as suicides. It does not seem to me that Holland's analysis is the most profitable line to take for those seeking to acquit the hunger-striker.

Surely, it might be argued, just what is missing from the debate is a clear reference to the *intention* of the hunger-striker. The intention of Oates was not to end his life but to save his companions. The intention of Fr. Kolbe was to save the Jewish father. The intention of the soldier who throws himself on the grenade is to save the lives of his comrades. And the intention of the hunger-striker is to put pressure on the government to accede to his demands. The suicide simply intends his death—by shooting himself, drowning himself, by not acting to save himself from life-threatening circumstances, by so arranging the circumstances that his death is brought about. And this is what distinguishes suicide from these cases of heroic self-sacrifice or legitimate protest.

But this is not sufficient. In Oates's case, he must surely be held to intend his death in *some* sense. If he did not knowingly and intentionally go to his *death*, he would not have accomplished his purpose: if his companions thought that he might survive, they would perhaps have risked their lives to go out and search for him. It is only his death that absolves them from this obligation. In a real sense, Oates intended to terminate his life. Similarly, Kolbe intended to go to execution in the other's place, he must have intended to present himself for execution—otherwise he would not have succeeded in his purpose. Must not the hunger-striker, too, intend his death—particularly if, as in present circumstances, the first death did not cause the government to waver? (It appears that the hunger-strikers were prepared to have three or four die before they hoped for victory.) And the hunger-striker who, before lapsing into a coma, instructs his family not to have him revived by medical intervention—surely he must in some sense intend his death as further pressure on the government.

But suppose we accept that in these cases they all in some sense intend to die but that this is secondary to their primary intention—saving lives, pressuring the government, etc. They perhaps accept that they will die, thus intending it in this sense, but their overriding intention is otherwise; for we can have actions with multiple intentions. It is the overriding intention which gives the act its moral character. In the cases of self-sacrifice, the overriding intention is clearly not to die but to save others—borne out by the fact that, if there had been any *other* way of saving them, the act would not have been performed. We might consider that, because these deaths were in some sense not ends in themselves but instrumental in achieving other ends and purposes, they are not to be counted suicides. This would permit us to define suicide as a self-killing in which the overriding intention is simply to end one's life and there is no further independent objective involved in the action. Let us call such self-killings *noninstrumental* in order to distinguish them from *instrumental* self-killings where the acts are performed for some other purposes such as heroism, the salvation of others, political protest, or whatever.[12]

This is an attractive thesis. It allows us clearly to distinguish the cases of Oates, Kolbe, and others—all instrumental self-killings—from the true cases of suicide. The hunger-striker, too, is clearly acquitted of the suicide verdict since his is an instrumental self-killing, undertaken for the purpose of political protest or whatever. Notice, however, that we now have to include in our definition of nonsuicidal self-killings all sorts of cases. The Buddhist monk who burns himself to death in front of the American Embassy is not a suicide. The person who shoots himself on learning that he is incurably ill in order to save his family from the pain and trouble of looking after him is not a suicide. Anyone who acts to bring about his own death for *any* reason other than that of simply bringing about his own death is not a suicide.

I am prepared to accept these self-killings as nonsuicidal, but many people who invoke the intention of the agent to discriminate between suicide and nonsuicide would be unhappy with these cases. Let me quote what a Maynooth theologian, Denis O'Callaghan, wrote in the *Irish Times à propos* the present hunger-strike: "The suicide verdict turns on a fact—does the hunger-striker intend his death (as the Czech student Jan Palach did when he burned himself to death in protest against the Russian invasion of his country) or is he prepared to accept death possibly as the inevitable side-effect of a protest action on which he has embarked?" Clearly the implication is that, while Jan Palach necessarily intended his death (even though his is a case of instrumental self-killing) and hence committed suicide, the hunger-striker *may* be described as not intending his death at all but merely accepting it as an unintended side-effect of the protest.

What I take to be implied here is the principle of double effect as it has been invoked by Catholic theologians, particularly though by no means exclusively in cases involving the killing of others, especially in abortions. There has been an enormous amount of discussion of this principle and of the sorts of cases to which the principle claims to apply. I am thinking not only of the classic cases from obstetric practice (as treated by Philippa Foot and Jonathan Bennett)[13] but all those complicated examples in the recent literature: the "trolley problem" where Edward is on a runaway railway trolley whose brakes have failed and who can only steer the trolley so as to kill five people on the main line or one person on a branch line; the potholers trapped in the cave with water rising and the only exit blocked by a fat man, where the alternative to drowning for the party is to blow the fat man out of the hole with dynamite; the miraculous health pebble floating towards the island where the only alternative is to direct it to one beach saving thereby five lives or another where it will save only one.[14]

The principle of double effect is primarily about acts and their effects, and not primarily about agents' intentions, as is sometimes asserted. The principle can be stated roughly as follows: when an agent is faced with an action which he foresees has two effects, one good and other evil, he may perform the action under the following conditions:

1. The action must itself be a good action or at least morally neutral;
2. The performance of the action must bring about at least as much good as evil;
3. The evil effect must not be a means to achieving the good effect;
4. The agent must have a justifying and sufficient reason for acting rather than refraining from acting.

That the action must not itself be an evil action is clearly demanded by the context of the whole principle—a morality where there are certain actions which are absolutely forbidden. Thus we cannot suppose that we can perform *any* morally evil act no matter what the good which will come about. Within this tradition direct killing of an innocent person may never be justified. The second condition requires that the good and evil consequences must be at least balanced. The principle could not be invoked in cases where an act leads to a trivial good and a great evil. The third condition merely states that the end can never justify the means. We are not therefore discussing doing evil acts which have good results, but rather acts which are morally permissible where the good resulting is coterminous with the evil, or, we might say, at least as immediate. Finally, the fourth condition makes it clear that it is only in rare cases, where we have serious and morally convincing reasons for acting rather than not acting, that the principle can be invoked.

Now one of the points I want to bring out in this account of the double effect principle is that, though I believe it to be an adequate account, it has not brought into the reckoning the *intention* of the agent. It is true of course that, if the agent is permitted to do the action by the principle, he must not intend the evil consequences but only the good. But this intention is not the morally specifying feature of the action. It is not simply because he can exclude from his intention the evil consequences of the act that the act is permissible. Rather it is because it is an act of a certain sort—good or at least morally neutral, with two effects, etc.—that he is permitted to perform it, and of course we can add that in its performance he must not will the evil.

Let me construct a story to try to bring this point out. A submarine with a full crew of 125 men is holed under water in the forward section. If a certain bulkhead door is not closed immediately, the submarine will lose its buoyancy and will sink, making rescue impossible because of the depth, and all will be lost. Behind the bulkhead door are five crewmen who will certainly be killed by drowning should the door be closed. The captain may act to close the door according to the principle of double effect. Why? The act—closing the bulkhead door—is not evil in itself, rather morally neutral. Clearly the good effect (saving 120 men) is not outweighed by the evil effect. Nor is the good effect achieved by means of the evil effect. The proof of this is that the door would still be closed even if the men were not there. It is not their *deaths* that save the other men. And clearly the captain has a morally justifying reason for acting rather than doing nothing. Notice that the captain's *intention* is not really all that relevant—we need not talk about his only intending the good and excluding from his intention the evil effects to permit the action. Of course he must not intend their deaths or take pleasure in their suffering (for example, in the case where one of the five has been his wife's lover). But it is not *this* which makes the act permissible.

Compare this story with another in which the principle would not apply. The submarine is holed on the bottom but is awaiting rescue. Unfortunately air is running out and, in order to save the majority of the crew, the captain shoots five crew members and disposes of their bodies through torpedo tubes. This would I think violate the principle in a number of ways. The act—shooting them—would be held to be directly evil, thus contradicting the first condition. Even though the good results would outweigh the evil, as in our first story, the third condition would be violated. It is by their *deaths* that he brings about the good effect (sufficient air for the rest). The proof is that unless the five die—that is, stop breathing—the good effect cannot come about. So despite having a good reason for acting, he must refrain from shooting them. What he cannot do, I think, is say: I am shooting them but of course I do not intend their deaths, only the saving of the others.

Let me apply this interpretation of the principle of double effect to the case of the potholers and the fat man. We could argue that blowing the fat man to pieces is directly killing him and therefore is ruled out as a candidate for the act of double effect—since it violates our first condition. The act is not morally neutral or good; as a direct killing, it is evil. This is why, in abortion cases, provided we view the fetus as a fully human person, operations like craniotomy (crushing the skull of the fetus and removing it) cannot be justified by the principle of double effect—they are held to be direct killings of the innocent and therefore absolutely wrong, regardless of the doctor's intention, or the good which will result.

I do not of course wish to exclude intention from the description of the act. The acts themselves—closing the bulkhead door, shooting the crew members, blowing up the fat man, etc.—must of course be voluntary intentional acts in order to be candidates for the principle of double effect. What I am saying is that the principle is concerned about the *act which is intended*—how it can be described, its effects, etc.—and not, as is commonly thought, about the *intention of the act* itself.

But notice what we have to take for granted here. In the abortion case, it is presupposed that the act of killing the fetus is intrinsically evil while the act of letting the mother die is not. In the potholing example, we must make a similar judgment. But could it be argued that we have in both these cases an act—performing an operation, causing an explosion—which has two effects, one good and the other evil, and that the act itself is morally neutral? It is here that the principle of double effect as I have outlined it gets confused with a quite different set of problems, those of describing an action—what proximate effects are to be counted as part of the description of the action itself (I did not kill him, I only moved my hand with a knife in it)? What moral difference is there between positive and negative actions, between acting and refraining, between killing and letting die? All these have been receiving considerable attention in the literature and I content myself with merely referring to them.[15] (Clearly Catholic theology tries to draw a distinction between craniotomy [direct killing] and hysterectomy of a diseased womb which contains a living fetus [indirect killing] on some such grounds.) What I am saying is that the principle of double effect is misstated if it is held to differentiate between acts on the agent's intention alone.

Incidentally this is the source of the worry that Anscombe has about the principle of double effect, when she asserts that the denial of the principle has been the corruption of non-Catholic thought and its abuse the corruption of Catholic thought.[16] The notion of the agent's intention which could be "directed" like a searchlight, on to the good effect but missing out the bad effects, she suggests, owes a lot to Cartesian psychology, with the intention viewed as an interior state of mind which could be produced at will.

Thus I find that O'Callaghan's attempt to distinguish the hunger-striker (not intending his death but merely accepting it as a necessary consequence, an inevitable side-effect of his action) from the case of Jan Palach (who directly intends his death) begs too many questions. I would prefer to define suicide as the act of a person who noninstrumentally intends his death, and allow all instrumental self-killings to evade the verdict on suicide. After all, in the religious tradition we are presupposing as background, what makes the suicide that most evil of persons is that he simply wants to turn his back on life, to reject the gift of life whatever happens.

We could devise a sort of postmortem verification of this. Suppose that the dead person is miraculously revived for an instant after death. What would his reaction be? The "true" suicide, the noninstrumental self-killer, will ask to be put back to death, so to speak—he literally does not wish to continue living. The self-sacrificer—Oates, Kolbe—would not react in this way at all. They would be delighted with revivification. (They would of course ask whether their actions had their desired effect—were the others saved? And they might say that they were prepared to do it again if necessary. But their *deaths* were not what they wanted.) The hunger-striker is perhaps a slightly different case. He would presumably ask—did the government give in? If the demands had been granted, then there would be no question of "redying." If not? Well, the very determined person would not say—put me back to death. He would say—I shall begin another hunger-strike unless the government.... And it is this difference which makes him not a case of the "true" suicide.

Thus, I would say that the real act of suicide is noninstrumental self-killing in which the horror, for the religious person, of the rejection of God's gift and indeed of God himself are manifest. I recognize that the religious sin of suicide becomes, on this definition, an almost inconceivable act. The suicide is the person who kills himself for no other reason than to terminate his life. His motives must be curious—a sort of black, "religious" pessimism, arising from a hatred of self, of the world, of existence itself, which is presented as a total and final rejection of meaning and of God. (The desire for annihilation is difficult for the person who believes in an immortal soul or in an afterlife—because such a person believes that you *cannot* actually end your existence. I can only suggest that such is the rejection of God by this true antitheist that he must be seen as saying: I reject existence utterly and I destroy deliberately, out of a sort of disgust at life, all that I can destroy—my bodily existence.) Such a suicide seeks an end to self-hood out of disgust at existence. Another conceivable motivation is that of a suicide who kills himself as the ultimate act of egotism, the final and irrevocable act of freedom in which he asserts his ego against the world and against even a nonexistent god. So Kirillov, in Dostoyevsky's *The Devils,* shoots himself as an act of self-will: "I cannot understand how an atheist could know that there is no god and not kill himself at once.... I am bound to shoot myself because the most important point of my self-will is to kill myself.... I am killing myself to show my defiance and my new terrible freedom." Out of these barely conceivable cases, we can begin to discern the depth of the religious condemnation of suicide as the worst and most ultimate of sins.

These are of course extremely *rare* cases—almost all the acts which are commonly called "suicide" are not of this type at all. Most are what I am calling instrumental self-killings. We must remember however that this does not of itself mean that they are all morally permissible. Clearly, within the "life as a gift" thesis, one can only put one's life at risk for a grave and justifying cause, for a morally worthy cause. Oates and Kolbe did so in order to save others at the expense of their own lives. The moral judgment on the hunger-striker we have been considering may not turn on the suicide question, but it does turn on the morally worthy, on the grave and serious reasons for acting in this way. My personal opinion is that the recent hunger-strike was never justified within that religious tradition. To back up this judgment would require a consideration of the political and military struggle in Northern Ireland at the present time, and the detailed reasons for the hunger-strike—and a very different paper.[17]

Notes

1. The medical certificates were amended to record the cause of death as "starvation," after protests by the families of the dead hunger-strikers at the original pathologist's report which recorded "self-imposed starvation." The coroner found that the cause of death was "starvation, self-imposed."

2. Richard Brandt, "The Morality and Rationality of Suicide," in *Moral Problems,* J. Rachels, ed. (New York: Harper & Row, 1971), pp. 375–76 [see this volume, chapter 21].

3. Ibid., p. 376 [see chapter 21].

4. R. F. Holland, "Suicide," in *Talk of God* (Royal Institute of Philosophy Lectures, volume 2, 1967–68), p. 82.

5. G. K. Chesterton, *Orthodoxy* (London: Sheed and Ward, 1939), p. 115.

6. Schopenhauer, *The World as Will and Representation*, section 69.

7. Chesterton, (note 5), p. 119.

8. A. Phillips Griffiths, "Wittgenstein, Schopenhauer, and Ethics," in *Understanding Wittgenstein* (Royal Institute of Philosophy Lectures, volume 7, 1974), p. 112.

9. R. G. Frey, "Suicide and Self-Inflicted Death," in *Philosophy* 56 (1981): 193–202 [see this volume, chapter 12].

10. Émile Durkheim, *Suicide: A Study in Sociology* (London: Routledge and Kegan Paul, 1952), pp. 41–42.

11. Holland, (note 4), pp. 89–91.

12. This is the definition of suicide given by Joseph Margolis in "Suicide," in *Ethical Issues in Death and Dying*, T. L. Beauchamp and S. Perlin, eds. (Englewood Cliffs, N.J.: Prentice-Hall, 1978), pp. 92–97. Margolis wishes to distinguish the case of the person who rationally and noninstrumentally wishes to end his life from cases where the person acts irrationally (e.g., mental illness) or instrumentally (e.g., self-sacrificing deaths).

13. Philippa Foot, "The Problem of Abortion and the Doctrine of the Double Effect," in *The Oxford Review* 5 (1967); Jonathan Bennett, "Whatever the Consequences," in *Analysis* 26 (1966).

14. E.g., Judith Jarvis Thomson, "Killing, Letting Die and the Trolley Problem," in *The Monist* 59 (1976); R A. Duff, "Intentionally Killing the Innocent," in *Analysis* 33 (1973).

15. E.g., Daniel Dinello, "On Killing and Letting Die," in *Analysis* 31 (1971); Bruce Russell, "On the Relative Strictness of Negative and Positive Duties," in *American Philosophical Quarterly* 14 (1977).

16. G. E. M. Anscombe, "War and Murder," in *Nuclear War and Christian Conscience*, Walter Stein, ed. (London: Merlin Press, 1961), p. 50.

17. This paper was first read to the Philosophy Staff Seminar at the University of Warwick, and a revised version to the Staff Seminar at the New University of Ulster. I am grateful for the helpful discussion and criticism I received.

14

Mastering the Concept of Suicide
Glenn C. Graber

All of us mastered the use of the concept of suicide in the course of learning our native language. We know that certain deaths are appropriately classified as suicides (for example, the deaths of Romeo, Juliet, Ernest Hemingway), whereas certain others are clearly not suicides (for example, the deaths of John F. Kennedy, Lyndon Johnson).* The difficulty comes when we try to classify them as we do.

What Is Suicide?

Let us consider some cases that result in death in different ways:

A. Arnold is fired from his job, the only job for which his training and his interests equip him. Upon returning home to tell his wife, whom he loves dearly, he finds a note saying that she has left him for another man—in fact, the very man who has just been given his former job. As he lights the stove to fix himself a lonely dinner, it explodes and his expensive home burns to the ground—which reminds him that he has allowed the fire insurance to lapse. After thinking through his plight for several hours, he

Reprinted by permission of the University of Tennessee Press. Glenn C. Graber's "The Rationality of Suicide" from *Suicide and Euthanasia: The Rights of Personhood,* eds. Samuel E. Wallace and Albin Eser. Copyright © 1981 by The University of Tennessee Press.

*There are, of course, some borderline cases in which we are unsure, even after all the facts are clear, whether to call a death suicide (several such cases are noted below). An advantage of the technique of analysis employed herein is that it allows us to make use of the insights we gain from examining clear cases to decide whether these borderline cases are appropriately classified as suicides.

takes a pistol (the only item that survived the fire) and blows his brains out.

B. Bernice is whistling a merry tune as she washes dishes, but when she touches the switch to turn on the garbage disposal, she is electrocuted and dies.

C. Clyde has a song in his heart as he eats his breakfast, but when he takes a sip of his coffee (into which his wife has mixed a generous amount of strychnine), he slumps over dead.

Case *A* clearly is a case of suicide. Cases *B* and *C*, just as clearly, are not. What precisely is the difference between them?

The reply that first comes to mind is to say that Arnold killed himself by his own action, whereas Bernice and Clyde were killed by somebody or something other than themselves. The trouble is that there is a wholly reasonable sense in which Bernice and Clyde can be said to have killed themselves by their own actions, too. After all, Bernice reached out her hand and touched the switch. The electricity did not come to her. (Contrast the case of someone struck by lightning.) And Clyde picked up the cup and drank from it. (Contrast someone who is held down and has poison injected into his veins.) Thus, the fact that one's death results from one's own action is not sufficient to qualify it as suicide. Some cases of accidental death (Bernice) and murder (Clyde) also have this feature.

What we need is to find some feature of the cases that distinguishes Arnold's action in relation to his death from the actions of Bernice and Clyde. One possibility is the difference between characteristic effects and unusual or uncharacteristic effects. This criterion would distinguish the cases cited so far in the proper way. To put a gun to one's temple and pull the trigger (as Arnold did) or to remain in a closed room in which gas is escaping as someone we will call Donna—Case *D*—did, characteristically causes death. In contrast, to put a cup of coffee to one's lips and drink does not characteristically cause death. It is only in the unusual circumstance in which there is poison in the coffee that a drink of it will kill. Bernice's death is likewise an uncharacteristic effect of her action, for it is only when something has gone wrong with the wiring (which is not the usual condition) that it will be a fatal act to touch a wall switch.

However, this criterion will not serve to distinguish suicide from other kinds of death in all cases. It is possible to commit suicide by means of abnormal or uncharacteristic conditions if we know about them in advance. If one knows, for example, that there is a short in a particular wall switch, then one could commit suicide by stepping into a bucket of water and then touching the switch. If Clyde had watched his wife pour the poison into his coffee and knew that it was poison but deliberately drank it anyway, we would judge that he committed suicide. In these cases, death is an uncharacteristic result of the action, but it is a suicide nevertheless. Hence we cannot define suicide in these terms.

These counterexamples suggest another possibility. Perhaps knowledge is the key to the distinction between suicide and other kinds of deaths. At least one theorist has thought so. The sociologist Émile Durkheim defined suicide as "all cases of death resulting directly or indirectly from a positive or negative act of the victim himself, which he knows will produce this result."[1]

This definition does not seem adequate. It does not distinguish between the following two cases, the first of which seems clearly to be suicide and the second of which seems equally clearly not to be.

E. Edgar is a wartime secret agent who is captured by the enemy. Knowing that he will be tortured mercilessly to the death, he takes a cyanide capsule from a hidden compartment in his shoe, bites into it, and dies.

F. Francine is another wartime secret agent who is captured. She has heard before about these particular captors and knows that they always torture to the death any agent who refuses to divulge the information they are after. Nevertheless, she refuses to tell them anything. After three painful days, she dies from their tortures.

The difference between these two cases is a subtle one, but since it is both real and important to the analysis of suicide, we will take time here to bring the difference into focus. In order to do this, we must note some preliminary points about the nature of action.

A single action has multiple effects. For example, Edgar's action not only has the consequence of bringing about his death but has the additional effects of guaranteeing that he does not divulge whatever strategic information he knows ("Dead men tell no tales") and of sparing him the pain of tortures that would otherwise be inflicted upon him. It may have still other effects as well. If we suppose (as is not unlikely) that one of Edgar's captors had been assigned the responsibility of searching captured agents in order to find concealed poisons and if the commanding officer is as ruthless as his procedures for treatment of captives suggest that he is, then Edgar's action of taking the poison may have the additional consequence of prompting the execution of one of his captors.

Some effects are causally independent of other effects. For example, consider the two consequences: Edgar's guaranteeing the protection of his secrets and his bringing about the execution of his captor who failed to find the poison. Neither of these is directly causally related to the other. The captor is executed, not because the secrets were successfully protected but because he failed to carry out an assigned responsibility. Imagine that Edgar had not succeeded in guaranteeing the protection of his secrets. Imagine, for example, that he had inadvertently left a written statement of them intact in his pocket. The chances are good that his captor would still have been executed. The fact that the soldier had failed to do his assigned duty would remain as a basis for punishment. Thus these two consequences are both effects of Edgar's swallowing the poison, but they are causally independent of each other.

Now we must consider the element of intention in action. Some of the effects of a given action are intended. More specifically, whatever goals the agent hoped or planned to achieve by performing the action are intended effects of the action. It is reasonable to assume that both Edgar and Francine had the same ultimate goal in mind in doing what they did; both wanted to protect the secret information in their possession. Thus this is clearly an intended effect of their respective actions. In addition, it is likely that Edgar was also influenced by the realization that death from the poison would spare him the pain of torture. Hence this can plausibly be interpreted as a second, coordinate goal of his action and thus another intended effect of it.

Some effects of an action are not intended effects. Consider the consequence of the execution of one of Edgar's captors who failed to find the concealed poison. Surely this was not an intended effect, and Edgar was probably not even aware of it. Of course, it is possible that he did know beyond reasonable doubt what would happen. Even if he knew, however, it would still seem a mistake to say that he intended for it to happen. Awareness of this consequence played no role at all in his decision to act as he did. His interest was in protecting his secret information in the best way he knew. The realization that an enemy soldier would die as a result of his action made him neither more nor less inclined to act. The consequence was, then, a by-product, a side-effect, or an incidental effect of his action, perhaps foreseen but not intended. This brings us to our final point about action: some of the effects of an action that are foreseen are nevertheless not intended effects.

It is important to establish this last point because it provides the key to the distinction between Edgar and Francine and, ultimately, the basis for criticism of Durkheim's definition of suicide. For Francine, her own death was a by-product or a side-effect of her action and not an intended effect. Her goal was to protect her secret information in the best way she knew—by remaining silent. She would have done the same thing if she had not known what her captors would do to her as a result or if she had known that they would not kill her, and her realization that these particular captors would surely kill her made her neither more nor less inclined to talk. (This may be too strong. She may have been tempted to talk in order to save her life, but she resisted the temptation and remained silent.) Thus her death was a foreseen but unintended consequence of her action.

Edgar's situation is importantly different from this. His death was not a side-effect of his action. Rather it was a part of the means he used to achieve the goal. His taking the poison caused his death, which in turn provided the guarantee that his secret information would be protected (assuming now that he remembered to destroy any notes).

The upshot of all this is that knowledge of the consequences is not what distinguishes suicide from nonsuicide, as Durkheim believed. Both Edgar and Francine knew that they were going to die. What makes the difference between suicide and nonsuicide is the intention of the agent. Edgar intended to die, and thus his death was suicide. Francine, in contrast, did not intend to die. Her death was a side-effect of her action, and thus she was not a suicide.

Now we have the key to the proper analysis of suicide. The crucial difference between suicide and other kinds of death is to be found in the intentions or purposes of the person who dies. This can be seen clearly in the cases discussed so far. Arnold, Donna, and Edgar (our three suicides) all did what they did with the express intention of bringing about their own deaths. Bernice, Clyde, and

Francine, in contrast, had no such intention. Bernice was trying to get rid of the garbage. Clyde wanted to drink some coffee. Francine was interested in protecting the national security of her country. None of the nonsuicides acted with the intention of dying; all of the suicides did act as they did for this purpose.

Thus our suggestion passes the first test of adequacy for a proposed analysis. It matches our preanalytic judgment about what is suicide and what is not. The crucial difference between suicide and other kinds of death is to be found in the intentions or purposes of the person who dies.

However, there is still some work to be done. In the first place, we need to formulate the suggestion into an explicit analysis so that we can see more clearly precisely what it involves. One way of doing this is proposed by Joseph Margolis, who defines suicide as "the deliberate taking of one's life in order simply to end it, not instrumentally for any ulterior purpose."[2] This description might fit the cases of Arnold and Donna. If someone had asked them, just prior to their acts, why they were preparing to take their lives, each might have answered by saying something like "My life is meaningless; I simply want to end it." This is the sort of thing Margolis has in mind.

However, Margolis's definition does not fit Case E—Edgar. If we had asked Edgar whether his purpose in taking the poison was simply to bring about his own death, he would undoubtedly have answered with a resounding "No!" He had two ulterior purposes: to protect his secrets and to prevent the pain of torture. If he could have found any way to reach these goals that did not involve his death, he would not have ended his life. For him death was a means or instrument to an ulterior purpose, not something he wanted in itself. And yet we have agreed that his death was suicide. Hence Margolis's proposal for a definition of suicide must be rejected, since it does not match our practical classifications in this sort of case.

Indeed, there is a plausible aspect in the cases of Arnold and Donna that would put even them outside Margolis's analysis. Suppose they explained their actions by saying, "I am in despair, and I want to end this awful anguish." The natural interpretation of this is to say that ending their anguish is for them an ulterior purpose to which their deaths are means or instruments. Then, on Margolis's analysis of suicide, we would have to say that these deaths are not suicides. Surely this is mistaken.

R. B. Brandt works intention into the analysis of suicide in a more promising way. He proposes the following definition:

> "Suicide" is conveniently defined, for our purposes, as doing something which results in one's death, either from the intention of ending one's life or the intention to bring about some other state of affairs (such as relief from pain) which one thinks it certain or highly probable can be achieved only by means of death or will produce death.[3]

However, this analysis is too broad. By this definition, not only would Edgar's death qualify as suicide, but so would Francine's. Her goal is to protect her nation's secrets, but she is aware that it is highly probable that the same action that will

achieve this purpose (that is, her negative action of remaining silent) will also produce her death, since it is the known practice of her captors to kill agents who
remain silent. Yet we agreed earlier that Francine's death is not a suicide. Thus we
cannot be satisfied with Brandt's definition as it stands. It is too close to
Durkheim's definition.

We can produce an accurate analysis of suicide by amending Brandt's definition. It will not do simply to drop the whole phrase that reads: "or the intention
to bring about some other state of affairs (such as relief from pain) which one
thinks it certain or highly probable can be achieved only by means of death or will
produce death." What would be left is equivalent to Margolis's definition, which
we have already discarded as too narrow.

The analysis of suicide we want must include deaths (like Edgar's) that are
intentionally brought about as a means to some ulterior purpose, and it must
exclude deaths (like Francine's) that are foreseen but not intended consequences
of deliberate actions. Actually, we can achieve this quite easily. All we have to do
is to drop the last four words of Brandt's analysis: "or will produce death." It is this
phrase that brings in deaths that are foreseen side-effects of deliberate actions.

Incorporating into Brandt's definition the two changes we have made, we get
the following analysis of suicide: suicide is defined as doing something that results
in one's death in the way that was planned, either from the intention of ending
one's life or the intention to bring about some other state of affairs (such as relief
from pain) that one thinks it certain or highly probable can be achieved only by
means of death.

Let us test this analysis further by examining its implications for certain additional cases. First consider this pair of cases:

G. Gary is in constant and intense pain caused by terminal cancer. Somehow
    he manages to get hold of a large quantity of a painkilling drug, which
    he takes all at once, saying, "I want to die. It is the only way to get rid of
    this awful pain."

H. Helen's physical condition is just like Gary's. She takes the same amount
    of the same drug, but she says, "It is not my intent to die. I am taking this
    dosage because nothing less will completely relieve the pain and I am
    determined to get rid of the pain, even if it results in my death."

Our analysis compels us to say that Gary's death is suicide, but Helen's is not.
(This assumes, as we must in the absence of explicit evidence to the contrary, that
they both mean exactly what they say. The ultimate goal of the action in both
cases is to be rid of pain. For Gary death is a means to this end, but for Helen
death is a by-product of the means chosen, which is to take a dosage large enough
to guarantee that it is effective in relieving the pain.) There is another way of
specifying the difference between these two cases. Helen might not be disappointed if she were to wake up a day or two later to find that the pain had returned. Not dying is compatible with (although not dictated by) her expressed
motive that all she wants is temporary relief from the pain, a rest for a while from

the burden. Gary, however, would react differently. If he were to come out of a coma a day or two later and still be racked with pain, he would be bound to feel that he had failed to accomplish his purpose.

There is one more implication of this analysis that should be brought to attention. We have said that the classification of an act as suicide hinges on the person's intentions or purposes. Psychologists tell us, however, that many people who attempt suicide do not really want to die. Their actions are really desperate calls for help from other people. Of course, some of them take a stronger action than they had intended, or the intervention they had expected does not come, and they do die. By our analysis, these are not actually suicides. They are accidental deaths. Thus our definition entails that what police agencies and others regard as the clearcut cases of suicide may not be suicides at all. Just because someone is found hanging from a rope he tied around his own neck or dead from a self-administered dose of sleeping pills, this does not prove that he committed suicide. It may not have been his intention to die.

Suicide and Rationality

Is suicide ever rationally justified? It seems clear that it sometimes is. Let us begin with a closer look at the situation of our old friend Edgar, the wartime secret agent.

His only choice is between death today and death tomorrow after incalculable pain, and surely he is correct in choosing the former option. It is the only rational decision in such a situation. Think first about his appraisal of the facts of the situation. He has reliable evidence that it is the practice of these captors to kill captured agents. He would be hoping against hope if he expected his captors suddenly to become soft-hearted and spare his life. It would be equally unrealistic for him to think that his compatriots would risk the success of their cause (as well as their own lives) to rescue him. He must face the fact: he is doomed.

Now consider his appraisal of the values. It would also be irrational not to want to avoid torture. The pain of it is reason enough to want to avoid it, but Edgar must also consider the very real risk that he might break under torture and betray his cause.

We acknowledge the rational justification of suicide in this sort of case, whether in fiction or in real life. Our usual emotional reaction is admiration for the agent for having the courage to follow what is obviously the only sensible course of action. (Note that we have not said he is morally justified. This is still an open question that we will consider shortly.)

Let us now step back from this example and see if any general principles can be abstracted from it. The way to get at such a principle is to ask, what is it about Edgar's situation that leads us to think that it is rationally justified for him to take his life? The answer to this question seems obvious. Once we are convinced that Edgar has not made any errors in his appraisal of either facts or values in the situation (which is one important aspect of rationality, but not the whole story), what persuades us of the correctness of his decision to kill himself is our own perception that he is better off dead. If we measure the advantages and disadvantages of both options open to him, it appears clear that the choice to kill himself immediately is likely to produce a greater total value (or, what amounts to the same thing, a lesser total disvalue) than the other option. This, then, is our general principle of rational justification in suicide. *It is rationally justified to kill oneself when a reasonable appraisal of the situation reveals that one is really better off dead.*

The best way to see whether the principle really works in practice is to try to apply it to some specific cases. Let us look, for example, at the situations of the cancer patients Gary and Helen. Each of them is racked with pain from an incurable and terminal illness. Gary decides to kill himself, and Helen chooses a course of action that results in her death. Are their decisions rationally justified? Only a short period of life is left to them anyway, and it will be filled with extreme pain. In this respect, their situations parallel Edgar's. It would be unreasonable of them to expect a sudden spontaneous remission of the disease at this advanced stage or to expect a miracle cure in the near future. There are some additional values open to them that are not available to Edgar. Whereas Edgar has only his hostile captors to keep him company, Gary and Helen are surrounded by more or less sympathetic people—including their families and close friends. The value of these contacts cannot be ignored, and their decisions would be unjustified if they left these values out of account altogether. Surely Gary and Helen are not being unreasonable, however, if they question whether the continuation of these human contacts is worth the cost in pain. The value of the benefits of which immediate death would rob them is outweighed by the disvalue of the pain from which death would spare them. Hence we must say that they would be better off dead and that ending their lives is therefore rationally justified.

Several points about this argument call for comment. First, the judgment that a certain person would be better off dead must be made entirely from that person's own point of view. The fact that Gary is an emotional and financial burden to his family is, in itself, totally irrelevant to the issue of whether he would be better off dead. It might be significant in saying that the family would be better off if he were dead, but that is another matter entirely. Of course, if Gary is aware that he is a burden, this awareness will be detrimental to his welfare. Awareness of being a burden, however, is different from the fact of being a burden, and only the former counts toward saying that he would be better off dead.

The second point is more complicated—and more controversial. We must acknowledge a person's own tastes and preferences, but we must not extend a blanket acceptance of all the value judgments of that person. If, for example, a woman prefers chocolate ice cream to pistachio, we cannot say she is mistaken, but if she prefers eating mud pies to eating ice cream, then surely she is mistaken about values. Objective values set the limits for legitimate and reasonable preferences. Among things that are of roughly equivalent value (for example, ice cream of different flavors, foods of different kinds of roughly equal nutritional value, styles of music, literature, or art), the choice between them is left entirely to the individual's taste, but if the value that the person places upon a thing (for example, mud pies) is too far out of line with its objective value, then the preference is labeled as unreasonable.

This principle is not limited in application only to trivial matters. The same value governs the choice of an occupation and a lifestyle. The choice between a career as a lawyer and one as a teacher is largely a matter of individual taste, but it would be unreasonable (economic considerations aside) for one to devote one's whole life to collecting odd bits of string.

The same reasoning applies in the case of Gary. We may feel that if we were in Gary's situation, we would rather endure the pain in order to be able to continue to enjoy association with other human beings. Nevertheless, if Gary himself is not afraid of death (with the resulting loss of human contacts) and prefers it to a continuation of the pain, we have no right to impose our preferences upon him by insisting that he is not rationally justified in ending his life. On the other hand, if Gary were to say that he saw no value at all in human associations or no disvalue at all in death, he would be mistaken and we ought not to endorse his mistaken judgment.

In other sorts of cases, it is much more difficult to form a judgment about the rationality of suicide. Let us look at one troublesome case:

I. Irene used to be an especially active young woman. She was a professional dancer, and all her favorite avocations were strenuous physical activities like swimming and tennis. As the result of an automobile accident, she is now paralyzed from the waist down, and the functioning of her arms and hands is impaired. She decides to kill herself, saying, "I would be better off dead than living as an invalid."

Is her decision rationally justified?

It must be admitted that she faces something less than a full and complete life. She will never again be able to participate in the kinds of physical activities that mean so much to her (and also mean a great deal to many other people). Her life is diminished as a result of her accident. We acknowledge this when we speak of the accident as a misfortune or a tragedy and of its results as a loss.

However, a life thus diminished is not totally robbed of value. Irene still has a lot going for her. She has full use of her mental faculties, full ability to communicate, and partial mobility of arms and hands. She can maintain meaningful and satisfying relationships with other people, and if she put her mind to it, she could undoubtedly devise a number of projects within her capabilities with which to occupy her time. We all know of people who have managed to make satisfying lives for themselves in spite of handicaps even more severe than Irene's.

There is no guarantee that Irene will make a satisfying life for herself. We all also know of persons, some less severely handicapped than Irene, who have remained bitter about their losses and, as a result, have isolated themselves from others and refused to try to devise constructive ways to fill their time. It is hardly surprising to find that many of these people look back over their lives and judge that they would have been better off dead. A life of bitterness, isolation, and self-pity is not clearly superior to no life at all.

In the face of these conflicting possibilities, how are we to determine whether Irene's life is worth continuing? It is tempting to say that the judgment should be left entirely up to Irene. However, this is an evasion. Unless we are willing to aid her by constructing a set of rational criteria on which she can make her judgment, we will have done nothing but add the weight of responsibility to her already considerable burdens. Moreover, it is an open question whether she is in a better position to apply such criteria than is somebody else.

Another tempting response is to look to capabilities rather than to possibilities or probabilities as the basis for evaluating life prospects. We have said, for example, that Irene can maintain relationships and that she could devise projects. Whether she actually does any of these things is, presumably, up to her, but even if she fails to do them, the fact remains that she is capable of doing them. This might seem to be enough by itself to say that her prospective life is worth living.

The trouble is that it may not be within Irene's power to control whether she fulfills these capabilities. She may fight against bitterness only to find that she cannot prevent its setting in. She may actively try to devise projects to fill her time only to discover that she cannot develop an interest in any of them. How one reacts to a misfortune like Irene's is not decided by conscious choice or effort of will. It involves factors in the personality that have developed gradually over the whole of one's life and cannot be altered in any direct way. Irene's entire life has been oriented exclusively toward physical activities, and so she may not have any interest in or ability for the kind of quiet activities that are now her only hope. If she finds that these activities fail to satisfy her no matter how hard she tries to develop an interest in them, it would be neither surprising nor unreasonable for her to conclude that she would be better off dead.

There is one very important value that we have not yet considered in Irene's situation. In order to get at it, let us look at the following case.

J.   Jeremy is yet another secret agent who is captured, but his captors are very different from those who got hold of Edgar and Francine. Instead of brutal torture, these people go in for subtle and sophisticated techniques of brainwashing that render the subjects willing and eager to share any strategic information they happen to know. Jeremy knows of their methods, and he also knows (as a result of a battery of psychological tests that were taken in the course of his training) that he is highly susceptible to such influence. He bites a cyanide capsule because he does not want to become the sort of person who would willingly betray his cause.

What this case brings out is the value of personal ideals and personal integrity. Jeremy has set certain ideals for the kind of person he wants to be; among other things, he wants to be loyal to his country. Departure from this ideal might not cause him any pain. If the brainwashing is totally effective, he might not feel any pangs of conscience when he betrays his country. He might even be proud of doing so because after the brainwashing is completed, he will have become a different kind of person than he is now—the kind whose loyalties are directed toward the cause of his captors. The trouble is that he does not now want to become the kind of person he would then be.

This is what is so insidious and frightening about techniques of brainwashing. They affect what is most dear to the victim. They alter one's ideals for the kind of person one wants to be and thus violate personal integrity. In an important sense, they destroy the *person* and put a different person in its place.

Irene might view her prospects in a way parallel to Jeremy's line of thought. She might be fairly sure that, in time, she could adjust to life as an invalid and find satisfaction in it. She can remember that she has enjoyed short periods in bed with minor illnesses, and she can imagine herself becoming totally engrossed in television soap operas, syrupy novels, and needlework. She also realizes that she finds a certain amount of pleasure in the pity and solicitude of those who come into contact with her, and she can imagine that this aspect of her nature will expand as time goes on.

However, she does not want to become this sort of person. She has always regarded this part of her nature as unworthy and has worked to suppress it, and the prospect of its becoming dominant in her personality is repugnant to her. She would rather end her life than to become this sort of person.

Some General Conclusions

In the course of this discussion, we have reached some general conclusions about the rationality of suicide. It might be helpful to repeat them in a list here:

1. Some suicides are rationally justified (Edgar and Gary, for example).
2. Some suicides are not rationally justified.
3. It is rationally justified to kill oneself if a reasonable appraisal of the situation reveals that one is really better off dead. This is the criterion of rational justification for suicides.
4. The judgment that a certain person is (or is not) better off dead should be justified exclusively:
   a. From the person's own point of view;
   b. Within limits, on the basis of the person's own tastes and preferences;
   c. On the basis of actual preferences (present and future), rather than abstract capabilities.
5. The prospective suicide's judgment of whether he or she would be better off dead is not the last word on the matter. The person may be mistaken.
   a. The person may make a wrong prediction about the degree to which his or her present values are likely to be satisfied. ("I'll never be able to keep up my career now that I am blind.")
   b. The person may make a wrong prediction about the nature of his or her future values. ("I'll never learn to enjoy the kind of activities open to me now that I am confined to a wheelchair.")
   c. The person may have mistaken values.

6. In judging whether a person would be better off dead, we must take into account not only the person's present and future values but also his or her personal ideals and personal integrity (Jeremy, for example).

Notes

1. *Suicide,* trans. Spaulding and Simpson (Glencoe, Ill.: The Free Press, 1951), p. 44.

2. *Negativities: The Limits of Life* (Columbus: Charles E. Merrill Publishing Co., 1975), p. 26.

3. "The Morality and Rationality of Suicide," in *A Handbook for the Study of Suicide,* ed. Seymour Perlin (New York: Oxford University Press, 1975), p. 363 [see chapter 21 in this volume].

15

Suicide: Its Nature and Moral Evaluation
Joseph Kupfer

T his paper has two purposes: to clarify what suicide is and to discuss its moral evaluation. These are not so easily kept separate, since it is just the traditional condemnation of suicide that often inhibits us from thinking of justified life-taking as suicide. We should not, however, so define suicide that it is logically impossible to have a justified suicide. Some suicides may be justified, even obligatory or noble. Consequently, I shall try to give an analysis of suicide that permits a range of moral evaluation. I shall proceed on the assumption that one way to develop an understanding of suicide is to examine a variety of cases: the ascription of suicide being sometimes clear, sometimes problematic.

I

Let's begin with cases that are clearly suicide, and see what makes them clear. Consider someone who has just lost his business and with it his life savings. He is crushed but not pathologically depressed or "out of his mind." He knows what he is doing and thinks it over for quite a while. He then proceeds to "take his own life." Or, consider someone in prison for life. He tries living in prison for several years, but after much self-searching decides that life like this really isn't worth living. He chooses to die rather than live a circumscribed life.

Both of these seem to me to be clear cases of suicide, however well or poorly justified. What makes them such? I think that here it pays to be obvious. The individual chose to end his own life and took the appropriate action. Clearly, there were other options and the individual wanted to die. It wasn't as if death was about

From the *Journal of Value Inquiry* 24 (1990): 67–81. © Kluwer Academic Publishers. Reprinted by the kind permission of Kluwer Academic Publishers.

to occur anyway or the individual didn't really want to die but saw no other way to accomplish his goal(s). In clear cases, the individual chooses to die and is causally responsible for his demise. It doesn't matter that he or we can say things like, "He died in order to be spared penury or tedium." Almost every suicide is for a "reason" besides the death itself. Very few people kill themselves just to "see what it would be like." Or, as in the murder in Camus's *Stranger*, for no apparent reason or because of the sun's strong rays. It is just these reasons and their diversity that need to be considered, later, in evaluating suicides.

Let's now consider examples of nonsuicides. However, they cannot be all that clear cut. In that they are relevant to the topic of suicide, they must involve people knowingly acting in ways which eventuate in their deaths. Without this component there wouldn't be the temptation to consider them suicides, and they would have no bearing on our discussion at all.

Imagine someone who is terminally ill and ends her life. Perhaps to spare loved ones or herself a couple of weeks of suffering—it doesn't really matter. What matters is that she has no control over whether she will die soon, only how soon and how. Similar considerations hold for people on death row. They are simply carrying out the will of the state themselves, hastening their end by doing so. We do better to call this auto-euthanasia or "hastening the end." They have not *chosen* to die in the sense that there are other "live" options.[1] It's rather that dying now is preferable to dying soon. In order for an act to be a suicide, then, the agent must have the option of a rather indeterminate period of life.

I realize that this will not conform to everyone's intuition, and may seem overly stipulative. However, the amount of time given up by the death seems relevant in distinguishing suicides from nonsuicides. The difference between foregoing a day and giving up ten or twenty years of living is significant. Whether or not our options are restricted, in this and other kinds of action, makes a difference to the nature of the action performed.[2] Strictly speaking, it is a matter of *belief* concerning the amount of time left to live. An individual who expects to live quite a while but wouldn't (because of an unforeseen, impending disaster or affliction, for example) is still committing suicide. And someone who mistakenly believes his death is imminent is, nonetheless, not a suicide.

There is no clear demarcation as to how soon, how imminent and certain the death must appear to be in order to make it a nonsuicide. If someone believes he has a year or two to live, it looks more like suicide. A week or two, not. To be a success, a clarification of a concept need not do away with difficult or borderline cases. Such clarification may still enable important distinctions in a large group of situations, and even provide assistance in *some* tough ones.

Next, think of a religious martyr who knows that by continuing to criticize the authorities or preach her creed others will definitely kill her. She could stop performing the defiant actions, and so preserve her life, but she doesn't. It is this refusal to avoid the almost certain death that tempts us to consider her behavior a suicide. Even though she knows she will be killed, she can't be said to be choosing her death by continuing her defiant behavior. Why not?

Because she is choosing to do something other than die, namely, to criticize or preach. I am also assuming here that this is what she wants to do rather than to die. She truly wishes to live in order to continue her religious mission but she also feels compelled not to allow the authorities to interrupt her efforts. If, on the other hand, she wished to die, perhaps to become canonized, then her behavior would certainly look more suicidal, if not count as a suicide proper (this would probably also constitute *hubris* of sorts, and vitiate her candidacy for sainthood, but that's another matter). As we have hypothesized the case, there is an alternate description which corresponds to her intention to do something other than die: to criticize and preach. The death is incidental, though foreseen. Thus, even though she acted in such a way that her death was practically inevitable, she did not commit suicide.

To see this, consider a prisoner who breaks out of prison only to be apprehended on an open field by guards with high-powered rifles. They order him to stop. He hears them and knows that some of them will surely hit him, as he isn't very far away and cover is out of reach. For him to keep running is to commit suicide. His running is not like the zealot's criticizing or preaching. It has no nonsuicidal purpose. The escaped prisoner doesn't wish to live and is *simply* using the guards as the means to bring about his own death True, he *had* been trying to accomplish something else with his running, but now that it is futile, he would rather die than go back to prison and face whatever punishment and further incarceration might be in store for him.

The difference between these two cases is this. The religious zealot seeks an end other than her death even though she knows it is an inevitable outcome of her pursuit of this end. The escaped prisoner realizes that his end is unattainable, and would rather die than live without it. In this respect, he is like the despairing businessman or the person imprisoned for life who thinks that life isn't worth living. The difference lies in the prisoner's use of other people to bring about his death.

II

These cases call our attention to two interesting aspects of the issue: immediate causes of death other than the self; and alternate descriptions or intentions. The latter is more crucial and knotty.

As I see the issue, it doesn't matter whether the individual immediately, directly causes his own death or simply arranges for its occurrence. R. F. Holland seems to think that it does. He thinks that because the explorer Oates walked out into the freezing blizzard, he did not commit suicide. Nature killed him, therefore, no suicide. "That the blizzard is a natural phenomenon is something that makes a difference."[3] But if his death were not imminent and he was trying to die, then his action is indeed a suicide (assuming that he knows that freezing blizzards usually kill people).

Alternate descriptions or intentions, however, present a more difficult consideration. In the case of the martyr, it was argued that her death was incidental, though foreseen. Thus, even though she acted in such a way that her death was inevitable, she did not commit suicide. There is an alternate description/intention of her act: to criticize and preach. But this business of alternate intention and description requires greater scrutiny.

For instance, there is a big difference between an alternate intention and ulterior intention. Some cases of self-caused death are "overdetermined." An individual may wish to preach the word of God and also die so as to become a martyr. She intends to do more than one thing by her action. Here I am inclined to say that there is a suicide just in case the death is a sufficient reason for the death-provoking action (as was clearly true for the escaped convict).

This notion of alternate description/intention echoes the "Doctrine of Double Effect" which turns on "A distinction between what an individual foresees as a result of his voluntary action and what, in the strict sense, he intends."[4] An individual intends, in the strict sense, both what he aims at as ends as well as those things he aims at as means to those ends. On the other hand, a person does not intend the foreseen consequences of his actions where these are neither the ends aimed at nor the means to them. "The words 'double effect' refer to the two effects that an action may produce: the one aimed at, and the one foreseen but in no way desired."[5] . . .

The difference between the individual's death being intended as a means to the desired end and merely being foreseen as an unavoidable outcome helps distinguish between suicides and nonsuicides. The religious zealot does not commit suicide precisely because her death is not intended as a means to the end of preaching the word of God. Her death is so far from being the means to her end, in intention and fact, that it is actually a hindrance to it. On the other hand, where the individual's death is intended as a means to the end aimed at, then the individual is committing suicide.

This is so in the case of a captured spy. He swallows a cyanide capsule to avoid interrogation which he believes will force him to reveal important secrets. Isn't this a suicide? We might be tempted to say no because there appears to be an alternate intention/description: avoiding incriminating interrogation. But this is really just the purpose or end of the suicide. It does not constitute an alternate description because the end to which it refers includes death as its intended means. The spy intends to kill himself as the means to avoiding interrogation and the subsequent disclosure of state secrets. Not really like the martyr at all.

We might also note another feature of this case; the death is in fact *necessary* as a means to accomplish the intended end. Had he not died, the spy would not have avoided incriminating interrogation. However, this condition is not *required* for the act to be a suicide. There may *in fact* be other means at the individual's disposal which he is either ignorant of or chooses not to employ (for example, because they jeopardize others' lives).

What of an airplane pilot who must either crash his plane at sea and die, or bail out and kill thousands of innocent people? This is similar to the spy example in that the motive for the act is the welfare of others. However, the pilot does not commit suicide. In the case of the pilot there is an alternate intention/description: crashing the plane. His death, though foreseen, is incidental to crashing the plane. The pilot's death is not intended as the means to saving lives (or crashing the plane, for that matter). This is unlike the spy's situation. The spy could not expect to achieve his end simply by taking cyanide. He must intend for the cyanide to kill him in a way that the pilot does not intend for the plane crash to kill him.

Whether or not there is an alternate intention/description of the act has the following interesting upshot which helps differentiate the spy from the airplane pilot. This might be considered the "substitutability of method" condition. The spy could just as well choose other methods of killing himself such as hanging or leaping from a great height, and still accomplish his goal. This is because his death is intended. However, the pilot cannot kill himself by some method *other* than crashing the plane, such as cyanide, and thereby achieve the end he aims at. This suggests that in cases of suicide, because the death is intended, substitute methods are feasible, make sense in terms of achieving the goal. But that in nonsuicides, substituting a different "way to die" doesn't make sense because the death is merely foreseen and incidental to what is really aimed at, such as crashing the plane.

There are limits to the applicability of this "substitutability of method" condition. The inappropriateness of substitute methods doesn't guarantee that the act is a nonsuicide. For instance, imagine that I want to frame someone for my murder and so kill myself. But, the person to be framed would only kill in a certain way; he would employ a specific *modus operandi*. This limits the methods at my disposal in the way requisite for nonsuicides, as in the case of the airplane pilot. I cannot kill myself in some other way and still achieve my end, but the act is nonetheless a suicide. Therefore, the "substitutability of method" condition can be applied only positively, as sufficient for the act to be a suicide. Thus, where the individual *could* substitute different methods and achieve his end, the act *is* a suicide; but where he couldn't; where only this mode will do, the issue is in doubt. So, substitutability of method insures suicide, but nonsubstitutability of method does not insure that the act is not a suicide.

When an individual takes his own life, then, it is a suicide unless one of the following two conditions obtains. He expects to die soon and so doesn't "choose" to die. Or, there is an alternate description/intention such that his death is not intended as a means to the end aimed at. When the latter condition obtains, the individual's death is but a foreseen, incidental outcome of his action. Consequently, the prospect of dying is not sufficient to prompt the act which results in his death.

The similarity between the spy and pilot cases suggests that the distinction between suicide and nonsuicide which we have just labored to draw is not always of chief importance. When the act which results in the individual's death is morally correct, even praiseworthy, the evaluation of the act would seem to be more vital than its description.

III

Let's turn now to the moral evaluation of suicide. Suicides range along a moral continuum, stretching from the heroic, through the permissible, to the immoral. In this respect suicide is not very different from other types of actions; similar considerations govern their evaluations. There will be cases, of course, when it will be morally correct for us to do things with and to ourselves which it would not be correct to do with or to others. It may be morally correct, for instance, to sacrifice ourselves in situations in which it would be wrong for us to sacrifice another. It seems plausible to think that in general suicide requires less by way of justification than the taking of another's life.

It is, however, the taking of a life, and therefore requires justification or explanation. To this it may be objected that since it is the individual's *own* life, no such justification or explanation is needed. I think this is wrong. At best it means that a weaker justification or less compelling explanation is all that is required. Taking a life, even one's own, is to destroy something of apparent value. This places the burden of proof or defense on the side of the destruction. While more is no doubt needed to defend this view directly, the plausibility of the subsequent evaluative analysis of suicide should lend it indirect support.

In what follows I assume that the suicide under consideration involves no shirking of obligations to *others*. I assume this both for the sake of simplicity, and because such shirking doesn't differentiate suicide from other forms of default, such as someone running out on his or her family.[6]

IV

The following evaluative analysis groups suicide into three moral categories: the praiseworthy or laudable; the acceptable; and the immoral or wrongful suicide. This organization is based on the agent's valuation: the nature of the valuing itself as well as the object which is valued or disvalued.

The first group consists of morally praiseworthy or laudable suicides. They turn on the agent valuing something else more than her own life, and so are other-regarding. These suicides include those which are noble, honorable, and obligatory. They are clearly "justified" in the broad sense of the term, but they are more than merely justified, as we shall see.

A clear case of a noble suicide requires a clear suicide. The easy condition to satisfy is choice. The difficult one is no alternate description or intention. The noble suicide always intends to do more than simply kill himself. But if his own death is essential or integral to accomplishing this larger goal, then perhaps it can still be considered a suicide.

Sidney Carton, of Dickens's *Tale of Two Cities,* provides a good case. He purposely sacrifices his own life that another may escape and make the woman Sidney loves happy. His death is intended as the means to the end he aims at. The nobility of the act lies not just in the larger intention, but in the motive behind that intention. He dies in order that another may be happy because he cares about her happiness as an end, out of love. He is motivated by concern for another's welfare independent of benefits he might thereby receive. Anonymity in such matters testifies to nobility of motive. But even here I find degrees. For someone to sacrifice himself to a *cause,* for a *principle,* would seem even greater because less bound to the self. Carton acts the way he does because he loves a woman; he is acting from his affections and the act springs from self-concern to that extent. The individual who gives up his life on the basis of moral conviction or commitment is less self-involved (though it is his moral conviction to be sure). At the very least, the motive is more determined by moral considerations per se.

Suicides that put others, causes, or principles ahead of ourselves are noble. They are but extreme cases of putting others, causes, and principles ahead of ourselves in less dramatic and final ways. But even when concerned with self, the suicide is morally worthy if the concern is principled. Although less laudable than the noble, we might consider these sorts of suicide *honorable*: concerned with self but in light of a moral principle rather than merely some personal interest. Honorable suicides spring from such motives as the aim of preventing oneself from doing or submitting to something base, or to avoid dishonor. To avoid living a servile or degraded life, for instance, is a moral motive, springing as it does from concern for self-respect. In the obvious sense, this sort of case is not "other-regarding" since motivated by considerations of self. Although it is not concerned with other *people*, however, it can be construed as "other-regarding" in that the motivation is other than self: respect, commitment to an ideal, or fidelity to the principle of dignity. What is *valued* is something other than mere self; what is valued is a moral standard. This is not self-regarding in the sense of concern for one's interests, happiness, or suffering. We should, then, consider this sort of suicide honorable. It is less than noble by virtue of its attention to self, but morally elevated because of the role played by a moral ideal or principle.

The third sort of suicide which turns upon the value of something distinct from the self is the obligatory sort. The clearest cases of obligatory suicide are those involving the assumption of a role which carries with it known risk: risk to others as well as the role-performer. Because of this risk, an obligation to commit suicide is built into the role; it is a role-bound obligation. The case of the spy is a good one. Here, the individual takes on the role knowing that he is supposed to take his own life should that be the only or best way to avoid endangering his country. There may, of course, be other sorts of obligatory suicides. If the individual's death would save a great many lives, then he might be obliged to kill himself even though he didn't voluntarily assume a high-risk role. In general, then, the obligation to commit suicide seems to stem from either a special role or our relationship to others in general. This parallels the bases for all sorts of obligations.

V

The second group consists of suicides that are morally acceptable. This is an awkward term, but comes closest to capturing those actions which are neither praiseworthy nor blameworthy. They involve the agent's valuation of his own life. The valuing or disvaluing is basically self-regarding. The lives of others may enter in, sometimes importantly, but the primary concern is the agent's finding his own life deficient in value.

The first type are "justified" suicides. It is of course true that all the suicides in the first class are justified in the broad sense. The nobility of an act, for instance, justifies it. But I am here offering a narrower, more specialized sense of justification, one which I hope also to distinguish from permission. It might, therefore, help to think of this narrower, idiosyncratic use as the "simply" justified. Here we find the familiar case of the chronic sufferer. Our strongest intuitions seem to arise when the unrelieved, unrelievable pain occurs in someone whose death is fairly close, but not actually imminent (for then, given my earlier analysis, it would not be an instance of suicide at all).

We see it as understandable—for anyone—to take her life in such a situation. Human nature being what it is, someone who didn't take her life in such a situation usually would require great strength. It seems unreasonable to expect or demand that people endure great, chronic suffering to no particular end. Of course, the suffering need not be physical. The loneliness of an aged surviving spouse with no other family or friends might be an adequate justification for suicide. Such a life is filled with disvalue and very little value. This justifies suicide (whether it also obliges another to assist in the suicide is another question).

Justified suicides blend imperceptibly into those that are but permissible. Doubtless, there will be "hard" cases, cases which might be impossible to differentiate. But this does not vitiate the distinction. The distinction is helpful in separating those cases which evoke subtle differences in our reactions and intuitions. The permissible suicide has a weaker basis than the justified. We don't see the act as universally reasonable or acceptable; rather, it seems to depend on the particular circumstances and psychology of the individual. In this sense, the permissible suicide is more "subjective," depending on the values and horizon of the subject's life in a way that the justified suicide doesn't. Where the justified suicide seems acceptable for "anyone," the permissible suicide depends on this particular someone. Because of this, the warrant for believing that the person's life isn't worth living seems weaker than in justified suicide.

I have in mind the kind of cases exemplified in a recent play: *Whose Life Is It Anyway?* In *Whose Life Is It Anyway?* a sculptor suffers quadriplegia as a result of an auto accident. He is unable to continue with his life's work, but suffers no overwhelming physical pain. The incapacity is permanent and the individual makes an effort for a while to find something meaningful in his new life. That new life, however, requires permanent residence in the hospital. All in all, the quadriplegic finds life intolerable and would rather be dead.

Even so, there is considerable "waste" of talent, energy, human potential, and the like. It is such waste, among other things, that prompts us to condemn some suicides. The utilitarian perspective especially would have us weigh the loss to society against the individual's long-term unhappiness.

In the permissible suicide, the individual's life is not so much filled with disvalue as devoid of value. Where the presence of something bad, such as pain, justifies the justified suicide, it is the absence of good that permits the permissible suicide. This is why the belief in hopelessness seems more warranted in the justified suicide. In the permissible, however, there are more contingencies unaccounted for, more possibilities for a worthwhile life, after all.

The last sort of suicide in this group is the excusable. What differentiates the excusable suicide from the justified or permissible is a defect in the valuation itself. Not only does the agent find disvalue in his life, but the condition which determines his valuation is itself deficient, lacking something of value. When we think of excused suicides we might reasonably think of "excuses," the sorts of thing which mitigate the agent's responsibility. Of course, certain excuses just don't readily apply to suicide, such as inattention, clumsiness, or carelessness. For under such conditions, the act just wouldn't be a suicide.

Most typical among excusable suicides are those in which the person is of unsound mind, as in temporary insanity, or those in which the individual is "not himself," as in clinical depression. As Richard Brandt notes, when extremely depressed, people are unable to estimate their future prospects properly either because unable to imagine improvement in their situation or because their assessment of probabilities is distorted.[7] In both these cases, the individual is not responsible for his behavior due to diminished capacity. Consequently, his suicide or its attempt is excusable.

Another condition could also provide a basis for excusing suicide. Brandt points out that someone who has the mistaken belief that he is obliged to commit suicide, say to spare his family suffering, is also excused.[8] While he doesn't argue for this view, the thinking behind it seems to be this. Although the individual has done something wrong, he is not blameworthy because motivated by duty. Of course, it might help to know why the individual thought that he was under an obligation to kill himself. No doubt this mistaken belief is based on others, such as that his family is better off not seeing him suffer from a chronic illness, or the like. And sometimes the explanation for these other beliefs is itself some mental dysfunction. Willy Loman, for instance, thinks that by killing himself and providing his family with the insurance money, he will do right by them and make them happy. However, he believes this because he is losing his mind.

This gap in Brandt's suggestion, *why* the person holds the mistaken belief he does, reveals its narrowness. For it isn't just that the belief is mistaken; it must also be unwarranted, unreasonable. Even laudable suicides can be based on mistaken beliefs, provided they are justified under the circumstances (e.g., believing that my death really will free hundreds of prisoners). In the case of excusable suicides the mistaken belief is also unwarranted. The error arises from some mental dysfunction or some other mitigating flaw, such as gullibility or short-sightedness. The basis for the mistake must not lie sufficiently within the agent's control, however, or the suicide will not be excusable but wrongful.

Brandt's suggestion is also narrow in its scope. The mistaken belief need not concern an obligation to commit suicide, but could be about a variety of things, such as the worthlessness of one's own life or the worthwhileness of another's. Once again, what is crucial is that the belief be plainly unwarranted *and* that the explanation for holding the belief relieve the agent of the sort of responsibility which could make the suicide wrongful.

We sometimes hear people speak of suicides as "foolish," and it isn't at all clear whether this is meant to be or should be included in the "excused" category.

Is the "foolish" suicide another class altogether? A foolish suicide might involve impetuous or impulsive action, for example. Still another sort, of a different stripe altogether, concerns failure to appreciate the particular situation. As Austin says, "We can know the facts and look at them mistakenly or perversely, or not fully realize or appreciate something, or even be under a total misconception."[9]

Someone who misconstrues the wily retreat of his troops to mean that the battle is surely lost and his capture imminent fails to properly appreciate matters. Failures of imagination, to see a variety of possibilities, as well as failures of interpretations, then, may constitute the foolishness. It seems reasonable to see these sorts of cases as excusable suicides, provided that the individual is not responsible for his foolish-making flaw. I am not sure whether all so-called foolish suicides are excusable or whether the foolish must be accorded separate status. The above considerations, together with our ordinary use of the term, however, might incline us to think of the foolish as a subclass of the excusable. A more extensive analysis would require looking at instances of foolish but nonsuicidal behavior.[10]

VI

Our last group consists of immoral or "wrongful" suicides. These also tend to be self-regarding. Like those in our previous category, these people disvalue something in their lives. But the story is more complicated. The object of disvalue is usually something directly affecting them, but not necessarily. Consider our example of someone who commits suicide in order to "frame" someone else in order that this enemy may greatly suffer. In this admittedly fanciful case, the agent need not find his own life bad; rather, he just has to disvalue his enemy's life more than he values his own. In such a case, then, the agent values his own life less than something else.

This sort of suicide appears to be similar to the laudable kind in that the agent values his own life less than something else. However, it is actually an inversion of the laudable suicide for two reasons. First, because it devolves upon comparative disvalue rather than value. In our example of immoral suicide, the individual *disvalues* another's life more than he values his own. In laudable suicide, the individual *values* a principle, person, or duty more than he values his own life. Secondly, it is an inversion because the aim is evil or vicious rather than praiseworthy.[11]

Our first sort of wrongful suicide, then, involves committing the act as a means to some bad end. As with nonsuicide parallels, this sort of suicide is wrong because instrumental in bringing about some evil. Even if the individual fails to achieve his end, we usually condemn the act because of the sort of character it indicates: a malicious, spiteful, envious, or hateful nature. This points us to another kind of wrongful suicide, the kind which springs from weak character.

When a person kills himself to escape some perceived evil, the act may be cowardly. This is probably the clearest, most familiar sort of wrongful suicide due to character failing. Think here of the financier who loses his fortune in a stock market crash. Let's hypothesize that, although despondent, he is neither clinically depressed nor "out of his mind." He has thought things out quite rationally and just cannot "face" the future. But, what differentiates his suicide from that of the quadriplegic sculptor? It seems to be a matter of degree, depending on how devastating the loss, how irrevocable the condition, how truly bleak the prospects.

In cowardly suicide, the condition (actual or threatened) is not nearly as decisive and irrevocable as the quadriplegic's. The financier's setback is external; he is still able to manage money or use his talents in other ways. Thus, while his world is shattered, his ability to regroup and recoup is not. A fortune can be rebuilt in a way that use of limbs for sculpting cannot. Thus, the financier's "fortunes" are reversible in a way that the paralyzed sculptor's are not. The former sculptor's way of being in the world is no longer possible.

Suicide is the cowardly way out when the individual fails to acknowledge the true ranking of his own values. He is afraid to risk *trying* to realize goals within his reach which realistically could make his life worthwhile. Losing a prestigious job; being branded a criminal; having to rebuild a fortune or live a nonluxurious life—these are not sufficient bases for taking one's life. There's more to live for than there is for the quadriplegic and the individual has resources as well as promising options. The cowardly suicide is fleeing responsibility for his life and the arduous effort required to rebuild it. It is fair to say that the cowardly suicide goes beyond the disvaluing typical of the acceptable suicides. He *devalues* his life.

Mightn't the allegedly cowardly suicide be the result of the unwarranted mistaken belief that there is little possibility of recovery? And wouldn't this make the suicide excusable? Perhaps, but it would depend on *why* the individual holds this belief. It would depend on whether having the mistaken, unwarranted belief is *itself* excusable, whether the individual could reasonably be expected to reject or correct such a belief. If the result of stupidity or defensible ignorance, then probably so. However, the belief could be the product of a rationalization which conceals the truth. By concealing the truth from himself the individual avoids the effort needed to rebound from failure or misfortune. In such a case, the cause of the error might be within the agent's control, and the suicide blamable rather than excusable. Unlike the excusable suicide, the coward is responsible for the condition which gives rise to his mistaken, unwarranted belief that killing himself is good or right. More generally, someone who is truly a coward (rather than one who merely behaves in a cowardly way) is, by definition, responsible for being ruled by fear.[12]

A still stronger case can be made where someone commits suicide in order to avoid the ill effects of his own *immoral* act. Fleeing responsibility for doing something wrong, as with an embezzler about to be uncovered, seems more cowardly. The individual is avoiding the bad consequences which he has brought about by doing something wrong. Running away from the "punishment," whatever its source, seems more cowardly since the individual is trying to escape what he morally deserves rather than a misfortune which has simply befallen him. This sort of "moral" cowardice seems especially ignoble.

There may be other character weaknesses operating in the kind of case we are considering, such as pride or impatience or overweening ambition. But, without cowardice I don't think any of these vices are sufficient to motivate suicide.

We cannot appreciate what's really wrong with this sort of suicide unless we refer to character failings. To say that the individual is failing to discharge a duty to himself may be correct, but incomplete. It doesn't explain why, for one thing. And it doesn't capture all of what is wrong in the act, for another. It isn't that the agent doesn't see his duty or that he's overcome or that he simply doesn't care about himself. He does care about himself—perhaps too much or in the wrong way. He "gives up" because he can't bear to face an uphill struggle. This is very close to the quadriplegic's situation except that there the individual's life is more radically altered: it is cut off at its root. It isn't that he's afraid of facing tomorrow. Rather, he sees no meaning in tomorrow and thinks it futile to go through the charade of sublimating his energies in some sideline.

We have just seen how considerations of character are needed to inform our moral evaluations of suicide. But considerations of character must also be supplemented. We must enrich our moral vocabulary and by so doing enlarge our moral perspective. This is because there are suicides for which judgments of permissibility, excusability, or even immorality are simply inadequate. There is more to their moral story. The suicide of someone who has been oppressed and exploited, for example, is not merely permissible, it is also dreadful or awful. The suicide of one who has been wrongfully imprisoned is tragic. And when someone takes her life because filled with self-loathing, it is pitiable. On the other hand, when a fanatic or megalomaniac commits suicide, it seems grotesque. We fall woefully short of the task of evaluating suicide if we confine ourselves to the categories of moral judgment. In addition to the language of judgment, we must speak the language of moral understanding.

Notes

1. Of course, they have "chosen" to die in the sense that the behavior was within their control, that they performed a voluntary or deliberate act. It is just that their choice is severely circumscribed by the imminence of their death.

2. The degree to which our options are restricted typically makes a difference in the moral evaluation and assessment of responsibility of actions. Thus, if someone is being attacked and cannot escape, his standing and fighting is less courageous than one who has the option to avoid the harm altogether. And, when we are coerced we bear less moral responsibility for what we do than when uncoerced.

It may be that I am reluctant to call terminal deaths suicide because a vestige of disapprobrium still attaches to the idea of suicide in general and this kind of action seems morally permissible.

3. R. F. Holland, "Suicide," in *Moral Dilemmas*, ed. Richard Purtill (California: Wadsworth, 1985), p. 98. This case is complicated by the fact that Oates was actually dying. This, and not the "natural" means of his death, is relevant to his action not being a suicide.

4. Phillipa Foot, "Abortion," in *Virtues and Vices* (Berkeley: University of California Press, 1978), p. 20.

5. Foot, p. 20.

6. Holland nicely points out that consideration of duty-shirking "would be no more

a reason against suicide than it would be a reason against his walking out on them (family) ... so we do not learn from this example whether or not the suicide itself is especially objectionable" (p. 96).

7. Richard Brandt, "The Morality and Rationality of Suicide," in *Choice and Action*, ed. Charles Reid (New York: Macmillan, 1981), p. 461. It is important to distinguish between "ordinary" depression (despondency) and "depressive illness" or "clinical depression." The former may indeed be chronic but is compatible with the ability to deliberate rationally.

8. Brandt, p. 454

9. John Austin, "A Plea for Excuses," in *Philosophy of Law*, eds. Feinberg and Gross (Encino, Calif.: Dickenson, 1975), p. 324.

10. Consider a father who goes to pick up his daughter at the movies. When he doesn't see her, he drives off, assuming she had a ride with someone else. Is this excusable? Shouldn't he have gotten out and looked around a little, or at least have waited a while? The father's behavior isn't excusable because there just don't seem to be any extenuating or mitigating considerations, such as being preoccupied with a pressing problem or late for an appointment. Whatever caused his behavior—impatience, laziness—seems well within the father's control to resist.

Sometimes foolish behavior is excusable because it stems from psychosocial crises: mid-life crisis or teenage turbulence, for instance. These crises may be prompted by biochemical changes over which the individual has little if any control.

Or, consider the foolishness of Shakespeare's Romeo. He sees Juliet lying in the mausoleum, apparently lifeless. First of all, he doesn't even bother to check her pulse or breath. Perhaps this is excusable on grounds of youthful ignorance and the turmoil of their predicament. Secondly, he doesn't pause to ponder whether indeed his life is not worth living without his beloved. But perhaps this is also excusable in light of the fervor of his love and the shortsightedness of his vision. The latter seems to be a deep-seated character trait for which Romeo probably cannot be held much responsible.

11. Of course there may be considerable difficulty in ascertaining whether a particular end is evil or good, just as with laudable suicides. This is not grounds for objecting to the analysis offered here, the purpose of which is to provide an account of wrongful (as well as laudable) suicide. The account can be correct even though applying its categories may sometimes be problematic.

12. There may be cases of "mixed" suicide, in which the individual is, for instance, to some extent acting honorably, to some extent cowardly. An army officer might make a terrible, irresponsible decision which costs the lives of thousands of his men (Gallipoli). His superiors then leave him alone in a room with a gun, expecting him to do the honorable thing—kill himself. His suicide might be construed as honorable insofar as it saves the country turmoil and the army embarrassment. However, it might also be somewhat cowardly, insofar as the officer wishes to avoid the public humiliation and the great effort needed to start his life over.

PART THREE

Is Suicide Moral?
Is It Rational?

16

Preventing Suicide
Edwin S. Shneidman

In almost every case of suicide, there are hints of the act to come, and physicians and nurses are in a special position to pick up the hints and to prevent the act. They come into contact, in many different settings, with many human beings at especially stressful times in their lives.

A suicide is an especially unhappy event for helping personnel. Although one can, in part, train and inure oneself to deal with the sick and even the dying patient, the abruptness and needlessness of a suicidal act leaves the nurse, the physician, and other survivors with many unanswered questions, many deeply troubling thoughts and feelings.

Currently, the major bottleneck in suicide prevention is not remediation, for there are fairly well-known and effective treatment procedures for many types of suicidal states; rather it is in diagnosis and identification.[1]

Assumptions

A few straightforward assumptions are necessary in suicide prevention. Some of them:

Individuals who are intent on killing themselves still wish very much to be rescued or to have their deaths prevented. Suicide prevention consists essentially in recognizing that the potential victim is "in balance" between his wishes to live and his wishes to die, then throwing one's efforts on the side of life.

Suicide prevention depends on the active and forthright behavior of the potential rescuer.

Reprinted from the *American Journal of Nursing* 65 (May 1965):111–16, with the permission of Lippincott-Raven Publishers.

Most individuals who are about to commit suicide are acutely conscious of their intention to do so. They may, of course, be very secretive and not communicate their intentions directly. On the other hand, the suicidally inclined person may actually be unaware of his own lethal potentialities, but nonetheless may give many indirect hints of his unconscious intentions.

Practically all suicidal behaviors stem from a sense of isolation and from feelings of some intolerable emotion on the part of the victim. By and large, suicide is an act to stop an intolerable existence. But each individual defines "intolerable" in his own way. Difficulties, stresses, or disappointments that might be easy for one individual to handle might very well be intolerable for someone else—in *his* frame of mind. In order to anticipate and prevent suicide one must understand what "intolerable" means to the other person. Thus, any "precipitating cause"—being neglected, fearing or having cancer (the fear and actuality can be equally lethal), feeling helpless or hopeless, feeling "boxed-in"—may be intolerable for that person.

Although committing suicide is certainly an all-or-none action, thinking about the act ahead of time is a complicated, undecided, internal debate. Many a black-or-white action is taken on a barely pass vote. Professor Henry Murray of Harvard University has written that "a personality is a full Congress" of the mind. In preventing suicide, one looks for any indications in the individual representing the dark side of his internal life-and-death debate. We are so often surprised at "unexpected" suicides because we fail to take into account just this principle that the suicidal action is a decision resulting from an internal debate of many voices, some for life and some for death. Thus we hear all sorts of postmortem statements like "He seemed in good spirits" or "He was looking forward to some event next week," not recognizing that these, in themselves, represent only one aspect of the total picture.

In almost every case, there are precursors to suicide, which are called "prodromal clues." In the "psychological autopsies" that have been done at the Suicide Prevention Center in Los Angeles—in which, by interview with survivors of questionable accident or suicide deaths, they attempt to reconstruct the intention of the deceased in relation to death—it was found that very few suicides occur without casting some shadows before them. The concept of prodromal clues for suicide is certainly an old idea; it is really not very different from what Robert Burton, over 300 years ago in 1652, in his famous *Anatomy of Melancholy,* called "the prognostics of melancholy, or signs of things to come." These prodromal clues typically exist for a few days to some weeks before the actual suicide. Recognition of these clues is a necessary first step to lifesaving.

Suicide prevention is like fire prevention. It is not the main mission of any hospital, nursing home, or other institution, but it is the minimum ever-present peripheral responsibility of each professional; and when the minimal signs of possible fire or suicide are seen, then there are no excuses for holding back on lifesaving measures. The difference between fire prevention and suicide prevention is that the prodromal clues for fire prevention have become an acceptable part of our commonsense folk knowledge; we must also make the clues for suicide a part of our general knowledge.

Clues to Potential Suicide

In general, the prodromal clues to suicide may be classified in terms of four broad types: verbal, behavioral, situational, and syndromatic.

Verbal

Among the verbal clues we can distinguish between the direct and the indirect. Examples of direct verbal communications would be such statements as "I'm going to commit suicide," "If such and such happens, I'll kill myself," "I'm going to end it all," "I want to die," and so on. Examples of indirect verbal communications would be such statements as "Goodbye," "Farewell," "I've had it," "I can't stand it any longer," "It's too much to put up with," "You'd be better off without me," and, in general, any statements that mirror the individual's intention to stop his intolerable existence.

Some indirect verbal communications can be somewhat more subtle. We all know that in human communication, our words tell only part of the story, and often the main "message" has to be decoded. Every parent or spouse learns to decode the language of loved ones and to understand what they really mean. In a similar vein, many presuicidal communications have to be decoded. An example might be a patient who says to a nurse who is leaving on her vacation, "Goodbye, Miss Jones, I won't be here when you come back." If some time afterward she, knowing that the patient is not scheduled to be transferred or discharged prior to her return, thinks about that conversation, she might do well to telephone her hospital.

Other examples are such statements as "I won't be around much longer for you to put up with," "This is the last shot you'll ever give me," or "This is the last time I'll ever be here," a statement which reflects the patient's private knowledge of his decision to kill himself. Another example is, "How does one leave her body to the medical school?" The latter should never be answered with factual information until after one has found out why the question is being asked, and whose body is being talked about. Individuals often ask for suicide-prevention information for a "friend" or "relative" when they are actually inquiring about themselves.

Behavior

Among the behavioral clues, we can distinguish the direct and the indirect. The clearest examples of direct behavioral communications of the intention to kill oneself is a "practice run," an actual suicide attempt of whatever seriousness. Any action which uses instruments which are conventionally associated with suicide (such as razors, ropes, pills, and the like), regardless of whether or not it could have any lethal outcome, must be interpreted as a direct behavioral "cry for help" and an indication that the person is putting us on our alert. Often, the nonlethal suicide attempt is meant to communicate deeper suicidal intentions. By and large, suicide attempts must be taken seriously as indications of personal crisis and of more severe suicide potentiality.

In general, indirect behavioral communications are such actions as taking a lengthy trip or putting affairs into order. Thus the making of a will under certain peculiar and special circumstances can be an indirect clue to suicidal intention. Buying a casket at the time of another's funeral should always be inquired after most carefully and, if necessary, prompt action (like hospitalization) taken. Giving away prized possessions like a watch, earrings, golf clubs, or heirlooms should be looked on as a possible prodromal clue to suicide.

Situational

On occasion the situation itself cries out for attention, especially when there is a variety of stresses. For example, when a patient is extremely anxious about surgery, or when he has been notified that he has a malignancy, when he is scheduled for mutilative surgery, when he is frightened by hospitalization itself, or when outside factors (like family discord, for example, or finances) are a problem—all these are situational. If the doctor or nurse is sensitive to the fact that the situation constitutes a "psychological emergency" for that patient, then he is in a key position to perform lifesaving work. His actions might take the form of sympathetic conversation, or special surveillance of that patient by keeping him with some specially assigned person, or by requesting consultation, or by moving him so that he does not have access to windows at lethal heights. At the least, the nurse should make notations of her behavioral observations in the chart.

To be a suicide diagnostician, one must combine separate symptoms and recognize *and label* a suicidal syndrome in a situation where no one symptom by itself would necessarily lead one to think of a possible suicide.

In this [essay] we shall highlight syndromatic clues for suicide in a medical and surgical hospital setting, although these clues may also be used in other settings. First, it can be said that patient status is stressful for many persons. Everyone who has ever been a patient knows the fantasies of anxiety, fear, and regression that are attendant on illness or surgery. For some in the patient role (especially in a hospital), as the outer world recedes, the fantasy life becomes more active; conflicts and inadequacies and fears may then begin to play a larger and disproportionate role. The point for suicide prevention is that one must try to be aware especially of those patients who are prone to be psychologically overreactive and, being so, are more apt to explode irrationally into suicidal behavior.

Syndromatic

What are the syndromes—the constellations of symptoms—for suicide? Labels for four of them could be: depressed, disoriented, defiant, and dependent-dissatisfied.

1. Depressed: The syndrome of depression is, by and large, made up of symptoms which reflect the shifting of the individual's psychological interests from aspects of his interpersonal life to aspects of his private psychological life, to some intrapsychic crisis within himself. For example, the individual is less interested in

food, he loses his appetite, and thus loses weight. Or, his regular patterns of sleeping and waking become disrupted, so that he suffers from lack of energy in the daytime and then sleeplessness and early awakening. The habitual or regular patterns of social and sexual responses also tend to change, and the individual loses interest in others. His rate or pace or speed of talking, walking, and doing the activities of his everyday life slows down. At the same time, there is increased preoccupation with internal (intrapsychic) conflicts and problems. The individual is withdrawn, apathetic, apprehensive and anxious, often "blue" and even tearful, somewhat unreachable and seemingly uncaring.

Depression can be seen too in an individual's decreased willingness to communicate. Talking comes harder, there are fewer spontaneous remarks, answers are shorter or even monosyllabic, the facial expressions are less lively, the posture is more drooped, gestures are less animated, the gait is less springy, and the individual's mind seems occupied and elsewhere.

An additional symptom of the syndrome of depression is detachment, or withdrawing from life. This might be evidenced by behavior which would reflect attitudes, such as "I don't care," "What does it matter," "It's no use anyway." If an individual feels helpless he is certainly frightened, although he may fight for some control or safety; but if he feels hopeless, then the heart is out of him, and life is a burden, and he is only a spectator to a dreary life which does not involve him.

First aid in suicide prevention is directed to counteracting the individual's feelings of hopelessness. Robert E. Litman, chief psychiatrist of the Los Angeles Suicide Prevention Center, has said that "psychological support is transmitted by firm and hopeful attitude. We convey the impression that the problem which seems to the patient to be overwhelming, dominating his entire personality, and completely insidious, is commonplace and quite familiar to us and we have seen many people make a complete recovery. Hope is a commodity of which we have plenty and we dispense it freely."[2]

It is of course pointless to say "Cheer up" to a depressed person, inasmuch as the problem is that he simply cannot. On the other hand, the effectiveness of the "self-fulfilling prophecy" should never be overestimated. Often an integral part of anyone's climb out of a depression is his faith and the faith of individuals around him that he is going to make it. Just as hopelessness breeds hopelessness, hope—to some extent—breeds hope.

Oftentimes, the syndrome of depression does not seem especially difficult to diagnose. What may be more difficult—and very much related to suicide—is the apparent improvement after a severe depression, when the individual's pace of speech and action picks up a little. The tendency then is for everyone to think that he is cured and to relax vigilance. In reality the situation may be much more dangerous; the individual now has the psychic energy with which to kill himself that he may not have had when he was in the depths of his depression. By far, most suicides relating to depression occur within a short period (a few days to 3 months) after the individual has made an apparent turn for the better. A good rule is that any significant change in behavior, even if it looks like improvement, should be assessed as a possible prodromal index for suicide.

Although depression is the most important single prodromal syndrome for suicide—occurring to some degree in approximately one-third of all suicides—it is not the only one.

2. Disoriented: Disoriented people are apt to be delusional or hallucinatory, and the suicidal danger is that they may respond to commands or voices or experiences that other people cannot share. When a disoriented person expresses any suicidal notions, it is important to take him as a most serious suicidal risk, for he may be in constant danger of taking his own life, not only to cut out those parts of himself that he finds intolerable, but also to respond to the commands of hallucinated voices to kill himself. What makes such a person potentially explosive and particularly hard to predict is that the trigger mechanism may depend on a crazed thought, a hallucinated command, or a fleeting intense fear within a delusional system.

Disoriented states may be clearly organic, such as delirium tremens, certain toxic states, certain drug withdrawal states. Individuals with chronic brain syndromes and cerebral arteriosclerosis* may become disoriented. On the other hand, there is the whole spectrum of schizophrenic and schizoaffective disorders, in which the role of organic factors is neither clearly established nor completely accepted. Nonetheless, professional personnel should especially note individuals who manifest some degree of nocturnal disorientation, but who have relative diurnal lucidity. Those physicians who see the patients only during the daytime are apt to miss these cases, particularly if they do not read nurses' notes.

Suicides in general hospitals have occurred among nonpsychiatric patients with subtle organic syndromes, especially those in which symptoms of disorientation are manifested. One should look, too, for the presence of bizarre behavior, fear of death, and clouding of the patient's understanding and awareness. The nurse might well be especially alert to any general hospital patient who has any previous neuropsychiatric history, especially where there are the signs of an acute brain syndrome. Although dyspnea† is not a symptom in the syndrome related to disorientation, the presence of severe dyspnea, especially if it is unimproved by treatment in the hospital, has been found to correlate with suicide in hospitals.

When an individual is labeled psychotic, he is almost always disoriented in one sphere or another. Even if he knows where he is and what the date is, he may be off base about who he is, especially if one asks him more or less "philosophic" questions, like "What is the meaning of life?" His thinking processes will seem peculiar, and the words of his speech will have some special or idiosyncratic characteristics. In general, whether or not such patients are transferred to psychiatric wards or psychiatric hospitals, they should—in terms of suicide prevention—be given special care and surveillance, including consultation. Special physical arrangements should be made for them, such as removal of access to operable screens and windows, removal of objects of self-destruction, and the like.

3. Defiant: The Welsh poet, Dylan Thomas, wrote: "Do not go gentle into that

---

*Hardening of the arteries—Ed.
†Shortness of breath—Ed.

good night / ... rage, rage against the dying of the light." Many of us remember, usually from high school literature, Henley's "Invictus," "I am master of my fate / I am the captain of my soul." The point is that many individuals, no matter how miserable their circumstances or how painful their lives, attempt to retain some shred of control over their own fate. Thus a man dying of cancer may, rather than passively capitulate to the disease, choose to play one last active role in his own life by picking the time of his death; so that even in a terminal state (when the staff may believe that he doesn't have the energy to get out of bed), he lifts a heavy window and throws himself out to his death. In this sense, he is willful or defiant.

This kind of individual is an "implementer."[3] Such a person is described as one who has an active need to control his environment. Typically, he would never be fired from any job; he would quit. In a hospital he would attempt to control his environment by refusing some treatments, demanding others, requesting changes, insisting on privileges, and indulging in many other activities indicating some inner need to direct and control his life situation. These individuals are often seen as having low frustration tolerance, being fairly set and rigid in their ways, being somewhat arbitrary and, in general, showing a great oversensitivity to outside control. The last is probably a reflection of their own inability to handle their inner stresses.

Certainly, not every individual who poses ward-management problems needs to be seen as suicidal, but what personnel should look for is the somewhat agitated concern of a patient with controlling his own fate. Suicide is one way of "calling the shot." The nurse can play a lifesaving role with such a person by recognizing his psychological problems and by enduring his controlling (and irritating) behavior—indeed, by being the willing target of his berating or demanding behavior and thus permitting him to expend his energies in this way, rather than in suicidal activities. Her willingness to be a permissible target for these feelings and, more, her sympathetic behavior in giving attention and reassurance even in the face of difficult behavior are in the tradition of the nurturing nurse, even though this can be a difficult role continually to fulfill.

4. Dependent-dissatisfied: Imagine being married to someone on whom you are deeply emotionally dependent, in a situation in which you are terribly dissatisfied with your being dependent. It would be in many ways like being "painted into a corner"—there is no place to go.

This is the pattern we have labeled "dependent-dissatisfied."[4] Such an individual is very dependent on the hospital, realizing he is ill and depending on the hospital to help him; however, he is dissatisfied with being dependent and comes to feel that the hospital is not giving him the help he thinks he needs. Such patients become increasingly tense and depressed, with frequent expressions of guilt and inadequacy. They have emotional disturbances in relation to their illnesses and to their hospital care. Like the "implementer," they make demands and have great need for attention and reassurance. They have a number of somatic complaints, as well as complaints about the hospital. They threaten to leave the hospital against medical advice. They ask to see the doctor, the chaplain, the chief nurse. They request additional therapies of various kinds. They make statements like, "Nothing is being done for me" or "The doctors think I am making this up."

The reactions of irritability on the part of busy staff are not too surprising in view of the difficult behavior of such patients. Tensions in these patients may go up especially at the time of pending discharge from the hospital. Suicide prevention by hospital staff consists of responding to the emotional needs and giving emotional support to these individuals. With such patients the patience of Job is required. Any suicide threats or attempts on the part of such patients, no matter how "mild" or attention-getting, should be taken seriously. Their demand for attention may lead them to suicide. Hospital staff can often, by instituting some sort of new treatment procedure or medication, give this type of patient temporary relief or a feeling of improvement. But most of all, the sympathetic recognition on the part of hospital staff that the complaining, demanding, exasperating behavior of the dependent-dissatisfied patient is an expression of his own inner feelings of desperation may be the best route to preventing his suicide.

Coworkers, Family, Friends

Suicide is "democratic." It touches both patients and staff, unlettered and educated, rich and poor—almost proportionately. As for sex ratio, the statistics are interesting. Most studies have shown that in Western countries more men than women commit suicide, but a recent study indicates that in certain kinds of hospital settings like neuropsychiatric hospitals, a proportionately larger percentage of women kill themselves.[5] The information in this [essay] is meant to apply not only to patients, but to colleagues, and even to members of our families as well. The point is that only by being free to see the possibility of suicidal potential in everybody can suicide prevention of anybody really become effective.

In our society, we are especially loath to suspect suicide in individuals of some stature or status. For example, of the physicians who commit suicide, some could easily be saved if they would be treated (hospitalized, for example) like ordinary citizens in distress. Needless to say, the point of view that appropriate treatment might cause him professional embarrassment should never be invoked in such a way so as to risk a life being lost.

In general, we should not "run scared" about suicide. In the last analysis, suicides are, fortunately, infrequent events. On the other hand, if we have even unclear suspicions of suicidal potential in another person, we do well to have "the courage of our own confusions" and take the appropriate steps.

These appropriate steps may include notifying others, obtaining consultation, alerting those concerned with the potentially suicidal person (including relatives and friends), getting the person to a sanctuary in a psychiatric ward or hospital. Certainly, we don't want to holler "Fire" unnecessarily, but we should be able to interpret the clues, erring, if necessary, on the "liberal" side. We may feel chagrined if we turn in a false alarm, but we would feel very much worse if we were too timid to pull that switch that might have prevented a real tragedy.

Earlier in this [essay] the role of the potential rescuer was mentioned. One implication of this is that professionals must be aware of their own reactions and their own personalities, especially in relation to certain patients. For example, does he have the insight to recognize his tendency to be irritated at a querulous and demanding patient and thus to ignore his presuicidal communications? Every rescue operation is a dialogue: Someone cries for help and someone else must be willing to hear him and be capable of responding to him. Otherwise the victim may die because of the potential rescuer's unresponsiveness.

We must develop in ourselves a special attitude for suicide prevention. Each individual can be a lifesaver, a one-person committee to prevent suicide. Happily, elaborate pieces of mechanical equipment are not needed; "all" that is required are sharp eyes and ears, good intuition, a pinch of wisdom, an ability to act appropriately, and a deep resolve.

Notes

1. N. L. Farberow and Edwin Shneidman, eds., *The Cry for Help* (New York: McGraw-Hill, 1961).

2. Robert Litman, "Emergency Response to Potential Suicide," *Journal of the Michigan Medical Society* 62 (1963): 68–72.

3. Norman L. Farberow, Edwin Shneidman, and Leonard Calista, *Suicide among General Medical and Surgical Hospital Patients with Malignant Neoplasms* (Washington, D.C.: Veterans' Administration, 1963).

4. Edwin Shneidman and Norman Farberow, *Evaluation and Treatment of Suicidal Risk among Schizophrenic Patients in Psychiatric Hospitals* (Washington, D.C.: Veterans' Administration, 1962).

5. Sherman Eisenthal, N. L. Farberow, and Edwin Shneidman, "Follow-up of Neuropsychiatric Hospital Patients on Suicide Observation Status," *Public Health Reports* 81 (November 1964): 977–90.

17

The Ethics of Suicide
Thomas S. Szasz

An editorial in the *Journal of the American Medical Association* (March 6, 1967) declared that "the contemporary physician sees suicide as a manifestation of emotional illness. Rarely does he view it in a context other than that of psychiatry." It was thus implied, the emphasis being the stronger for not being articulated, that to view suicide in this way is at once scientifically accurate and morally uplifting. I submit that it is neither; that, instead, this perspective on suicide is both erroneous and evil: erroneous because it treats an act as if it were a happening; and evil, because it serves to legitimize psychiatric force and fraud by justifying it as medical care and treatment.

Before going further, I should like to distinguish three fundamentally different concepts and categories that are combined and confused in most discussions of suicide. They are: (1) suicide proper, or so-called successful suicide; (2) attempted, threatened, or so-called unsuccessful suicide; and (3) the attribution by someone (typically a psychiatrist) to someone else (now called a "patient") of serious (that is, probably successful) suicidal intent. The first two concepts refer to acts by an actually or ostensibly suicidal person; the third refers to the claim of an ostensibly normal person about someone else's suicide-proneness.

I believe that, generally speaking, the person who commits suicide intends to die; whereas the one who threatens suicide or makes an unsuccessful attempt at it intends to improve his life, not to terminate it. (The person who makes claims about someone else's suicidal intent does so usually in order to justify his efforts to control that person.)

Put differently, successful suicide is generally an expression of an individual's desire for greater autonomy—in particular, for self-control over his own death;

Reprinted from *The Antioch Review* 31 (Spring 1971): 7–17, with the permission of the author. Copyright © 1971 by Thomas Szasz.

whereas unsuccessful suicide is generally an expression of an individual's desire for more control over others—in particular, for compelling persons close to him to comply with his wishes. Although in some cases there may be legitimate doubt about which of these conditions obtains, in the majority of instances where people speak of "suicide" or "attempted suicide," the act falls clearly into one or the other group.

In short, I believe that successful and unsuccessful suicide constitute radically different acts or categories, and hence cannot be discussed together. Accordingly, I have limited the scope of this essay to suicide proper, with occasional references to attributions of suicidal intent. (The ascription of suicidal intent is, of course, a very different sort of thing from either successful or unsuccessful suicide. Since psychiatrists use it as if it designated a potentially or probably fatal "condition," it is sometimes necessary to consider this concept together with the phenomenon of suicide proper.)

I

It is difficult to find "responsible" medical or psychiatric authority today that does not regard suicide as a medical, and specifically as a mental health, problem.

For example, Ilza Veith, the noted medical historian, writing in *Modern Medicine* (August 11, 1969), asserts that "the act [of suicide] clearly represents an illness...."

Bernard R. Shochet, a psychiatrist at the University of Maryland, offers a precise description of the kind of illness it is. "Depression," he writes, "is a serious systemic disease, with both physiological and psychological concomitants, and suicide is a part of this syndrome." And he articulates the intervention he feels is implicit in this view: "If the patient's safety is in doubt, psychiatric hospitalization should be insisted on."[1]

Harvey M. Schein and Alan A. Stone, both psychiatrists at the Harvard Medical School, are even more explicit about the psychiatric coercion justified, in their judgment, by the threat of suicide. "Once the patient's suicidal thoughts are shared," they write,

> the therapist must take pains to make clear to the patient that he, the therapist, considers suicide to be a maladaptive action, irreversibly counter to the patient's sane interests and goals; that he, the therapist, will do *everything* he can do to prevent it; and that the potential for such an action arises from the patient's illness. It is equally essential that the therapist believe in the professional stance; if he does not he should not be treating the patient within the delicate human framework of psychotherapy.[2]

Schein and Stone do not explain why the patient's confiding in his therapist to the extent of communicating his suicidal thoughts to him should *ipso facto* deprive the patient from being the arbiter of his own best interests. The thrust of their argument is prescriptive rather than logical. They seek to justify depriving the patient of a basic human freedom—the freedom to grant or withhold consent for treatment: "The therapist must insist that patient and physician—together—communicate the suicidal potential to important figures in the environment, both professional and family.... Suicidal intent must not be part of therapeutic confidentiality." And further on they write: "Obviously this kind of patient must be hospitalized.... The therapist must be prepared to step in with hospitalization, with security measures, and with medication."

Schein and Stone thus suggest that the "suicidal" patient should have the right to choose his therapist; and that he should have the right to agree with his therapist and follow the latter's therapeutic recommendation (say, for hospitalization). At the same time, they insist that if "suicidal" patient and therapist disagree on therapy, then the patient should *not* have the right to disengage himself from the first therapist and choose a second—say, one who would consider suicidal intent a part of therapeutic confidentiality.

Many other psychiatric authorities could be cited to illustrate the current unanimity on this view of suicide.

Lawyers and jurists have eagerly accepted the psychiatric perspective on suicide, as they have on nearly everything else. An article in the *American Bar Association Journal* (September 1968) by R. E. Schulman, who is both a lawyer and a psychologist, is illustrative.

Schulman begins with the premise that "No one in contemporary Western society would suggest that people be allowed to commit suicide as they please without some attempt to intervene or prevent such suicides. Even if a person does not value his own life, Western society does value everyone's life."

But I should like to suggest, as others have suggested before me, precisely what Schulman claims no one would suggest. Furthermore, if Schulman chooses to believe that Western society—which includes the United States with its history of slavery, Germany with its history of National Socialism, and Russia with its history of Communism—really "values everyone's life," so be it. But to accept this assertion as true is to fly in the face of the most obvious and brutal facts of history.

II

When a person decides to take his life, and when a physician decides to frustrate him in this action, the question arises: Why should the physician do so?

Conventional psychiatric wisdom answers: Because the suicidal person (now called "patient" for proper emphasis) suffers from a mental illness whose symptom is his desire to kill himself; it is the physician's duty to diagnose and treat his illness: *ergo,* he must prevent the "patient" from killing himself and, at the same time, must "treat" the underlying "disease" that "causes" the "patient" to wish doing away with himself. This looks like an ordinary medical diagnosis and intervention. But it is not. What is missing? Everything. The hypothetical, suicidal "patient" is not ill; he has no demonstrable bodily disorder (or if he does, it does not "cause" his suicide); he does not assume the sick role: he does not seek medical help. In short, the physician uses the rhetoric of illness and treatment to justify his forcible intervention in the life of a fellow human being—often in the face of explicit opposition from his so-called "patient."

I do not doubt that attempted or successful suicide may be exceedingly *disturbing* for persons related to, acquainted with, or caring for the ostensible "patient." But I reject the conclusion that the suicidal person is, *ipso facto,* disturbed, that being disturbed equals being *mentally ill,* and that being mentally ill *justifies* psychiatric hospitalization or treatment. I have developed my reasons for this elsewhere, and need not repeat them here.[3] For the sake of emphasis, however, let me state that I consider counseling, persuasion, psychotherapy, or any other *voluntary measure,* especially for persons troubled by their own suicidal inclinations and seeking such help, unobjectionable, and indeed generally desirable, interventions. However, physicians and psychiatrists are usually not satisfied with limiting their help to such measures—and with good reason: from such assistance the individual may gain not only the desire to live, but also the strength to die.

But we still have not answered the question: Why should a physician frustrate an individual from killing himself? As we saw, some psychiatrists answer: Because the physician values the patient's life, at least when the patient is suicidal, more highly than does the patient himself. Let us examine this claim. Why should the physician, often a complete stranger to the suicidal patient, value the patient's life more highly than does the patient himself? He does not do so in medical practice. Why then should he do so in psychiatric practice, which he himself insists is a form of medical practice? Let us assume that a physician is confronted with an individual suffering from diabetes or heart failure who fails to take the drugs prescribed for his illness. We know that this often happens, and that when it does the patient may become disabled and die prematurely. Yet it would be absurd for a physician to consider, much less attempt, taking over the conduct of such a patient's life, confining him in a hospital against his will in order to treat his disease. Indeed, any attempt to do so would bring the physician into conflict with both the civil and the criminal law. For, significantly, the law recognizes the medical patient's autonomy despite the fact that, unlike the suicidal individual, he suffers from a real disease; and despite the fact that, unlike the nonexistent disease of the suicidal individual, his illness is often easily controlled by simple and safe therapeutic procedures.

Nevertheless, the threat of alleged or real suicide, or so-called dangerousness to oneself, is everywhere considered a proper ground and justification for involuntary mental hospitalization and treatment. Why should this be so?

Let me suggest what I believe is likely to be the most important reason for the profound antisuicidal bias of the medical profession. Physicians are committed to saving lives. How, then, should they react to people who are committed to throwing away their lives? It is natural for people to dislike, indeed to hate, those who challenge their basic values. The physician thus reacts, perhaps "unconsciously" (in the sense that he does not articulate the problem in these terms), to the suicidal patient as if the patient had affronted, insulted, or attacked him. The physician strives valiantly, often at the cost of his own well-being, to save lives; and here comes a person who not only does not let the physician save him, but, *horribile dictu,* makes the physician an unwilling witness to that person's deliberate self-destruction. This is more than most physicians can take. Feeling assaulted in the very center of their spiritual identity, some take to flight, while others fight back.

Some nonpsychiatric physicians will thus have nothing to do with suicidal patients. This explains why many people who end up killing themselves have a record of having consulted a physician, often on the very day of their suicide. I surmise that these persons go in search of help, only to discover that the physician wants nothing to do with them. And, in a sense, it is right that it should be so. I do not blame the doctors. Nor do I advocate teaching them suicide prevention—whatever that might be. I contend that because physicians have a relatively blind faith in their life-saving ideology—which, moreover, they often need to carry them through their daily work—they are the wrong people for listening and tasking to individuals, intelligently and calmly, about suicide. So much for those physicians who, in the face of the existential attack which they feel the suicidal patient launches on them, run for *their* lives. Let us now look at those who stand and fight back.

Some physicians (and other mental health professionals) declare themselves not only ready and willing to help suicidal patients who seek assistance, but all persons who are, or are alleged to be, suicidal. Since they, too, seem to perceive suicide as a threat, not just to the suicidal person's physical survival but to their own value system, they strike back and strike back hard. This explains why psychiatrists and suicidologists resort, apparently with a perfectly clear conscience, to the vilest methods: they must believe that their lofty ends justify the basest means. Hence the prevalent use of force and fraud in suicide prevention. The consequence of this kind of interaction between physician and "patient" is a struggle for power. The patient is at least honest about what he wants: to gain control over his life *and* death—by being the agent of his own demise. But the (suicide-preventing) psychiatrist is completely dishonest about what he wants: he claims that he only wants to help his patient, while actually he wants to gain control over the patient's life in order to save himself from having to confront his doubts about the value of his own life. Suicide is medical heresy. Commitment and electroshock are the appropriate psychiatric-inquisitorial remedies for it.

III

In the West, opposition to suicide, like opposition to contraception and abortion, rests on religious grounds. According to both the Jewish and Christian religions, God created man, and man can use himself only in the ways permitted by God. Preventing conception, aborting a pregnancy, or killing oneself are, in this imagery, all sins: each is a violation of the laws laid down by God, or by theological authorities claiming to speak in His name.

But modern man is a revolutionary. Like all revolutionaries, he likes to take away from those who have and to give to those who have not, especially himself. He has thus taken Man from God and given him to the State (with which he often identifies more than he knows). This is why the State gives and takes away so many of our rights, and why we consider this arrangement so "natural."

But this arrangement leaves suicide in a peculiar moral and philosophical limbo. For if a man's life belongs to the State (as it formerly belonged to God), then surely suicide is the taking of a life that belongs not to the taker but to everyone else.

The dilemma of this simplistic transfer of body-ownership from God to State derives from the fundamental difference between a religious and secular world view, especially when the former entails a vivid conception of a life after death, whereas the latter does not (or even emphatically repudiates it). More particularly, the dilemma derives from the problem of how to punish successful suicide. Traditionally, the Roman Catholic Church punished it by depriving the suicide of burial in consecrated ground. As far as I know, this practice is now so rare in the United States as to be practically nonexistent. Suicides are given a Catholic burial, as they are routinely considered having taken their lives while insane.

The modern State, with psychiatry as its secular-religious ally, has no comparable sanction to offer. Could this be one of the reasons why it punishes so severely—so very much more severely than did the Church—the *unsuccessful* suicide? For I consider the psychiatric stigmatization of people as "suicidal risks" and their incarceration in psychiatric institutions a form of punishment, and a very severe one at that. Indeed, although I cannot support this claim with statistics, I believe that accepted psychiatric methods of suicide prevention often aggravate rather than ameliorate the suicidal person's problems. As one reads of the tragic encounters with psychiatry of people like James Forrestal, Marilyn Monroe, or Ernest Hemingway, one gains the impression that they felt demeaned and deeply hurt by the psychiatric indignities inflicted on them, and that, as a result of these experiences, they were even more desperately driven to suicide. In short, I am suggesting that coerced psychiatric interventions may increase, rather than diminish, the suicidal person's desire for self-destruction.

But there is another aspect of the moral and philosophical dimensions of suicide that must be mentioned here. I refer to the growing influence of the resurgent idea of self-determination, especially the conviction that men have certain inalienable rights. Some men have thus come to believe (or perhaps only to believe that they believe) that they have a right to life, liberty, and property. This makes for some interesting complications for the modern legal and psychiatric stand on suicide.

This individualistic position on suicide might be put thus: A man's life belongs to himself. Hence, he has a right to take his own life, that is, to commit suicide. To be sure, this view recognizes that a man may also have a moral responsibility to his family and others, and that, by killing himself, he reneges on these responsibilities. But these are moral wrongs that society, in its corporate capacity as the State, cannot properly punish. Hence the State must eschew attempts to regulate such behavior by means of formal sanctions, such as criminal or mental hygiene laws.

The analogy between life and other types of property lends further support to this line of argument. Having a right to property means that a person can dispose of it even if in so doing he injures himself and his family. A man may give away, or gamble away, his money. But significantly, he cannot—our linguistic conventions do not allow it—be said to *steal from himself.* The concept of theft requires at least two parties: one who steals and another from whom something is stolen. There is no such thing as "self-theft." The term "suicide" blurs this very distinction. The etymology of this term implies that suicide is a type of homicide, one in which criminal and victim are one and the same person. Indeed, when a person wants to condemn suicide he calls it "self-murder." Schulman, for example, writes: "Surely, self-murder falls within the province of the law."

History does repeat itself. Until recently, psychiatrists castigated as sick and persecuted those who engaged in self-abuse (that is, masturbation); now they castigate as sick and persecute those who engage in self-murder (that is, suicide).

The suicidologist has a literally schizophrenic view of the suicidal person: He sees him as two persons in one, each at war with the other. One half of the patient wants to die; the other half wants to live. The former, says the suicidologist, is wrong; the latter is right. And he proceeds to protect the latter by restraining the former. However, since these two people are, like Siamese twins, one, he can restrain the suicidal half only by restraining the whole person.

The absurdity of this medical-psychiatric position on suicide does not end here. It ends in extolling mental health and physical survival over every other value, particularly individual liberty.

In regarding the desire to live as a legitimate human aspiration, but not the desire to die, the suicidologist stands Patrick Henry's famous exclamation, "Give me liberty, or give me death!" on its head. In effect, he says: "*Give him* commitment, *give him* electroshock, *give him* lobotomy, *give him* life-long slavery, but *do not let him choose* death!" By so radically invalidating another person's (not his own!) wish to die, the suicide-preventer redefines the aspiration of the Other as not an aspiration at all: The wish to die thus becomes something an irrational, mentally diseased being displays, or something that happens to a lower form of life. The result is a far-reaching infantilization and dehumanization of the suicidal person.

For example, Phillip Solomon writes in the *Journal of the American Medical Association* (January 30, 1967), that "We [physicians] must protect the patient from his own [suicidal] wishes." While to Edwin Shneidman, "Suicide prevention is like fire prevention."[4] Solomon thus reduces the would-be suicide to the level of an unruly child, while Shneidman reduces him to the level of a tree! In short, the suicidologist uses his professional stance to illegitimize and punish the wish to die.

There is, of course, nothing new about any of this. Do-gooders have always opposed autonomy or self-determination. In "Amok," written in 1931, Stefan Zweig put these words into the mouth of his protagonist: "Ah, yes, 'It's one's duty to help.' That's your famous maxim, isn't it? . . . Thank you for your good intentions, but I'd rather be left to myself. . . . So I won't trouble you to call, if you don't mind.

Among the 'rights of man' there is a right which no one can take away, the right to croak when and where and how one pleases, without a 'helping hand.' "

But this is not the way the scientific psychiatrist and suicidologist sees the problem. He might agree (I suppose) that, in the abstract, man has the right Zweig claimed for him. But, in practice, suicide (so he says) is the result of insanity, madness, mental illness. Furthermore, it makes no sense to say that one has a right to be mentally ill, especially if the illness is one that, like typhoid fever, threatens the health of other people as well. In short, the suicidologist's job is to try to convince people that wanting to die is a disease.

This is how Ari Kiev, director of the Cornell Program in Social Psychiatry and its suicide-prevention clinic, does it: "We say [to the patient], look, you have a disease, just like the Hong Kong flu. Maybe you've got the Hong Kong depression. First, you've got to realize you are emotionally ill.... Most of the patients have never admitted to themselves that they are sick...." (*New York Times*, February 9, 1969).

This pseudomedical perspective is then used to justify psychiatric deception and coercion of the crudest sort.

Here is how, according to the *Wall Street Journal* (March 6, 1969), the Los Angeles Suicide Prevention Center operates. A man calls and says he is about to shoot himself. The worker asks for his address. The man refuses to give it.

> "If I pull it [the trigger] now I'll be dead," he [the caller] said in a muffled voice. "And that's what I want." Silently but urgently, Mrs. Whitbook [the worker] has signalled a coworker to begin tracing the call. And now she worked to keep the man talking.... An agonizing 40 minutes passed. Then she heard the voice of a policeman come on the phone to say the man was safe.

But surely, if this man was able to call the Suicide Prevention Center, he could have, had he wanted, called for a policeman himself. But he did not. He was thus deceived by the Center in the "service" he got.

I understand that this kind of deception is a standard practice in suicide prevention centers, though it is often denied that it is. A report *(Medical World News,* July 28, 1967) about the Nassau County Suicide Prevention Service corroborates the impression that when the would-be suicide does not cooperate with the suicide-prevention authorities, he is confined involuntarily. "When a caller is obviously suicidal," we are told, "a Meadowbrook ambulance is sent out immediately to pick him up."

One more example of the sort of thing that goes on in the name of suicide prevention should suffice. It is a routine story from a Syracuse newspaper (*Syracuse Post Standard,* September 29, 1969). The gist of it is all in one sentence: "A 28-year-old Minoa [a Syracuse suburb] man was arrested last night on a charge of violation of the Mental Hygiene Law, after police authorities said they spent two hours looking for him in the Minoa woods." But this man has harmed no one; his only "offense" was that someone claimed he might harm himself. Why, then, should the police look for, much less arrest, him? Why not wait until he returns? Or why not look, offer help, but avoid arrest and coerced psychiatry?

These are rhetorical questions. For our answers to them depend on and reflect our concepts of what it means to be a human being.

IV

I submit, then, that the crucial contradiction about suicide viewed as an illness whose treatment is a medical responsibility is that suicide is an action but is treated as if it were a happening. As I showed elsewhere, this contradiction lies at the heart of all so-called mental illnesses or psychiatric problems.[5] However, it poses a particularly acute dilemma for suicide, because suicide is the only fatal "mental illness."

Before concluding, I should like to restate briefly my views on the differences between diseases and desires, and show that by persisting in treating desires as diseases, we only end up treating man as a slave.

Let us take, as our paradigm case of illness, a skier who takes a bad spill and fractures an ankle. This fracture is something that has happened to him. He has not intended it to happen. (To be sure, he may have intended it; but that is another case.) Once it has happened, he will seek medical help and will cooperate with medical efforts to mend his broken bones. In short, the person and his fractured ankle are, as it were, two separate entities, the former acting on the latter.

Let us now consider the case of the suicidal person. Such a person may also look upon his own suicidal inclination as an undesired, almost alien, impulse and seek help to combat it. If so, the ensuing arrangement between him and his psychiatrist is readily assimilated to the standard medical model of treatment: the patient actively seeks and cooperates with professional efforts to remedy his "condition."

But as we have seen this is not the only way, nor perhaps the most important way, that the game of suicide prevention is played. It is accepted medical and psychiatric practice to treat persons for their suicidal desires against their will. And what exactly does this mean? Something quite different from that to which it is often analogized, namely the involuntary (or nonvoluntary) treatment of a bodily illness. For a fractured ankle can be set whether or not a patient consents to its being set. That is because setting a fracture is a *mechanical act on the body*. But a threatened suicide cannot be prevented whether or not the "patient" consents to its being prevented. That is because, suicide being the result of human desire and action, suicide prevention is a *political act on the person*. In other words, since suicide is an exercise and expression of human freedom, it can be prevented only by curtailing human freedom. This is why deprivation of liberty becomes, in institutional psychiatry, a form of treatment.

In the final analysis, the would-be suicide is like the would-be emigrant: both want to leave where they are and move elsewhere. The suicide wants to leave life and embrace death. The emigrant wants to leave his homeland and settle in another country.

Let us take this analogy seriously. It is much more faithful to the facts than is the analogy between suicide and illness. A crucial characteristic that distinguishes open from closed societies is that people are free to leave the former but not the latter. The medical profession's stance toward suicide is thus like the Communists' toward emigration: the doctors insist that the would-be suicide survive, just as the Russians insist that the would-be emigrant stay home.

Whether those who so curtail other people's liberties act with complete sincerity, or with utter cynicism, hardly matters. What matters is what happens: the abridgement of individual liberty, justified, in the case of suicide prevention, by psychiatric rhetoric; and, in the case of emigration prevention, by political rhetoric.

In language and logic we are the prisoners of our premises, just as in politics and law we are the prisoners of our rulers. Hence we had better pick them well. For if suicide is an illness because it terminates in death, and if the prevention of death by any means necessary is the physician's therapeutic mandate, then the proper remedy for suicide is indeed liberticide.

Notes

1. Bernard Shochet, "Recognizing the Suicidal Patient," *Modern Medicine* 38 (May 1970): 114–23.

2. Harvey M. Schein and Alan A. Stone, "Psychotherapy Designed to Detect and Treat Suicidal Potential," *American Journal of Psychiatry* 125 (March 1969): 1247–51 (emphasis added).

3. Thomas S. Szasz, *Law, Liberty and Psychiatry* (New York: Macmillan, 1963); and *Ideology and Insanity* (Garden City, N.Y.: Doubleday, 1970).

4. Edwin Shneidman, "Preventing Suicide," *Bulletin of Suicidology* (July 1968): 19–25 [see chapter 16 in this volume].

5. Thomas S. Szasz, *The Myth of Mental Illness* (New York: Harper and Row, 1961).

18

The Ethics of
Suicide Prevention
Victor Cosculluela

Authors from various disciplines have brought forth reasons for preventing all, or at least virtually all, suicide. We will consider these arguments in an attempt to determine whether or not, and in what circumstances, bystanders are morally obliged or permitted to prevent a suicide from realizing his intentions. We shall reach a moderate conclusion: Some suicide may legitimately be prevented, but not all. Arguments for the view that all suicide should be prevented are unacceptable.

I will assume that totally uncoercive suicide prevention measures need no justification. For example, merely presenting the would-be suicide with one's antisuicide position requires no justification. Suggesting a psychotherapist for the person who seeks relief from his suicidal impulses also requires no justification. For the remainder of this paper I will have in mind coercive measures (e.g., involuntary hospitalization, medication, etc.).

The literature on suicide contains several arguments which are thought to justify the coercive prevention of all, or at least almost all, suicide. These arguments can be grouped into three categories: psychological, epistemological, and ethical arguments. All attempt to establish an ethical conclusion, but the first two categories are distinguished by the fact that they appeal to special claims about the psychology of suicide or about the limits of human knowledge. I will first consider psychological arguments; epistemological and ethical arguments will then be discussed.

Psychological arguments: (1) By far the most important psychological argument with respect to suicide prevention is the claim that suicide prevention is justified since suicide is always or virtually always a manifestation of mental illness. We are told that the suicidal option is almost always chosen under "pathological circum-

Reprinted from the *International Journal of Applied Philosophy* 9 (1994): 35–41 with permission of the editor.

stances or under the influence of diseased feelings."[1] So-called rational suicide is a rarity since most persons who commit suicide suffer from "clinically recognizable psychiatric illnesses often carrying an excellent prognosis."[2] It is then inferred that the therapist must not only "make clear to the patient that he (the therapist) ... believes such behavior arises from the patient's illness"; he must "do everything he can to prevent it, enlisting the rest of the staff in this effort." In fact, suicidal intent "must not be part of therapeutic confidentiality in a hospital setting."[3]

However, there is a great deal of disagreement on the relation between suicide and mental illness. First, even some of those who accept the claim that perhaps most of those who attempt suicide are limited in their capacity to think and act rationally by some mental illness admit that it would be extremely difficult to justify the claim that all suicide attempts result from mental illnesses.[4] Further, psychiatrist Thomas Szasz claims that the view that suicide is a manifestation of mental illness is "both erroneous and evil": erroneous since "it treats an act as if it were a happening"; and evil because it "serves to legitimize psychiatric force and fraud by justifying it as medical care and treatment."[5] Finally, some psychiatrists take a moderate view, regarding many suicides as mentally ill, while allowing that many make realistic estimations of their options.[6] It is therefore not surprising that after examining the psychiatric material pertaining to suicide, Margaret Battin reaches the conclusion that there is "clearly no consensus on the frequency of mental illness in suicide or suicide attempts"; in fact, estimates of the percentage of clearly mentally ill among suicides have ranged from as low as 20 percent to as high as 100 percent.[7] However, one point on which there is general agreement is that relatively few suicides are psychotic.[8] (It would be ironic if most suicides were psychotic since, on some estimates, the suicide rate for psychiatrists is almost seven times that of the general population.[9])

Even if we accept the claim that the desire to commit suicide is a manifestation of mental illness, that *in itself* would not justify preventive measures. The desire to produce a comprehensive metaphysical system might be (and perhaps has been) a manifestation of mental illness, but that in itself would not justify others in preventing its realization. Even the desire to recover from one's mental illness might be a by-product of the illness, but surely no one would suggest that this justifies perpetuating the patient's illness. So even if one could show that all suicidal desires are products of mental illness (which is clearly not the case), that alone would not justify preventive measures.

Although these examples show that the fact that a desire arises from mental illness is not *in itself* sufficient to justify the coercive prevention of its realization, one might claim that the self-harming aspect of suicide, when combined with the presence of mental illness, justifies the coercive prevention of suicide. However, even this claim is false, for we do not always consider it appropriate to prevent those with mental illnesses from realizing their desires, even when those desires are related to their illnesses and their fulfillment would cause the agent harm. For example, even if we discovered that a person's religious practices (e.g., fasting) were due in part to some minor neurosis, we would not (other-regarding factors aside) consider it appropriate to prevent the person from engaging in these practices, even if such practices were harmful to the agent.[10] However, more will be said below about the appeal to mental illness.

(2) Another psychological thesis used to justify suicide prevention measures asserts that potential suicides wish to be saved; suicidal behavior is a "cry for help." Suicidologist Edwin Shneidman is the main proponent of this view: "Individuals who are intent on killing themselves still wish very much to be rescued or to have their deaths prevented." Consequently, suicide prevention consists in recognizing that the potential suicide is ambivalent between his wishes to live and his wishes to die, then "throwing one's efforts on the side of life."[11]

In support of this view, one might appeal to the fact that a high percentage of would-be suicides appreciate being saved. However, this would only provide a limited defense since some survivors express bitterness over their "rescue."[12]

Shneidman's view is that potential suicides have serious doubts about suicide even though they also have proattitudes toward suicide. However, this in itself does not justify suicide prevention. Whenever one makes a difficult choice, it is likely that doubts will remain, but this in itself does not show that others are justified in preventing us from carrying out our decisions.[13] More will be said about the appeal to ambivalence below, after we discuss a third psychological argument.

(3) A third psychological thesis, which is repeated quite frequently in the literature, claims that the wish to die by suicide is usually transient. From this some immediately infer that every physician or psychotherapist is obliged to frustrate the desire to commit suicide.[14]

Here again it would be a mistake to use an invalid argument of the form: Since most potential suicides have a certain characteristic, this in itself justifies treating all potential suicides as if they had that characteristic. Even if the desire for suicide is transient in most cases, that in itself will not justify the claim that all suicide should be prevented. One can easily imagine cases in which individuals think long and hard on the suicidal option before choosing it.[15]

Further, why should the simple fact that a desire is transient justify others in preventing its realization? The desire to do something very good for others might be fleeting, but that in itself does not show that others are justified in preventing its realization. Clearly, the lifespan of a desire does not *itself* determine whether or not one should prevent its realization, otherwise one would have to say that a transitory desire to do good for others must be frustrated.

The appeal to the claim that *most* suicide results from mental illness, the appeal to the alleged ambivalence of *most* suicides, and the appeal to the alleged transitoriness of *most* suicidal impulses all fail to justify the claim that *all* suicide should be prevented. Further, since the mere fact that a desire springs from mental illness, the mere fact that one is ambivalent about it, and the mere fact that it is fleeting are each insufficient to show that the desire's realization should be prevented, it turns out that appealing to mental illness, ambivalence, or to the fleeting nature of suicidal impulses will not in *itself* justify suicide prevention *in any case whatsoever*. Further, even if one made an appeal to all three claims (i.e., the mental illness claim, the ambivalence claim, and the transitoriness claim), it seems that that in itself would not justify any preventive measures. Why, then, have so many authors appealed to these alleged facts in an attempt to justify coercive suicide prevention measures?

With respect to the mental illness claim, one reason may be that mental illness is related to something which is relevant to suicide prevention: the potential suicide's set of factual (nonmoral) beliefs. Whether or not someone has correct factual beliefs is relevant to the issue of paternalistic interference. If, for example, laymen want to take certain drugs in the belief that they will be cured of their ailments, when in fact they would be seriously harmed, laws which attempt to prevent them from obtaining the drugs without prescriptions may be justified.[16] Mental illness enters the picture when we realize the impact it can have on one's factual beliefs; depending on the severity of the illness, one might come to hold ludicrous factual beliefs: e.g., "Unless I kill myself, I'll become a werewolf." In cases where mental illness creates factual ignorance which gives rise to suicidal intentions, suicide prevention may be justified. Even in such a case, it would be inaccurate to say that the presence of mental illness justifies preventive measures; the mental illness simply happens in this case to be responsible for the factual ignorance which is partially responsible for the desire to commit suicide.

Mental illness is also relevant when it prevents someone from acting on his deepest desires, even though it may not involve factual ignorance. One might, for example, be the victim of irrational fears or compulsions which push one toward self-destruction, even though one may also have a rationally formed desire to live. Preventive measures seem justified in cases in which a person cannot control his own self-destructive behavior.

As for the appeals to ambivalence and transitoriness, they seem relevant to factual beliefs about one's deepest desires. If one is ambivalent, one may say, "I don't know what I want," and transitory desires often create confusion about what one "really" desires. Paternalistic prevention measures may be justified by the potential suicide's ignorance about his own deepest desires. However, it would be incorrect to say that the ambivalence alone, or the transitoriness alone, justifies preventive measures; rather, factual ignorance which would otherwise be likely to cause self-harm justifies paternalistic preventive measures. Ambivalence and transitoriness are relevant as possible sources of ignorance.

One might claim that transitoriness is itself directly relevant to the issue of whether preventive measures would be justified in cases of potential suicide. After all, one may *really* want *now* to kill oneself. However, if this desire would only last for, say, a minute, it may seem that that in itself is relevant to the issue of suicide prevention. One might propose a highly unusual case in which a potential suicide wants to kill himself yet is fully aware that his desire to do so is fleeting. Nevertheless, it seems to me that the transitory nature of his desire to commit suicide does not itself justify preventive measures. The potential suicide knows that he genuinely wants to kill himself, he knows that his desire is fleeting, and yet he still wants to fulfill the desire. Why should the mere fact that the desire is transient matter in this case when it does not matter in other cases (e.g., cases in which one has transient desires to do tremendous good for society)?

It might be said that in cases of suicidal desire, the transient desire would be terminal if fulfilled. But if death is precisely what the person wants, and if he is aware of the fact that his desire to commit suicide is fleeting, I fail to see how the *mere* fact of transitoriness counts. Transitoriness is related to factual ignorance (e.g., it may mask one's deeper desires and it may create the illusion that the transitory desire is actually enduring), but it is only because of this relation that it is relevant to the suicide prevention issue.

Epistemological arguments: (1) It is sometimes argued that we cannot predict with certainty what anyone will experience during the rest of his natural life. Since the future is unknowable, suicide cannot be rational and should be prevented; after all, a cure for one's ailments may appear tomorrow or even in a few moments.[17]

At least one problem with this argument is that rational action does not require certainty about the future; we are forced to act on probabilities. To demand absolute certainty where it cannot be had is itself irrational. In fact, one could easily turn this argument on its head and argue that since one cannot be certain that the next moment will not bring unspeakable agony and degradation, it is irrational to continue living.

When we accept the fact that we are forced to act on probabilities, we see at once that suicide may be based on a rational estimate of probabilities. I may have a terminal illness which I know will cause me horrific pain. Although it is logically possible that tomorrow a cure will be introduced, this may be hopelessly unlikely, and I may know that this is unlikely by consulting specialists in the field. No one would say, "You shouldn't have your gangrenous foot amputated since a miraculous cure is conceivable." Likewise, no one should say, "You shouldn't commit suicide to avoid horrible agony since a miraculous cure is conceivable."

(2) However, a more sophisticated epistemological argument might be developed using the ideas of Philip Devine. Devine argues that a precondition of rational choice is that one know what one is choosing, either by personal experience or by the testimony of others who have experienced it or something like it. So, it is not possible to choose death rationally. Nor is any amount of knowledge about what one hopes to escape by death helpful since "*rational choice between two alternatives requires knowledge of both.*"[18] Assuming that death is the annihilation of the person (i.e., there is no afterlife), Devine claims that death is "logically opaque" since it is logically impossible for one to experience death or learn about it from the testimony of others who have experienced it or something like it. Devine denies that sleep could give one information about the nature of death since "sleep, even when dreamless, presupposes the continuation of the self in being and the possibility of awakening." Likewise, near-death experiences will not help since "what one would learn about in that way is not death but apparent dying."[19]

Unfortunately, Devine's argument for the conclusion that one cannot rationally choose death faces several seemingly devastating objections.[20] Consequently, no plausible case for suicide prevention can rely on it. He claims that rational choice between two alternatives requires knowledge of both, but since death is logically opaque, suicide cannot be a rational choice. However, Devine's argument would also establish that it is irrational to choose to continue living since the alternative, death, is unknowable. Thus, we reach the absurd conclusion that choosing to live and choosing to die are both irrational. Further, it is sometimes rational to choose an unknown alternative to a known evil; if a known evil is bad enough, it may be rational to take a chance on an unknown option. Finally, Devine's claim that death is unknowable is itself suspect; if, as he supposes, death is annihilation, it is hard to see what more must be known about it; as one critic put it: "To know that death is annihilation is to know all there is to know."[21]

Ethical arguments: (1) The ethical arguments for suicide prevention do not rely on special psychological or epistemological claims. One such argument claims that "every human life is of value,... so every human life is to be saved."[22]

Even if every human life is of value, it does not follow that every human life is of "absolute value," that its value overrides all other considerations. Even if we admit that life has value, this alone will not justify suicide prevention since we do not accept preventive measures in every case in which someone is considering whether or not to abandon something valuable. Others are not justified in preventing a person from abandoning certain experiences (e.g., instances of pleasure) simply because of the alleged intrinsic value of those experiences. The mere fact that something is valuable does not entail that one can legitimately be forced to accept it.

(2) So far we have focused only on the would-be suicide. One might, however, try to defend suicide prevention measures on the ground that suicide involves deep suffering for others (e.g., the suicide's family and friends). Naturally, one will have to balance this suffering against the negative features of preventive measures; we are not entitled to prevent people from acting in certain ways on the ground that others would be slightly annoyed otherwise. Further, this justification will not apply to those would-be suicides who do not have important relations to others.

None of the arguments considered, whether psychological, epistemological, or ethical, justifies preventive measures in all cases of potential suicide. The psychological arguments from mental illness, transitoriness, and ambivalence turned out to be only indirectly relevant; such features alone never justify preventive measures, but they are relevant to the would-be suicide's beliefs and self-control. In that sense, mental illness, ambivalence, and the transitoriness of many suicidal impulses are facts which are indirectly relevant to the issue of suicide prevention. The epistemological arguments proved unsound partly because of their assumptions about rationality. The argument which appeals to Devine's view of the "logical opaqueness" of death involves all the problems associated with that view. Further, the mere fact that life is valuable will not justify suicide prevention since we do not accept preventive measures with respect to other actions that involve the abandonment of intrinsic goods. Finally, the argument which tries to justify suicide prevention measures by appealing to other-regarding considerations will justify some instances of prevention, but not all.

Exposing the limitations of these arguments, however, is quite different from discovering the conditions under which suicide prevention is permissible or obligatory. We have already admitted that other-regarding considerations may justify suicide prevention measures. They may even make such measures obligatory. If the harm to others would otherwise be great, preventive measures may be obligatory. Further, if suicide would involve the agent in a serious shirking of duties to others besides the duty to refrain from causing them pain, preventive measures may be justified or even obligatory, depending on the weight of the duties in question and the weight of the agent's reasons for wanting to commit suicide. Before we are entitled to interfere in someone's liberty because of that person's duties to others, it seems that the duties in question must be quite weighty.

Let us ignore other-regarding considerations for the moment and ask: Are we ever justified in preventing suicide because of factors pertaining only to the would-be suicide? The affirmative answer seems correct, and we have already indicated one such factor: the would-be suicide's factual beliefs. When a person is about to engage in self-harming behavior, others are permitted (or perhaps even obliged) to stop him if the behavior is being undertaken on the basis of factual ignorance. For example, it is unthinkable that others should idly watch as a person drinks a poisonous liquid in the belief that it is nonpoisonous. It is unthinkable that informed persons should do nothing while another leaps carelessly from an airplane in the mistaken belief that he is equipped with a parachute. Likewise, since suicide involves not only self-harm but self-killing, suicide prevention measures may be justified if the suicide's intention to kill himself arises from factual ignorance. For example, if a person intends to kill himself in the mistaken belief that he has a terminal illness, a bystander who is aware of the individual's health is justified in preventing the suicide in order to correct the individual's beliefs.

It might be thought that if an action would serve someone's interests, then one should not stop that person from performing that action even if it would be performed on the basis of factual ignorance. However, such a view does not respect the agent's wish to make informed decisions. For example, plastic surgery might serve a person's interests, but if the patient believes, perhaps because of deception, that he is actually undergoing another operation, it would ordinarily be wrong not to prevent the plastic surgery. Likewise, if I know that walking on a slippery floor might maximize a person's overall self-interest (by allowing him to sue for thousands of dollars), even though a certain amount of harm is involved, I am not ordinarily justified in allowing the person to walk on the slippery portion of the floor.

Sometimes the factual ignorance which justifies suicide prevention concerns the would-be suicide's deepest desires. Even if the agent is informed about all relevant external factors, suicide prevention may be justified when the agent is ignorant about what he "really" wants. Here ambivalence and transitoriness play their part; they serve as warning signs to bystanders that the agent may be ignorant about his deepest desires or about the duration of his suicidal desires. However, what counts is the agent's ignorance concerning his own desires, not the agent's ambivalence or the transitoriness of his desires; ambivalence is a symptom of the ignorance in question, while transitory desires may distract one from one's deeper desires.

However, even when a person is suffering from factual ignorance, suicide prevention might still be unjustified. Some have argued that in cases where the individual is irretrievably psychotic, repeatedly applying suicide prevention measures may be illegitimate even though the patient suffers from delusions.[23] Suicide prevention measures for psychotic patients may involve extremely degrading procedures. For example, the patient may be completely deprived of privacy of any kind, even the minimal privacy achieved by the wearing of clothing. Even more degrading procedures may be necessary to prevent suicide in such cases. But it seems doubtful that we have the right to degrade the potential suicide to this level. In the case of the irretrievably psychotic patient who has repeatedly expressed his determination to kill himself, the measures necessary to prevent him from doing so involve an unacceptable degree of degradation. I suggest that it would be better to allow the patient to commit suicide, even on the basis of delusions, than to subject him to long-term profoundly degrading or profoundly painful suicide prevention measures. So even when the would-be suicide suffers from factual ignorance, preventive measures may not be justified. They will not be so when they involve long-term severe degradation or pain for the potential suicide. (This example also brings out the point that to say that suicide prevention is justified in a certain case does not entail that any measure one chooses is justified; the least degrading and painful method must be adopted.)

The account suggested by our remarks so far is that suicide prevention measures are justified only if (i) the individual's suicidal intentions rest on factual ignorance, or (ii) the agent is not in control of his own behavior, or (iii) suicide would involve the agent in a serious shirking of duties to others and his reasons for suicide do not justify such a violation of duty.

I think, however, that we should add a fourth member to this list: (iv) the individual's suicidal intentions rest on grossly irrational *ethical* beliefs which he would abandon if a bystander were to enlighten him. Suppose, for instance, that Jones believes that all those who have ever lied are obliged to kill themselves, and he is preparing to act accordingly. It seems that temporary preventive measures are in order. However, if the ethical beliefs in question are deeply held convictions which form part of the core of the potential suicide's value system, interference cannot be justified by the claim that the ethical belief are false; ignoring other-regarding considerations, it is illegitimate to force others to act contrary to their core value system.[24]

If any of these four conditions is present, and the measures do not involve long-term severe pain or degradation, suicide prevention will be justified (assuming the bystander does not have unrelated duties that override his right to prevent the suicide: e.g., the duty to prevent the accidental launching of nuclear weapons). Suicide prevention will be obligatory when these conditions are satisfied *and* the bystander is not under an at least equally weighty duty which would require him to refrain from preventing the suicide. In virtually every case in which preventive measures are permissible, they will also be obligatory.

However, we will have to add a very important qualification to this account. So far, we have assumed that bystanders are aware of the potential suicide's mental state (i.e., his beliefs and level of self-control) and his duties to others. In many cases, however, they will simply have no idea what the potential suicide's beliefs are, or whether he has strong duties to others, or whether he is in control of himself. For example, if I happen to see a stranger who is about to leap to his death from a bridge, I will ordinarily have no time to come to know his mental state and his duties to others. It seems to me that in cases in which we have no reliable evidence concerning the potential suicide's beliefs or his duties to others or his self-control, we should try to prevent the suicide (assuming we do not have overriding duties that are incompatible with doing so). The reason is that temporarily preventing an informed person who is in control of himself from committing suicide is morally better than doing nothing while, say, a confused person kills himself, especially since, in all likelihood, the would-be suicide could make another attempt if this one were prevented and since the suicidal option is irreversible if successful.

Before concluding, I will consider two objections to suicide prevention. First, Szasz has claimed that suicide prevention involves "a far-reaching infantilization and dehumanization of the suicidal person."[25] We have admitted that in some cases this is so. However, not all suicide prevention measures involve infantilization and dehumanization. If someone is about to kill himself on the basis of the false belief that he has a terminal illness, and I stop him in order to correct his beliefs, this does not involve dehumanization or infantilization. In fact, one might say that I am respecting his wishes, since, presumably, he would not want to die because of easily correctable errors.[26] Szasz has in mind psychiatrists who take any suicidal thoughts as sufficient grounds for extremely coercive and degrading measures. Clearly, he is right to object to this policy. But it would be a mistake to generalize from these instances to the conclusion that all suicide prevention involves dehumanization or infantilization.

A second objection, formulated by Robert Martin, asserts that preventive measures of any sort are justified only when they spare the agent future regret. But *suicide* prevention does not spare the agent future regret since, if the suicide were successful, the agent would simply cease to exist; successful suicide attempts cannot result in future regrets. Therefore, suicide prevention is illegitimate. No matter how foolish the decision to commit suicide, preventive measures are not justified since the agent would not thereby be spared future regret. A man who kills himself unaware that treatment was available which could have cured him "won't be worse off than had we intervened, because after his death he won't be *any* way; and because before death he desired death and got it."[27]

This line of reasoning would also force one to accept the conclusion that preventing someone from unknowingly taking a drug that would induce a permanent coma would be illegitimate since one would not spare the person future regret. Further, if a mentally disturbed person decided to attempt flight from the tenth floor, it would be illegitimate to prevent him from doing so; he wanted to fly and will not feel any regrets (being insane, he will not realize the implications of his decision in mid-flight). Clearly, these consequences are unacceptable, but no more unacceptable than Martin's conclusion.

Martin assumes that the potential suicide's present desire is simply for death. It has been pointed out that this is simplistic; the suicide's desire is to commit suicide on the basis of knowledge. So by allowing someone to commit suicide on the basis of erroneous factual beliefs, one ignores the person's desire for informed suicide.[28] (However, as mentioned earlier, it may sometimes be legitimate to let hopelessly psychotic individuals commit suicide even on the basis of their delusions.)

We can summarize the account of suicide prevention developed above as follows:

(I) Where the potential suicide's state of mind (i.e., his beliefs and level of self-control) and his duties to others are known, suicide prevention measures are permissible if and only if the following conditions obtain:

    (1) At least one of the following is the case: (i) the suicidal intention rests on factual ignorance, (ii) the potential suicide is not in control of his actions, (iii) suicide would involve the agent in a serious shirking of duties to others which his reasons for suicide do not justify, or (iv) the suicidal intention rests on grossly irrational ethical beliefs which the potential suicide would abandon if he were enlightened by a bystander.
    (2) The preventive measures do not involve long-term profound degradation or profound pain for the potential suicide.

(II) Where the potential suicide's state of mind and his duties to others are known, suicide prevention will be obligatory if and only if

    (1) it is permissible (since it satisfies the conditions for the permissibility of suicide prevention just rehearsed) and
    (2) the bystander contemplating preventive measures is not under an at least equally weighty duty which would require him to refrain from preventing the suicide.

(III) Where the potential suicide's state of mind or his duties to others are unknown, temporary preventive measures are called for since, for example, it is better to temporarily prevent an informed person who is in control of himself from committing suicide than to do nothing while a confused or compulsive person kills himself.[29]

Notes

    1. Erwin Ringel, "Suicide Prevention and the Value of Human Life," in *Suicide: The Philosophical Issues,* ed. M. P. Battin and D. J. Mayo (London: Peter Owen, 1980), 206.
    2. George Murphy, "Suicide and the Right to Die," *American Journal of Psychiatry* 130 (April 1973): 472.
    3. Benjamin B. Wolman, ed., *International Encyclopedia of Psychiatry, Psychology, Psychoanalysis, and Neurology* (New York: Aesculapius Publishers, Inc., 1977), s.v. "Suicidal Patients: Hospital Treatment," by Alan A. Stone, 14–15.
    4. John Moskop and H. Tristram Engelhardt, "The Ethics of Suicide: A Secular View," in *Suicide: Theory and Clinical Aspects,* ed. L. D. Hankoff and Bernice Einsidler (Littleton: PSG Publishing Co., 1979), 56.
    5. Thomas S. Szasz, "The Ethics of Suicide," in *Suicide: The Philosophical Issues,* ed. M. P. Battin and D. J. Mayo, 186 [see chapter 17 in this volume].
    6. Jerome A. Motto, "The Right to Suicide: A Psychiatrist's View," in *Suicide: The Philosophical Issues,* ed. M. P. Battin and D. J. Mayo, 212-19.
    7. Margaret P. Battin, *Ethical Issues in Suicide* (Englewood Cliffs: Prentice-Hall, 1982), 5.

8. Ibid., 4.

9. Jacques Choron, *Suicide* (New York: Charles Scribner's Sons, 1972), 37.

10. A plausible explanation for our unwillingness to interfere in this kind of case is that paternalistic interference in such cases compromises the person's individuality in that it prevents her from acting on her basic intrinsic values, some of which are of a religious nature. See Elliot D. Cohen, "Paternalism That Does Not Restrict Individuality: Criteria and Applications," *Social Theory and Practice* 12 (1986): 309–35.

11. Edwin S. Shneidman, "Preventing Suicide," in *Suicide: Right or Wrong?* ed. John Donnelly (Amherst, N.Y.: Prometheus Books, 1990), 154 [see chapter 16 in this volume].

12. Choron, *Suicide,* 50; Battin, *Ethical Issues in Suicide,* 156.

13. Robert M. Martin, "Suicide and False Desires," in *Suicide: The Philosophical Issues,* ed. M. P. Battin and D. J. Mayo, 146.

14. Murphy, "Suicide," 472-73.

15. One might appeal to a rule-utilitarian argument here: Preventing all suicide has a higher utility than preventing none. However, even if we ignore well-known objections to rule-utilitarianism, this argument relies on a false dichotomy; obviously, we are not forced to pick between a policy of preventing all suicide and a policy of preventing none.

16. The example comes from Alan H. Goldman, *Moral Knowledge* (London and New York: Routledge, 1988), 145.

17. Ringel, "Suicide Prevention," 206.

18. Philip E. Devine, "On Choosing Death," in *Suicide: The Philosophical Issues,* ed. M. P. Battin and D. J. Mayo, 139, emphasis added.

19. Ibid., 140–41.

20. David J. Mayo, "The Concept of Rational Suicide," *The Journal of Medicine and Philosophy* 11 (1986): 151.

21. Ibid.

22. Ringel, "Suicide Prevention," 208.

23. Eliot Slater, "Choosing the Time to Die," in *Suicide: The Philosophical Issues,* ed. M. P. Battin and D. J. Mayo, 202.

24. The claim that the paternalistic restriction of a person's self-regarding conduct is justified only when it does not compromise the individuality of the person by preventing her from acting on her basic intrinsic values is defended in Cohen, "Paternalism."

25. Thomas Szasz, "The Ethics of Suicide," 194.

26. The idea that paternalistic interference may be a way of respecting a person's true wishes is suggested in Ruth Mackin, "Refusal of Psychiatric Treatment: Autonomy, Competence, and Paternalism," in *Psychiatry and Ethics,* ed. R. B. Edwards (Amherst, N.Y.: Prometheus Books, 1982), 339–40.

27. Robert M. Martin, "Suicide and False Desires," 149. Martin qualifies his claim by admitting that other-regarding considerations might justify suicide prevention measures.

28. Arthur M. Wheeler, "Suicide Intervention and False Desires," *The Journal of Value Inquiry* 20 (1986): 241–44.

29. I thank Alan Goldman, Howard Pospesel, and Elliot Cohen for some extremely valuable critical remarks.

19

Theistic and Nontheistic Arguments
Milton A. Gonsalves

S uicide is here taken in the strict sense as *the direct killing of oneself on one's own authority.*

Direct killing is an act of killing that is directly voluntary; that is, death is intended either as an end or as a means to an end. Either the action is capable of only one effect and that effect is death, or the action is capable of several effects, including death, and among these death is the effect intended, either for its own sake or as a means to something else.

Indirect killing is an act of killing that is indirectly voluntary; death is not intended, either as an end or as a means to an end, but is only permitted as an unavoidable consequence. The action is capable of at least two effects, one of which is death, and the agent intends, not death, but the other effect. To avoid misunderstanding it is better not to speak of the indirect killing of oneself as killing at all, but as the deliberate exposure of one's life to serious danger. Such exposure is not what is meant by suicide.

The killing is not suicide unless it is done *on one's own authority.* Two others might be thought of as having authority in the matter: God and the state. God, having a supreme dominion over human life, could order a woman to kill herself, but to know God's will in such a case, a special revelation would be needed, for which there is no provision in philosophical ethics. The state, supposing that it has the right of capital punishment, might appoint a man condemned to death to be his own executioner. Whatever be the morality of such an uncommon and questionable practice, it is not suicide according to the accepted definition.

From Milton A. Gonsalves, "Suicide," in *Fagothey's Right and Reason: Ethics in Theory and Practice* (Columbus: Merrill Publishing Co., 1989), pp. 246–48. © 1989. Reprinted by permission of Prentice-Hall, Inc., Upper Saddle River, N.J.

Suicide can be committed positively, by the performance of some death-dealing act against oneself; or negatively, by omitting to use the ordinary means of preserving one's life. It is suicide to starve oneself to death, to refuse to avoid an oncoming train, to neglect to use the ordinary remedies against an otherwise fatal disease.

Among the arguments proposed in favor of the moral permissibility of suicide are the following:

1. It is understood that no one should commit suicide for whom life holds out some hope or promise, and that people suffering from temporary despondency should be prevented from harming themselves, but there are always some for whom life has become an intolerable and irremediable burden. They are useless to society and to themselves. It is better for all concerned that they retire from the scene of life through the ever open door.

2. It is an act of supreme personal self-determination to summon death when life's value has been spent. A person is expected to manage his or her life intelligently and not to be merely passive in the face of inexorable nature. When reason shows that life has no more to offer, it is folly to drag out life to its last bitter breath. The person preserves dignity and self-mastery by ending his or her life at the moment when all its worth and meaning are exhausted.

3. A person is allowed to choose a lesser evil to avoid a greater. Since there are worse evils than death, why cannot death be chosen as the lesser evil? There is nothing unnatural about it. If it is not wrong to interfere with nature to prolong life, as medical science does, why should it be wrong to interfere with nature to shorten life? In both cases it is done for the benefit of the person concerned and by his or her own consent.

4. Even admitting that God has given us our life, yet it is truly a gift. A gift belongs to the receiver, who may now do whatever he or she wills with it. No gift is expected to be retained indefinitely at the expense and to the harm of the receiver. When its possession becomes more injurious than its surrender, it should be in accordance with the will of a good God and a wise use of his gift to relinquish it.

5. To suppose that suicide in any way defrauds God of his supreme right is to have a very naive idea of God. No creature could possibly defraud God of anything. In giving us the gift of life, God knew how we would use it and expected us to use our intelligence and freedom in managing it. He allows us to destroy animals and plants, other life, for our purposes. Why should our own life be withdrawn from our control?

6. In the case of self-defense we have the right to destroy other human lives for our own safety. The state claims the same right in war and capital punishment. It seems, then, that God can and sometimes does give us direct ownership over human life. Why must it be only over others' lives? The reasons for suicide are often stronger than for self-defense, either personal or national. Why not kill ourselves when we have become our own greatest enemy?

These rather persuasive arguments are countered by opposing arguments:

1. Suicide is often regarded as an act of cowardice and a refusal to face life

courageously. We take the easy way out when we thrust the burdens we cannot bear onto the shoulders of our dependents. But not all are in this case; rather, they themselves are a burden on others. Yet they must not forget the worth of their own person. Who can be called useless? Suffering has no earthly value and might be called the worst of earthly disvalues, but its moral and spiritual value can be tremendous. Courage and patience cannot be discounted in any moral appraisal of human life.

2. It is a natural prompting of well-ordered self-love to keep one's person in being against all destructive forces. There are times when one must face death without flinching, but there is something inordinate in willfully acting as that destructive force oneself. Everything naturally seeks its own being and tends to keep itself in being as long as possible. Intelligence is meant to promote, not counteract, that natural urge.

3. The lesser of two physical evils may be chosen when there is no moral evil involved, but moral evil may never be chosen to avoid a physical evil. Medical science is an intelligent use and development of the remedies nature provides to preserve life. To use them to destroy life is not wise management but a wrecking of what has been entrusted to our care. I would be free to wreck myself if I were responsible only to myself, but this is not so if there is a God to whom I am ultimately responsible.

4. Life is a gift from God, but some gifts are given outright and others have strings attached. All God's gifts are restricted, not because of any lack in his generosity, but because he has to make us responsible for their use when he entrusts them to our freedom. Freedom itself is perhaps his greatest gift, but we are not allowed, though we are able, to misuse it. Life has been given, and its allotted span goes with the gift. It is not ours to decide when we have had enough of it and to tell God that we are quitting.

5. We can never actually defraud God, but we are not allowed even to *try* or to be willing to do what would defraud God were he not infinitely beyond all possible harm. God allows us to destroy animals and plants because they are not persons and are provided for our use and consumption. Human life is not on the same level as other life; personhood makes the difference.

6. In self-defense the defender kills the attacker not on his or her own authority but on God's authority implicit in the defender's own natural right to life. The defender has no ownership over the attacker's life but only repels force by force, a situation the attacker brought on by the crime. The state also acts on authority given to it by God as a natural society, authority not to be used in any way the state pleases but only in defense against the nation's internal and external destroyers. The suicide is both attacker and attacked, and there is no defense. Crime and punishment are here simultaneous and extreme. The suicide is simultaneously executioner and murderer.

It can be readily seen that from a nontheistic viewpoint there is no argument against suicide. A person who acknowledges no being higher than himself or herself assumes supreme dominion over his or her life and can do away with it at pleasure. The fact that a theistic philosophy sees life as a gift from God does not of itself make suicide wrong, for an outright gift may be used or abandoned in any way the recipient wishes. The case against suicide, then, requires proof that God's gift of life to us is not an outright but a restricted gift, that he has not given us full ownership and control over our person with the right to consume and destroy it at our discretion, but he has given us only the use of ourselves, the right of stewardship and management, for which he will demand an account. Since philosophy cannot ask God what he willed to do, its only recourse is to show that God not only did not but *could not* give us full ownership over ourselves as persons.

The reason that God must reserve to himself full mastership over human life is the peculiar nature of a rational and free being, such as the human being is. We can attain the end for which we have been created only by freely choosing to do morally good acts. These acts take time, and the length of each person's life is the opportunity allotted for doing them. It is for God and not for us to say when we have done enough well enough to deserve the end. The suicide equivalently tells God that He will have to take the deeds performed and virtues developed so far, and that He will simply get no more. The creature thus tries to dictate what God will have to be satisfied with, in contradiction to what God in creating has a right to demand from His creature. God cannot give such authority to a creature without making the creature supreme over Him. The suicide, by making further works of his or her own impossible, invades God's exclusive right, is a rebel against the creator, and commits moral wrong.

20

Voluntary Death, Property Rights, and the Gift of Life
David M. Holley

Are there any moral reasons why a person who finds life unsatisfactory should not choose death? One approach to answering this question would be to consider the communal obligations people have. Sometimes we have obligations which could not be fulfilled if we were to choose death. However, it is not difficult to imagine cases in which obligations to the community are minimal or are unlikely to be capable of fulfillment or possibly even more likely to be fulfilled by death. Furthermore, the choice of death may on occasion be beneficial either to the individual or the community (see for example Hume, 1963:593–95). So unless it could be shown that obligations to the community were particularly strong, they might on occasion be outweighed by other moral considerations.

An alternative approach to answering this question which goes back at least as far as Plato is to consider whether the choice of death is inappropriate because it is a violation of duties an individual has toward God. Typically such a view is built upon some metaphorical account of the relationship between God and our lives. In this paper I will discuss two such accounts and the arguments connected with them about the impermissibility of choosing death. Part one will be devoted to what might be called the property metaphor: the idea that our lives belong to God and hence that we are usurping God's prerogative when we choose to destroy them. In part two I will consider the use of a gift metaphor, in particular the claim that our lives are gifts of God and that to take them without God's permission indicates extreme ingratitude. I will try to show that arguments based on either metaphor are insufficient without an adequate account of God's intentions. In part three I develop several accounts of God's purposes in terms of some additional metaphors and

Reprinted by permission of the Journal of Religious Ethics, Inc., from the *Journal of Religious Ethics* 17, no. 1 (Spring 1989): 103–21. Copyright © 1989 by the Journal of Religious Ethics, Inc.; all rights reserved.

relate these to the basic argument. Part four considers what types of exceptions an approach based on duties to God might allow. Part five is a more general reflection on the significance of metaphorical thinking for moral decision-making.[1]

I

The idea that life belongs to God is deeply rooted in the Judeo-Christian tradition. In the Psalms we read, "The earth is the Lord's and everything in it" (Ps. 24: 1 NIV). Many biblical images also suggest thinking about our lives as God's property: potter and clay (Jer. 18:1–8; Rome. 9:20–22), shepherd and sheep (Ps. 23), master and slave (Matt. 18:23–35), and so on.

The basis for the claim that we are God's property is the doctrine of creation. According to this doctrine the whole world owes its existence to the creative work of God. There are various philosophical views of the nature and basis of property rights, but it is hard to imagine a stronger claim than might be made by one who creates and sustains the whole universe.

A classical philosophical account of the moral basis of property rights is to be found in Locke's writings, and it is interesting that Locke not only acknowledges that God has property rights; he appeals to those rights in arguing that the individual may not morally choose death:

> ...Men being all the Workmanship of one Omnipotent, and infinitely wise Maker; All the Servants of one Sovereign Master, sent into the World by his order and about his business, they are his Property, whose Workmanship they are, made to last during his, not one anothers Pleasure.... Every one ... is bound to preserve himself; and not to quit his Station willfully.... (Locke, 1970:289)

If we accept the idea that our lives are God's property, then to choose death would be to destroy what belongs to God. To be sure, it is not always wrong to destroy the property of another. There can be compelling moral reasons for doing so; saving a life, for example. But one is not justified in destroying the property of another without a compelling moral reason. So it would seem to follow that we have a duty to God to go on living unless we have a moral reason sufficient to override this duty.

The fact that we have found life somewhat unpleasant would probably not be a sufficiently compelling reason: If I find that my neighbor has painted his house a disgusting shade of pink, that gives me no right to destroy the house. Of course, the house may be something that I can get away from, and my own life is not something I can avoid. But suppose I am limited in such a way that I can't easily avoid seeing the house: I have a disease that has made me bedfast. My room has only one window, and whenever I look out all I can see is a solid wall of pink. I may implore the owner to change things and thereby make my life more pleasant. But the unpleasantness in my experience does not in and of itself justify destruction or defacement of the property.

On the other hand, what if it was more than just a little unpleasantness? What if my life involves significant suffering? I suspect that we can imagine cases in which the destruction of property might be justified if it was the only way to avoid significant suffering. However, several factors come into play here. For example, how valuable is the property? We are ordinarily inclined to think that the more valuable the property, the greater the justification required for its destruction. I need a much stronger excuse for destroying your treasured Stradivarius than I would if I broke your pencil. To some extent, the value involved may be relative to the owner. So if God is the owner of my life, then my justification for destroying my life might need to be quite strong if the value God places on my life is very great.

But surely, we may think, whatever value God might place on my continued existence cannot outweigh my own interest in alleviating my suffering. That depends. It depends on whether in fact your suffering is in your own best interest. If, somehow, continuing to live in spite of your suffering would be of benefit to you, then it is not a matter of asserting your interest against God's rights, but rather asserting your false conception of your interest against God's rights. You may insist that your personal autonomy to make whatever decision you choose should be respected even if you wrongly assess what is in your interest. But that is not the issue. God is not going to force you to live if you choose not to. The only question is whether the choice to end your life is a morally correct one, and if in fact the justification for ending your life is based upon an incorrect evaluation of your interest, then that cannot override God's interest in your continued existence. You may, of course, ask how someone with some false belief about a situation ought to act, but that is not the same as asking what action is objectively right.

All of this hinges on the question of what a person's interests are, and I suspect that differences in judgment about that are very closely related to differing judgments about the moral justifiability of suicide. It is perhaps important to notice that the question of whether suffering is in an individual's interest is very closely related to the question of whether God has a morally sufficient reason for allowing suffering. A believer who thought that God did in fact have a morally sufficient reason might at least have cause to wonder whether his or her own suffering was not personally beneficial.

One assumption of this whole discussion is that God does not want his property destroyed. Ordinarily we make that assumption of a property owner, but there are clearly times when it doesn't apply. If a property owner knows that his or her property is causing a significant amount of misery or suffering, then it is at least possible that the owner would want to eliminate the suffering. A compassionate owner might be willing to accept the destruction of his or her property in order to achieve this goal. If we assume that God is perfectly benevolent, then perhaps he would not want a life to continue at the cost of significant suffering. In that case one who destroyed his or her own life would not be infringing upon God's rights, but merely carrying out his wishes.

It may be objected that God has not given us the authority to make such decisions. But clearly we have been given a great deal of discretion about the use of much of God's property. So maybe we should accept the responsibility here also. If a person's life gets bad enough and has no prospect of getting better, then perhaps that person should use the God-given power of choice to decide to end that life. If God wants the person's good, perhaps that is just what he would want.

Again, the issue seems to revolve around the problem of judging what our interest is. Thinking of our lives as God's property will not in and of itself give us much guidance about that. We would need to know something more about what God intends for his property. I shall return to that question later. For now it is enough to notice that the property argument does not appear sufficient to establish as strong a prohibition as most theists would like.

Even if it did, however, there is another problem with this kind of argument. It seems to presuppose the moral justifiability of a person's being property. When Plato uses this argument, it is explicitly based on the analogy of slavery:

> If one of your slaves should kill himself when you had not indicated you wanted him to die, would you not be angry with him and punish him if you had someone to punish? Then perhaps on the basis of this it would not be unreasonable that one must not kill himself but must wait until god sends some necessity.... (Bluck, 1955:62c)

Baruch Brody (1974:601) has suggested that it is possible for a theist to hold to the moral permissibility of God's owning people as follows: The wrong in slavery lies not in the fact that a human being is owned. It is in the fact that one human being is owned by another human being. While we have no right to possess each other, there is nothing morally objectionable about all of us being God's possessions.

There may be something to this. God's "ownership" of a human life is clearly very different from the human institution of slavery. But once we begin to take into account the differences, there is cause to wonder whether speaking of the relation in terms of property is appropriate at all. Even if God does not treat us merely as objects, the logic of property-owning seems to suggest the appropriateness of treating the thing owned in such a way. So perhaps it would be better to avoid the metaphor rather than qualifying it to the point where it loses significant meaning.[2]

What does a believer intend to assert by the claim that life belongs to God? I would suggest that the claim is primarily an assertion of God's authority. To say that life belongs to God is to say that there is something which is rightly in God's control and beyond human authority. To be a property owner is one way of possessing authority, but there are others as well, and it is significant that a great many "authority metaphors" have been traditionally applied to God. The relationships of father-child, king-people, and commander-army are illustrative of some of the ways in which God's authority is conceived. Interestingly, in the passage from Locke quoted earlier the image appealed to is one of a servant who has been given a particular task: obeying the orders of the one who has assigned the task. A closely related image, found in both Christian and non-Christian sources, is that of a sentinel who has been assigned to guard a post and must wait to be relieved of duty by the commander. Cicero (1897:250) quotes Pythagoras as forbidding us to "abandon the station or post of life without the orders of our commander, that is of God."

In section three I will consider the significance of assertions of God's authority in relation to the question at hand. For the moment, however, let us turn to a different metaphor, the idea that life is a gift of God.

II

A number of theologians have made the claim that life is a gift. However, in some the ideas of gift and property seem to have been mixed together. For example, Aquinas says that suicide is unacceptable because

> life is a gift made to man by God, and it is subject to him who is *master of death and life*. Therefore a person who takes his own life sins against God, just as he who kills another's slave injures the slave's master, or just as he who usurps judgment in a matter outside his authority also commits a sin. (Aquinas, 1975:2a2ae, Q64, Art. 5)

The basis of the argument is not so much that life is a gift as it is the claim that God has authority over matters like making and destroying life. The analogy used to illustrate this authority is similar to Plato's, being based on the authority of a master over slaves. Someone who kills a slave destroys the master's property, and when we take our own life, we are destroying one of God's slaves.

A more direct use of the gift metaphor may be found in an argument by Paul Ramsey:

> The immorality of choosing death as an end is founded upon our religious faith that life is a *gift*. A gift is not given if it is not received as a gift. no more than a gift can be given out of anything other than kindness or generosity (to give out of flattery or duplicity or to curry favor is not a gift). To choose death as an end is to throw the gift back in the face of the giver; it would be to defeat his gift-giving. (Ramsey, 1978:146)

In this passage it is the "logic of gift-giving" which furnishes the basis of the argument. The choice of death is seen as a rejection of God's gift, and, hence, a contemptible expression of ingratitude.

The belief that life is a gift, like the belief that life belongs to God, is rooted in the doctrine of creation. In the tradition God freely chooses to bring the world into being, and human life is the crown of God's creation. God is the source of any individual's life, and we are all the recipients of God's creative work.

Like all metaphors, the idea of life as a gift tends to direct our attention toward certain features of our experience. For example, we notice the "unearned, undeserved character of many benefits we all enjoy, including existence itself"

(Camenisch, 1981:26). To speak of life as a gift reminds us that our lives are not owed to us as an employer might owe wages. Rather, life is something we enjoy due to the beneficence of the Creator. Implicit in this, of course, is the affirmation that life is good. Although it is possible to speak of worthless gifts, the theistic context of a wise and benevolent giver assures us of the value of what we have received.

Furthermore, this gift language leads us to think of certain responses as being appropriate and others inappropriate. To receive a valuable gift ordinarily calls for a response of gratitude, and our response is revealed not only in what we say about the gift, but the way we treat it. Paul Camenisch (1981:9) asks rhetorically, "Would not most persons agree that I had committed a morally censurable violation if, having told my old philosophy professor that I was grateful for the gift of a rare edition of Kant's works, I then gave them to a paper recycling drive?" The contemptibleness in such an act is not merely the waste of a valuable commodity. It is also my utter disregard and disrespect for one who deserves my gratitude.

It may be said that if something is really a gift, then it becomes my property to do with as I please. Otherwise it is merely a loan. However, to speak in this way is to separate the phenomenon of gift-giving from its relational context. In at least some cases my treatment of a gift is by extension an act toward the giver. If my father gives me a valued family heirloom, say a watch, and I give it to my four-year-old child to play with, my father would be justified in feeling hurt. I have shown by my act that I do not value what he places great value on, and in knowing that the watch was valuable to him, I demonstrate my disregard for his feelings and our relationship.

The need to show special concern in our treatment of gifts is most clearly apparent in cases where the gift is most closely associated with the one who gives it. Included in this class are those gifts which we make ourselves. Emerson writes in his essay on "Gifts,"

> The only gift is a portion of thyself. Thou must bleed for me. Therefore the poet brings his poem; the shepherd, his lamb; the farmer, corn; the miner, a gem; the sailor, coral and shells; the painter, his picture; the girl, a handkerchief of her own sewing. This is right and pleasing, for it restores society in so far to its primary basis, when a man's biography is conveyed in his gifts....(Emerson, 1906:291)

The more clearly connected a gift is with the giver, the more it functions as a token or sign of the giver. Hence, abusing the gift comes closer to an act of disrespect toward the one who gives it.

In the case of the gift of life, human creation is conceived of as very closely related to and expressive of God's nature. All of creation is like a work of art which God produces, and human beings are so much an expression of the divine nature that mankind is said to be made in the image of God. Hence, the value that we place upon our lives by the way we treat them is very closely tied to our attitude toward the giver of life. It is in this kind of context that Ramsey can say that choosing death is like throwing God's gift back in his face.

There is something a little strange in speaking about a duty to be grateful, partly because talk of duties and obligations seems at odds with our idea that gratitude should be somehow spontaneous. However, in our experience of gift-giving there is something very close to obligation. When we have been given something valuable and beneficial, we often want to show our gratitude by giving something in return. If carried too far, this impulse can turn an occasion of gift-giving into something like a business relationship. (He has given me such and such, so I owe him something of comparable value.) However, even in genuine gift-giving, there is often a feeling of indebtedness. This is particularly true in cases where we are given something which we need or value and could not have acquired on our own.

In such cases there may be nothing we can do in return except use the gift in such a way as to demonstrate our gratitude and please the giver. If my grandmother provides the means for me to get a college education, I am indebted to her. I owe her more than I could repay. My "debt" would not be repaid, however, by graduating from college and earning enough money to give her back what she has spent. That may or may not be possible or appropriate. More to the point, I am under obligation to use the opportunity she has provided me to the best of my ability, to study hard, not to squander my time, and so forth.

I owe a debt to my family, but again this is not the kind of debt which can be discharged by any kind of direct payment. As Kenneth Schmitz points out, "Even when my father was alive, I could not return a father's love to him, except by receiving it as a son and by loving my own children with a love not unlike his" (Schmitz, 1982:54).

In our lives we receive benefits of many types, some of which we are aware of, and some of which are unknown. The donors are both those who stand in close relationship to us and nameless givers who know nothing of us. We are recipients of a cultural tradition which allows us to live the kind of lives we live. The proper way to "repay" our benefactors is to enjoy and help to enrich the tradition which we will pass on.

Returning to the gift of life, we have an example of a benefit which we could not possibly repay. Our gratitude can only be expressed by living our lives in a way that would please the giver of this gift. Swinburne writes that one source of an obligation to obey God arises out of the fact that

> he is our creator and sustainer. We depend for our existence at each instant on his will. Now many would hold that men have an obligation to please their benefactors. A man who makes no effort to please those who have done much for him is generally felt to be behaving in an immoral way. (Swinburne, 1974:214)

When we begin to speak about using the gifts we have received in a way which would please our benefactors, we are very close to another metaphor which has been intertwined in theological writings with the gift metaphor: that of stewardship. James Gustafson makes the connection as follows:

... [P]eople owe allegiance to the one who provides them with life and its possibilities. To be the recipient of life is to have a sense of indebtedness to the giver
of life. It is to be oriented toward nature and other persons in an attitude of cus-
todianship, of deputyship, for all that is and is to be is given and not earned, available and not possessed. The human community is the caretaker and the cultivator
of what has been given out of God's goodness. (Gustafson, 1975:97)

The vision of a lifestyle devoted to responsible use of the benefits we have received seems to arise quite naturally out of conceiving life as a gift. One who takes
seriously the claim that life is a gift comes to think of what has been given as
something to be gratefully received and used in accordance with the intentions of
the giver. The gift, like my grandmother's gift of a college education, becomes
both a benefit and a trust. I am entrusted with the responsible use of what I have
been given.

Earlier I quoted Paul Ramsey's rejection of suicide based on the claim that
life is a gift. Immediately after the passage quoted, Ramsey goes on to assert that

life is a *trust*. And not to accept our life as a trust, to abandon our trusteeship, evi-
dences a denial that God is trustworthy, or at least some doubt that he knew what
he was doing when he called us by our own proper names and trusted us with life.
We are stewards and not owners of our lives. (Ramsey, 1978:147)

The property metaphor discussed earlier also leads to the view that we are not
owners of our lives. In that way of thinking the reason is simply that we are owned
by another. Here the issue is not so much who owns us as it is what our responsibilities are in the light of the fact that we have received something of great value.
Our indebtedness to our benefactor makes it morally unacceptable to treat our
lives in any way we choose. We are obligated to use what we have in the way it was
intended by its wise and benevolent giver. This makes us trustees or stewards,
responsive to the wishes of the one who has entrusted us with life.

Seen in this light, the choice of death seems to violate the duty to live our
lives in a way which indicates our grateful reception of what we have been given.
However, this conclusion can be questioned. Tom Beauchamp has asked whether
choosing death in the face of misery necessarily indicates ingratitude:

The removal of misery is a truly good effect and the intention to produce it
cannot by itself be a condemnable motive, even if suicide is the unfortunate
means to the end of the misery; additionally, it cannot be regarded as evil or
sinful in intent if accompanied by a sincere expression of gratitude to God.
(Beauchamp, 1980:89)

Whether or not Beauchamp is correct depends, I think, on how we conceive
the purpose of the gift of life. If it is given for our enjoyment, then it makes sense
when faced with misery and little prospect of future enjoyment to express our
thanks and "cash in our ticket." But in standard theistic accounts God gives us our
lives in order to develop in us the capacities needed for becoming genuinely loving

people who are able to receive his love. In other words, the world is more like a training ground than an amusement park. Given such an account, the removal of misery may not be sufficient justification for "taking ourselves out of school." Our expression of gratitude for an instruction we were not willing to undergo would be hollow words.

A more radical objection to the argument based on the gift metaphor may be found in a recent book by M. Pabst Battin. She argues that there are some gifts for which thanks or gratitude are not appropriate:

> A gift may be unattractive, ill-fitting, or spoiled. It may be damaging to one's health or one's values. It may be unnecessary, burdensome, or embarrassing.

Applying thus to the gift of life, Battin suggests,

> If it is a good life—say, one involving a healthy, handsome body, an intelligent and sane mind, reasonable financial security, a peaceful political environment, deep human relationships, and so forth—we might consider ourselves obliged to express gratitude.... But if the life you are given is an unsatisfactory one—one involving a diseased and deformed body, severe poverty, desperate political repression, terrifying insanity, unbearable grief or deprivation—we would be very much less likely, if the analogy with ordinary gift-giving situations holds, to claim that you are obliged to be grateful for it. Gratitude in such a circumstance might seem impossible or perverse. (Battin, 1982:43)

The argument in effect questions the fundamental assumption involved in using the gift metaphor: that life is good. It is, of course, possible to question that assumption. However, to raise such a question is neither more nor less than an expression of the classic problem of evil. How can God be morally vindicated of the charge of giving me such a miserable life?

I need not try to answer that question here. It is sufficient to point out that given the assumption that God is benevolent, wise, etc., it follows that there is an explanation for the misery and suffering in the world. A believer who is confident about that might reasonably affirm that even in unfortunate and tragic circumstances God is working to produce something very good and that the value of an individual life may not be fully apparent.

Much depends here on our perspective on the purpose of the gift. Battin writes as if we could easily look at our lives and by some standard like the balance of pleasure over pain evaluate them to be satisfactory, much as we would evaluate a hotel room. However, the believer's confidence that life is good is not based on the possibility of making such an evaluation. In fact, much of religious tradition is devoted to reminding believers to expect suffering, persecution, trials, etc. The confidence of the believer that life is good is based upon the believer's confidence that God is good. If I know that my life comes from God and that God is both wise and good, I can be sure that, whatever the appearances, I have been given a good gift....

III

In the last section, questions about the gift of life led us to a consideration of the purpose of the gift. Unless some account of what God intends to achieve with our lives is brought in, it is not at all clear why when life becomes difficult we might not be permitted to gratefully give it back. Ramsey's assertion that giving it back amounts to throwing it back in God's face only makes sense in light of some account of what God is trying to accomplish in us.

In attempting to give such an account, a believer tends to introduce into the discussion several additional metaphors. One of these is the idea that life is a school or training ground. God's intention is to educate or develop us in a way that will enable us to use our full potentialities. An alternative, though related, account is that life is a hospital and we are being treated for a sinful nature which threatens to destroy us.

Thinking about life as a school or training ground leads us to think about the need for discipline that will enable us to learn our lessons well. We may have to sacrifice some things in order to do what is required of us. If the school is like an army boot camp, or even a law school, we may find ourselves pushed to the limit. This is not to suggest that the experience need be unpleasant. There may be satisfaction as we see our progress and acquire new skills and knowledge. There may even be intimations of the transformation that we are undergoing. But if we take the matter seriously, our focus will be on learning as much from the experience as we can. And, of course, implicit in the school metaphor is the goal of graduation.

The hospital metaphor focuses our attention on the need for endurance and perhaps struggle as we fight the disease. Like the school experience, this is something which may demand much of us, and like school much of what happens will seem beyond our control. There may be feelings of helplessness or even despair. There may be temptations to give in to the disease process. But there is also hope in the possibility of a cure and release from the hospital. Thinking of life as a hospital leads us to expect the possibility of unpleasant or painful treatment. This is not to say that everything about the experience will be unpleasant, but our expectations when we are undergoing a cure are very different from what we expect to find at a resort.

Earlier I suggested that the main point of the believer's claim that life belongs to God is to assert God's authority and to deny that we should be in complete control. The metaphors we are considering now provide a way of thinking about that authority. If life is a school, then God is the teacher. He is in charge of our lessons and we will progress as we submit to the structure he has developed. There may be times when we think we know better than the teacher what we need. However, even in the case of human teachers, our refusal to accept the teacher's authority can result in missing something vital, and in the case of a teacher who knows our needs perfectly, the assertion of our own authority would be foolish.

The physician is also an authority figure. When I am sick, I put myself under a physician's care. I accept the treatment plan which the physician provides. Of course, with a human physician I can question that treatment plan, for the physician may not know adequately what is best, given my needs and values. But if I had an all-knowing and perfectly benevolent physician, it would not make sense to assert my autonomy in the face of his treatment plan. Such a physician would know what I needed much better than I did. And if perchance my condition were complicated by a disease which clouded my own powers of judgment, there would be even more basis for the physician's assumption of authority.

The metaphors suggest the possibility of basing God's moral authority on his knowledge and benevolence. He knows what is best for us and is seeking to produce it. If we accept such a claim, then some decisions we might make could be outside the legitimate scope of our authority. If life is a hospital, then a decision to end life may be like checking out of the hospital. Even if we have the freedom to do so, there are good reasons for leaving the decision in the hands of another. God's judgment of when we are cured takes precedence over our own. We run the risk of doing much harm to ourselves if our judgment is in error.

Similarly, a perfectly wise and benevolent teacher might be in a position to judge when we were ready to graduate, when we were mistaken about the matter ourselves. To try to make the judgment on our own would be unwise in that we are attempting to act on the basis of inadequate information. This is, I think, essentially the point made by Aquinas when he says that life is subject to God's power and that one who takes a life, including his own, "usurps judgment in a matter outside his authority."[3] To act on the basis of inadequate knowledge can be not only an intellectual failing but a moral failing as well, particularly when the action risks serious harm. So if we are under the authority of a wise and benevolent teacher, it may be morally wise to leave certain decisions in his hands....

IV

The theistic perspective leads, then, to a reluctance to consider the choice of death a morally acceptable option. Can any exceptions be admitted? One possible basis for exceptions might be cases of individual revelation. Since the prohibition is based upon inadequate knowledge, it is conceivable that God might in some cases enlighten one that school is over. Some classical commentators made this kind of appeal in attempts to justify the action of the biblical Samson (Judges 16). However, given the possibility of self-deception, there is in the tradition a strong bias in the other direction.

What considerations might be sufficient to outweigh the presumption against the choice of death? One factor might be extremely limited options. Suppose an individual has a choice between accepting death or performing an act which would violate important moral duties. Being faithful to moral requirements would in many cases outweigh the obligation to preserve and protect the gift of life. Hence, martyrdom might be consistent with an acceptance of God's authority and gratitude for his work. To perform apostasy or engage in some other disgraceful activity would reflect a greater concern for life than for doing God's will.

Related to this are cases of "sacrificial suicide" in which an individual gives up his or her own life on behalf of others. There are some significant puzzles about whether and when the term "suicide" is appropriate which I will not address here.[4] I will only suggest that heroic obedience to a moral ideal might be a reason for accepting probable or even certain death. Since the point of the training one is undergoing has to do with developing characteristics like loving concern, acts of sacrifice might be an indication of a willingness to be obedient and faithful no matter what.

We must be cautious here for several reasons. One is that an act of sacrifice might be foolhardy rather than courageous. One who throws away his life with little or no prospect of helping others or in pursuit of a trivial goal may show insufficient recognition of the preciousness of God's gift. A second reason for caution is that apparently altruistic actions are not always what they seem. In a theistic ethic an act of sacrifice performed to help another may be acceptable, whereas an act done because of a wish for death might not be. Obviously, we are not usually in a very good position to separate our motives neatly, but though we can imagine a multitude of borderline cases, we can also think of clear instances of acts primarily motivated by an intention to help others and acts done primarily for some other reason.[5]

The choice of death in obedience to a specific duty or a moral ideal suggests an attitude of regarding life as precious though not clinging to it at all costs. Another type of case involving a willingness to give up life is that of the terminally ill patient who refuses extraordinary means of life support. In certain circumstances, such a decision can represent a recognition and acceptance of God's sovereignty. When there is no reasonable expectation of recovery, a believer might take that as an indication that the life God has entrusted to her care is now to be given back. Bonhoeffer claims in his *Ethics* (1955:122) that the life of the body is both "a gift that is to be preserved and a sacrifice that is to be offered." Either a careless risk of life or a dogged determination to hang on to it could reveal an inadequate recognition of its value.

On the other hand, while refusing to accept unrealistic attempts to preserve life can reflect a willingness to leave the matter in God's hands, a decision to take active measures to end one's life cannot. One recent article suggests an inconsistency here:

> Many of those who believe that suicide and (active) euthanasia are prohibited on religious grounds also claim that it is sometimes morally permissible to let a person die when he so requests or consents. But frequently the person's decision to have his treatment terminated is based on judgments about whether he or anyone else would benefit by his staying alive. When such judgments are part of the justification for letting a person die, they need not be infallible. Why should they have to be infallible when they are part of the argument for self-interested suicide? (Lombardi, 1984:66)

The main problem with this line of argument is that it conceives the believer to be making a quasi-utilitarian assessment of benefits. It is true that one who refuses life-sustaining treatment may judge it not beneficial in the sense that it is unlikely to be effective. But that is not at all the same as judging whether it would be beneficial to die or to stay alive. A believer might plead ignorance on the second question and rely on her best judgment on the first. The judgment that a treatment is not likely to be successful could be sufficient reason for refusing it. But from the theistic viewpoint it is not sufficient basis for taking matters into one's own hands.

There can be difficult and troubling cases for one who holds this perspective. For example, would it ever be right to directly take your life to avoid cruel treatment, or to avoid the possibility of doing wrong (say, revealing under torture information that could be used to harm others), or to avoid the effects of a degenerative disease? I do not propose to give an account of what a theist should say about all of these cases, though I would point out that judgment of the right action in these and other cases is separate from the matter of assessing blame. A theist might judge almost all cases of self-inflicted death to be wrong and yet think that emotional distress, ignorance, or other mitigating factors make blame very rarely appropriate. Rather than clearing up the vanities of judgments, my intent here is merely to indicate how an approach based on duties to God might suppose a general rejection of the choice of death, though coherently allowing for certain types of exceptions.

V

The importance of metaphors for our thinking has recently been stressed by some writers (for example, Lakoff and Johnson, 1980; and Gerhart and Russell, 1984). This paper may serve as an illustration of how metaphors can play a central role in our moral evaluations. Though the context from which I have drawn the various metaphors is a religious one and religious traditions are rich sources for metaphors and images, the use of metaphorical thinking to aid in moral judgment is a feature of nonreligious views as well. Consider Hume's judgment on suicide:

> That Suicide may be consistent with interest and with our duty to ourselves, no one can question, who allows that age, sickness, or misfortune, may render life a burden, and make it worse even than annihilation....[B]oth prudence and courage should engage us to rid ourselves at once of existence when it becomes a burden. (Hume, 1963:595)

Hume's thinking, like that of religious writers, is influenced by a key metaphor. Only in his case, it is not life as a gift but life as a burden.

The metaphors one uses will help to determine what facts are seen as significant, what questions are important, and what principles are relevant. A burden is typically something unpleasant. Our most fundamental way of dealing with burdens is to try to get rid of them as soon as possible. To be sure, there are times when we may have a duty to carry a particular burden. But when we conceive of something as burdensome, that creates a bias in our minds, leading us to ask such questions as, "How can I be freed of this?" A burden is something that weighs us down, and to think of life as a burden inclines us toward looking for ways of removing the weight.

Contrast this way of thinking with the conception of life as a gift. To think of life as a gift is to be predisposed to look for its good qualities and ways of gratefully using it. When we conceive of something as a gift, we do not typically think of how we can be rid of it. Of course, there are gifts we would like to be rid of— most of us have at least two or three such items lurking in the garage or gathering dust on the top shelves of our closets. However, the idea that something is a gift, in and of itself, tends to make us reluctant to discard it....

Moral philosophers have typically concentrated on developing an adequate system of moral principles. However, even with such a system, the task of describing the situation to which these principles will be applied can be an equally formidable moral task. Each of us must put the data together in a way which makes sense within our interpretive framework. We do not come to experience with a blank tablet, but through the filters of our philosophical presuppositions and religious traditions and cultural biases we "knit together" our account of the way things are, and a crucial feature of that account will in many cases be metaphors and images in terms of which the data are ordered....

It is possible to examine a metaphor and find it one-sided, misleading, or even incoherent. In my discussion of life as God's property, I suggested that by the time appropriate qualifications are made, the idea loses significant meaning. In general, we test metaphors in the way we would test any belief that has been called into question, by coherence with the rest of our beliefs. One may be reluctant to abandon a treasured and habitual metaphor, but that is not a problem unique to this pattern of thought. Many of our beliefs can be held inviolate with enough ingenuity. We can rationally discuss our metaphors, and sometimes it will be rational to alter them, qualify them, or give them up entirely. However, before we can engage in such a process, we must recognize their presence and the power they have to influence our moral thinking.[6]

Notes

1. For purposes of this discussion I will assume the truth of standard Judeo-Christian accounts of the nature of God and the world. Obviously one way to question arguments appealing to duties to God is to challenge the existence of God or assumptions about God's nature. But my concern here is with understanding whether duties to God (assuming that God exists) are relevant to moral decisions about the question at issue.

2. For a discussion of some problems involved in thinking of human beings as owned see Kluge (1981 94–96).

3. For a discussion of the bearing of limited human knowledge on this issue see Novak (1975:72ff.).

4. For a helpful discussion of this issue see McGray (1983).

5. The widely discussed Captain Oates case exhibits some of the borderline characteristics which make it difficult to classify. Oates apparently hoped he would not wake from

the night's sleep. There is also some question of whether his action had any significant probability of helping the cause. See Donnelly (1978:101).

6. An earlier version of this paper was read at a 1983 N.E.H. summer seminar at the University of Virginia on "Principles and Metaphors in Biomedical Ethics." The seminar leader, Dr. James Childress, was especially helpful in stimulating my thinking and providing encouragement.

References

Aquinas, Thomas. 1975. *Summa Theologiae,* Vol. 38. New York: McGraw-Hill Book Company.

Battin, M. Pabst. 1982. *Ethical Issues in Suicide.* Englewood Cliffs, N.J.: Prentice-Hall.

Beauchamp, Tom. 1980. "Suicide." Pp. 67–108 in Tom Regan (ed.), *Matters of Life and Death.* Philadelphia: Temple University Press.

Bluck, R. S. 1955. *Plato's Phaedo.* Indianapolis, Ind.: The Bobbs-Merrill Company.

Bonhoeffer; Dietrich. 1955. *Ethics.* New York: Macmillan.

Brody, Baruch. 1974. "Morality and Religion Reconsidered." Pp. 592–603; in Baruch Brody (ed.), *Readings in the Philosophy of Religion: An Analytic Approach.* Englewood Cliffs, N.J.: Prentice-Hall.

Camenisch, Paul. 1981. "Gift and Gratitude in Ethics." *The Journal of Religious Ethics* 9/1 (Spring): 1–34.

Cicero, Marcus Tullius. 1897. "Cato Major, An Essay on Old Age." Pp. 216–62 in *Cicero's Three Books of Offices and Other Moral Works.* New York and London: Harper and Brothers, Publishers.

Donnelly, John. 1978. "Suicide and Rationality." Pp. 88-105 in John Donnelly (ed.), *Language, Metaphysics, and Death.* New York: Fordham University Press.

Emerson, Ralph Waldo. 1906. *Essays: First and Second Series.* London: J. M. Dent and Sons, Ltd.

Gerhart, Mary, and Allan Russell. 1984. *Metaphoric Process: The Creation of Scientific and Religious Understanding.* Fort Worth, Tex.: Texas Christian University Press.

Gustafson, James. 1975. *Can Ethics Be Christian?* Chicago: The University of Chicago Press.

Hume, David. 1963. "Of Suicide." Pp. 585–96 in *Essays: Moral, Political, and Literary.* London: Oxford University Press.

Kluge, Eike-Henner W. 1981. *The Ethics of Deliberate Death.* Port Washington, N.Y.: National University Publications.

Lakoff, George, and Mark Johnson. 1980. "Conceptual Metaphors in Everyday Language." *The Journal of Philosophy* LXXVII: 453–86.

Locke, John. 1970. *Two Treatises on Government.* Cambridge: The University Press

Lombardi, Joseph. 1984. "Suicide and the Service of God." *Ethics* 95 (October): 56–67.

McGray, James. 1983. "Bobby Sands, Suicide, and Self-Sacrifice." *Journal of Value Inquiry* 17: 65–75.

Novak, David. 1975. *Suicide and Morality.* New York: Scholars Studies Press, Inc.

Ramsey, Paul. 1978. *Ethics at the Edges of Life: Medical and Legal Intersections.* New Haven: Yale University Press.

Schmitz, Kenneth. 1982. *The Gift: Creation.* Milwaukee, Wisc.: Marquette University Press.

Swinburne, R. G. 1974. "Duty and the Will of God." *Canadian Journal of Philosophy* IV/2 (December): 213–27.

21

The Morality and Rationality of Suicide

Richard B. Brandt

F rom the point of view of contemporary philosophy, suicide raises the following distinct questions: whether a person who commits suicide (assuming that there is suicide if and only if there is intentional termination of one's own life) is morally blameworthy, reprehensible, sinful in all circumstances; whether suicide is objectively right or wrong, and in what circumstances it is right or wrong, from a moral point of view; and whether, or in which circumstances, suicide is the best or the rational thing to do from the point of view of the agent's personal welfare.

The Moral Blameworthiness of Suicide

In former times the question of whether suicide is sinful was of great interest because the answer to it was considered relevant to how the agent would spend eternity. At present the practical issue is not as great, although a normal funeral service may be denied a person judged to have committed suicide sinfully. The chief practical issue now seems to be that persons may disapprove of a decedent for having committed suicide, and his friends or relatives may wish to defend his memory against moral charges.

The question of whether an act of suicide was sinful or morally blameworthy is not apt to arise unless it is already believed that the agent morally ought not to have done it: for instance, if he really had very poor reason for doing so, and his act foreseeably had catastrophic consequences for his wife and children. But, even if a given suicide is morally wrong, it does not follow that it is morally reprehen-

Originally published in the *Handbook for the Study of Suicide,* edited by Seymour Perlin, pp. 61–76. Copyright © 1975 by Oxford University Press, Inc. Reprinted by permission.

sible. For, while asserting that a given act of suicide was wrong, we may still think that the act was hardly morally blameworthy or sinful if, say, the agent was in a state of great emotional turmoil at the time. We might then say that, although what he did was wrong, his action is *excusable,* just as in the criminal law it may be decided that, although a person broke the law, he should not be punished because he was *not responsible,* that is, was temporarily insane, did what he did inadvertently, and so on.

The foregoing remarks assume that to be morally blameworthy (or sinful) on account of an act is one thing, and for the act to be wrong is another. But, if we say this, what after all does it *mean* to say that a person is morally blameworthy on account of an action? We cannot say there is agreement among philosophers on this matter, but I suggest the following account as being safe from serious objection: "*X* is morally blameworthy on account of an action *A*" may be taken to mean "*X* did *A,* and *X* would not have done *A* had not his character been in some respect below standard; and in view of this it is fitting or justified for *X* to have some disapproving attitudes including remorse toward himself, and for some other persons *Y* to have some disapproving attitudes toward *X* and to express them in behavior." Traditional thought would include God as one of the "other persons" who might have and express disapproving attitudes.

In case the foregoing definition does not seem obviously correct, it is worthwhile pointing out that it is usually thought that an agent is not blameworthy or sinful for an action unless it is a *reflection on him;* the definition brings this fact out and makes clear why.

If someone charges that a suicide was sinful, we may now properly ask, "What defect of character did it show?" Some writers have claimed that suicide is blameworthy because it is *cowardly,* and since being cowardly is generally conceded to be a defect of character, if an act of suicide is admitted to be both objectively wrong and also cowardly, the claim to blameworthiness might be warranted in terms of the above definition. Of course, many people would hesitate to call taking one's own life a cowardly act, and there will certainly be controversy about which acts are cowardly and which are not. But at least we can see part of what has to be done to make a charge of blameworthiness valid.

The most interesting question is the general one: which types of suicide in general are ones that, even if objectively wrong (in a sense to be explained below), are not sinful or blameworthy? Or, in other words, when is a suicide *morally excused* even if it is objectively wrong? We can at least identify some types that are morally excusable.

1. Suppose I *think* I am morally bound to commit suicide because I have a terminal illness and continued medical care will ruin my family financially. Suppose, however, that I am mistaken in this belief, and that suicide in such circumstances is not right. But surely I am not morally blameworthy; for I may be doing, out of a sense of duty to my family, what I would personally prefer not to do and is hard for me to do. What defect of character might my action show? Suicide from a genuine sense of duty is not blameworthy, even when the moral conviction in question is mistaken.

2. Suppose that I commit suicide when I am temporarily of unsound mind, either in the sense of the M'Naghten rule that I do not know that what I am doing is wrong, or of the Durham rule that, owing to a mental defect, I am substantially unable to do what is right. Surely, any suicide in an unsound state of mind is morally excused.

3. Suppose I commit suicide when I could not be said to be temporarily of unsound mind, but simply because I am not myself. For instance, I may be in an extremely depressed mood. Now a person may be in a very depressed mood, and commit suicide on account of being in that mood, when there is nothing the matter with his character—or, in other words, his character is not in any relevant way below standard. What are other examples of being "not myself," of emotional states that might be responsible for a person's committing suicide, and that might render the suicide excusable even if wrong? Being frightened; being distraught; being in almost any highly emotional frame of mind (anger, frustration, disappointment in love); perhaps just being terribly fatigued.

So there are at least three types of suicide which can be morally excused even if they are objectively wrong. The main point is this: Mr. X may commit suicide and it may be conceded that he ought not to have done so, but it is another step to show that he is sinful, or morally blameworthy, for having done so. To make out that further point, it must be shown that his act is attributable to some substandard trait of character. So, Mrs. X after the suicide can concede that her husband ought not to have done what he did, but she can also point out that it is no reflection on his character. The distinction, unfortunately, is often overlooked. St. Thomas Aquinas, who recognizes the distinction in other places, seems blind to it in his discussion of suicide.

The Moral Reasons for and Against Suicide

Persons who say suicide is morally wrong must be asked which of two positions they are affirming: Are they saying that every act of suicide is wrong, *everything considered*; or are they merely saying that there is always some moral obligation—doubtless of serious weight—not to commit suicide, so that very often suicide is wrong, although it is possible that there are *countervailing considerations* which in particular situations make it right or even a moral duty? It is quite evident that the first position is absurd; only the second has a chance of being defensible.

In order to make clear what is wrong with the first view, we may begin with an example. Suppose an army pilot's single-seater plane goes out of control over a heavily populated area; he has the choice of staying in the plane and bringing it down where it will do little damage but at the cost of certain death for himself, and of bailing out and letting the plane fall where it will, very possibly killing a good many civilians. Suppose he chooses to do the former, and so, by our definition, commits suicide. Does anyone want to say that his action is morally wrong? Even Immanuel Kant, who opposed suicide in all circumstances, apparently would not wish to say that it is; he would, in fact, judge that this act is not one of suicide, for he says, "It is no suicide to risk one's life against one's enemies, and even to sacrifice it, in order to preserve one's duties towards oneself."[1] St. Thomas Aquinas, in his discussion of suicide, may seem to take the position that such an act would be wrong, for he says, "It is altogether unlawful to kill oneself," admitting as an exception only the case of being under special command of God. But I believe St. Thomas would, in fact, have concluded that the act is right because the basic intention of the pilot was to save the lives of civilians, and whether an act is right or wrong is a matter of basic intention.[2]

In general, we have to admit that there are things with some moral obligation to avoid which, on account of other morally relevant considerations, it is sometimes right or even morally obligatory to do. There may be some obligation to tell the truth on every occasion, but surely in many cases the consequences of telling the truth would be so dire that one is obligated to lie. The same goes for promises. There is some moral obligation to do what one has promised (with a few exceptions); but, if one can keep a trivial promise only at serious cost to another person (i.e., keep an appointment only by failing to give aid to someone injured in an accident), it is surely obligatory to break the promise.

The most that the moral critic of suicide could hold, then, is that there is *some* moral obligation not to do what one knows will cause one's death; but he surely cannot deny that circumstances exist in which there are obligations to do things which, in fact, will result in one's death. If so, then in principle it would be possible to argue, for instance, that in order to meet my obligation to my family, it might be right for me to take my own life as the only way to avoid catastrophic hospital expenses in a terminal illness. Possibly the main point that critics of suicide on moral grounds would wish to make it that it is never right to take one's own life *for reasons of one's own personal welfare,* of any kind whatsoever. Some of the arguments used to support the immorality of suicide, however, are so framed that if they were supportable at all, they would prove that suicide is *never* moral.

One well-known type of argument against suicide may be classified as *theological.* St. Augustine and others urged that the Sixth Commandment ("Thou shalt not kill") prohibits suicide, and that we are bound to obey a divine commandment. To this reasoning one might first reply that it is arbitrary exegesis of the Sixth Commandment to assert that it was intended to prohibit suicide. The second reply is that if there is not some consideration which shows on the merits of the case that suicide is morally wrong, God has no business prohibiting it. It is true that some will object to this point, and I must refer them elsewhere for my detailed comments on the divine-will theory of morality.[3]

Another theological argument with wide support was accepted by John Locke, who wrote: "…Men being all the workmanship of one omnipotent and infinitely wise Maker; all the servants of one sovereign Master, sent into the world by His order and about His business; they are His property, whose workmanship they are made to last during His, not one another's pleasure.…Every one…is bound to preserve himself, and not to quit his station wilfully.…"[4] And Kant: "We have been placed in this world under certain conditions and for specific purposes. But a suicide opposes the purpose of his Creator, he arrives in the other world as one who has deserted his post; he must be looked upon as a rebel against God. So long as we remember the truth that it is God's intention to preserve life, we are bound to regulate our activities in conformity with it. This duty is upon us until the time comes when God expressly commands us to leave this life. Human beings are sentinels on earth and may not leave their posts until relieved by another beneficent hand."[5] Unfortunately, however, even if we grant that it is the duty of human beings to do what God commands or intends them to do, more argument is required to show that God does *not* permit human beings to quit this life when their own personal welfare would be maximized by so doing. How does one draw the requisite inference about the intentions of God? The difficulties and contradictions in arguments to reach such a conclusion are discussed at length and perspicaciously by David Hume in his essay "On Suicide," and in view of the unlikelihood that readers will need to be persuaded about these, I shall merely refer those interested to that essay.[6]

A second group of arguments may be classed as arguments *from natural law*. St. Thomas says: "It is altogether unlawful to kill oneself, for three reasons. First, because everything naturally loves itself, the result being that everything naturally keeps itself in being, and resists corruptions as far as it can. Wherefore suicide is contrary to the inclination of nature, and to charity whereby every man should love himself. Hence suicide is always a mortal sin, as being contrary to the natural law and to charity."[7] Here St. Thomas ignores two obvious points. First, it is not obvious why a human being is morally bound to do what he or she has some inclination to do. (St. Thomas did not criticize chastity.) Second, while it is true that most human beings do feel a strong urge to live, the human being who commits suicide obviously feels a stronger inclination to do something else. It is as natural for a human being to dislike, and to take steps to avoid, say, great pain, as it is to cling to life.

A somewhat similar argument by Immanuel Kant may seem better. In a famous passage Kant writes that the maxim of a person who commits suicide is "From self-love I make it my principle to shorten my life if its continuance threatens more evil than it promises pleasure. The only further question to ask is whether this principle of self-love can become a universal law of nature. It is then seen at once that a system of nature by whose law the very same feeling whose function is to stimulate the furtherance of life should actually destroy life would contradict itself and consequently would not subsist as a system of nature. Hence this maxim cannot possibly hold as a universal law of nature and is therefore entirely opposed to the supreme principle of all duty."[8] What Kant finds contradictory is that the motive of self-love (interest in one's own long-range welfare) should sometimes lead one to struggle to preserve one's life, but at other times to end it. But where is the contradiction? One's circumstances change, and, if the argument of the following section in this chapter is correct, one sometimes maximizes one's own long-range welfare by trying to stay alive, but at other times by bringing about one's demise.

A third group of arguments, a form of which goes back at least to Aristotle, has a more modern and convincing ring. These are arguments to show that, in one way or another, a suicide necessarily does harm to other persons, or to society at large. Aristotle says that the suicide treats the *state* unjustly.[9] Partly following Aristotle, St. Thomas says: "Every man is part of the community, and so, as such, he belongs to the community. Hence by killing himself he injures the community."[10] Blackstone held that a suicide is an offense against the king "who hath an interest in the preservation of all his subjects," perhaps following Judge Brown in 1563, who argued that suicide cost the king a subject—"he being the head has lost one of his mystical members."[11] The premise of such arguments is, as Hume pointed out, obviously mistaken in many instances. It is true that Freud would perhaps have injured society had he, instead of finishing his last book, committed suicide to escape the pain of throat cancer. But surely there have been many suicides whose demise was not a noticeable loss to society; an honest man could only say that in some instances society was better off without them.

It need not be denied that suicide is often injurious to other persons, especially the family of a suicide. Clearly it sometimes is. But, we should notice what this fact establishes. Suppose we admit, as generally would be done, that there is some obligation not to perform any action which will probably or certainly be injurious to other people, the strength of the obligation being dependent on various factors, notably the seriousness of the expected injury. Then there is *some* obligation not to commit suicide, when that act would probably or certainly be injurious to other people. But, as we have already seen, many cases of *some* obligation to do something nevertheless are *not* cases of a duty to do that thing, *everything considered*. So it could sometimes be morally justified to commit suicide, even if the act will harm someone. Must a man with a terminal illness undergo excruciating pain because his death will cause his wife sorrow—when she will be caused sorrow a month later anyway, when he is dead of natural causes? Moreover, to repeat, the fact that an individual has some obligation not to commit suicide when that act will probably injure other persons does not imply that, everything considered, it is wrong for him to do it, namely, that in all circumstances suicide *as such* is something there is some obligation to avoid.

Is there any sound argument, convincing to the modern mind, to establish that there is (or is not) *some moral obligation* to avoid suicide *as such*, an obligation, of course, which might be overridden by other obligations in some or many cases? (Captain Oates may have had a moral obligation not to commit suicide as such, but his obligation not to stand in the way of his comrades getting to safety might have been so strong that, everything considered, he was justified in leaving the polar camp and allowing himself to freeze to death.)

To present all the arguments necessary to answer this question convincingly would take a great deal of space. I shall, therefore, simply state one answer to it which seems plausible to some contemporary philosophers. Suppose it could be shown that it would maximize the long-run welfare of everybody affected if people were taught that there is a moral obligation to avoid suicide—so that people would be motivated to avoid suicide just because they thought it wrong (would have anticipatory guilt feelings at the very idea), and so that other people would be inclined to disapprove of persons who commit suicide unless there were some excuse (such as those mentioned in the first section). One might ask: how could it maximize utility to mold the conceptual and motivational structure of persons in this way? To which the answer might be: feeling in this way might make persons who are impulsively inclined to commit suicide in a bad mood, or a fit of anger or jealousy, take more time to deliberate; hence, some suicides that have bad effects generally might be prevented. In other words, it might be a good thing in its effects for people to feel about suicide in the way they feel about breach of promise or injuring others, just as it might be a good thing for people to feel a moral obligation not to smoke, or to wear seat belts. However, it might be that negative moral feelings about suicide as such would stand in the way of action by those persons whose welfare really is best served by suicide and whose suicide is the best thing for everybody concerned.

When a Decision to Commit Suicide Is Rational from the Person's Point of View

The person who is contemplating suicide is obviously making a choice between future world-courses: the world-course that includes his demise, say, an hour from now, and several possible ones that contain his demise at a later point. One cannot have precise knowledge about many features of the latter group of world-courses, but it is certain that they will all end with death some (possibly short) finite time from now.

Why do I say the choice is between *world*-courses and not just a choice between future life-courses of the prospective suicide, the one shorter than the other? The reason is that one's suicide has some impact on the world (and one's continued life has some impact on the world), and that conditions in the rest of the world will often make a difference in one's evaluation of the possibilities. One *is* interested in things in the world other than just oneself and one's own happiness.

The basic question a person must answer, in order to determine which world-course is best or rational for him to choose, is which he *would* choose under conditions of optimal use of information, when *all* of his desires are taken into account. It is not just a question of what we prefer *now*, with some clarification of all the possibilities being considered. Our preferences change, and the preferences of tomorrow (assuming we can know something about them) are just as legitimately taken into account in deciding what to do now as the preferences of today. Since any reason that can be given today for weighting heavily today's preference can be given tomorrow for weighting heavily tomorrow's preference, the preferences of any time-stretch have a rational claim to an equal vote. Now the importance of that fact is this: we often know quite well that our desires, aversions, and preferences may change after a short while. When a person is in a state of despair—perhaps brought about by a rejection in love or discharge from a long-held position—nothing but the thing he cannot have seems desirable; everything else is turned to ashes. Yet we know quite well that the passage of time is likely to reverse all this; replacements may be found or other types of things that are available to us may begin to look attractive. So, if we were to act on the preferences of today alone, when the emotion of despair seems more than we can stand, we might find death preferable to life; but if we allow for the preferences of the weeks and years ahead, when many goals will be enjoyable and attractive, we might find life much preferable to death. So, if a choice of what is best is to be determined by what we want not only now but later (and later desires on an equal basis with the present ones)—as it should be—then what is the best or preferable world-course will often be quite different from what it would be if the choice, or what is best for one, were fixed by one's desires and preferences now.

Of course, if one commits suicide there are no future desires or aversions that may be compared with present ones and that should be allowed an equal vote in deciding what is best. In that respect the course of action that results in death is different from any other course of action we may undertake. I do not wish to suggest the rosy possibility that it is often or always reasonable to believe that next week "I shall be more interested in living than I am today, if today I take a dim view of continued existence." On the contrary, when a person is seriously ill, for instance, he may have no reason to think that the preference-order will be reversed—it may be that tomorrow he will prefer death to life more strongly.

The argument is often used that one can never be *certain* what is going to happen, and hence one is never rationally justified in doing anything as drastic as committing suicide. But we always have to live by probabilities and make our estimates as best we can. As soon as it is clear beyond reasonable doubt not only that death is now preferable to life, but also that it will be every day from now until the end, the rational thing is to act promptly.

Let us not pursue the question of whether it is rational for a person with a painful terminal illness to commit suicide; it is. However, the issue seldom arises and few terminally ill patients do commit suicide. With such patients matters usually get worse slowly so that no particular time seems to call for action. They are often so heavily sedated that it is impossible for the mental processes of decision leading to action to occur; or else they are incapacitated in a hospital and the very physical possibility of ending their lives is not available. Let us leave this grim topic and turn to a practically more important problem: whether it is rational for persons to commit suicide for some reason other than painful terminal physical illness. Most persons who commit suicide do so, apparently, because they face a nonphysical problem that depresses them beyond their ability to bear.

Among the problems that have been regarded as good and sufficient reasons for ending life, we find (in addition to serious illness) the following: some event that has made a person feel ashamed or lose his prestige and status; reduction from affluence to poverty; the loss of a limb or of physical beauty; the loss of sexual capacity; some event that makes it seem impossible to achieve things by which one sets store; loss of a loved one; disappointment in love; the infirmities of increasing age. It is not to be denied that such things can be serious blows to a person's prospects of happiness.

Whatever the nature of an individual's problem, there are various plain errors to be avoided—errors to which a person is especially prone when he is depressed

—in deciding whether, everything considered, he prefers a world-course containing his early demise to one in which his life continues to its natural terminus. Let us forget for a moment the relevance to the decision of preferences that he may have tomorrow, and concentrate on some errors that may infect his preference as of today, and for which correction or allowance must be made.

In the first place, depression, like any severe emotional experience, tends to primitivize one's intellectual processes. It restricts the range of one's survey of the possibilities. One thing that a rational person would do is compare the world-course containing his suicide with his best alternative. But his *best* alternative is precisely a possibility he may overlook if, in a depressed mood, he thinks only of how badly off he is and cannot imagine any way of improving his situation. If a person is disappointed in love, it is possible to adopt a vigorous plan of action that carries a good chance of acquainting him with someone he likes at least as well; and if old age prevents a person from continuing the tennis game with his favorite partner, it is possible to learn some other game that provides the joys of competition without the physical demands.

Depression has another insidious influence on one's planning; it seriously affects one's judgment about probabilities. A person disappointed in love is very likely to take a dim view of himself, his prospects, and his attractiveness; he thinks that because he has been rejected by one person he will probably be rejected by anyone who looks desirable to him. In a less gloomy frame of mind he would make different estimates. Part of the reason for such gloomy probability estimates is that depression tends to repress one's memory of evidence that supports a nongloomy prediction. Thus, a rejected lover tends to forget any cases in which he has elicited enthusiastic response from ladies in relation to whom he has been the one who has done the rejecting. Thus his pessimistic self-image is based upon a highly selected, and pessimistically selected, set of data. Even when he is reminded of the data, moreover, he is apt to resist an optimistic inference.

Another kind of distortion of the look of future prospects is not a result of depression, but is quite normal. Events distant in the future feel small, just as objects distant in space look small. Their prospect does not have the effect on motivational processes that it would have if it were of an event in the immediate future. Psychologists call this the "goal-gradient" phenomenon; a rat, for instance, will run faster toward a perceived food box than a distant unseen one. In the case of a person who has suffered some misfortune, and whose situation now is an unpleasant one, this reduction of the motivational influence of events distant in time has the effect that present unpleasant states weigh far more heavily than probable future pleasant ones in any choice of world-courses.

If we are trying to determine whether we now prefer, or shall later prefer, the outcome of one world-course to that of another (and this is leaving aside the questions of the weight of the votes of preferences at a later date), we must take into account these and other infirmities of our "sensing" machinery. Since knowing that the machinery is out of order will not tell us what results it would give if it were working, the best recourse might be to refrain from making any decision in a stressful frame of mind. If decisions have to be made, one must recall past reactions, in a normal frame of mind, to outcomes like those under assessment. But many suicides seem to occur in moments of despair. What should be clear from the above is that a moment of despair, if one is seriously contemplating suicide, ought to be a moment of reassessment of one's goals and values, a reassessment which the individual must realize is very difficult to make objectively, because of the very quality of his depressed frame of mind.

A decision to commit suicide may in certain circumstances be a rational one. But a person who wants to act rationally must take into account the various possible "errors" and make appropriate rectification of his initial evaluations.

The Role of Other Persons

What is the moral obligation of other persons toward those who are contemplating suicide? The question of their moral blameworthiness may be ignored and what is rational for them to do from the point of view of personal welfare may be considered as being of secondary concern. Laws make it dangerous to aid or encourage a suicide. The risk of running afoul of the law may partly determine moral obligation, since moral obligation to do something may be reduced by the fact that it is personally dangerous.

The moral obligation of other persons toward one who is contemplating suicide is an instance of a general obligation to render aid to those in serious distress, at least when this can be done at no great cost to one's self. I do not think this general principle is seriously questioned by anyone, whatever his moral theory; so I feel free to assume it as a premise. Obviously the person contemplating suicide is in great distress of some sort; if he were not, he would not be seriously considering terminating his life.

How great a person's obligation is to one in distress depends on a number of factors. Obviously family and friends have special obligations to devote time to helping the prospective suicide—which others do not have. But anyone in this kind of distress has a moral claim on the time of any person who knows the situation (unless there are others more responsible who are already doing what should be done).

What is the obligation? It depends, of course, on the situation, and how much the second person knows about the situation. If the individual has decided to terminate his life if he can, and it is clear that he is right in this decision, then, if he needs help in executing the decision, there is a moral obligation to give him help. On this matter a patient's physician has a special obligation, from which any talk about the Hippocratic oath does not absolve him. It is true that there are some damages one cannot be expected to absorb, and some risks which one cannot be expected to take, on account of the obligation to render aid.

On the other hand, if it is clear that the individual should not commit suicide, from the point of view of his own welfare, or if there is a presumption that he should not (when the only evidence is that a person is discovered unconscious, with the gas turned on), it would seem to be the individual's obligation to intervene, prevent the successful execution of the decision, and see to the availability of competent psychiatric advice and temporary hospitalization, if necessary. Whether one has a right to take such steps when a clearly sane person, after careful reflection over a period of time, comes to the conclusion that an end to his life is what is best for him and what he wants, is very doubtful, even when one thinks his conclusion a mistaken one; it would seem that a man's own considered decision about whether he wants to live must command respect, although one must concede that this could be debated.

The more interesting role in which a person may be cast, however, is that of adviser. It is often important to one who is contemplating suicide to go over his thinking with another, and to feel that a conclusion, one way or the other, has the support of a respected mind. One thing one can obviously do, in rendering the service of advice, is to discuss with the person the various types of issues discussed above, made more specific by the concrete circumstances of his case, and help him find whether, in view, say, of the damage his suicide would do to others, he has a moral obligation to refrain, and whether it is rational or best for him, from the point of view of his own welfare, to take this step or adopt some other plan instead.

To get a person to see what is the rational thing to do is no small job. Even to get a person, in a frame of mind when he is seriously contemplating (or perhaps has already unsuccessfully attempted) suicide, to recognize a plain truth of fact may be a major operation. If a man insists, "I am a complete failure," when it is obvious that by any reasonable standard he is far from that, it may be tremendously difficult to get him to see the fact. But there is another job beyond that of getting a person to see what is the rational thing to do; that is to help him *act* rationally, or *be* rational, when he has conceded what would be the rational thing.

How either of these tasks may be accomplished effectively may be discussed more competently by an experienced psychiatrist than by a philosopher. Loneliness and the absence of human affection are states which exacerbate any other problems; disappointment, reduction to poverty, and so forth, seem less impossible to bear in the presence of the affection of another. Hence simply to be a friend, or to find someone a friend, may be the largest contribution one can make either to helping a person be rational or see clearly what is rational for him to do; this service may make one who was contemplating suicide feel that there is a future for him which it is possible to face.

Notes

1. Immanuel Kant, *Lectures on Ethics,* New York: HarperTorchbook (1963), p. 150 [see this volume, chapter 4, p. 51].

2. See St. Thomas Aquinas, *Summa Theologica*, Second Part of the Second Part, Q. 64, Art. 5 [chapter 2 of this volume]. In Article 7, he says: "Nothing hinders one act from having two effects, only one of which is intended, while the other is beside the intention. Now moral acts take their species according to what is intended, and not according to what

is beside the intention, since this is accidental as explained above" (Q. 43, Art. 3: I-II, Q. 1, Art. 3, as 3). Mr. Norman St. John-Stevas, the most articulate contemporary defender of the Catholic view, writes as follows: "Christian thought allows certain exceptions to its general condemnation of suicide. That covered by a particular divine inspiration has already been noted. Another exception arises where suicide is the method imposed by the State for the execution of a just death penalty. A third exception is *altruistic* suicide, of which the best known example is Captain Oates. Such suicides are justified by invoking the principles of double effect. The act from which death results must be good or at least morally indifferent; some other good effect must result: The death must not be directly intended or the real means to the good effect: and a grave reason must exist for adopting the course of action" [*Life, Death and the Law* (Bloomington, Ind.: Indiana University Press, 1961), pp. 250–51]. Presumably the Catholic doctrine is intended to allow suicide when this is required for meeting strong moral obligations; whether it can do so consistently depends partly on the interpretation given to "real means to the good effect." Readers interested in pursuing further the Catholic doctrine of double effect and its implications for our problem should read Philippa Foot, "The Problem of Abortion and the Doctrine of Double Effect," *The Oxford Review* 5 (1967): 5–15.

3. R. B. Brandt, *Ethical Theory* (Englewood Cliffs, NJ.: Prentice-Hall, 1959), pp. 61-82.

4. John Locke, *Two Treatises of Government*, ch. 2.

5. Kant, *Lectures on Ethics*, p. 154 [see this volume, chapter 4, p. 54].

6. This essay appears in collections of Hume's works [see chapter 3 in this volume].

7. For an argument similar to Kant's, see also St. Thomas Aquinas, *Summa Theologica*, II, II, Q. 64, Art. 5 [chapter 2 in this volume].

8. Immanuel Kant, *The Fundamental Principles of the Metaphysic of Morals*, trans. H. J. Paton (London: The Hutchinson Group, 1948), ch. 2.

9. Aristotle, *Nicomachean Ethics*, Bk. 5, Ch. 10, p. 1138a.

10. St. Thomas Aquinas, *Summa Theologica*, II, II, Q. 64, Art. 5 [see this volume, chapter 2, p. 41].

11. Sir William Blackstone, *Commentaries*, 4:189; Brown in *Hales* v. *Petit*, I Plow, 253, 75 E.R 387 (C.B. 1563). Both cited by Norman St. John-Stevas, *Life, Death, and the Law*, p. 235.

22

On Choosing Death
Philip E. Devine

A celebrated Epicurean argument runs as follows: since death is annihilation, since (in Aristotle's phrase) "nothing is thought to be any longer good or bad for the dead,"[1] it follows not that death is the greatest of all evils but that death is no evil at all. Fear of death is irrational, because there is nothing of the appropriate sort—no state or condition of ourselves as conscious beings—to be afraid of in death.[2] This Epicurean argument supports the common contention that death may sometimes be an object of rational choice.

I wish to discuss critically this view, and to attempt to support the claim (for which the testimony of sensitive persons is overwhelming) that there is something uncanny about death, especially one's own.[3] I do not want to deny that a suicide can be calmly and deliberately, and in that sense rationally, carried out. But then someone might calmly and deliberately do something blatantly foolish or even pointless, and it is sometimes rational to act quickly and with passionate fervor. But if, as seems plausible, a precondition of rational choice is that one know *what* one is choosing, either by experience or by the testimony of others who have experienced it or something very like it, then it is not possible to choose death rationally. Nor is any degree of knowledge of what one desires to escape by death helpful, since rational choice between two alternatives requires knowledge of both. The issue is not whether pain (say) is bad, but whether a certain degree of pain is worse than death. It might seem at least that progressively more intense misery gives progressively stronger reasons for killing oneself, but the situation is rather like this. If one is heating a metal whose melting point one does not know at all, one knows that the more heat one applies, the closer one gets to melting the

From *The Ethics of Homicide* (Ithaca, N.Y.: Cornell University Press, 1978), pp. 138–43. Reprinted with the permission of the author.

metal. But it does not follow that it is possible to know—before the metal actually starts melting—that one has even approached the melting point.

It is necessary, however, seriously to consider the contention that there are experiences—being flayed and kept alive by ingenious means afterwards for instance—in preference to which it is clearly rational to choose death. At this point in the argument it is necessary to separate the claim that such a choice would be rationally required (that it would not be rational to decide to continue to live under such circumstances) from the claim that it is rationally permitted (that it might be rational both to decide to live and to decide to die). As far as the first of these possibilities is concerned, I do not see how someone could be considered irrational if he decides to show what a human being is capable of enduring. As for the second, while it is true that suicide under such circumstances has a powerful appeal, so does suicide in many other circumstances as well, such as when one will otherwise be exposed to disgrace and dishonor of an extreme sort, or when one is convinced that one's unbearable emotional difficulties will never be resolved. Perhaps all these kinds of suicide are rational too (although contemporary defenders of the possibility of rational suicide do not commonly think so), but if so their rationality is not of the calculative sort. We are dealing, that is, not with a situation concerning which rational men will exhibit a range of estimates, but with a situation in which one man's estimate is as good as another, because what is being done is a comparison with an unknown quality.

I do not mean to imply that we can have no knowledge of what death is, that we cannot for instance teach a child the meaning of "death." But consider what we can do. We can show the child a corpse, but a corpse is not a dead person (that is, not in the required sense of something which is dead and a person, something one of *us*—except in a stretched sense—could be), but only what a person leaves behind when he dies. We can make the child a witness at a deathbed, but to do that is simply to show a living person becoming a corpse. We can tell the child that death is not seeing friends any more (and so on), but somehow he will have to learn how to take these negatives properly, since otherwise death will be confused with all one's friends' leaving town. Finally, we can tell him a myth, even a subdued one such as "death is everlasting sleep," or that death is the absence of life, much as nakedness is the absence of clothing. (In nakedness, of course, the person who existed clothed continues to exist unclothed.) And that such mythology is logically appropriate is part of what I shall call the opaqueness of death.

The opaqueness of death does not result from uncertainty as to our condition afterward, although what I am getting at is sometimes expressed in such terms. My point is rather that it is folly to think that one can housebreak death by representing it as annihilation. One might—considering that the opaqueness of death is a *logical* opaqueness—be tempted to compare the qualms I have expressed about rationally choosing death with skeptical qualms about our right to believe that the sun will rise tomorrow, which rest on the logical difference between inductive and deductive reasoning. To press this comparison would be a mistake, however, for two reasons. First, we routinely have to make choices based on inductive evidence, whereas we do not routinely choose to die or to go on living. Second, the myths cited indicate that the opaqueness of death is a real element in human motivation and self-understanding, an element that cannot be neglected even, or especially, if one considers these myths all to be false.

Human beings characteristically find themselves in profound imaginative and intellectual difficulty when they attempt to envisage the end of their existence. This difficulty is not lessened by the experience of sleep, since sleep, even when dreamless, presupposes the continuation of the self in being and the possibility of an awakening. (I say the possibility, since someone might die before he wakes, and Sleeping Beauty remains alive though asleep even if Prince Charming never arrives.) Nor is the difficulty lessened by interviewing those whose hearts have stopped and who have revived, since what one would learn about in that way is not death but apparent dying.

The difficulty does not lie, at least not centrally, in imagining a world without me, but rather in connecting this world with my (self-regarding) concerns. (Altruistic and disinterested concerns are not at issue at this particular point, since they do not bear on the question of why death can be an evil for the dead person himself. In any case, an altruistic suicide can be rational or irrational in a straightforward way: I might be rational in believing that my suicide will protect my comrades from the secret police, whereas if I lived I would talk and they would be captured and tortured to death, and I might be quite unrealistic in my calculation of the effect my self-immolation will have on public opinion.) Even my aversions, my desires not to experience certain things, do not connect easily with such a world, since there is for instance a logical gap between "freedom from pain" resulting from the nonexistence of the subject of pain and ordinary painless existence. To put the point another way, if I am contemplating suicide, I am not trying to choose (not centrally, that is) "between future world-courses: the world-course which contains [my] demise, say, an hour from now, and several possible ones which contain [my] demise at a later point."[4] What I am contemplating is much more intimate than a world-course. It is my own (self-chosen) death, and such a choice presents itself inevitably as a leap in the dark.

But the decision to kill oneself—it might be argued—need not reflect a preference of death over life, but rather of one (shorter) life over another, or of one (speedier) death over another. The clearest cases of preferences of this sort are choices it would be odd to call suicide. I might take a remedy that makes my present life more tolerable, while somewhat shortening its length, or I might, being tied up and about to be hanged, decide to jump rather than wait to be pushed. Self-execution is in a class apart from ordinary suicide in any case, as any reader of the Phaedo might confirm, and it may be possible to speak of self-execution even in cases where the person convicted does what the executioner ought to do, and commutes, with his own hand, a painful and degrading death to one that is relatively painless. The distinction between choosing death rather than life and choosing one kind of life or death rather than another does not turn, in any case, on the nearness of the death in question. A remedy that makes present life more tolerable may shorten a life expectancy of forty years to thirty-five, or of a week to a day. And if a twenty-year-old should choose irrevocably to be killed at seventy, it would, I think, be fair to say that he had chosen death (at seventy) in preference to old age.

One can perhaps get a better grip on what is involved here by comparing the choice of death with other radical and irreversible choices. (Some first-time choices, e.g., to visit London, present no problem, since one knows that one can always cut one's losses if things do not turn out as desired.) In many of these choices one can be guided, in part at any rate, by the experience of those who have gone before, but this will not always work, since there had to be a first person to undergo a sex-change operation, take LSD, and so on. Choices of this sort are not necessarily irrational, but if rational... their rationality must be explained in terms of the general rationality of risk-taking (which is supported to a degree by experience). This notion does not seem to apply in the case of choosing death. The difference between these choices and that of death is a logical one. While it is logically possible (even if not possible in this particular case) to get an idea of what it is like to have taken LSD, from someone who has done so, death is of necessity that from which no one returns to give tidings.

One might, indeed, attempt to explain our fear of death in precisely these terms: fear of death is fear of the unknown. Of course this is a metaphor, since the opaqueness of death is logical rather than epistemological. But the unknown is attractive as well as fearful, and death has in fact, alongside its fearfulness, the attractiveness which is a feature of the limits of human experience. It does not seem possible, on these premises alone, to resolve the tension between death's fearfulness and its attractiveness.

Notes

1. *Nicomachean Ethics* 1115a 25, trans. W. D. Ross, in Richard McKeon, ed., *The Basic Works of Aristotle* (New York: Random House, 1941), p. 975.

2. Lucretius, *De Rerum Natura,* 111, 870 ff.

3. I'd like to discuss these, that is, without falling into the logical errors criticized by someone like Paul Edwards. See his article "My Death," in Paul Edwards, ed., *Encyclopedia of Philosophy* (New York, 1967), vol. 5.

4. Richard B. Brandt, "The Morality and Rationality of Suicide," p. 117 [see this volume, chapter 21, p. 232].

23

The Art of Suicide
Joyce Carol Oates

In the morning of life the son tears himself loose from the mother, from the domestic hearth, to rise through battle to his destined heights. Always he imagines his worst enemy in front of him, yet he carries the enemy within himself—a deadly longing for the abyss, a longing to drown in his own source, to be sucked down to the realm of the Mothers. His life is a constant struggle against extinction, a violent yet fleeting deliverance from ever-lurking night. This death is no external enemy, it is his own inner longing for the stillness and profound peace of all-knowing nonexistence, for all-seeing sleep in the ocean of coming-to-be and passing away.

C. G. Jung, *Symbols of Transformation*

Not only the artist, that most deliberate of persons, but all human beings employ metaphor: the conscious or unconscious creation of concrete, literal terms that seek to express the abstract, the not-at-hand, the ineffable. Is the suicide an artist? Is Death-by-Suicide an art form, the employment of a metaphor so vast, so final, that it obliterates and sweeps into silence all opposition? But there are many suicides, there are many deaths, some highly conscious and others groping, perplexed, perhaps murderous, hardly conscious at all: a succumbing to the gravitational pull of which Jung speaks in the quotation above, which takes him away from the "realm of the Mothers"—but only for a while, until his life's energy runs its course, and he is drawn down into what Jung calls, in metaphorical language that is beautiful, even seductive, the "profound peace of all-knowing nonexistence." Yet if we were to push aside metaphor, if we were no longer even to speak in a reverential tone of Death, but instead of Deadness—mere, brute, blunt, flat, distinctly unseductive Deadness—how artistic a venture is it, how meaningfully can it engage our deepest attention?

My thesis is a simple one: apart from circumstances which insist upon self-destruction as the inevitable next move, the necessary next move that will preserve one's dignity, the act of suicide itself is a consequence of the employment of false metaphors. It is a consequence of the atrophying of the creative imagination: the failure of the imagination, not to be confused with gestures or freedom, or rebellion, or originality, or transcendence. To so desperately confuse the terms of our finite contract as to invent a liberating Death when it is really brute, inarticulate Deadness that awaits—the "artist" of suicide is a groping, blundering, failed artist, and his art-work a mockery of genuine achievement.

The "artistic" suicide—in contrast to the suicide who acts in order to hasten an inevitable end, perhaps even to alleviate terrible pain—is always mesmerized by the imaginative act of self-destruction, *as if it were a kind of creation.* It is a supreme gesture of the will, an insistence upon one's absolute freedom; that it is "contrary to nature," a dramatic violation of the life-force, makes the gesture all the more unique. One can determine one's self, one's identity, by choosing to put an end to that identity—which is to say, an end to finitude itself. The suicide who deliberates over his act, who very likely has centered much of his life around the possibility of the act, rejects our human condition of finitude (all that we are not, as well as all that we are); his self-destruction is a disavowal, in a sense, of what it means to *be* human. But does the suicide who is transfixed by metaphor suffer a serious derangement of perception, so that he contemplates the serene, transcendental, Platonic "all-knowing nonexistence" while what awaits him is merely a biological death—that is, deadness?

In Sylvia Plath's famous poem "Lady Lazarus" the young woman poet boasts of her most recent suicide attempt in language that, though carefully restrained by the rigorous formal discipline of the poem, strikes us as very close to hysteria. She is a "smiling woman," only thirty; and like the cat she has nine times to die. (Though in fact Plath's next attempt, an attempt said not to have been altogether serious, was to be her last.) She is clearly proud of herself, though self-mocking as well, and her angry contempt for the voyeurs crowding around is beautifully expressed:

> What a million filaments.
> The peanut-crunching crowd
> Shoves in to see
>
> Them unwind me hand and foot—
> The big strip tease.
> Gentlemen, ladies

These are my hands
My knees
I may be skin and bone,

Nevertheless, I am the same, identical woman.

Dying
Is an art, like everything else.
I do it exceptionally well.
I do it so it feels like hell.
I do it so it feels real.
I guess you could say I've a call.

In this poem and in numerous others from the collections *Ariel* and *Winter Trees* the poet creates vivid images of self-loathing, frequently projected onto other people or onto nature, and consequently onto life itself. It is Sylvia Plath whom Sylvia Plath despises, and by confusing her personality with the deepest layer of being, her own soul, she makes self-destruction inevitable. It is not *life* that has become contaminated, and requires a radical exorcism; it is the temporal personality, the smiling thirty-year-old woman trapped in a failing marriage and overburdened with the responsibilities of motherhood, in one of the coldest winters in England's recorded history. Unable to strike out at her ostensible enemies (her husband Ted Hughes, who had left her for another woman; her father, long dead, who had "betrayed" her by dying when she was a small child), Plath strikes out at the enemy within, and murders herself in her final shrill poems before she actually turns on the gas oven and commits suicide. If her death, and even many of her poems, strike us as adolescent gestures it is perhaps because she demonstrated so little self-knowledge; her anguish was sheer emotion, never translated into coherent images. Quite apart from the surreal figures of speech Plath employs with such frenzied power, her work exhibits a curious deficiency of imagination, most evident in the autobiographical novel *The Bell Jar,* in which the suicidal narrator speaks of her consciousness as trapped inside a bell-jar, forced to breathe again and again the same stale air.

"There is but one truly serious philosophical question," Camus has said in a statement now famous, "and that is suicide." Camus exaggerates, certainly, and it is doubtful whether, strictly speaking, suicide is a "philosophical" problem at all. It may be social, moral, even economic, even political—especially political; but is it "philosophical"? Marcus Aurelius noted in his typically prudent manner: "In all that you do or say or think, recollect that at any time the power of withdrawal from life is in your hands," and Nietzsche said, perhaps less somberly, "The thought of suicide is a strong consolation; one can get through many a bad night with it." But these are *problems,* these are *thoughts*; that they are so clearly conceptualized suggests their detachment from the kind of anguish, raw and undifferentiated, that drove Sylvia Plath to her premature death. The poet Anne Sexton liked to claim that suicides were a special people. "Talking death" for suicides is "life." In Sexton's third collection of poems, *Live or Die,* she included a poem characterized by remarkable restraint and dignity, one of the most intellectual (and despairing) works of what is loosely called the "confessional mode." Is suicide a philosophical problem? Is it intellectual, abstract, cerebral? Hardly:

> Since you ask, most days I cannot remember.
> I walk in my clothing, unmarked by that voyage.
> Then the almost unnameable lust returns.
>
> For then I have nothing against life.
> I know well the grass blades you mention,
> the furniture you have placed under the sun.
>
> But suicides have a special language.
> Like carpenters they want to know *which tools*.
> They never ask *why build*.

In Sexton the gravitational pull toward death seems to preclude, or exclude, such imaginative speculations as those of Camus; *that* death is desirable is never questioned.

Of course there are the famous suicides, the noble suicides, who do not appear to have been acting blindly, out of a confused emotional state: there is Socrates who acquiesced courteously, who did not choose to flee his execution; there is Cato; Petronius; Jesus of Nazareth. In literature there are, famously, Shakespeare's Othello, who *rises* to his death, and Shakespeare's Antony and Cleopatra, both of whom outwit their conquerors by dying, the latter an "easy" death, the former an awkward, ghastly Roman death, poorly executed. Macbeth's ferocious struggle with Macduff is a suicidal gesture, and a perfect one, as is Hamlet's final combat with the enemy most like himself in age and spirit. The Hamlet-like Stavrogin of Dostoyevsky's monumental *The Possessed* worries that he may lack the "magnanimity" to kill himself, and to rid the world of such a loathsome creature as he; but he acquires the necessary strength and manages to hang himself, a symbolic gesture tied up clearly with Dostoyevsky's instinct for the logic of self-destruction as a consequence of modern man's "freedom" (i.e., alienation) from his nation.

Is the subjective act, then, nursed and groomed and made to bring forth its own sort of sickly fruit, really a public, political act? "Many die too late, and a few die too early," Nietzsche says boldly. "The doctrine still sounds strange: *Die at the right time!*" Nietzsche does not address himself to the less-than-noble; he is speaking, perhaps, not to individuals at all but to trans-individual values that, once healthy, are now fallen into decay, and must be hastened to their inevitable historical end. If until recent times death has been a taboo subject in our culture, suicide has been nothing short of an obscenity: a sudden raucous jeering shout in a genteel gathering. The suicide does not play the game, does not observe the rules; he leaves the party too soon, and leaves the other guests painfully uncomfortable. The world which has struck them as tolerable, or even enjoyable, is, perhaps to a more discerning temperament, simply impossible: like Dostoyevsky's Ivan Karamazov, he respectfully returns his ticket to his Creator. The private gesture becomes violently and unmistakably public, which accounts for the harsh measures taken to punish suicides—or the bodies of suicides—over the centuries.

It is possible to reject society's extreme judgment, I think, without taking up an unqualified cause for the "freedom" of suicide, particularly if one makes sharp distinctions between kinds of suicides—the altruistic, the pathological, and the metaphorical. It is in metaphorical self-murder that what is murdered is an aspect of the self, and what is attained is a fictitious "transcendence" of physical circumstance.

But can one freely choose a condition, a state of being, that has never been experienced except in the imagination and, even there, *only in metaphor*? The wish "I want to die" might be a confused statement masking any number of unarticulated wishes: "I want to punish you, and you, and you"; "I want to punish the loathsome creature that appears to be myself"; "I want to be taken up by my Creator, and returned to the bliss of my first home"; "I want to alter my life because it is so disappointing, or painful, or boring"; "I want to silence the voices that are always shouting instructions"; "I want—I know not what." Rationally one cannot "choose" Death because Death is an unknown experience, and perhaps it isn't even an "experience"—perhaps it is simply nothing, and one cannot imagine nothing. The brain simply cannot fathom it, however glibly its thought-clusters may verbalize *nonexistence, negation of being, Death,* and other nonreferential terms. There is a curious heckling logic to the suicide's case, but his initial premise may be totally unfounded. *I want to die* may in fact be an empty statement expressing merely an emotion: *I am terribly unhappy at the present time.*

Still, people commit suicide because it is their deepest, most secret wish, and if the wish is too secret to be consciously admitted it will manifest itself in any number of metaphorical ways. We can list some of them—alcoholism, accidents, self-induced malnutrition, wretched life-choices, a cultivation of melancholy. The world is there, the world *is,* not awaiting our interpretations but unresisting when we compose them, and it may be that the mere semblance of the world's acquiescence to our metaphor-making leads us deeper and deeper into illusion. Because passion, even misdirected and self-pitying and claustrophobic, is always appealing, and has the power to drown out quieter, more reasonable voices, we will always be confronted by the fascination an intelligent public will feel for the most skillfully articulated of death-wishes.

24

The Morality of Physician-Assisted Suicide
Robert F. Weir

n March 1989, twelve physicians published an article on the provision of care to hopelessly ill patients. Unfortunately, many of the substantive points in that article received insufficient attention from readers because the authors' call for appropriate, continually adjusted care for terminally ill patients was overshadowed by a portion of the document in which ten of the authors agreed that "it is not immoral for a physician to assist in the rational suicide of a terminally ill person."[1]

In June 1990, Jack Kevorkian, a retired pathologist in Michigan, gained international media attention by enabling Janet Adkins, a woman in the early stage of Alzheimer's disease, to terminate her life with the help of his "suicide machine."[2] The features of the case were so unusual that physicians, ethicists, and attorneys in health law who were interviewed by journalists were unanimous in judging this particular act of physician-assisted suicide deplorable.[3]

In March 1991, Timothy Quill, an internist in New York, published a detailed account of the suicide of one of his patients identified only as "Diane," a patient with acute myelomonocytic leukemia who requested and received his assistance in killing herself with an overdose of barbiturates.[4] Given the features of this particular case, some of the professionals in medicine, ethics, and law interviewed by the media judged Dr. Quill's action to have been morally acceptable, even if against the law in New York.[5]

The issue of physician-assisted suicide (PAS) is not limited to these well-publicized examples. The American Hospital Association estimates that many of the 6,000 daily deaths in the United States are orchestrated by patients, relatives, and physicians, although how many of these deaths are assisted suicides is

From *Law, Medicine and Health Care* 20 (1992): 116–26. Reprinted by the permission of the American Society of Law, Medicine, and Ethics and the author.

unknown.[6] In a 1990 *New York Times*-CBS poll, taken two weeks after the initial publicity of the Adkins case, 53 percent of the respondents said that physicians should be allowed to assist a severely ill person in terminating his or her own life.[7] Moreover, PAS is beginning to be addressed as a separate ethical issue in the medical literature, without being lumped together with the related but different issue of voluntary euthanasia.[8]

The legal status of PAS is also being tested in an unprecedented manner. The Hemlock Society, having failed three years ago to get "The Humane and Dignified Death Act" on the ballot in California, successfully worked with a coalition called Washington Citizens for Death with Dignity to get Initiative 119 on the ballot in Washington in November 1991. The wording of this initiative, using language that blurs the differences between PAS and voluntary euthanasia, simply asked voters: "Shall adult patients who are in a medically terminal condition be permitted to request and receive from a physician aid-in-dying?"[9]

Given these events, the time has come for a serious discussion of the morality and legality of physician-assisted suicide. I hope to contribute to that discussion by first analyzing the concept of assisted suicide and describing the diversity of possible legal responses to acts of PAS. I will then provide an ethical analysis of PAS by discussing the cases of Janet Adkins and "Diane," sorting out the competing ethical arguments about this issue, and making some recommendations for professional practice and public policy.

The Concept of Assisted Suicide

As is true for all suicides, an assisted suicide involves someone (a person outside a clinical setting, or a patient in a clinical setting) who has suicidal motives, intends to die, does something to cause his or her death, and is noncoerced in deciding to kill himself or herself. However, in contrast to "normal" suicides, an assisted suicide requires aid from a physician, a relative, or friend of the person wanting to commit suicide, or some other person who carries out the role of "enabler." The enabler can assist the suicidal person in any number of ways: by supplying information (e.g., from the Hemlock Society) on the most effective ways of committing suicide, purchasing a weapon of self-destruction, providing a lethal dose of pills or poison, giving the suicidal person encouragement to carry out the lethal deed, or helping in the actual act of killing (e.g., by helping the person take the pills, pull the trigger of a gun, close the garage doors, or turn on the gas). Also in contrast to suicide, an act of assisted suicide is an illegal act in many jurisdictions, punishable by fines and/or short-term imprisonment.

Given the surreptitious nature of most physician-assisted suicides, it is reasonable to think that most of these death-enabling acts by physicians are done outside hospitals and nursing homes. However, because cases of PAS can take place inside as well as outside clinical settings, such acts need to be distinguished from (1) acts of abating life-sustaining treatment and (2) acts of voluntary euthanasia. The reasons for drawing the distinctions are twofold: to help in accurately describing clinical cases that are conceptually different in important ways, and to provide an explanation for the differing ethical and legal assessment of these three kinds of clinical situations (any of which can, and usually do, result in a patient's death) that is found among physicians, nurses, ethicists, attorneys, legislators, and the rest of our society.

Acts of abating life-sustaining treatment are now a common feature of medical practice, whether the decision to abate treatment involves withholding treatment, decelerating treatment, or withdrawing a modality of treatment (e.g., a ventilator, a feeding tube) that has already been started.[10] From the perspectives of biomedical ethics and the law, a decision by an autonomous patient to abate life-sustaining treatment should be respected and carried out by the patient's physician in virtually all cases. In a similar manner, a reasonable decision by the surrogate of a nonautonomous patient to have life-sustaining treatment stopped should also be respected and carried out by the patient's physician, as long as the decision is based on (1) the earlier, known preferences of the patient or (2) a reasonable assessment of the patient's best interests. A physician who abates life-sustaining treatment for either of these reasons—the patient's preferences or the patient's current best interests—is practicing morally responsible medicine and runs virtually no risk of civil or criminal liability, as demonstrated by a survey of all the relevant case law over the past two decades.[11]

Nevertheless, questions sometimes arise as to whether a patient who refuses life-sustaining treatment is thereby trying to commit suicide, and whether physicians who cooperate with a patient's refusal of life-sustaining treatment could be successfully prosecuted, after the patient's death, for having assisted with the patient's suicide. The answer to both questions is negative, based on existing case law.[12] Although it is possible that some patients who refuse treatment are suicidal, the judicial cases involving this question have all been decided by the courts in the same way.

Numerous courts, with a unanimous voice, have given two reasons for rejecting claims that patients who refuse life-sustaining treatment are actually engaged in suicide: (1) the patient's intention in refusing treatment, and (2) the "underlying cause" of the patient's death when the patient dies without the treatment. The intention of such patients is not self-destruction, according to the courts, but freedom to control the course of their medical care.[13] In addition, the courts have reasoned that patients who refuse life-sustaining treatment do not thereby cause their deaths, but merely submit to the natural causes that are shutting down one or more critical bodily functions.[14] In the words of the *Conroy* court:

> Declining life-sustaining medical treatments may not properly be viewed as an attempt to commit suicide. Refusing medical intervention merely allows the disease to take its natural course.... In addition, people who refuse life-sustaining medical treatment may not harbor a specific intent to die, rather, they may fervently wish to live, but to do so free of unwanted medical technology, surgery, or drugs, and without protracted suffering.... Recognizing the right of a terminally ill person to reject medical treatment respects that person's intent, not to die, but to suspend medical intervention.... The difference is between self-infliction or self-destruction and self-determination.[15]

Of course patients are different, and clinical cases almost always differ in important details. Consequently, a physician who cooperates with a patient in abating life-sustaining treatment *can* be assisting a patient to commit suicide, if the patient is suicidal. However, the clinical cases that have been subjected to judicial analysis in a number of jurisdictions indicate that acts of abating treatment and acts of assisting suicide are usually distinguishable, because of differences in the motivation, intention, and causative role of the person whose life is at stake.

Acts of voluntary euthanasia, when such acts of intentional killing at a patient's request actually occur, are more clearly distinguishable from acts of assisting suicide. The most obvious difference is the difference in final agency. In acts of assisted suicide, the person who does the actual killing is the person who wants to die. In acts of voluntary euthanasia, the person who does the killing is someone (e.g., a physician, a nurse, a relative) other than the person who wants to die. If a physician is involved, the difference in personal involvement is between providing a suicidal patient with a prescription that would be lethal if taken by the patient in certain amounts, compared with the physician personally administering a lethal injection to the patient at the patient's request.

In addition to this difference, there are other differences that frequently distinguish acts of assisted suicide from acts of voluntary euthanasia. First, a patient who requests to be killed by a physician (or someone else) is usually unable to commit suicide, for either physiological or psychological reasons. The combination of (1) having decided that death is preferable to the continuation of a personal existence that has become intolerable (e.g., because of intractable pain or extensive paralysis), but (2) being unable to carry out the act of self-destruction means that the patient has to request that someone else do the act of killing if the intended result of death is to occur.

Second, the methods used to do the killing are usually different. The most commonly used method in cases of physician-assisted suicide seems to be sleeping pills, with a physician enabling the suicide to take place by providing the prescription for the drugs and/or discussing the required doses and preferable means of drug administration with the patient. By contrast, virtually any physician who would decide, for reasons of mercy, to kill a patient at the patient's request would choose another method to do it, most commonly an injection of potassium chloride or a bolus of air.

A related difference between acts of assisted suicide and acts of voluntary euthanasia is the certainty of the patient's death as a result of the physician's involvement. A physician who responds to a patient's request for assistance in committing suicide cannot be certain, merely by providing a prescription or discussing dosage, either that the patient will follow through with the attempt at self-destruction or that the attempt at causing his or her death will actually work. By contrast, any physician willing to act on a patient's request to be killed is almost certainly going to have sufficient medical and pharmacological knowledge to ensure that when he or she gives an injection with the intention of killing the patient, the patient's death will be certain and immediate.

A final difference between acts of assisted suicide and acts of voluntary

euthanasia, namely the legal liability involved, is also significant. In assisted suicide cases, a physician (or other person) who enables the act of self-killing to be
done runs the risk of a relatively mild legal penalty or, in some jurisdictions, no
legal penalty at all, a point I will expand on later. By contrast, a physician who kills
a patient at the patient's request—even for reasons of mercy—runs the risk of
being prosecuted for murder or manslaughter.

Assisted suicide, even when the person in the role of "enabler" is a physician,
is therefore conceptually different from (1) treatment abatement and (2) voluntary
euthanasia, although the deaths of patients are the frequent results in each
instance. In clinical practice, when the clarity of different concepts can sometimes
be blurred, acts of PAS at the very least usually differ from acts of abating life-
sustaining treatment, and always differ from acts of voluntary euthanasia. For
patients (e.g., some patients with metastatic cancer, or endstage heart or lung or
renal disease, or AIDS) who request the assistance of a physician in committing
suicide, this difference can be very real: they need more help from the physician
than merely abating treatment, but less help than would be required if they were
asking the physician to kill them.

The Legal Status of Physician-Assisted Suicide

The cases of Janet Adkins and "Diane," occurring in different states and under very
different circumstances, illustrate the legal ambiguity that exists on the issue of
assisted suicide. According to early reports of the Adkins case, the specific reason
that Jack Kevorkian was willing to use his "suicide machine" in Michigan was his
discovery that Michigan was one of the states having no legislative statute that
defined assisted suicide as an illegal act.[16] The ensuing controversy about the case
in Michigan and elsewhere continued for months, in large part because of the slow-
ness and diversity in response to the case by various legal authorities in the state.

From the outset, attorneys in Michigan acknowledged that the legal status of
assisted suicide, whether done by a physician or someone else, was "murky." Not only
was there no legislative statute making assisted suicide a crime, there was also no clear
case law to provide legal precedent in the state. Two possible precedents, a 1920
Michigan Supreme Court decision and a 1983 Michigan Court of Appeals ruling,
were not sufficiently clear to determine the legal consequences that faced Kevorkian.[17]

Nevertheless, some state officials decided that legal steps had to be taken, lest
Michigan become a "haven" for persons seeking assistance in killing themselves.
The result, acted out over several months, was a series of three events: an unsuccessful attempt to convict Kevorkian of first-degree murder, a successful effort in
a civil suit two months later to bar Kevorkian from using his machine again or
building another one, and a long-running debate in the Michigan legislature over
proposed legislation that would make assisted suicide a crime punishable by a
combination of financial penalty and a short prison sentence.[18]

Uncertainty about the legal status of assisted suicide also played a role in the
case of "Diane," as indicated by Timothy Quill's published account of the case

and the early media reports. Quill's account never specifically states that assisted suicide is illegal in New York, nor does it say that he inquired about the legality of his helping Diane to terminate her life. Instead, Quill simply alludes to the legal "boundaries" he was exploring by enabling Diane to kill herself, the possible legal "repercussions" that might occur if a family member had to help her, and his decision not to tell the medical examiner that the cause of the patient's death had been suicide. Quill's final reference to the law is his comment, "I am not sure the law, society, or the medical profession would agree" with the decision to help Diane.[19]

Initial media reports offered differing interpretations of the legal status of assisted suicide in New York. The Rochester (Monroe County) district attorney said, when asked in March about the state statute on assisted suicide, that persons convicted of aiding in a suicide could be sentenced to one to four years in prison, but added that he knew of no prosecutions of physicians and had not yet decided whether to submit the case to a grand jury.[20] Three weeks later another report, citing the same district attorney, stated that a person convicted in New York of aiding a successful suicide could be sentenced to as many as fifteen years in prison.[21]

The district attorney soon decided not to prosecute Quill, pointing out that, because "Diane" had never been identified, there was no cadaver to be examined medically for evidence of a crime. That decision was rescinded after a journalist discovered Diane's identity and located her dead body in a college anatomy lab.[22] In July, a grand jury in Rochester declined to indict Quill, even though the members of the jury knew that traces of barbiturates had been found in the cadaver.[23] In August, the disciplinary board of the New York State Health Department decided that "no charge of misconduct was warranted" against Quill, noting the longstanding patient-physician relationship in the case and the fact that Quill "himself did not directly participate in any taking of life."[24]

As demonstrated by these cases, the legal status of assisted suicide varies from state to state. In contrast to acts of suicide and attempted suicide, both of which were decriminalized in all the states in the 1970s, acts of assisted suicide remain legally problematic.

Legislative statutes in twenty-six states make assisted suicide a criminal act, either as (1) a unique offense governed by a specific statute or (2) a class (e.g., second degree) of murder or manslaughter.[25] For states having specific statutory prohibitions of assisted suicide, the punishment is usually a fine (in the $1,000–2,000 range) and the possibility of one or more years in prison. In states lacking a specific statute on assisted suicide, anyone assisting in suicide may be legally liable under the state's criminal code for murder or manslaughter or possibly under the common law in the state.

Whether a person, including someone who is a physician, who assists in a suicide will be reported and prosecuted is another question. In particular, the question of prosecution depends on a number of factors related to time, circumstance, and public opinion. It seems reasonable to think, for example, that the publicity and public outcry over the Adkins case made an effort to prosecute Kevorkian unavoidable, even with a weak legal basis for the case.

By contrast, the wide public acceptance of Quill's role in "Diane's" suicide made successful prosecution so unlikely that, even with the legislative statute on assisted suicide, the district attorney initially decided not to file charges. The subsequent decisions by the grand jury and the disciplinary board of the state health department confirmed the political correctness of that initial decision not to prosecute. Nevertheless, a prudent physician in any state should understand that he or she runs some legal risk, however slight, in assisting a patient to commit suicide.

Ethics in the Michigan and New York Cases

Even if the criminal law were not a factor in PAS cases, such cases would still be subject to ethical analysis. For that reason, it is important to examine the ethics that seem to have characterized the cases of Janet Adkins and "Diane," at least to the extent we know the facts of the cases as portrayed in published materials. How did the cases differ morally, and what difference do those differences make in an ethical analysis?

In the Adkins case, the first problematic aspect of the case is that Janet Adkins was not a patient of Dr. Kevorkian. She was a fifty-four-year-old woman with a diagnosis of Alzheimer's disease, who lived in Portland and asked her husband to telephone Kevorkian in Detroit after they read about him in a magazine and saw him discuss his "suicide machine" on a television show. The only relationship that existed between them prior to her death was based on two short conversations in Detroit (one at dinner, and one during a forty-minute "consultation") two days before the suicide occurred in the back of Kevorkian's old Volkswagen bus.

Other problematic aspects of the Adkins case involve several steps that Kevorkian failed to take in making an assessment of Adkins's medical condition and providing her with medical advice. Having obtained her medical records from two physicians in Oregon and Washington, he apparently did not consult with any other specialists on Alzheimer's disease, in Detroit or elsewhere, regarding the difficulties of diagnosing this condition, accurately describing the progressive dementia involved, and managing some of the symptoms (e.g., anxiety, depression) that can be treated with medication. He did not, according to media accounts of the videotaped "consultation," make much effort to assess her physical condition or her mental state, and even less effort to ascertain whether she was capable of making a voluntary, informed decision to end her life with his machine. He also did not suggest medical alternatives that she and her husband, who was present at the time, might want to consider. Indeed, his actions did not convey any sense that an act of PAS should be done with great reluctance and as an act of last resort, only when an arduous effort to change the patient's mind has failed.

Finally, given that he was talking with a woman understandably anxious about both the early and long-term disabilities connected with Alzheimer's disease, it is surprising that Dr. Kevorkian did not recommend procedural safeguards to Adkins and her husband before providing her with the means to kill herself with successive intravenous injections of saline, thiopental, and potassium chloride. At the very least, it would have seemed reasonable for him to recommend that she (with her husband, and possibly with her three sons) seek a second medical opinion, psychological counseling, and contact with a local Alzheimer's disease organization or support group before taking the irreversible step that would result in her death.

The case of "Diane" is significantly different, except that both patients committed suicide without their husbands, children, or friends present. "Diane" was a forty-five-year-old patient of Timothy Quill, and had been his patient for at least eight years.[26] He knew her medical history, much of her personal history, her husband and college-age son, her virtues and values, her fears and weaknesses, and the importance she placed on avoiding a lingering, suffering death. He knew she had successfully battled against vaginal cancer, alcoholism, and depression, only to develop acute leukemia that, at best, offered her a 25 percent chance of complete remission following chemotherapy and bone marrow transplantation. Quill thought those odds were sufficiently good to recommend treatment; "Diane," after beginning chemotherapy, reached a different conclusion.

As much as anything, "Diane's" case reveals a physician-patient relationship characterized by mutual respect, shared information, numerous conversations, honesty, informed choice, and an emphasis on patient autonomy. Of course the only version we have of the case facts is the version supplied by Dr. Quill. Nevertheless, he clearly indicates that when she refused the chemotherapy, he thought she was making a mistake. Having given her information regarding treatment options and likely outcomes, arranged meetings with two oncologists, and discussed her limited life expectancy in the absence of treatment, he thought she should opt for treatment—to the point that he did not tell her of the painful deaths of the last four hospital patients with acute leukemia.

When "Diane" refused chemotherapy and subsequently indicated a strong desire to control when and how she died, Dr. Quill took several steps over the course of several months. As a former hospice physician, he helped her understand comfort care and become a hospice patient. He made sure she was not depressed, recommended that she see a psychologist, provided transfusions and antibiotics to her as an outpatient, and encouraged her to say goodbyes to relatives and friends. Fearing that she might botch a suicide attempt and/or involve her family in helping her commit suicide, he told her about suicide information that is available through the Hemlock Society.

When she later asked for barbiturates for sleep, he made sure that she knew the correct amount to use for sleep—and for suicide. He met with her regularly, and solicited a promise from her to see him one last time before she planned to kill herself. With sadness, he had no doubt that "she knew what she was doing."

What difference do these differences between the two cases make, in terms of the ethics of medical practice? Both physicians say that they understood themselves to be acting outside the realm of currently accepted medical practice, but believed what they were doing was compassionate, beneficent, and necessary. Yet the reported facts of the two cases reveal physicians whose apparent motives, intentions, and actions were drastically different.

Jack Kevorkian seems (according to the reports in the media) to have been insensitive, negligent in several ways, and more interested in publicity than in the person who came for help. Timothy Quill, although acting contrary to conventional medical practice and being liable for criminal prosecution in New York, appears (through his account of the case) to have been genuinely concerned about his patient and her family. Because of that concern, he seems to have given "Diane" reasonable medical options, several informed choices, responsible medical and moral advice, and appropriate palliative care during the terminal phase of her life. In my view, his involvement in enabling her to commit suicide was also morally responsible.

The Case against Physician-Assisted Suicide

(1) The Medical Profession Is Committed to Healing

The most common argument against PAS has two variants, both of which are based on the view that physicians constitute a unique profession that is defined, at least in part, by a traditional group morality stipulating standards of care and of behavior by members of the group. One version of this argument involves a direct appeal to the Hippocratic Oath, dating from the fourth century B.C.E. In particular, current opponents of PAS appeal to the portion of the Oath that declares: "I will neither give a deadly drug to anybody if asked for it, nor will I make a suggestion to this effect."[27]

The second, more general version of this argument emphasizes the centrality of healing in defining who physicians are and what they do in their professional role.[28] For some persons who advocate this view of medicine, the notion that physicians might, even in rare instances, assist patients to commit suicide is automatically and without exception ruled out of bounds for any member of the medical profession. As stated by David Orentlicher, "Treatment designed to bring on death, by definition, does not heal and is therefore fundamentally inconsistent with the physician's role in the patient-physician relationship."[29]

(2) Physicians Should Not Cause Death

A related argument asserts that there is no difference between PAS and voluntary euthanasia. Once a physician moves beyond abating life-sustaining treatment, so the argument goes, it does not really matter whether the physician's participation in helping to hasten the patient's death at the patient's request is by prescribing barbiturates or by injecting a lethal agent. Both acts "encourage doctors to use their skills to kill their patients."[30] According to Leon Kass, there is little difference between a physician's role as an accomplice to death or as an agent of death: assisting in a patient's death "is as much in violation of the venerable proscription against euthanasia as were the physician to do it himself."[31]

(3) Patients Should Not Request Physician-Assisted Suicide

This argument also has two variants, both of which address the moral responsibility of patients in the relationships they have with physicians. One version, the simpler of the two, states that patients should never ask their physicians to help them commit suicide, given that (a) many persons regard suicide as an immoral act and (b) physician participation in enabling that act of self-destruction to occur may constitute criminal action.

The second version of this argument is based on the difference between negative and positive moral rights, as these rights apply to the relationship between a patient and that patient's physician. A decision made by a patient to forgo mechanical ventilation, feeding tubes, or some other life-sustaining treatment involves the *negative* right (or liberty right) of treatment refusal. A correlate of this negative right is the obligation of the patient's physician not to interfere with or thwart that negative right unless the physician has some overriding obligation of another sort.

By contrast, a request by a patient for a physician's assistance in committing suicide can be interpreted as involving a *positive* right (or welfare right), or at least a claim to that effect. The difference is important: the patient does not merely request to be left alone by the physician, but tries to impose a moral obligation on the physician to help the patient accomplish the desired end of self-destruction. That claim, whether based on merit or need, is weak, and certainly need not be regarded as imposing an obligation on the physician who receives it.[32]

(4) Physician-Assisted Suicide Would Lead to Mistrust and Abuses

This view, a form of the "slippery slope" argument, projects two unfortunate consequences that would follow from the widespread acceptance and/or legalization of PAS. One of these consequences would be damage to the relationship of trust that, one hopes, exists between patients and their physicians. According to David Orentlicher, even a discussion of assisted suicide could damage the patient-physician relationship in two different ways: it could raise questions in the patient's mind about the value the physician attaches to the patient's present life of disability and suffering, and it could raise doubts in the patient's mind about the physician's commitment to provide effective treatment for the patient's current medical conditions. Either way, a physician's willingness even to discuss the possibility of assisted suicide "might seriously undermine" the patient's trust in the physician.[33]

The other consequence, that of abuses by physicians in assisting patients to commit suicide, would be equally serious. As vividly illustrated by the actions of Jack Kevorkian, some physicians would undoubtedly agree to help patients kill themselves without determining whether a given patient is clinically depressed, whether appropriate other medical opinions have been secured, whether the request for help is necessary, whether alternatives to assisted suicide have been explored, or whether relatives and friends who would be psychologically harmed by an unexpected suicide are aware of what may happen. The fact that "Diane's" case was handled in a better manner is of little comfort, according to this argument, since it merely demonstrates that virtually all cases of PAS involve physicians acting alone, with no scrutiny from their peers, the courts, or anybody else.[34]

(5) Physician-Assisted Suicide Is Unnecessary

Patients turn to their physicians for help in committing suicide for any number of reasons. Chief among these reasons is a desire to avoid the prolonged pain and suffering, both physical and psychological, often involved in the course of a chronic and/or terminal condition. Frequently having witnessed the long, painful deaths of relatives in hospital settings, patients sometimes ask their physicians to help them avoid the same fate. Concerned that physicians will be unable to control the pain or effectively manage the symptoms of their chronic medical conditions, they conclude that suicide, perhaps requiring assistance from a physician or someone else, is their only alternative.

Such reasoning is wrong, according to advocates of hospice programs. In this argument, the availability of hospice care throughout the country precludes the need for patients to seek suicide, thus making the participation of physicians in assisting suicide unnecessary. Some physicians may, out of ignorance regarding effective pain control, "agree with patients that their suffering is intolerable and worthy of assisted suicide when in fact the pain may be easily treatable."[35] A preferable alternative is for physicians to learn how to relieve patients' pain more effectively, manage the symptoms of their conditions more appropriately, and assure them that prolonged suffering need not be the fate that awaits them.[36]

Do these five arguments, taken singly or as a collective argument, make a persuasive case that physicians should never agree to assist their patients in committing suicide? I think not, for the following reasons. Critics of PAS who use the first argument take an undeniably important, defining feature of the medical profession, but emphasize it to the exclusion of other ways of describing who physicians are and what they do professionally. Healing the sick and injured is surely one of the goals of medicine, but not in isolation from other appropriate medical goals. Preventing disease, saving and prolonging lives, relieving pain and suffering, ameliorating disabling conditions, and avoiding undue harm to patients are also important medical goals that represent defining features of medicine as a profession.

Some of these goals of medicine, it is important to note, are appropriate even when patients cannot he healed—and even when some patients turn to their physicians for help in putting an end to an existence they have come to regard as intolerable. The achievement of these appropriate medical goals is more important than a literal adherence to an ancient oath whose religious and moral framework is of such limited relevance to contemporary medicine that the oath is frequently altered when used in medical school convocations and increasingly replaced entirely by other kinds of oaths, including those written by medical students themselves.

The second argument, the one equating PAS with voluntary euthanasia, is simply misplaced in the debate over PAS. It is true, of course, that euthanasia has for centuries been regarded as contrary to morally responsible medical practice, but the intentional killing of patients is not the ethical issue involved in PAS. Physicians do not cause the deaths of patients in these cases; the patients cause their own deaths, a legal act in all fifty states, subsequent to receiving some type of enabling help from their physicians. Thus critics of PAS who assert that physicians are thereby killing patients are either (a) mistaken about the differences between assisted suicide and voluntary euthanasia or (b) intentionally blurring the differences between these two acts to score points with the emotive language of "killing."

The third argument is largely true, in my view, because it appropriately indicates that patients should not make unreasonable demands on physicians. Patients should be hesitant to try to involve their physicians in acts of assisted suicide, just as any of us should refrain from encouraging other persons to participate in actions that may be contrary to their value systems. Equally important, when patients with chronic, progressively deteriorating, or terminal conditions do ask their physicians for help in committing suicide, they should understand that they have no justifiable reason for thinking that their physicians are obligated to render such help. Physician-assisted suicide should be motivated by compassion for a patient, not a misplaced sense of moral obligation.

The last two arguments, the ones stating that PAS is dangerous and unnecessary, are only partially true. Abuses in the name of physician-assisted suicide will undoubtedly take place in the future, as they undoubtedly already do. Whether the abuses will be greater than at present is impossible to say. What is possible to say, however, is that PAS seems to be both necessary and morally justifiable in rare cases and, if handled correctly by morally responsible physicians, need not threaten the foundation of trust that is crucial to patient-physician relationships.

The occasional necessity of PAS is illustrated by the case of "Diane," who requested assistance from Timothy Quill in terminating her life even though she was receiving appropriate medical care as a hospice patient. Unfortunately, even hospice care fails, for some patients, to provide them with sufficient personal control over the terminal phase of their lives. "Diane's" case also suggests that a patient's level of trust in a physician may be increased, not undermined, when a caring physician indicates a reluctant willingness to help the patient bring her or his life to an end.

The Case for Physician-Assisted Suicide

Having provided this critical assessment of arguments against PAS, I will now put forth five arguments that may prove to be persuasive in justifying some cases of physician participation in assisted suicide. Taken together, the arguments claim that PAS is occasionally justifiable as a compassionate way for physicians to respond to current medical reality by alleviating patient suffering, optimizing patient control, and minimizing harm to the patient and other persons important to the patient. Taken individually, the arguments suggest that physicians should, in rare cases, consider assisting their patients to commit suicide, for any of five reasons.

(1) To Respond to Current Medical Reality

Change is a regular part of medicine, whether the change takes the form of new diagnostic tools, new research discoveries, new victories over old diseases, new diseases, new health problems, new drugs, new life-sustaining technologies, or new concerns over matters pertaining to biomedical ethics, health economics, and health law. Change is surely a factor in the medical problems that patients bring their physicians, with adult patients now presenting more medical problems that are chronic or degenerative in nature than ever before.[37] Added to this factor is another one: patients are living increasingly longer lives, with the combination of chronic medical conditions and extended life expectancy representing the distinct possibility, for some persons, that remaining alive will be regarded as offering nothing other than more disability, more financial and personal hardship, and more suffering.

The good news is that many adults are now capable, with the help of pharmacological and technological advances in medicine, of having long lives with a remarkable health status that would have been unachievable earlier in this century and unimaginable before that. The bad news is that some adults are caught in an existential situation dominated by intractable pain, severe disability, progressive dementia, a deteriorating neurological condition, a terminal condition, or some combination of these that makes life seem not to be worth living. An unknown number of these persons decide that death is a preferable option to the suffering that life holds for them and, for their own personal reasons, ask their physicians to help them end the suffering.

It is this part of medical reality—the realistic limits of physicians to heal all their patients and effectively relieve suffering—that represents the ethical core of the debate over PAS. Rather than quoting a passage from the Hippocratic Oath about what physicians cannot do for their patients, contemporary physicians should address medical reality as it currently exists in their patients—some with terminal conditions, and an increasing number with chronic and degenerative diseases—and consider again what they might do for that small minority of patients who find their lives to be intolerable and who, perhaps as a last resort, turn to their physicians for help in bringing about death.

(2) To Alleviate Patient Suffering

Virtually anyone who is ill suffers from time to time. For some patients, suffering is primarily physical in nature, with the particular forms of suffering including nausea, dyspnea, fever, hunger, thirst, diarrhea, and pain. For other patients, suffering is partially or perhaps primarily psychological in nature, with individuals experiencing anxiety, depression, denial, loneliness, helplessness, anger, and fear. Much of this suffering, whether physiological or psychological in nature, can be effectively managed with empathic support, medications, various other medical and surgical interventions, nursing care, psychological counseling, stress-reduction techniques, and rest.

But for Janet Adkins, "Diane," and an unknown number of other patients, the multiple efforts made by themselves, their families and friends, and their physicians to alleviate their suffering ultimately do not work. Janet Adkins, it seems, experienced substantial psychological suffering brought on by thoughts about the losses she had already experienced (she could no longer read literature or play the piano). Additional psychological suffering was undoubtedly created by the anxiety and fear of wondering what her remaining years with Alzheimer's disease would be like for herself and her family.

"Diane" experienced the physical suffering caused by her disease-related bone pain, weakness, infections, fatigue, and fever, but she preferred this suffering to the suffering she would have experienced through hospitalization, chemotherapy, radiation therapy, and bone marrow transplantation. In addition, she seems to have experienced substantial psychological suffering that included anger at an insensitive oncologist, anxiety over losing control of her living and dying, fear about increasing discomfort and dependence, fear about additional pain, and an overwhelming sense of injustice regarding the leukemic condition that struck soon after she had conquered her other health problems.

The ethical challenge that is presented to physicians by such cases is direct and sharp: should I, having exhausted all other therapeutic possibilities, respond affirmatively to a request for help made by one of my patients? Should I, with the intention of alleviating the life-ruining suffering that my patient is experiencing, be willing to assist the patient in committing suicide? In at least some cases, the appropriate answer is yes.[38]

(3) To Optimize Patient Control

The desire to have control over one's living, dying, and death is a factor in assisted suicide cases that matches the desire for suffering to be ended. Janet Adkins was willing to travel from Portland to Seattle for experimental treatment, then to fly (with her husband) to Detroit to make use of the "suicide machine" in order to end her life before it was ravaged further by Alzheimer's disease. Although legitimate questions have been raised about her mental status at the time, there seems to be little doubt that, if she was still autonomous in the days before her death, her choice to kill herself was a choice to control her destiny instead of permitting her disease to control her.

The desire for personal control is even clearer in "Diane's" case. Quill states that "Diane," having overcome her earlier medical problems, "took control of her life" and developed "a strong sense of independence and confidence." When she went against Quill's medical advice and the wishes of her family in refusing chemotherapy, she "articulated very clearly that it was she who would be experiencing all the side effects of treatment." Later, when "Diane" knew she was dying, Quill says that it was "extraordinarily important to 'Diane' to maintain control of herself and her own dignity during the time remaining to her." In describing his own participation in the case, Quill states that he felt he was "setting her free to get the most out of the time she had left, and to maintain dignity and control on her own terms until her death."[39]

For physicians in such cases, the option of trying to optimize patient control represents the ultimate challenge of how far one is willing to go to respect the autonomy of patients. If (as seems clear in "Diane's" case, but not Janet Adkins's case) the patient who requests assistance is autonomous, the patient is therefore capable of making an informed, deliberative, and voluntary decision regarding her or his health care. If personal control over one's living and dying is highly valued by the patient, the decisions made about health care will reflect that value. In extreme cases the desire to remain autonomous and in control sometimes includes a request for help from a physician—a request for help in exercising control over one's final exit.

(4) To Minimize Harm to the Patient and Others

The ethical principle of nonmaleficence has considerable importance in medicine. Throughout the history of medicine, physicians have been expected to avoid intentionally or negligently harming their patients. Given that patients are frequently harmed in a variety of ways in clinical contexts, the ethical requirement placed on physicians is that of trying to ensure that patients are not harmed on balance in the course of efforts to heal them or otherwise promote their welfare.

Traditionally, the ultimate harm to befall a patient has been considered to be death. As a consequence, two longstanding moral rules of medical practice have been derived from this professional aversion to having any intentional (or negligent) role in a patient's death: "do not kill" and "do not assist another person's death."

In the great majority of cases, these moral rules continue to apply. However, patients can be harmed in several significant ways short of death, through the invasion of their important interests, the impairment of their mental or psychological welfare, physical injury, and technological abuse.[40] Moreover, most thoughtful persons have some sort of informal ranking or other cataloging of harmful events that could take place in their lives that would represent, to them, a fate worse than death.

Janet Adkins, "Diane," and unknown other persons have concluded that remaining alive under terrible, worsening circumstances is a fate worse than death. The important question is whether physicians should have any role in facilitating one harmful event (a patient's self-destruction) in order to help the patient avoid other harms (e.g., intractable pain, progressive dementia, loss of personhood, incalculable damage to a family) that the patient regards as worse. In rare cases, the appropriate answer is affirmative, both for the sake of the patient and for persons loved by the patient.

(5) To Act Out of Compassion

... In my view, the only acceptable motive for physicians to have in enabling a patient to commit suicide is that of compassion. In many instances, of course, compassionate physicians decide, for good moral reasons, not to help patients achieve the sort of self-deliverance that they seek. In other, much less frequent instances, compassionate physicians sometimes decide that the plea for help from a patient for whom life has become intolerable is a request that cannot and should not be rejected. Either moral choice, if motivated by compassion, can be correct, depending on the facts of individual cases.

Justifiable Practice and Public Policy

For PAS to be justifiable, several conditions have to be met. First, a morally responsible physician who is asked to assist in a suicide should determine if the patient is suffering from treatable clinical depression and, if so, recommend treatment for that condition. In addition, the physician should try to determine if the patient's pain and other suffering are, in fact, refractory to treatment.

A second condition is for the physician to determine that assisted suicide is a moral last resort, in the sense that there are no effective medical options available that are acceptable to the patient. No medical treatment is available that will reverse or cure the patient's condition, no life-sustaining treatment is being used that could be abated at the patient's request, and no intervention (even hospice care) seems to provide the relief and release the patient desperately seeks.

A third condition consists of several conversations between the physician and the patient, with at least one of the conversations including one or more of the patient's closest relatives and friends. From the physician's perspective, these conversations, whether done within a few days or over several weeks, should have several purposes: to determine that the patient is autonomous and the decision to commit suicide is rational, to recommend a second medical opinion and other appropriate professional help, to make sure that no acceptable alternatives to assisted suicide are available, to determine that the request for assistance is necessary, and to make sure that the patient's close relatives and friends are informed about the prospective suicide. The consent of the patient's family to the contemplated suicide is not required, but they should at least be aware, in general terms, of what may happen so that the psychological harm they experience will be lessened when they find out that the suicide has taken place....

I have some tentative recommendations that might contribute to the discussion. A preferable alternative to the current patchwork of state laws on assisted suicide would be for the National Conference of Commissioners on Uniform State Laws (NCCUSL), working with appropriate medical groups, to develop model legislation on PAS that might be adopted throughout the country, so that physicians practicing in any state could have greater certainty regarding the legality (or illegality) of PAS. My hope is that this new legislation will remove PAS from the criminal statutes in all states, so that physicians who decide for reasons of compassion to engage in PAS will no longer have to be secretive and deceptive with their professional colleagues about having done so.

In my view, the legal restrictions on assisted suicide should be lifted only for physicians. Given the ease with which emotionally unstable, demented, and suicidal individuals could be "assisted" in their deaths by numerous other persons with questionable motives, the NCCUSL and/or various state legislatures may decide to maintain the legal liability attached to acts of assisted suicide when performed by persons other than physicians.

Physicians, of course, should not be given a legal blank check. Physicians who receive requests for help in committing suicide with regret and sadness, who give serious consideration to such requests only in carefully limited circumstances, and who meet the conditions for morally responsible PAS should not face legal penalties. By contrast, physicians who are irresponsible in taking requests for PAS, who fail to exercise appropriate care in working with patients seeking PAS, and who are careless in providing patients with the means of self-destruction should face penalties for such negligence, perhaps including losing their licenses to practice medicine.

One final point. The case for PAS has been developed with great reluctance, both because I wish such activity by physicians were unnecessary and because I am uncomfortable advocating an ethical position that departs from much traditional thinking about ethics in medicine. However, I am convinced that PAS is sometimes necessary, that it is an alternative not to be automatically rejected by morally responsible physicians, and that it is, in at least some instances, justifiable as the right and compassionate thing to do.

References

I want to thank Christine Cassel, M.D., and Richard Caplan, M.D., for their helpful comments on an earlier draft of this paper.

1. S. H. Wanzer, D. D. Federman, S. J. Edelstein, et al., "The Physician's Responsibility Toward Hopelessly Ill Patients: A Second Look," *N Engl J Med* 1989;320:844–49.

2. "Physician Aids in Suicide," *Chicago Tribune.* June 6, 1990:A1.

3. "As Memory and Music Faded, Oregon Woman Chose Death," *New York Times,* June 7, 1990:A1.

4. T. E. Quill, "A Case of Individualized Decision Making," *N Engl J Med* 1991; 324:691–94.

5. "Doctor Says He Agonized, but Gave Drug for Suicide," *New York Times,* March 6, 1991:A1.

6. C. K. Cassel, D. E. Meier, "Morals and Moralism in the Debate over Euthanasia and Assisted Suicide," *N Engl J Med* 1990;323:750–52.

7. "Giving Death a Hand: Rending Issue," *New York Times,* June 19, 1990:A22.

8. A. R. Demac, "Thoughts on Physician-Assisted Suicide," *West J Med* 1988;148: 228–30; D. Orentlicher, "Physician Participation in Assisted Suicide," *JAMA* 1989;262:1844–45.; R. F. Weir, "Physicians and Assisted Suicide," *Iowa Medicine* 1990;80:534.; R. F. Weir, "Is Assisted Suicide Justifiable?" *Iowa Medicine* 1991;81:27.; D. E. Weissman, "Physician Assisted Suicide," *Bioethics Bulletin* 1991;4:3–4.

9. D. M. Gianelli, "A Right to Die," *American Medical News,* January 7, 1991:9.

10. R. F. Weir, *Abating Treatment with Critically Ill Patients.* New York: Oxford University Press; 1989.

11. R. F. Weir, L. Gostin, "Decisions to Abate Life-Sustaining Treatment for Nonautonomous Patients," *JAMA* 1990;264:1846–53.

12. L. H. Glantz, "Withholding and Withdrawing Treatment: The Role of the Criminal Law," *Law, Med & Health Care* 1988;15:231–41.

13. *Commissioner of Corrections* v. *Myers,* 399 NE2d 452 (Mass 1979).; *Satz* v. *Perlmutter,* 362 So2d 160, 163 (Fla Dist Ct App 1978), *Aff'd,* 379 SO2d 359 (Fla 1980).; *Bartling* v. *Superior Court,* 163 CalApp3d 186, 209 CalRptr 220 (1984).; *Bouvia* v. *Superior Court,* 179 CalApp3d 1127, 22, CalRptr 297 (CalApp2d Dist 1986), *Review Denied* (Cal June 5, 1986).;

In Re Requena, 213 NJ Super 475, 517 A2d 886 (NJ Super Ct Ch Div), *Aff'd,* 243 NJ Super 443, 517 A2d 869 (Super Ct App Div 1986).; *Delio* v. *Westchester County Medical Center,* 12g AD2d 1, 516 NYS2d 677 (App Div 2d Dep't 1987).; *In Re Gardner,* 534 A2d 947 (Maine 1987).

14. Ibid.

15. *In Re Conroy,* 98 NJ 321, 486 A2d 1209 (1985).

16. *Chicago Tribune, New York Times,* supra notes 2 and 3.

17. M. Williams, "Ethics, Patient's Right to Die Weighed in Kevorkian Case," *American Medical News,* January 28, 1991:18.

18. "Michigan Judge Bars Doctor from Using Suicide Machine," *New York Times,* February 6, 1991:A15.; "MEA Exclusive: Officials Knew Kevorkian's Plans Beforehand," *Med Ethics Advisor* 1991;7:25–27.

19. Quill, supra note 4.

20. *New York Times,* supra note 5.

21. D. M. Gianelli, "NY Case Reopens Debate on Doctor-Assisted Suicide," *American Medical News,* March 25, 1991:1.

22. "Doctor who Aided Patient Suicide May Be Tried," *New York Times,* July 22, 1991:B12.

23. "Jury Declines to Indict a Doctor Who Said He Aided in a Suicide," *New York Times,* July 27, 1991:A1.

24. "State Won't Press Case on Doctor in Suicide," *New York Times,* July 17, 1991.

25. C. K. Smith, "Assistance in Compassionate Suicide: Still No Legal Right," *Hemlock Quarterly* 1990;41:6–7.

26. Quill, supra note 4.

27. *Chicago Tribune, JAMA,* supra notes 2 and 8.

28. W. Gaylin, L. R. Kass, E. D. Pellegrino, M. Siegler, "Doctors Must Not Kill," *JAMA* 1988;259:2139–40.; L. R. Kass, "Neither for Love nor Money: Why Doctors Must Not Kill," *Public Interest* 1989;94:25–46.; F. J. Brescia, "Killing the Known Dying: Notes of a Death Watcher," *J Pain Sym Man;*6:337–39.

29. Orentlicher, supra note 8.

30. D. J. Rothman, "M.D. Doesn't Mean 'More Deaths'," *New York Times,* April 20, 1991:A15.

31. *Chicago Tribune,* supra note 2.

32. *Abating Treatment with Critically Ill Patients,* supra note 10.

33. Orentlicher, supra note 8.

34. *New York Times,* supra note 30.

35. Weissman, supra note 8.

36. K. M. Foley, "The Relationship of Pain and Symptom Management to Patient Requests for Physician-Assisted Suicide," *J Pain Synr Man* 1991;6:289–97.

37. M. P. Battin, "Euthanasia: The Way We Do It, the Way They Do It," *J Pain Synr Man* 1991;6:298–305.

38. Institute of Medical Ethics Working Party on the Ethics of Prolonging Life and Assisting Death, "Assisted Death," *Lancet* 1990;336:610–13.; S. C. Klagsbrun, "Physician-Assisted Suicide: A Double Dilemma," *J Pain Synr Man* 1991;6:325–28.

39. Quill, supra note 4.

40. Weir, supra note 10.

25

Is There a Right to Die?

Leon R. Kass

To speak of rights in the very troubling matter of medically managed death is ill suited both to sound personal decisionmaking and to sensible public policy. There is no firm philosophical or legal argument for a "right to die."

t has been fashionable for some time now and in many aspects of American public life for people to demand what they want or need as a matter of rights. During the past few decades we have heard claims of a right to health or health care, a right to education or employment, a right to privacy (embracing also a right to abort or to enjoy pornography, or to commit suicide or sodomy), a right to clean air, a right to dance naked, a right to be born, and a right not to have been born. Most recently we have been presented with the ultimate new rights claim, a "right to die."

This claim has surfaced in the context of changed circumstances and burgeoning concerns regarding the end of life. Thanks in part to the power of medicine to preserve and prolong life, many of us are fated to end our once-flourishing lives in years of debility, dependence, and disgrace. Thanks to the respirator and other powerful technologies that can, all by themselves, hold comatose and other severely debilitated patients on this side of the line between life and death, many who would be dead are alive only because of sustained mechanical intervention. Of the 2.2 million annual deaths in the United States, 80 percent occur in health care facilities; in roughly 1.5 million of these cases, death is preceded by some explicit decision about stopping or not starting medical treatment. Thus, death in America is not only medically managed, but its timing is also increasingly subject to deliberate choice. It is from this background that the claims of a right to die emerge.

I do not think that the language and approach of rights are well suited either

Leon R. Kass, "Is There a Right to Die?" *Hastings Center Report* (January–February 1993): 34–43. © Leon R. Kass. Reprinted by permission.

This paper is a contribution to a volume of essays, *Old Rights and New,* edited by Robert A. Licht, published in 1993 by the American Enterprise Institute.

to sound personal decisionmaking or to sensible public policy in this very difficult and troubling matter. In most of the heart-rending end-of-life situations, it is hard enough for practical wisdom to try to figure out what is morally right and humanly good, without having to contend with intransigent and absolute demands of a legal or moral right to die. And, on both philosophical and legal grounds, I am inclined to believe that there can be no such thing as a *right* to die—that the notion is groundless and perhaps even logically incoherent. Even its proponents usually put "right to die" in quotation marks, acknowledging that it is at best a misnomer.

Nevertheless, we cannot simply dismiss this claim, for it raises important and interesting practical and philosophical questions.... The former Euthanasia Society of America, shedding the Nazi-tainted and easily criticized "E" word, changed its name to the more politically correct Society for the Right to Die before becoming Choice In Dying. End-of-life cases coming before the courts, nearly always making their arguments in terms of rights, have gained support for some sort of "right to die." The one case to be decided by a conservative Supreme Court, the *Cruzan* case, has advanced the cause, as I will show.

The voter initiatives to legalize physician-assisted suicide and euthanasia in Washington and California were narrowly defeated, in part, because they were badly drafted laws; yet the proponents of such practices seem to be winning the larger social battle over principle. According to several public opinion polls, most Americans now believe that "if life is miserable, one has the right to get out, actively and with help if necessary." Though the burden of philosophical proof for establishing new rights (especially one as bizarre as a "right to die") should always fall on the proponents, the social burden of proof has shifted to those who would oppose the voluntary choice of death through assisted suicide. Thus it has become politically necessary—and at the same time exceedingly difficult—to make principled arguments about why doctors must not kill, about why euthanasia is not the proper human response to human finitude, and about why there is no right to die, natural or constitutional. This is not a merely academic matter: our society's willingness and ability to protect vulnerable life hang in the balance.

An examination of "right to die" is even more interesting philosophically. It reveals the dangers and the limits of the liberal—that is, rights-based—political philosophy and jurisprudence to which we Americans are wedded. As the ultimate new right, grounded neither in nature nor in reason, it demonstrates the nihilistic implication of a new ("postliberal") doctrine of rights, rooted in the self-creating will. And as liberal society's response to the bittersweet victories of the medical project to conquer death, it reveals in pure form the tragic meaning of the entire modern project, both scientific and political.

The claim of a right to die is made only in Western liberal societies—not surprisingly, for only in Western liberal societies do human beings look first to the rights of individuals. Also, only here do we find the high-tech medicine capable of keeping people from dying when they might wish. Yet the claim of a right to die is also a profoundly strange claim, especially in a liberal society founded on the primacy of the right to life. We Americans hold as a self-evident truth that governments exist to secure inalienable rights, first of all, to self-preservation; now we are being encouraged to use government to secure a putative right of self-destruc-tion. A "right to die" is surely strange and unprecedented, and hardly innocent. Accordingly, we need to consider carefully what it could possibly mean, why it is being asserted, and whether it really exists—that is, whether it can be given a prin-cipled grounding or defense.

A *Right* to Die

…A right, whether legal or moral, is not identical to a need or a desire or an interest or a capacity. I may have both a need and a desire for, and also an interest in, the possessions of another; and the capacity or power to take them by force or stealth—yet I can hardly be said to have a right to them. A right, to begin with, is a species of liberty. Thomas Hobbes, the first teacher of rights, held a right to be a *blameless* liberty. Not everything we are free to do, morally or legally, do we have a right to do: I may be at liberty to wear offensive perfumes or to sass my parents or to engage in unnatural sex, but it does not follow that I have a right to do so. Even the decriminalization of a once-forbidden act does not yet establish a legal right, not even if I can give reasons for doing it. Thus, the freedom to take my life—"I have inclination, means, reasons, opportunity, and you cannot stop me, and it is not against the law"—does not suffice to establish the *right* to take my life. A true right would be at least a blameless or permitted liberty, at best a praise-worthy or even rightful liberty, to do or not to do, without anyone else's interfer-ence or opposition.

Historically, the likelihood of outside interference and opposition was in fact the necessary condition for the assertion of rights. Rights were and are, to begin with, *political* creatures, the first principles of liberal politics. The rhetoric of claiming rights, which are in principle always absolute and unconditional, per-forms an important function of defense, but only because the sphere of life in which they are asserted is limited. Rights are asserted to protect, by deeming them blameless of rightful, certain liberties that others are denying or threatening to curtail. Rights are claimed to defend the safety and dignity of the individual against the dominion of tyrant, king, or prelate, and against those high-minded moralizers and zealous meddlers who seek to save man's soul or to preserve his honor at the cost of his life and liberty.

To these more classical, negative rights against interference with our liberties, modern thought has sought to add certain so-called welfare rights—rights that entitle us to certain opportunities or goods to which, it is argued, we have a rightful claim on others, usually government, to provide. The rhetoric of welfare rights extends the power of absolute and unqualified claims beyond the goals of defense against tyranny and beyond the limited sphere of endangered liberties; for these reasons their legitimacy as rights is often questioned. Yet even these ever-expanding lists of rights are not unlimited. I cannot be said to have a right to be loved by those whom I hope will love me, or a right to become wise. There are many good things that I may rightfully possess and enjoy, but to which I have no claim if they are lacking. Most generally, then, having a right means having a *justified* claim against others that they act in a fitting manner: either that they refrain from interfering or that they deliver what is justly owed. It goes without saying that the mere assertion of a claim or demand, or the stipulation of a right, is insufficient to establish it; making a claim and actually having a rightful claim to make are not identical. In considering an alleged right to die, we must be careful to look for a *justifiable* liberty or claim, and not merely a desire, interest, power, or demand.

Rights seem to entail obligations: one person's right, whether to noninterference or to some entitled good or service, necessarily implies another person's obligation. It will be important later to consider what obligations on others might be entailed by enshrining a right to die.

A Right *to Die*

Taken literally, a right to die would denote merely a right to the inevitable; the certainty of death for all that lives is the touchstone of fated inevitability. Why claim a right to what is not only unavoidable, but is even, generally speaking, an evil? Is death in danger of losing its inevitability? Are we in danger of bodily immortality? Has death, for us, become a good to be claimed rather than an evil to be shunned or conquered?

Not exactly and not yet, though these questions posed by the literal reading of "right to die" are surely germane. They hint at our growing disenchantment with the biomedical project, which seeks, in principle, to prolong life indefinitely. It is the already available means to sustain life for prolonged periods—not indefinitely, but far longer than is in many cases reasonable or desirable—that has made death so untimely late as to seem less than inevitable, that has made death, when it finally does occur, appear to be a blessing.

For we now have medical "treatments" (that is, interventions) that do not treat (that is, cure or ameliorate) specific diseases, but do nothing more than keep people alive by sustaining vital functions. The most notorious such device is the respirator. Others include simple yet still artificial devices for supplying food and water and the kidney dialysis machine for removing wastes. And, in the future, we shall have the artificial heart. These devices, backed by aggressive institutional policies favoring their use, are capable of keeping people alive, even when comatose, often for decades. The "right to die," in today's discourse, often refers to—and certainly is meant to embrace—a right to refuse such life-sustaining medical treatment.

But the "right to die" usually embraces also something more. The ambiguity of the term blurs over the difference in content and intention between the already well-established common-law right to refuse surgery or other unwanted medical treatments and hospitalization and the newly alleged "right to die." The former permits the refusal of therapy, even a respirator, even if it means accepting an increased risk of death. The latter permits the refusal of therapy, such as renal dialysis or the feeding tube, *so that* death *will* occur. The former seems more concerned with choosing how to live while dying; the latter seems mainly concerned with a choice *for death*. In this sense the claimed "right to die" is not a misnomer.

Still less is it a misnomer when we consider that some people who are claiming it demand not merely the discontinuance of treatment but positive assistance in bringing about their deaths. Here the right to die embraces the (welfare!) right to a lethal injection or an overdose of pills administered by oneself, by one's physician, or by someone else. This "right to die" would better be called a right to assisted suicide or a right to be mercifully killed—in short, a right *to become dead*, by assistance if necessary.

This, of course, looks a lot like a claim to a right to commit suicide, which need not have any connection to the problems of dying or medical technology. Some people in fact argue that the "right to die" through euthanasia or medically assisted suicide grows not from a right to refuse medical treatment but rather from this putative right to commit suicide (suicide is now decriminalized in most states). There does seem to be a world of moral difference between submitting to death (when the time has come) and killing yourself (in or out of season), or between permitting to die and causing death. But the boundary becomes fuzzy with the alleged right to refuse food and water, artificially delivered. Though few proponents of a right to die want the taint of a general defense of suicide (which though decriminalized remains in bad odor), they in fact presuppose its permissibility and go well beyond it. They claim not only a right to attempt suicide but a right to succeed, and this means, in practice, a *right to the deadly assistance of others*. It is thus certainly proper to understand the "right to die" in its most radical sense, namely, as a right to become or to be made dead, by whatever means.

This way of putting the matter will not sit well with those who see the right to die less as a matter of life and death, more as a matter of authority or dignity. For them the right to die means the right to continue, despite disability, to exercise control over one's own destiny. It means, in one formulation, not the right to become dead, but the right to choose the manner, the timing, and the circumstances of one's death, or the right to choose what one regards as the most humane or dignified way to finish out one's life. Here the right to die means either the right to self-command or the right to death with dignity—claims that would oblige others, at a minimum, to stop interfering, but also, quite commonly, to "assist self-command" or to "provide dignity" by participating in bringing one's life to an end, according to plan. In the end, these proper and high-minded demands for autonomy and dignity turn out in most cases to embrace also a right to become dead, with assistance if necessary.

This analysis of current usage shows why one might be properly confused about the meaning of the term "right to die." In public discourse today, it merges all the aforementioned meanings: right to refuse treatment even if, or so that, death may occur; right to be killed or to become dead; right to control one's own dying; right to die with dignity; right to assistance in death. Some of this confusion inheres in the term; some of it is deliberately fostered by proponents of all these "rights," who hope thereby to gain assent to the more extreme claims by merging them with the more modest ones. Partly for this reason, however, we do well to regard the "right to die" at its most radical—and I will do so in this essay—as a right to become dead, by active means and if necessary with the assistance of others. In this way we take seriously and do justice to the novelty and boldness of the claim, a claim that intends to go beyond both the existing common-law right to refuse unwanted medical treatment and the so-called right to commit suicide all by oneself....

Having sought to clarify the meaning of "right to die," we face next the even greater confusion about who it is that allegedly has such a right. Is it only those who are "certifiably" terminally ill and irreversibly dying, with or without medical treatment? Also those who are incurably ill and severely incapacitated, although definitely not dying? Everyone, mentally competent or not? Does a senile person have a "right to die" if he is incapable of claiming it for himself? Do I need to be able to claim *and act* on such a right in order to have it, or can proxies be designated to exercise my right to die on my behalf? If the right to die is essentially an expression of my autonomy, how can anyone else exercise it for me?

Equally puzzling is the question, Against whom or what is a right to die being asserted? Is it a liberty right mainly against those officious meddlers who keep me from dying—against those doctors, nurses, hospitals, right-to-life groups, and district attorneys who interfere either with my ability to die (by machinery and hospitalization) or with my ability to gain help in ending my life (by criminal sanctions against assisting suicide)? If it is a right to become dead, is it not also a welfare right claimed against those who do not yet assist—a right demanding also the provision of the poison that I have permission to take? (Compare the liberty right to seek an abortion with the welfare right to obtain one.) Or is it, at bottom, a demand asserted also *against nature,* which has dealt me a bad hand by keeping me alive, beyond my wishes and beneath my dignity, and alas without terminal illness, too senile or enfeebled to make matters right?

The most radical formulations, whether in the form of "a right to become dead" or "a right to control my destiny" or "a right to dignity," are, I am convinced, the complaint of human pride against what our tyrannical tendencies lead us to experience as "cosmic injustice, directed against me." Here the ill-fated demand a right not to be ill-fated; those who want to die, but cannot, claim a right to die, which becomes, as Harvey Mansfield has put it, a tort claim against nature. It thus becomes the business of the well-fated to correct nature's mistreatment of the ill-fated *by making them dead.* Thus would the same act that was only yesterday declared a crime against humanity become a mandated act, not only of compassionate charity but of compensatory justice!

Why Assert a Right to Die?

Before proceeding to the more challenging question of the existence and ground of a "right to die," it would be useful briefly to consider why such a right is being asserted, and by whom. Some of the reasons have already been noted in passing:

- fear of prolongation of dying due to medical intervention; hence, a right to refuse treatment or hospitalization, even if death occurs as a result;

- fear of living too long, without fatal illness to carry one off, hence, a right to assisted suicide;
- fear of the degradations of senility and dependence; hence, a right to death with dignity;
- fear of loss of control; hence, a right to choose the time and manner of one's death.

Equally important for many people is the fear of becoming a burden to others—financial, psychic, social. Few parents, however eager or willing they might be to stay alive, are pleased by the prospect that they might thereby destroy their children's and grandchildren's opportunities for happiness. Indeed, my own greatest weakening on the subject of euthanasia is precisely this: I would confess a strong temptation to remove myself from life to spare my children the anguish of years of attending my demented self and the horrible likelihood that they will come, hatefully to themselves, to resent my continued existence. Such reasons in favor of death might even lead me to think I had a *duty* to die—they do not, however, establish for me any right to become dead.[1]

But the advocates of a "right to die" are not always so generous. On the contrary, much dishonesty and mischief are afoot. Many people have seen the advantage of using the language of individual rights, implying voluntary action, to shift the national attitudes regarding life and death, to prepare the way for the practice of terminating "useless" lives.[2]

Many who argue for a right to die mean for people not merely to have it but to exercise it with dispatch, so as to decrease the mounting socioeconomic costs of caring for the irreversibly ill and dying. In fact, most of the people now agitating for a "right to die" are themselves neither ill nor dying. Children looking at parents who are not dying fast enough, hospital administrators and health economists concerned about cost-cutting and waste, doctors disgusted with caring for incurables, people with eugenic or aesthetic interests who are repelled by the prospect of a society in which the young and vigorous expend enormous energy to keep alive the virtually dead—all these want to change our hard-won ethic in favor of life.

But they are either too ashamed or too shrewd to state their true intentions. Much better to trumpet a right to die, and encourage people to exercise it. These advocates understand all too well that the present American climate requires one to talk of rights if one wishes to have one's way in such moral matters. Consider the analogous use of arguments for abortion rights by organizations which hope thereby to get women—especially the poor, the unmarried, and the nonwhite—to exercise their "right to choose," to do their supposed duty toward limiting population growth and the size of the underclass.

This is not to say that all reasons for promoting a "right to die" are suspect. Nor do I mean to suggest that it would never be right or good for someone to elect to die. But it might be dangerous folly to circumvent the grave need for prudence in these matters by substituting the confused yet absolutized principle of a "right to die," especially given the mixed motives and dangerous purposes of some of its proponents.

Truth to tell, public discourse about moral matters in the United States is

much impoverished by our eagerness to transform questions of the right and the
good into questions about individual rights. Partly, this is a legacy of modern liberalism, the political philosophy on which the genius of the American republic
mainly rests. But it is augmented by American self-assertion and individualism,
increasingly so in an age when family and other mediating institutions are in
decline and the naked individual is left face to face with the bureaucratic state.

But the language of rights gained a tremendous boost from the moral abso-
lutism of the 1960s, with the discovery that the nonnegotiable and absolutized
character of all rights claims provides the most durable battering ram against the
status quo. Never mind that it fuels resentments and breeds hatreds, that it ignores
the consequences to society, or that it short-circuits a political process that is more
amenable to working out a balanced view of the common good. Never mind all
that: go to court and demand your rights. And the courts have been all too willing
to oblige, finding or inventing new rights in the process.

These sociocultural changes, having nothing to do with death and dying,
surely are part of the reason we are now confronted with vociferous claims of a
right to die. These changes are also part of the reason why, despite its notorious
difficulties, a right to die is the leading moral concept advanced to address these
most complicated and delicate human matters at the end of life. Yet the reasons
for the assertion, even if suspect, do not settle the question of truth, to which, at
long last, we finally turn. Let us examine whether philosophically or legally we can
truly speak of a right to die.

Is There a Right to Die?

Philosophically speaking, it makes sense to take our bearings from those great
thinkers of modernity who are the originators and most thoughtful exponents of
our rights-based thinking. They above all are likely to have understood the purpose, character, grounds, and limits for the assertion of rights. If a newly asserted
right, such as the right to die, cannot be established on the natural or rational
ground for rights offered by these thinkers, the burden of proof must fall on the
proponents of novel rights, to provide a new yet equally solid ground in support
of their novel claims.

If we start at the beginning, with the great philosophical teachers of natural
rights, the very notion of a right to die would be nonsensical. As we learn from
Hobbes and from John Locke, all the rights of man, given by nature, presuppose
our self-interested attachment to our own lives. All natural rights trace home to the
primary right to life, or better, the right to self-preservation—itself rooted in the
powerful, self-loving impulses and passions that seek our own continuance, and
asserted first against deadly, oppressive polities or against those who might insist
that morality requires me to turn the other cheek when my life is threatened.[3] . . .

Because death, my extinction, is the evil whose avoidance is the condition of
the possibility of my having any and all of my goods, my right to secure my life
against death—that is, my rightful liberty to self-preservative conduct—is the

bedrock of all other rights and of all politically relevant morality. Even Hans Jonas, writing to defend "the right to die," acknowledges that it stands alone, and concedes that "every other right ever argued, claimed, granted, or denied can be viewed as an extension of this primary right [to life], since every particular right concerns the exercise of some faculty of life, the access to some necessity of life, the satisfaction of some aspiration of life."[4] It is obvious that one cannot found on this rock any right to die or right to become dead. Life loves to live, and it needs all the help it can get.

This is not to say that these early modern thinkers were unaware that men might tire of life or might come to find existence burdensome. But the decline in the will to live did not for them drive out or nullify the right to life, much less lead to a trumping new right, a right to die. For the right to life is a matter of nature, not will.

Locke addresses and rejects a natural right to suicide, in his discussion of the state of nature:

> But though this be a state of liberty, yet it is not a state of license; though man in that state has an uncontrollable liberty to dispose of his person or possessions, yet he has not liberty to destroy himself, or so much as any creature in his possession, but where some nobler use than its bare preservation calls for it. The state of nature has a law of nature to govern it, which obliges everyone; and reason, which is that law, teaches all mankind who will but consult it, that, being all equal and independent, no one ought to harm another in his life, health, liberty, or possessions.[5]

Admittedly, the argument here turns explicitly theological—we are said to be our wise Maker's property. But the argument against a man's willful "quitting of his station" seems, for Locke, to be a corollary of the natural inclination and right of self-preservation.

Some try to argue, wrongly in my view, that Locke's teaching on property rests on a principle of self-ownership, which can then be used to justify self-destruction: since I own my body and my life, I may do with them as I please. As this argument has much currency, it is worth examining in greater detail. Locke does indeed say something that seems at first glance to suggest self-ownership:

> Though the earth and all inferior creatures be common to all men, *yet every man has a property in his own person;* this nobody has a right to but himself. The labor of his body and the work of his hands we may say are properly his.[6]

But the context defines and constricts the claim. Unlike the property rights in the fruits of his labor, the property a man has in his own person is inalienable: a man cannot transfer title to himself by selling himself into slavery. The "property in his own person" is less a metaphysical statement declaring self-ownership, more a political statement denying ownership by another. This right removes each and every human being from the commons available to all human beings for appropriation and use. My body and my life are my property *only in the limited sense* that they are *not yours.* They are different from my alienable property—my house, my car, my shoes. My body and my life, while mine to use, are not mine to dispose of. In the deepest sense, my body is nobody's body, not even mine.[7]

Even if one continues, against reason, to hold to strict self-ownership and self-disposability, there is a further argument, one that is decisive. Self-ownership might enable one at most to justify *attempting* suicide; it cannot justify a right to succeed or, more important, a right to the assistance of others. The designated potential assistant-in-death has neither a natural duty nor a natural right to become an actual assistant-in-death, and the liberal state, instituted above all to protect life, can never countenance such a right to kill, even on request. A right to become dead or to be made dead cannot be sustained on classical liberal grounds.

Later thinkers in the liberal tradition, including those who prized freedom above preservation, also make no room for a "right to die." Jean-Jacques Rousseau's complaints about the ills of civil society centered especially and most powerfully on the threats to life and limb, from a social order whose main purpose should have been to protect them.[8] And Immanuel Kant, for whom rights are founded not in nature but in reason, holds that the self-willed act of self-destruction is simply self-contradictory.

> It seems absurd that a man can injure himself (*volenti non it injuria* [Injury cannot happen to one who is willing]). The Stoic therefore considered it a prerogative of his personality as a wise man to walk out of his life with an undisturbed mind whenever he liked (as out of a smoke-filled room), not because he was afflicted by actual or anticipated ills, but simply because he could make use of nothing more in this life. And yet this very courage, this strength of mind—of not fearing death and of knowing of something which man can prize more highly than his life—ought to have been an ever so much greater motive for him not to destroy himself, a being having such authoritative superiority over the strongest sensible incentives; consequently, it ought to have been a motive for him not to deprive himself of life.
>
> Man cannot deprive himself of his personhood so long as one speaks of duties, thus so long as he lives. That man ought to have the authorization to withdraw himself from all obligation, i.e., to be free to act as if no authorization at all were required for this withdrawal, involves a contradiction. To destroy the subject of morality in his own person is tantamount to obliterating from the world, as far as he can, the very existence of morality itself, but morality is, nevertheless, an end in itself. Accordingly, to dispose of oneself as a mere means to some end of one's own liking is to degrade the humanity in one's person (*homo noumenon*), which, after all, was entrusted to man (*homo phenomenon*) to preserve.[9]

It is a heavy irony that it should be autonomy, the moral notion that the world owes mainly to Kant, that is now invoked as the justifying ground of a right to die. For Kant, autonomy, which literally means self-legislation, requires acting in accordance with one's true self—that is, with one's rational will determined by a universalizable, that is, rational, maxim. Being autonomous means not being a slave to instinct, impulse, or whim, but rather doing as one ought, as a rational being. But autonomy has now come to mean "doing as you please," compatible no less with self-indulgence than with self-control. Herewith one sees clearly the triumph of the Nietzschean self, who finds reason just as enslaving as blind instinct and who finds his true "self" rather in unconditioned acts of pure creative will.

Yet even in its willful modern meaning, "autonomy" cannot ground a right to die. First, one cannot establish on this basis a right to have someone else's assistance in committing suicide—a right, by the way, that would impose an obligation on someone else and thereby restrict his autonomy. Second, even if my choice for death were "reasonable" and my chosen assistant freely willing, my autonomy cannot ground his right to kill me, and, hence, it cannot ground my right to become dead. Third, a liberty right to an assisted death (that is, a right against interference) can at most approve assisted suicide or euthanasia for the mentally competent and alert—a restriction that would prohibit effecting the deaths of the mentally incompetent or comatose patients who have not left explicit instructions regarding their treatment. It is, by the way, a long philosophical question whether all such instructions must be obeyed, for the person who gave them long ago may no longer be "the same person" when they become relevant. Can my fifty-three-year-old self truly prescribe today the best interests for my seventy-five-year-old and senile self?

In contrast to arguments presented in recent court cases, it is self-contradictory to assert that a proxy not chosen by the patient can exercise the patient's rights of autonomy. Can a citizen have a right to vote that would be irrevocably exercised "on his behalf," and in the name of his autonomy, by the government?[10] Finally, if autonomy and dignity lie in the free exercise of will and choice, it is at least paradoxical to say that our autonomy licenses an act that puts our autonomy permanently out of business.

It is precisely this paradox that appeals to the Nietzschean creative self, the bearer of so many of this century's "new rights." As Mansfield brilliantly shows, the creative ones are not bound by normality or good sense:

> Creative beings are open-ended. They are open-ended in fact and not merely in their formal potentialities. Such beings do not have interests; for who can say what is in the interest of a being that is becoming something unknown? Thus the society of new rights is characterized by a loss of predictability and normality: no one knows what to expect, even from his closest companions.[11]

The most authentic self-creative self revels in the unpredictable, the extreme, the perverse. He does not even flinch before self-contradiction; indeed, he can display the triumph of his will most especially in self-negation. And though it may revolt us, who are we to deny him this form of self-expression? Supremely tolerant of the rights of others to their own eccentricities, we avert our glance and turn the other moral cheek. Here at last is the only possible philosophical ground for a right to die: arbitrary will, backed by moral relativism. Which is to say, no ground at all.

Is There a Legal Right to Die?

Such foreign philosophic doctrines, prominent among the elite, are slowly working their relativistic way through the broader culture. But in America, rights are still largely defined by law. Turning, then, from political and moral philosophy to American law, we should be surprised to discover any constitutional basis for a legal right to die, given that the framers understood rights and the role of government more or less as did Locke. Perusal of the original Constitution of 1757 or of the Bill of Rights finds absolutely nothing on which even the most creative of jurists could try to hang such a right.

But the notorious due process clause of the Fourteenth Amendment, under the ruling but still oxymoronic "substantive due process" interpretation, has provided such a possible peg, as it has for so many other new rights, notwithstanding the fact that the majority of states at the time the Fourteenth Amendment was ratified had laws that prohibited assisting suicide. The one "right-to-die" case to reach the Supreme Court, *Cruzan by Cruzan* v. *Director, Missouri Department of Health* (decided by a five-to-four vote in June 1990) explored the Fourteenth Amendment in connection with such a right.[12] This case may well have prepared the way for finding constitutional protection, at least for a right-to-refuse-life-sustaining-treatment-in-order-that-death-may-occur.

The parents of Nancy Cruzan, a comatose young woman living for seven years in a persistent vegetative state, petitioned to remove the gastrostomy feeding and hydration tube in order that Nancy be allowed to die. The trial court found for the parents but the Missouri Supreme Court reversed; when the Cruzans appealed, the United States Supreme Court took the case to consider "whether Cruzan has a right under the United States Constitution which would require the hospital to withdraw life-sustaining treatment from her under the circumstances."

At first glance, the Court's decision in *Cruzan* disappointed proponents of a right to die, because it upheld the decision of the Missouri supreme court: it held that Missouri's interest in safeguarding life allowed it to demand clear and convincing evidence that the incompetent person truly wished to withdraw from treatment, evidence that in Nancy Cruzan's case was lacking. Nevertheless, the reasoning of the majority decision was widely interpreted as conceding such a right to die for a competent person—a misinterpretation, to be sure, but not without some ground.

Chief Justice William Rehnquist, writing for the majority, scrupulously avoided any mention of a "right to die," and he wisely eschewed taking up the question under the so-called right of privacy. Instead, following precedent in Fourteenth Amendment jurisprudence and relying on the doctrine that informed consent is required for medical invasion of the body, he reasoned that "the principle that a competent person has a constitutionally protected *liberty interest* in refusing unwanted medical treatment may be inferred from our previous decisions." (A "liberty interest" is a technical term denoting a liberty less firmly protected by the due process clause than a "fundamental right"; generally speaking, restrictions on the latter may be justified only by a compelling state interest but restraints on the former may be upheld if they do not unduly burden its exercise.) But on the crucial question of whether the protected liberty interest to refuse medical treatment embraces also refusing *life-sustaining* food and water, Rehnquist waffled skillfully:

> Petitioners insist that under the general holdings of our cases, the forced admin-istration of life-sustaining medical treatment, and even of artificially-delivered food and water essential to life, would implicate a competent person's liberty interest. Although we think the logic of the cases discussed above would embrace such a liberty interest, the dramatic consequences involved in refusal of such treatment [namely, death] would inform the inquiry whether the deprivation of that interest is constitutionally permissible. *But for purposes of this case, we assume that the United States Constitution would grant a competent person a constitutionally pro-tected right to refuse life-saving hydration and nutrition.* (p. 2852) (Emphasis added)

Because the decision in *Cruzan* concerned an incompetent person incapable of exercising "a hypothetical right to refuse treatment or any other right," the right that Rehnquist was willing to assume had no bearing on the decision. But the chief justice could have put the matter differently. He might have said, "Whether or not a competent person has such a right, Nancy Cruzan, being incompetent, does not." True, he drew back from accepting in his own name the petitioner's claim, indicating instead that an inquiry would still be needed to determine whether a state may constitutionally deprive a competent person of his "liberty interest" to elect death by refusing artificial hydration and nutrition. But he was willing to stipulate for the purposes of this case—(one suspects that he really means for the purpose of getting a majority on his side in this case)—a constitu-tionally protected right-to-refuse-treatment-so-that-death-will-occur. This stipu-lation, missing the qualification "for the purposes of this case," was heralded in many newspapers and magazines around the country as establishing a constitu-tional right to die for competent persons.

Justice Sandra Day O'Connor, apparently the swing vote in the case, wrote a concurring opinion solely to indicate why the stipulated right was a right indeed. It is clear from her opinion that, if the case had in fact involved a competent patient, a right-to-elect-death-by-refusing-food-and-water would have been judi-cially established, for she would have sided with the four-member minority who were ready to grant it even to incompetents:

> I agree that a [constitutionally] protected liberty interest in refusing unwanted medical treatment may be inferred from our prior decisions…and that the refusal of artificially delivered food and water is encompassed within that liberty interest. I write separately to clarify why I believe this to be so. (p. 2856)

What Chief Justice Rehnquist treats as hypothetical, Justice O'Connor treats as actual, and she presents her argument for its establishment. In the end she even speaks about the need to safeguard similar liberty interests for incompetents, giving shockingly little attention to the duty of the state to protect the life of

incompetent people against those who would exercise on their behalf their putative right to die.[13]

Only Justice Antonin Scalia, writing a separate concurring opinion, seems to
have gotten it right, insisting that the Constitution has absolutely nothing to say in
this matter. He argues, first, that the liberty protected by the Fourteenth Amendment could not and does not include a "right to suicide," and second, that arguments attempting to separate the withdrawal of the feeding tube from Nancy
Cruzan from ordinary suicide all fail. He reasons (to me convincingly) that a right
to refuse treatment here means necessarily a right to put an end to her life.

> What I have said above is not meant to suggest that I would think it desirable, if
> we were sure that Nancy Cruzan wanted to die, to keep her alive by the means at
> issue here. I only assert that the Constitution has nothing to say about the sub-
> ject. To raise up a constitutional right here we would have to create out of
> nothing (for it exists neither in text nor tradition) some constitutional principle
> whereby, although the State may insist that an individual come in out of the cold
> and eat food, it may not insist that he take medicine; and although it may pump
> his stomach empty of poison he has ingested, it may not fill his stomach with
> food he has failed to ingest. (p. 2863)

Yet paradoxically, Justice Scalia's powerful argument, which identifies the
refusal of food and water as suicide, may come back to haunt us, especially when
conjoined with Justice O'Connor's insistence that such right of refusal is already
constitutionally protected. For should Justice O'Connor's view prevail, Justice
Scalia's powerful intellect will have provided the reasons for regarding the newly
protected right as indeed a right to die. The elements are all in place for inventing
a constitutional right to suicide and, in the case of competents, for assistance with
suicide, that is, a right to die. Justice Scalia's worry is not misplaced:

> I am concerned, from the tenor of today's opinions, that we are poised to confuse
> that enterprise [legislating with regard to end-of-life decisions] as successfully as
> we have confused the enterprise of legislating concerning abortion. (p. 2859)

Almost no one seems to have noticed a painful irony in this proceeding[14] The
Fourteenth Amendment prohibits the states from depriving persons not only of
liberty but also of life and property, without due process of law. A so-called
vitalist state, like Missouri, has at least for now been vindicated in its efforts to protect an incompetent person's life against those who assert the superiority of his
"liberty interest" to elect death by starvation. But no thought seems to have been
given to the conduct of the so-called nonvitalist states, like New Jersey, that go the
other way and give the benefit of incompetency to death—all in the name of liberty. In abandoning those vulnerable persons whom others insist have lives no
longer worth living, these states come much closer to violating the strict letter of
the Fourteenth Amendment's insistence that the state not take life than does Missouri in allegedly thwarting Cruzan's liberty to elect death.

The Tragic Meaning of "Right to Die"

The claim of a "right to die," asserted especially against physicians bent on prolonging life, clearly exposes certain deep difficulties in the foundations of modern society. Modern liberal, technological society rests especially upon two philosophical pillars raised first in the seventeenth century, at the beginning of the modern era: the preeminence of the human individual, embodied in the doctrine of natural rights as espoused first by Hobbes and Locke; and the idea of mastery of nature, attained through a radically new science of nature as proposed by Francis Bacon and René Descartes.

Both ideas were responses to the perceived partial inhospitality of nature to human need. Both encouraged man's opposition to nature, the first through the flight from the state of nature into civil society for the purpose of safeguarding the precarious rights to life and liberty; the second through the subduing of nature for the purpose of making life longer, healthier, and more commodious. One might even say that it is especially an opposition to death that grounds these twin responses. Politically, the fear of violent death at the hands of warring men requires law and legitimate authority to secure natural rights, especially life. Technologically, the fear of death as such at the hands of unfriendly nature inspires a bolder approach, namely, a scientific medicine to wage war against disease and even against death itself, ultimately with a promise of bodily immortality.

Drunk on its political and scientific successes, modern thought and practice have abandoned the modest and moderate beginnings of political modernity. In civil society the natural rights of self-preservation, secured through active but moderate self-assertion, have given way to the nonnatural rights of self-creation and self-expression; the new rights have no connection to nature or to reason, but appear as the rights of the untrammeled will. The "self" that here asserts itself is not a natural self, with the predictable interests given it by a universal human nature with its bodily needs, but a uniquely individuated and self-made self. Its authentic selfhood is demonstrated by its ability to say no to the needs of the body, the rules of society, and the dictates of reason. For such a self, self-negation through suicide and the right to die can be the ultimate form of self-assertion.

In medical science, the unlimited battle against death has found nature unwilling to roll over and play dead. The successes of medicine so far are partial at best and the victory incomplete, to say the least. The welcome triumphs against disease have been purchased at the price of the medicalized dehumanization of the end of life: to put it starkly, once we lick cancer and stroke, we can all live long enough to get Alzheimer's disease. And if the insurance holds out, we can die in the intensive care unit, suitably incubated. Fear of the very medical power we engaged to do battle against death now leads us to demand that it give us poison.

Finally, both the triumph of individualism and our reliance on technology (not only in medicine) and on government to satisfy our new wants-demanded-as-rights have weakened our more natural human associations—especially the family, on which we all need to rely when our pretense to autonomy and mastery is eventually exposed by unavoidable decline. Old age and death have been taken out of the bosom of family life and turned over to state-supported nursing homes and hospitals. Not the clergyman but the doctor (in truth, the nurse) presides over the end of life, in sterile surroundings that make no concessions to our finitude. Both the autonomous will and the will's partner in pride, the death-denying doctor, ignore the unavoidable limits on will and technique that nature insists on. Failure to recognize these limits now threatens the entire venture, for rebellion against the project through a "right to die" will only radicalize its difficulties. Vulnerable life will no longer be protected by the state, medicine will become a death-dealing profession, and isolated individuals will be technically dispatched to avoid the troubles of finding human ways to keep company with them in their time of ultimate need.

That the right to die should today be asserted to win release from a hyperpowerful medical futility is thus more than tragic irony: it is also very dangerous. Three dangers especially stand out.

First, the right to die, especially as it comes to embrace a right to "aid-in-dying," or assisted suicide, or euthanasia, will translate into an obligation on the part of others to kill or help kill. Even if we refuse to impose such a duty but merely allow those to practice it who are freely willing, our society would be drastically altered. For unless the state accepts the job of euthanizer, which God forbid that it should, it would thus surrender its monopoly on the legal use of lethal force, a monopoly it holds and needs if it is to protect innocent life, its first responsibility.

Second, there can be no way to confine the practice to those who knowingly and freely request death. The vast majority of persons who are candidates for assisted death are, and will increasingly be, incapable of choosing and effecting such a course of action for themselves. No one with an expensive or troublesome infirmity will be safe from the pressure to have his right to die exercised.

Third, the medical profession's devotion to healing and refusal to kill—its ethical center—will be permanently destroyed, and with it, patient trust and physicianly self-restraint. Here is yet another case where acceding to a putative personal right would wreak havoc on the common good.

Nothing I have said should be taken to mean that I believe life should be extended under all circumstances and at all costs. Far from it. I continue, with fear and trembling, to defend the practice of allowing to die while opposing the practice of deliberately killing—despite the blurring of this morally bright line implicit in the artificial food and water cases, and despite the slide toward the retailing of death that continues on the sled of a right to refuse treatment. I welcome efforts to give patients as much choice as possible in how they are to live out the end of their lives. I continue to applaud those courageous patients and family members and those conscientious physicians who try prudently to discern, in each case, just what form of treatment or nontreatment is truly good for the patient, even if it embraces an increased likelihood of death. But I continue to insist that we cannot serve the patient's good by deliberately eliminating the patient. And if we have no right to do this to another, we have no right to have others do this to ourselves. There is, when all is said and done, no defensible right to die.

Notes

1. For my "generosity" to succeed, I would, of course, have to commit suicide without assistance and without anyone's discovering it—i.e., well before I were demented. I would not want my children to believe that I suspected them of being incapable of loving me through my inevitable decline. There is another still more powerful reason for resisting this temptation: is it not unreasonably paternalistic of me to try to order the world so as to free my children from the usual intergenerational experiences, ties, obligations, and burdens? What principle of family life am I enacting and endorsing with my "altruistic suicide"?

2. Here is a recent example from a professor of sociology who objected to my condemnation of Derek Humphry's *Final Exit*:

> Is Mr. Kass absolutely opposed to suicide? Would he have dissuaded Hitler? Would he disapprove of suicide by Pol Pot? ... If we would welcome suicide by certain figures on limited occasions, should we prolong the lives of people who lived useless, degrading or dehumanized lives; who inflicted these indignities upon others; or who led vital lives but were reduced to uselessness and degradation by incurable disease? (*Commentary*, May 1992, p. 12).

3. Harvey C. Mansfield Jr., "The Old Rights and the New: Responsibility vs. Self-Expression," in *Old Rights and New*, ed. Robert A. Licht (Washington, D.C.: American Enterprise Institute, 1993).

4. Hans Jonas, "The Right to Die," *Hastings Center Report* 8, no. 4 (1978): 31–36, at 31.

5. John Locke, *Second Treatise on Civil Government*, ch. 2, "Of the State of Nature," para. 6.

6. Locke, *Second Treatise*, ch. 5, "Of Property," para. 27. Emphasis added.

7. Later, in discussing the extent of legislative power, Locke denies to the legislative, though it be the supreme power in every commonwealth, arbitrary power over the individual and, in particular, power to destroy his life. "For nobody can transfer to another more power than he has in himself; and nobody has an absolute arbitrary power over himself, or over any other to destroy his own life, or take away the life or property of another." *Second Treatise*, ch. 9, "Of the Extent of the Legislative Power," para. 135. Because the state's power derives from the people's power, the person's lack of arbitrary power over himself is the ground for restricting the state's power to kill him.

8. See, for example, Rousseau, *Discourse on the Origin and Foundations of Inequality among Men*, note 9, especially paragraphs four and five.

9. Immanuel Kant, *The Metaphysical Principles of Virtue*, trans. James Ellington (Indianapolis: Bobbs-Merrill, 1964), pp. 83–84. My purpose in citing Kant here is not to defend Kantian morality—and I am not myself a Kantian—but simply to show that the thinker who thought most deeply about rights in relation to *reason* and *autonomy* would have found the idea of a "right to die" utterly indefensible on these grounds.

10. The attempt to ground a right to die in the so-called right to privacy fails for the same reasons. A right to make independent judgments regarding one's body in one's private sphere, free of governmental interference, cannot be the basis of the right of someone else, appointed by or protected by government, to put an end to one's bodily life.

11. Mansfield, "The Old Rights and the New." This permanent instability of "the self" defeats the main benefit of a rights-based politics, which knows how to respect individual rights precisely because they are understood to be rooted in a common human nature, with reliable common interests, both natural and rational. The self-determining self,

because it is variable, also turns out to be an embarrassment for attempts to respect prior acts of self-determination, as in the case of living wills. For if the "self" is truly constantly being re-created, there is no reason to honor today "its" prescriptions of yesterday; for the two selves are not the same.

12. 110 S. Ct. 2841 (1990).

13. Justice William Brennan, in his dissenting opinion, denies that the state has even a legitimate interest in—much less a duty toward—someone's life that could ever outweigh the person's choice to avoid medical treatment. And in the presence of a patient who can no longer choose for herself, the state has an interest *only* in trying to determine as accurately as possible "how she would exercise her rights under these circumstances.... *[U]ntil* Nancy's wishes have been determined, the only [!] state interest that may be asserted is an interest in safeguarding the accuracy of that determination." (This is, by the way, a seemingly impossible task, given the view of the self that is implicit in Justice Brennan's reasoning.) Not the security of the life but the self-assertion of the self-determining will is, for Justice Brennan, the primary interest of the state. We see here how Nietzschean thinking threatens to replace classical American liberalism, even in constitutional interpretation.

14. A notable exception is Yale Kamisar, professor of law at the University of Michigan Law School. In my view, Kamisar is our finest legal commentator on this subject. See his "When Is There a Constitutional 'Right to Die'? When Is There No Constitutional 'Right to Live'?" *Georgia Law Review* 25 (1991): 1203–42.

26

Suicide and Rights
Margaret Pabst Battin

C laims that suicide is wrong because life is of intrinsic value, or because suicide harms others, or because permissible attitudes toward suicide may lead to coercion and abuse, are opposed by the view that a person nevertheless has the *right* to end his or her life if he or she so chooses, and that this right overrides other objections to suicide. Furthermore, the person's right to suicide precludes paternalistic intervention if that would impede the exercise of this right. In this chapter we shall consider the philosophical view that suicide is a matter of right.

There are two things that we should notice about this view. First, to say that the right to suicide overrides other objections to suicide does not show these objections to be erroneous or unfounded. For instance, to say that the right to suicide overrides the inherent value of human life is not to say that human life is not of value—it may be of great value, great enough so that one person may not destroy *another's* life; it may be only to say that the value of human life is not so great that one may not bring one's own life to an end. Similarly, to say that the right to suicide overrides objections that may be made on grounds of harms to others is not to say that such harms do not occur or should not be noticed. And to say that the right to suicide overrides the risk of abuse and manipulation is not to say that these risks are not real but only that we ought not compromise the choices of some individuals in order to protect others.

Second, under the more common versions of the view that suicide is a right, it is said to be a right held by all persons. Many ethical theorists, even of nonlibertarian stripe, grant that persons whose lives are hopelessly blighted by intolerable, incurable illness or pain have a right to end their lives; under the view to be

From *Ethical Issues in Suicide* by Margaret Pabst Battin, © 1995. Reprinted by permission of Prentice-Hall, Inc., Upper Saddle River, N.J. This is an abridged version of the original chapter.

explored here, however, *all* persons have this right—even those who are young, healthy, and prospering—though of course persons whose lives are blighted may be much more likely to choose to exercise this right.

First, however, we must consider whether there is such a right.

Suicide as a Right

The claim that suicide is a right is hardly new. Schopenhauer, for instance, although he held that suicide is always metaphysically foolish, asserts that a person nevertheless has a right to end his or her life: "...it is quite obvious that there is nothing in the world to which every man has a more unassailable title than to his own life and person."[1] Indeed although the terminology of rights is of much later usage, and the notion that women are holders of rights is later still, the notion that an individual is entitled to end his life if he chooses is already at work in a great many classical Greek and Roman sources. In a metaphor used by several Stoic writers, Cicero says:

> An actor need not remain on the stage until the very end of the play; if he wins applause in those acts in which he appears, he will have done well enough. In life, too, a man can perform his part wisely without staying on the stage until the play is finished.[2]

Josephus's Eleazar speaks of suicide as a "privilege";[3] so does Seneca, who holds that a person may exercise this privilege "as soon as Fortune seems to be playing him false."[4] Although the Stoics condemn frivolous suicide, they do in general hold that a man has a right to end his life if its disadvantages outweigh its advantages. They also hold that the right to determine the precise circumstances and style of one's own death is among one's most fundamental rights, least easily overridden by the claims of others. Seneca says, "Every man ought to make his life acceptable to others besides himself, but his death to himself alone. The best form of death is the one we like."[5]

The most forceful assertions that suicide is a right occur after the many centuries of the medieval Church's strict opposition to suicide; of particularly strong impact was Rousseau's novel *Heloise* (1761), where Saint-Preux asserts that to rid oneself of the "misery of life" is "the most simple of nature's rights of which no man of sense yet ever entertained a doubt."[6] Among the Romantic thinkers and the philosophers influenced by them, suicide in any circumstances is seen as an ultimate human right. Nietzsche is representative in insisting: "Suicide is man's right and privilege."[7]

But when we interpret suicide as a right, the strategy changes. Here one begins by assuming suicide to be (at least) a prima facie right, but then considers circumstances in which this initial right may be overriden. This tactic might succeed in religious argumentation: One could assume that human beings have a right to end their lives (in virtue, say, of their responsibilities for self-determination under the

doctrine of free will), but that God's edicts override this right by prohibiting suicide in all but certain (rare) kinds of cases. Or, to use a similar strategy in reinter-
preting the Aristotelian point, we might assume that all persons have a right to end
their lives, but that for those persons whose deaths would constitute an injury to the
state this right is overridden. In fact this latter kind of analysis is sometimes used in
contemporary discussions of the morality of suicide, even when the right to suicide is said to be overridden for almost everyone. In these analyses emphasis is typically placed on the injury that exercising one's right to suicide would cause to
other individuals and to society: This is the basis for overriding that right after all.
Thus to grant that persons have a right to suicide is not to say that they may kill
themselves whenever they wish; one can advocate a rights-based analysis of suicide
and yet hold that this right, unlike most other rights, is one that is almost always
overridden. Before we can consider the implications of construing suicide as a
right, however, we must first discover whether such a notion is intelligible at all.

We can distinguish several different ways in which the claim that suicide is a
right might be understood. According to one, which is widespread in popular culture, the right to suicide is understood as a kind of property right; this view is
based on a conception of one's own life as belonging to oneself, rather than, say,
to the state or to God. The second view, perhaps equally widespread, sees suicide
as a right in virtue of one's general freedom to act as one wishes, provided only
that one does not thereby harm others or violate moral rules. Third, in an interesting but needless to say controversial view, one may treat suicide as a *natural*
right, one among the fundamental liberties of humankind. In all these views an
individual has the right to end his or her life provided there are no overriding considerations; what is of interest, then, are the circumstances in which rights of these
sorts are overrideable by other claims.

"It's My Life": The Argument from Private Ownership

A frequent theme in a number of historical eras is the notion that a person's life is
"his own" or "her own"; this supports the argument that the individual may therefore do as he or she wishes with that life, even if that means ending it in suicide.
In the classical literature this notion has been understood on the model of
freedom from slavery; indeed, for the Stoics, the possibility of suicide is proof that
one is not a slave.[8] Enlightenment and eighteenth-century thinkers, in contrast,
interpret this notion as supporting a counterargument to the medieval religious
claim that suicide is wrong because man's life belongs to God. As H. J. McClosky
puts it, the argument for a right to suicide is Locke's traditional view, that man is
the property of God, "turned on its head":

> . . . it is akin to saying that the man who is a decider, a chooser who has a will of
> his own possesses himself, is his own "property," and as such, has property rights
> in and to his person. His autonomy is his most precious possession, and gives him
> his property right in and to himself.[9]

Variants of the medieval antisuicide argument from divine ownership still occur in contemporary authors; the Russian emigré Berdyaev, for instance, writes:

> People who do not think [that suicide is murder] make much of the fact that a murderer takes a life which does not belong to him. Their argument turns on the proposition that since my life is my own, I can take it without committing murder in the same way that I can take my own money without being a thief. But this argument is false and superficial. My life is not solely my own, it does not belong to me absolutely, it belongs to God first. He is the absolute owner; my life also belongs to my friends, to my family, to society, and finally to the entire world which has need of me. Absolute private ownership is a false principle, generally speaking.[10]

But the argument from private ownership, denied by Berdyaev in order to argue against suicide, can also be used in its positive form to argue against suicide. For instance, a seventy-four-year-old Washington, D.C., man with Parkinson's Disease was told by his physician, after a serious suicide attempt, that if he didn't "want his life" he "might as well give it to a useful cause," and enjoined on that basis to refrain from further suicide attempts but to volunteer as a subject for potentially dangerous medical research.[11] Here the physician's underlying argument suggests that although one has the right to dispose of one's property if one wishes, one ought to give it to someone or some cause that can make further use of it, like an outgrown coat, rather than destroy it altogether.

More frequently, however, the conception of one's life as one's own is used to argue in favor of libertarian practices with respect to suicide. This argument has received extensive public exposure in recent years in Brian Clark's play *Whose Life Is It, Anyway?*[12] about a quadriplegic's determined quest for freedom from the medical measures forcing him to continue his life.

But the private-property argument is not without its conceptual difficulties. One might object that life, unlike land, money, livestock, articles of clothing or household goods, is not the kind of thing that can be *property*, for nontransferable property is not property at all. Kluge considers the following reply:

> What we own—in any full-blooded sense of that term—we can disown, give away, sell or otherwise dispose of so that it becomes the property of someone else. We cannot do this with our lives. Therefore, whatever the unique relationship this bears to us, it cannot be one of ownership.[13]

We do, perhaps metaphorically, speak of selling oneself into slavery or devoting oneself to a cause as "giving one's life" to someone else; we certainly speak of self-sacrificial heroes as having "given their lives." We speak of "trading" our lives for certain benefits, of "relinquishing" them, "discarding" them, and even of "throwing one's life away." These locutions strongly suggest an underlying metaphor of life as an item of disposable property. But, it could be argued, the analogy on which the private ownership argument for suicide is based is an unsound one, at least assuming a no-afterlife metaphysics: In ordinary property-destruction cases the owner of the property continues to exist (and be benefitted or harmed) after destroying his or her property, whereas in suicide the owner is the destroyed property. "It's *my* life," we might point out, bears a misleading grammatical resemblance to "it's *my* whistle" or "it's *my* house," since the possessor of a life will not survive the surrender of this property, but the possessor of a whistle or a house will.

There is no doubt that the notion of one's life as "one's own" is widely current in libertarian popular thinking; interestingly, it is an argument one very often hears from adolescents and young adults. Nevertheless it is not at all clear that the underlying notion of one's life as one's private property is philosophically coherent. "It's *my* life" may express an important sentiment, but not necessarily that one's life is an item among one's belongings.

The Argument from Freedom

A closer approach to the notion implicit in the sentiment "it's *my* life" can be achieved by considering suicide not as a property right, but as a right generated by one's natural freedoms. On this view one may end one's life in virtue of one's liberty to do as one chooses, provided that one's actions do not harm others or infringe on their rights and provided that there are no contravening obligations or duties. Where there are, one's right is said to be overridden.

There are three major conceptions of rights under which we might interpret the notion of a right to suicide: the Hobbesian notion of *liberty rights*; the notion of *noninterference rights*; and what is sometimes referred to as the notion of *welfare rights*. I will call them all "simple" rights, as distinguished from the natural rights we will consider later. In the first of these conceptions, to say that a person has a right to do something means that he or she has no obligation not to do it: If Jones has a right to visit a fortune-teller, then Jones has no obligation or duty not to visit a fortune-teller, although there may be other good reasons (e.g., prudence) for her not to do so. In the second basic conception of rights, to have a right means not only that the person has no obligation not to do the act, but that other persons have corresponding obligations not to interfere. If Smith has a right to sail to Bermuda, then you and I have no right to prevent him from getting into his boat. The third conception of rights incorporates the previous two, but imposes still stronger claims: It involves positive provisos that others, at least where they can do so without serious risk to themselves and without violating other moral canons, are to assist in the exercise of that right. If Brown has been captured by robbers and lashed to a tree, her right to freedom from unlawful restraint, if it is a welfare right, obliges us to release her, if we can do so without risking capture ourselves and without violating other moral rules. To say that we have a *right* to suicide, then, might be to say any one of these things: That a person has no obligation not to kill herself (as she might, for instance, if she has dependent children), that other persons have no basis for interference in any attempt she may make at suicide (and thus that suicide-prevention social and police services, if legitimate at all, require special justification), or that other persons (though not necessarily any specific persons) have an obligation not only not to interfere but to assist her in killing herself, if that should be her choice.

Of contemporary authors who treat suicide as a right at all, most take it as a liberty right, though some take it as a right that imposes claims upon others. What presents continuing philosophical problems is the matter of determining when, and under what circumstances, the right to suicide can be overridden. The psychiatrist Jerome Motto, for instance, asserts

> From a psychiatric point of view, the question as to whether a person has the right to cope with the pain in his world by killing himself can be answered without hesitation. He does have that right.... The problem we struggle with is not whether the individual has the right to suicide; rather, we have a two-fold dilemma stemming from the fact that he does have it. Firstly, what is the extent to which the exercise of that right should be subject to limitations? Secondly, when the right is exercised, how can we eliminate the social stigma now attached to it?[14]

Bioethicists Lebacqz and Engelhardt argue that

> Since arguments in principle against suicide do not succeed, there is a prima facie right to kill oneself. The question of suicide thus becomes a question of distributive justice—of balancing this right against the legitimate claims of others.[15]

Some simple rights are fairly easily overridden—my prima facie right to pick my nose, say, is quickly overridden by the sensibilities of the other diners at the table; other simple rights are not—my right to plant a vegetable garden is not overridden by my neighbor's preference for looking at flowers. Of course arbitrating the way in which duties, obligations, and the consequences of actions override rights of various sorts is the stuff of ordinary moral life, and while some cases are easy, others are not. But they may be particularly difficult with respect to suicide. Is an eighteen-year-old girl's prima facie right to suicide overridden by the devastating consequences her death would have for her parents, and by their fundamental interest in watching her grow? Perhaps so. Is an eighty-one-year-old woman's right to suicide instead of death by terminal cancer overridden by her adult children's conservative religious convictions? Perhaps not. But these cases raise one of the central problems posed by treating suicide as a right: What conditions or circumstances, exactly, would override this right?

Nor is this the only sort of problem posed by treating suicide as a right. A second major issue concerns claims for noninterference and assistance on the part of others. Suppose, for instance, that Jones has a right to suicide, and that her right is not overridden by any other considerations. Does this entail that Smith has an obligation to stay out of Jones's way as she ends her life? More strongly, might Smith have an obligation to help Jones do the deed? In some relatively simple cases, we may be able to posit successful answers to questions such as these, but this is far from producing a coherent and complete set of principles governing overridings and obligations on the part of others. This is not to say that the notion of suicide as a right is not a philosophically useful one, but that if we choose to use it, a good part of the philosophical work still remains to be done.

However, there are several pitfalls in treating suicide as a right. First and most important, to treat suicide as a right which can be overridden by other duties and obligations to other persons may provide unequal treatment for individuals whose grounds for suicide are the same, but who differ in their surrounding circumstances or their relationships to others. Of two persons afflicted with an identical terminal illness, for instance, one might have a right to suicide while the other's right is overridden, if one is free from family relationships and the other is not, even though the reasons for the suicide might be the same. Second, to treat suicide as a right may grant equal license to those whose reasons for suicide are not equally good. If suicide is a right overrideable primarily on the basis of duties and obligations to others, two potential suicides whose interpersonal relationships and commitments to others are similar may have the same right, or lack thereof, to kill themselves, even though they have vastly different reasons for doing so. Furthermore, the person who chooses suicide on rational grounds and the person whose reasons are superficial or pathological might seem not only to have equal rights to end their lives, but equal claims to noninterference or assistance in doing so. Third, to treat suicide as a right, regardless of which model of rights we accept, may seem to impose obligations on others in a uniform way regardless of their own individual characteristics and sensitivities. If suicide is conceived of as a liberty right, no person, however close, would be said to have an obligation to intervene or to assist. If suicide is understood as a welfare right, then other persons generally might be said to have an obligation to help the individual to his or her end.

No doubt these pitfalls could be avoided with a complex system of rights, overridings, and obligations, which would not give such simplistic results. But as a complex system is developed, it will begin to take more substantial account of the grounds upon which rights, overridings, and obligations with respect to suicide might be based. Developing a complex system would indeed reveal the real deficiency of the views of suicide as a right that we have considered so far: They do nothing to identify the grounds upon which such a right is based. If suicide is a right simply as a function of one's freedom to do as one chooses, then it will be very difficult to show why, in any case in which others are at all adversely affected, the right to suicide is not always almost immediately overridden, and how it could ever impose claims for assistance upon others. Suicide might be a right, but only a right as substantial as the right to pick one's nose: something you may do just if nobody minds. But if a "right" to suicide is only this strong, we have somehow not done justice to those traditional assertions with which we began. Clearly something much stronger is meant.

There is still another problem with the view that suicide is a simple right. As James Bogen points out, an account of suicide in terms of rights, duties, and obligations may not really answer the moral questions in suicide: It may tell us what we are allowed to do, but not what we *ought* to do.[16] To establish that I have a right to suicide does not establish that my committing suicide is a good or bad thing to do, any more than establishing that I have a right to vote for a certain candidate establishes that that is a good way to cast my vote.

However, there is still another way of treating suicide as a right, which may overcome these problems to some extent: It is to consider suicide as a *natural* right. This may bring with it some preliminary answer to the question of how readily a right to suicide can be overridden, and, further, some indication—however tentative—of when suicide may be a good thing to do. After all, the kinds of things to which we believe we have *natural* rights are things we believe are important to have and, on the whole, are good to do.

Suicide as a Natural Right

Thus a third way in which we might understand the claim that suicide is a right is to group suicide among the fundamental or natural rights of humankind. These more basic rights, as distinct from the simple rights we have been considering in the previous sections, are rights of the sort identified in the classical manifestoes: the American Constitution and its Bill of Rights, the French Declaration of the Rights of Man, the Communist Manifesto, and the 1948 U.N. Declaration of Human Rights, among others. The rights listed, of course, vary from one manifesto to another, variously including rights to life, liberty, ownership of property; freedom of assembly, speech, and worship; rights to education, employment, political representation and medical care. However, although the manifestoes vary considerably in their contents, the conception underlying them is similar: They declare that certain universal, general, fundamental rights are held by individuals in virtue of their being human. Although in practice violations do occur, at least in theory natural rights cannot be easily overridden, and then only for some compelling reason of the public interest.

Could suicide be a *natural* right? This would place it on a par with the rights to life, liberty, freedom of speech and worship, political representation, and the pursuit of happiness, equally deserving of protection where this right threatens to be abridged. It would demand recognition in law, custom, medicine, and religion, as another pillar of an enlightened, moral society. The right to die when and how one wishes, and for reasons of one's own choosing, would be as basic as the right to live.

Two principal problems are encountered with this way of construing the right to suicide. First, there is no precedent for the claim; in particular, none of the great human-rights manifestoes mentions any right to suicide. Recent legislation in most U.S. states does establish a so-called right to die; however, use of this latter expression is restricted to medical situations that involve only the withholding of heroic means of prolonging the lives of those already terminally ill. The right to die, as it is used in this legislation, is the right only not to have one's dying prolonged; it is not interpreted as the right to end an otherwise continuing life. Thus, that there is, in these jurisdictions, a legal right to die by refusing treatment in terminal illness does not establish that there is a larger right to suicide. Of course that a right to suicide is not mentioned in any of the major manifestoes, or in legislation, does not show that there is no such right; it can perhaps be established on other independent grounds.

A second principal objection to construing suicide as a natural right is that this view cannot take adequate account of the pathology involved in most actual suicide cases. It can hardly be disputed that there is pathology involved in much— or perhaps even most—suicide that is reported and studied today. But this does not disprove the existence of such a right: it may mean only that the exercise of this right will often be subject to paternalistic constraints of the sort we have previously discussed. After all, we regularly countenance the abridgement of other natural rights in nonnormal or pathological circumstances, as for instance when we limit the liberty, freedom of speech, right of association, and even the pursuit of happiness among the criminal and mentally ill.

These two objections aside, we may wonder what positive evidence there is for the existence of such a right. To base it on the larger right of autonomy or self-determination may be merely to treat it as a simple right, a position that in the end might prove quite weak. Alternatively the right to end one's life might be said to be self-evident: A natural, fundamental right that cannot and need not be derived from other rights, interests, or duties. Or, it may be based on a larger, positive right; this is the view advanced by Rousseau's Saint-Preux, who finds it rooted in the general fundamental right to pursue one's own good.

> The more I reflect, the more I am convinced that the question may be reduced to this fundamental proposition: Every man has a right by nature to pursue what he thinks good, and avoid what he thinks evil, in all respects which are not injurious to others. When our life, therefore, becomes a misery to ourselves, and is of advantage to no one, we are at liberty to put an end to our being. If there is any such thing as a clear and self-evident principle, certainly this is one.[17]

But while Rousseau's text, like that of many other thinkers, asserts the self-evidence of the right to suicide, other thinkers just as strongly assert the self-evidence of the contrary principle: that suicide is forbidden. Pursuing this line of thought, Wittgenstein writes

> If suicide is allowed then everything is allowed. If anything is not allowed then suicide is not allowed. This throws a light on the nature of ethics, for suicide is, so to speak, the elementary sin.[18]

What is extraordinary about the issue of suicide is the self-certainty with which both sides are argued: the one, that suicide is an individual's natural right; the other, not only that it is not a natural right, but is strictly forbidden. Furthermore, the thinkers on both sides appeal to the self-evidence of their positions. Yet, since the right in question is said to be self-evident, further justification of it presumably cannot be given—in much the same way that further justification was said to be superfluous for the fundamental principle of the value of life. Consequently, if conflicting principles are urged as self-evident, it may appear that this dispute cannot be resolved. Let us look, however, at the kinds of arguments put forward by those concerned with the right to end one's life.

The Right to Suicide and the Right to Life

But perhaps suicide is incompatible with the natural or fundamental right to life; if so, this would suggest that a right to suicide cannot also be a natural right, and is perhaps not a right at all. This issue is addressed by various thinkers, including Joel Feinberg[19] and Antony Flew.[20] Feinberg points out that the Jeffersonian tradition in political theory, embodied in such documents as the U.S. Bill of Rights, describes the right to life not only as universal but also as *inalienable*; that is, it cannot be abrogated by any individual or institution, presumably including oneself. But if one cannot surrender or waive one's right to life, then, it may seem, one does not have a right to end one's life. This argument suggests, Feinberg observes, that there is no such thing as a right to suicide.

However, Feinberg also observes although the right to life is inalienable, there is attached to this right no requirement that it be exercised.[21] If, setting aside for the moment the right to life, we inspect the list of other rights that, under our prevailing assumption of the natural-rights framework, are "generally held to be natural rights—liberty, property, fraternity, the pursuit of happiness, freedom of worship, free speech—it will be apparent that in no case, except perhaps liberty, is it suggested that an individual is *required* to exercise the right. The right to worship is a natural right, let us say, but does not preclude not worshipping at all. The right to property does not require one to own anything; one can elect poverty if one wishes. In other words, a right is something neither necessary nor obligatory, but optional; it is what one may do if one chooses. If the right to life is a natural right, then it guarantees an individual the right to live if he or she chooses, but does not obligate or compel him or her to do so. Another way to put this is to say that the natural right to life, along with other natural rights like liberty, free association, and freedom of worship, are *rights* only, not duties: There is no duty to worship, to associate with one's fellows, or to speak freely, and there is no *duty* to live.

However, this invites the reply that a distinction is to be made between natural rights that are discretionary, such as free speech, and those that are mandatory, like liberty, education, and, for Hegelians, the right to punishment. Children have a right to education, this position claims, but attendance at school is not simply a matter of their or their parents' discretion; it is required. Man has a natural right to liberty, Mill argued, but even where abridgement of liberty is self-respecting only, as in selling oneself into slavery, an individual has no right to preclude his or her own freedom.[22] Similarly one could argue that the right to life is a natural right, but unlike discretionary rights such as free speech, free assembly, or freedom of worship, it must be exercised: One has a duty to remain alive.

But the case for the existence of mandatory *rights* (to be distinguished from generally recognized duties) is weak. This is because one can always claim that the exercise of certain rights is required only to prevent abuses of them; these rights are not in themselves duties. For instance, although compulsory school attendance may make it appear that the right to education is mandatory, compulsory attendance policies may not in fact reflect any moral obligation on the part of children to attend school, but serve to prevent infringements on children's rights to attend school, both by virtue of the children's own immature judgment, and coercion by adults who would prefer to use children's labor or companionship for their own ends. The argument that the right to life is mandatory, similarly, can always be countered by the claim that exercise of this right is essential to guarantee it for all. If some people were to fail to exercise their right to life and choose instead to die, so this argument goes, the possibilities of coercion and abuse toward others would become enormous. Thus the fact that we insist that people stay alive does not show that they have no right to end their lives, but only that we regard the consequences of allowing them to exercise their right to do so as potentially disastrous for others. Indeed this might be regarded as an example of a natural right routinely overridden to serve some compelling reason of the public interest.

We should also point out that the individual who chooses to die does not lose his or her *right* to life. To commit suicide is not to abridge one's right to life; it is to abridge one's life. Similarly, though slaves no longer have freedom, they have a right to freedom, albeit often unrecognized by the societies within which they live. Refusal to worship, own property, vote, or speak freely does not abridge one's rights to do these things, and it would be misleading to speak of persons who refuse as having waived, abrogated, relinquished, or surrendered their rights to do them. A person may, of course, lose some or perhaps all of his rights. But this does not occur through nonexercise of them, but rather through some other circumstances, such as by contract or as a consequence of misdeed: One may lose one's right to financial independence by becoming married or, as proponents of capital punishment claim, one's right to life by committing murder. Thus refusal to exercise one's right to life by committing suicide does not entail that one loses that right. If this is so, a right to kill oneself may be compatible even with the *inalienable* right to life.

Perhaps the analogy between the right to life and other inalienable natural rights is weak, since failure to exercise it at one time precludes any further enjoyment of it: Effective suicide prevents any opportunity for future exercise of the right to life. But effective suicide does not terminate one's right to life; if an individual who had committed suicide were to become alive again, we would be unlikely to say that she no longer had any right to live. Of course earlier historical periods have not seen the matter quite this way; suicide was a felony offense in most of late medieval and early modern Europe, and those whose suicide attempts were ineffective could be put to death as a penalty.[23] The contemporary suicide attempter, on the other hand, is with very few exceptions no longer subject to criminal penalties, but is resuscitated and encouraged to live.

The Basis of a Natural Right to Suicide

That the natural right to life need not be exercised does not entail, however, that suicide is a natural right; this must be independently established. But to justify the natural or fundamental rights is a notoriously difficult and disputatious task. As we've noted the principal manifestoes do not agree even on the less contentious items, and argumentation among philosophers about the foundations of natural rights are unending. Nevertheless, I think we can sketch the outlines of a defense of suicide as a natural right.

One might assume, as I have proposed elsewhere, an account of fundamental or natural rights as grounded in human dignity.[24] This view considers persons to have natural or fundamental rights to do or have certain sorts of things just because things of that sort tend to promote human dignity. Perhaps this notion of dignity is vague, but it is also, as Ronald Dworkin puts it, "powerful,"[25] and we can intuitively grasp the way in which such things as liberty, freedom of speech, education, freedom of association, and other basic rights tend on the whole to promote human dignity. On the other hand we do not have natural rights to things like alcoholism, because alcoholism on the whole does not promote human dignity, even though we may be free (i.e., have a simple right) to become alcoholic if we wish, provided it harms no one and contravenes no other obligation. This sort of view, and I think it is a plausible one, would suggest that suicide is in fact a matter of natural right because it tends, on the whole, to promote human dignity.[26]

This assertion may seem to fly in the face of the most evident fact. Clearly, suicide as we know it does *not* tend on the whole to promote human dignity; it is a dismal, pathetic affair. Consider, for instance, the ubiquitous "get-even" suicides, consciously or subconsciously intended to produce guilt, remorse, or injury to another person; obviously, suicide of this sort displays human nature at its least sublime. Or, again, consider the suicide of isolation: the elderly man, living alone in a shabby rented room, without family, without friends, without social contacts of any real kind. To claim that suicide is a natural right because it tends on the whole to promote human dignity clearly misdescribes these cases, and encourages us to overlook the very real tragedies that are played out here.

But as we've said earlier and ought to repeat often, the fact that suicide in this culture is very strongly associated with depression, disturbance, or mental illness does not prove that the connection is necessary, or that a person must be mentally ill to consider such a thing. Were it not for the cultural taboo and the inherited notions of suicide as crime and as sin, suicide might indeed be much more common and accepted than it now is. [Some think] that suicide might be a boon to those afflicted by terminal illness or old age; [others speculate] that it could become the *preferred* way of death. In such worlds the pathological cases we now see would represent only a tiny, aberrant fraction of the whole.

But can *suicide* in fact promote human dignity, as would have to be the case to consider suicide a natural right? This question, central to the issue of whether suicide can be considered a natural right, requires sustained, careful, and unbiased thought. One might begin by mentioning certain exemplary names: Cato, Socrates, Charlotte Perkins Gilman, Szmul Zygielbojm, and Captain Oates. One might attend carefully to the notion of rational suicide, and the ways in which one's values may sometimes take precedence over the continuation of one's life. One might consider whether some self-deaths could not be understood paradoxically, as a kind of "self-preservation," a kind of self-respect and protection of one's fundamental interests. "I am what I have been," suicides sometimes seem to say, "but cannot be any more." They are based, as it were, on a self-ideal: a conception of one's own value and worth, beneath which one is not willing to slip. Of course, one's self-ideal may be distorted by depression, psychosis, or other illnesses of the mind, but then again, it may be realistic, sensitive, and intact, and form at least part of the basis of the notion of human dignity with which we began. Whether the threat to one's self-ideal is from physical illness and pain, as in euthanatic suicide, or from the destruction of other persons or values upon which one's life is centrally focused, as in self-sacrificial suicide, or from a fundamental refusal to submit to the conditions of life in a degraded world, as in suicides of principle and social protest, the import is the same: One chooses death instead of further life, because further life would bring with it a compromise of that dignity without which one cannot consent to live.

But, again, what about the cases in which suicide is clearly the product of pathology, as are the majority of cases with which we are familiar today? Here the answer, as we've seen, is simple: The right to suicide, although a fundamental human right, is overridden, because the individual is not competent to exercise it in a way that might achieve its end. As we've said, we regularly countenance abridgement of other fundamental rights in cases of pathology or disturbance. For example, although we find that liberty, in general, promotes human dignity, and people can achieve full stature only if they are free, we nevertheless confine those who are criminal, incompetent by reason of very young or old age, or insane. But if we permit the abridgement of other natural human rights in circumstances like these, there is no reason why we should not permit the abridgement of the right to suicide in certain circumstances too. These abridgements might curtail suicide among the depressed or temporarily disturbed, while permitting it, for instance, among the terminally ill.

Let us recall David Wood's example of the suicide of the architect who pioneered high-rise apartment buildings and has regretted what he has done.[27] Is this a suicide of dignity, and so one to which he has a fundamental right? Or is it a suicide like most of those with which we are empirically familiar, the product of a disturbed, irrational mind? We can imagine the case either way: as the final, desperate act of self-loathing, occurring as the confused climax of long years of self-reproach; but we can also imagine it as a considered courageous statement of principle, a dignified final act transcending one's own defeat. If it is the former, we can imagine reminding the man that he has obligations to his family, his friends, his gods, and himself, and doing what we can to prevent the act. But if it is the latter, such objections seem petty, and the interference perverse: We can only admire his attainment of a difficult human ideal. Can one imagine telling Cato that he ought not kill himself because his accounts are incomplete or because it would disrupt the activities of his slaves? We admire acts of dignity in other realms, but sometimes forget that they can—though perhaps not often—occur in suicide too.

Of course to claim that a person has a right to end his or her life because to do so would further human dignity is not to claim that that person may not also have duties to live, and/or duties that presuppose living. Socrates weighed his choice of death against his duties to his two small sons and reaffirmed his choice; St. Paul weighed his duties to the Church against his desire to see Christ, and stayed alive. Many of the duties generated by human relationships would seem to preclude suicide; many of the traditional arguments against suicide are attempts to argue for duties that presuppose living, and hence are thought to justify legal and cultural suicide prohibitions that assure that the duty of living is performed by all. But it is not clear how strong duties to others must be in order to override a *natural* right to suicide. Furthermore, just as some of a person's interests can be satisfied without her continuing to live, some of a person's duties can also be fulfilled despite her death (payment of debts, for example). Some duties may be overridden by various other considerations: The duty to provide conjugal companionship, for example, may be overridden by the right to avoid pain. On the other hand the right to suicide may be so strong that other duties very rarely touch it at all. If there is a *natural* right to end one's life when one chooses, one of the most substantial and crucial areas of normative ethics would become the weighing of other duties against this right.

Rights and the Role of Others

Whether suicide is a right is not merely an abstract question; crucial practical consequences depend upon it. If a given act is a matter of right, then any abridgement of that right calls for justification; exercise of it does not. For instance, any abridgement of the right to liberty calls for justification (e.g., the need for military draft in time of war), whereas any exercise of the right to liberty does not. If there is a right to end one's life when one so chooses, then justification must be provided in order to interfere with an individual's plans for suicide. This would be true whether those who interfere are help-line volunteers, police, psychiatrists, legislators formulating legal sanctions against suicide, insurance companies withholding death benefits to survivors of suicide,[28] health-insurance plans refusing coverage in cases of injury during an incomplete suicide attempt, or hospital, prison, military, or other institutional personnel who seek to interrupt the suicide attempts of individuals in their care. Any person or institution seeking to prevent an individual from taking his or her life would have to be able to provide good reason for doing so. This would be just as true in emergency situations as at other times.

This is not to require, of course, that a complete and explicit statement of justification be produced prior to any interference, at least in emergency situations or first-time attempts; one might advocate a policy whereby temporary intervention is permitted just in order to discover the circumstances of the case. Further intervention would be appropriate in cases in which suicide is not autonomously chosen or where the individual has obligations (say, to dependent children) strong enough to override any rights; intervention would also be appropriate in cases where the evidence is inadequate. In principle, however, justification for intervention in any suicide attempt would always be required, and the individual considered free to do as he or she chooses unless such justification can be found.

As things now stand, just the reverse assumption is made. Suicide interveners do not have to justify their actions either before or after the fact, whereas persons who wish to end their lives—if they are ever permitted to do so—are in general expected to provide adequate justification for their choice. That it is not a legal wrong to prevent a suicide presupposes that suicide is not a right. The assumption is that the act of suicide requires special justification, whereas suppression of it does not. But if suicide is a right, the prospective suicide cannot be required to produce a reason for his or her actions. The only issues that remain are concerned with whether the right may be overridden for any reason.

Furthermore, a right may not only impose upon others an obligation to refrain from interference, but also one to render assistance. In a recent paper Peter Williams argues that there cannot be such a thing as a right to die (he has in mind euthanasia situations) because there is no corresponding duty on the part of others to do the killing.[29] But this is precisely the issue. If there is a right to die (which can be exercised either in euthanasia or suicide), this means that there may also be an obligation on the part of others—though it is not now legally or morally recognized—either to perform euthanasia for the individual, or to assist him or her in carrying out his or her own self-killing. If the right is a natural right, the obligations it imposes on others may be still stronger. In the most extreme example, consider the case of a quadriplegic, who because of the complete and permanent paralysis of all her limbs is unable to terminate her own life. If we agree that this person has no obligation to continue to endure her condition or, more strongly, has the right, like anyone else, to end her life if she so chooses, we must confront an additional issue: Does someone else—whether physician, family member, friend, or state official—have an obligation to administer to this person the means of death she chooses? If we acknowledge the right, we must be prepared to acknowledge a corresponding duty, and if we hold that suicide is a fundamental right, we must be prepared to ensure that the duty is met. Of course not all rights give rise to corresponding obligations on the part of others to provide means for satisfaction of that right: U.S. citizens, for example, have a right to foreign travel, but this fact does not obligate the government or any individuals to provide the means for it. On the other hand U.S. citizens also have a right to legal counsel; here, in contrast, the state does assume the obligation to provide counsel, in the form of public defenders, for those who cannot obtain it for themselves.

Thus if the right to end one's life is in fact a right, we must still settle the issue of whether it is a simple liberty right or a natural right, and whether it does or does not impose obligations on others. Most authors who recognize a right to suicide treat it as a liberty-right only, one not imposing obligations. But there are some historical precedents for treating suicide as a right that does impose obligations of assistance upon others: The Roman citizen could expect his slave to hold the sword upon which he would fall, and the Roman city at Marseilles maintained a public supply of poisons for use in suicide, to which it granted access to any citizen who could present an adequate set of reasons for suicide to the Senate.[30] Nor have such notions been confined to ancient Rome. The Sorbonne physician Binet-Sanglé called in 1919 for the establishment of public thanatoria or euthanasia parlors where the client could choose from among electrocution, poison, gases, narcotics, and a variety of other means a method of reaching an "individually styled" death.[31] Doris Portwood, on the other hand, resists what we might call this bureau-cratization of suicide but claims that aging and ill persons have a right to assis-tance in suicide from their intimates and friends.[32] Of course the existence of such practices and claims does not entail that entitlement to assistance in suicide is a matter of moral right, but they should encourage us to reexamine our beliefs and practices in this regard.

In 1961 Nobel physicist Percy Bridgman, then almost eighty years old and suf-fering from terminal cancer, shot himself. He left the following final note: "It isn't decent for society to make a man do this thing himself. Probably this is the last day I will be able to do it myself."[33] Bridgman's case may serve well to test the range of moral views on the role of others in suicide. If we adopt the traditional religious or social arguments against suicide or the stricter versions of the view that life is of value, Bridgman did himself, his family, and his society wrong. If, on the other hand, we adopt the stronger versions of the thesis that suicide is a right, society failed Bridgman in its final obligation, as Bridgman himself clearly believed. Of course the relationship between the rights of individuals and the obligations of others is a complex issue, but this is no reason to ignore Bridgman's claim.

Notes

1. Arthur Schopenhauer, "On Suicide," in *Studies in Pessimism in Complete Essays of Schopenhauer,* trans. T. Bailey Saunders (New York: Wiley Books Co., 1942), p. 25.

2. Cicero, *On Old Age,* vol. 7, "Death Has No Sting," trans. Michael Grant (Baltimore: Penguin Books, 1969), p. 241.

3. Flavius Josephus, *The Jewish War VII* 325 (London: William Heinemann, 1928), p. 597.

4. Seneca, *Letters from a Stoic* (Baltimore: Penguin Books, 1969), Letter 70, p. 63.

5. Ibid.

6. Rousseau, *Julie, or the New Heloise,* Letter 114.

7. Nietzsche, *The Dawn of Day (Morgenrote),* original edition, 1881 (Stuttgart: Kroner Verlag, 1953), p. 210.

8. See Seneca's description of the Spartan boy, Letter 70, p. 80.

9. H. J. McClosky, "The Right to Life," *Mind* 84, no. 332 (July 1975): 416–17.

10. Nicholas Berdyaev, "On Suicide," *Approach: A Literary Quarterly,* no. 43 (Spring 1962): 6–27. Reprinted from *Christianisme Social: Revue Internationale et Sociale pour un monde chrétien,* 1953. Trans. Elizabeth Bellenson and Helen Fowler, citation from p. 15.

11. Victor Hasenoehrl, private conversation.

12. Brian Clark, *Whose Life Is It, Anyway?* (New York: Dodd, Mead, 1978).

13. Eike-Henner W. Kluge, *The Practice of Death* (New Haven, Conn.: Yale University Press, 1975), p. 119.

14. "The Right to Suicide: A Psychiatrist's View," in M. Pabst Battin and David J. Mayo, eds., *Suicide: The Philosophical Issues* (New York: St. Martin's Press, 1980), p. 213.

15. Karen Lebacqz and H. Tristran Engelhardt, "Suicide," in Dennis J. Horan and David Mayo, eds., *Death, Dying, and Euthanasia* (Washington, D.C.: University Publications of America, 1977), p. 669.

16. James Bogen, "Suicide and Virtue," in Battin and Mayo, eds., *Suicide: The Philo-sophical Issues,* pp. 286–92.

17. Rousseau, *Julie, or the New Heloise,* Letter 114, p. 167.

18. Ludwig Wittgenstein, *Notebooks 1914–1916.* Trans. G. E. M. Anscombe, R. Rhees, and G. H. Von Wright (Oxford: Clarendon, 1961), p. 91e. He concludes this paragraph, however, the last entry in his notebooks of 1914 to 1916, by conjecturing "Or is even suicide in itself neither good nor evil?"

19. Joel Feinberg, "Voluntary Euthanasia and the Inalienable Right to Life," *Philosophy and Public Affairs* 7 (1978): 112.

20. Antony Flew, "The Right to Death," MSS, University of Reading.

21. Feinberg, "Voluntary Euthanasia," pp. 104ff.

22. This thesis is argued in John Stuart Mill's *On Liberty* (1859); however, Mill does not discuss suicide in this or any other text.

23. See Alvarez's quotation of a disturbing description of the hanging of a suicide attempter in London, circa 1860, in *The Savage God: A Study of Suicide* (New York: Random House, 1972), p. 43.

24. See my "Suicide: A Fundamental Human Right?" in Battin and Mayo, eds., *Suicide: The Philosophical Issues,* pp. 267–85.

25. Ronald Dworkin, *Taking Rights Seriously* (Cambridge, Mass.: Harvard University Press, 1977, 1978), p. 198. Dworkin bases his account of rights in two independent notions, the "vague but powerful idea of human dignity," and the "more familiar idea of political equality." See also his newer *Life's Dominion* (New York: Knopf, 1993), especially chapter 7.

26. This account appears to resemble Jean Baechler's defense of suicide as "an inalienable human privilege" [*Suicides* (New York: Basic Books, 1979), p. 34] based on the right to freedom, the right to happiness, and the right to dignity (p. 50). See especially his chapter 2, "The Humanity of Suicide," pp. 38–52.

27. "Suicide as Instrument and Expression," in Battin and Mayo, *Suicide: The Philosophical Issues,* pp. 151–60.

28. One justification for the two-year exclusion clauses now common in life-insurance policies might be to protect the insurers against persons who deliberately insure themselves and then commit suicide in order to have their beneficiaries collect the proceeds, but such clauses do not take account of other nonfraudulent grounds for suicide that might arise within a two-year period. It may be reasonable to expect insurance companies to protect themselves with exclusion clauses against financially motivated suicide, but perhaps not clauses based on a stipulated length of time. It is not at all clear that this sort of justification would apply in cases of health insurance.

29. Peter Williams, "Rights and the Alleged Rights of Innocents to Be Killed," *Ethics* 87 (1977): 383–94.

30. Valerius Maximus, *Memorabilia,* Book II, Chapter 6, recounts an aged woman's appearance before the magistrates to request permission to commit suicide.

31. Dr. Binet-Sanglé, *L'Art de Mourir. Défense et Technique du Suicide Secondé.* (Paris: Albin Michel, 1919). See especially Part II, Chapter II, "Choix du Procédé, euthanasique."

32. Doris Portwood, *Commonsense Suicide: The Final Right* (New York: Dodd, Mead, 1978).

33. Percy Bridgman, letter in *Bulletin of the Atomic Scientists,* quoted by Max Delbrück, "Education for Suicide," interview in *Prism,* a publication of the American Medical Association, 2 (1974), p. 20.

The Supreme Court on Physician-Assisted Suicide

DENNIS C. VACCO, ATTORNEY GENERAL OF NEW YORK, ET AL., PETITIONERS v. TIMOTHY E. QUILL ET AL.

No. 95-1858

SUPREME COURT OF THE UNITED STATES

1997 U.S. LEXIS 4038

January 8, 1997, Argued

June 26, 1997, Decided

PRIOR HISTORY: ON WRIT OF CERTIORARI TO THE UNITED STATES COURT OF APPEALS FOR THE SECOND CIRCUIT.

DISPOSITION: 80 F.3d 716, reversed.

SYLLABUS:

In New York, as in most States, it is a crime to aid another to commit or attempt suicide, but patients may refuse even lifesaving medical treatment. Respondent New York physicians assert that, although it would be consistent with the standards of their medical practices to prescribe lethal medication for mentally competent, terminally ill patients who are suffering great pain and desire a doctor's help in taking their own lives, they are deterred from doing so by New York's assisted-suicide ban. They, and three gravely ill patients who have since died, sued the State's Attorney General, claiming that the ban violates the Fourteenth Amendment's Equal Protection Clause. The Federal District Court disagreed, but the Second Circuit reversed, holding (1) that New York accords different treatment to those competent, terminally ill persons who wish to hasten their deaths by self-administering prescribed drugs than it does to those who wish to do so by directing the removal of life-support systems, and (2) that this supposed unequal treatment is not rationally related to any legitimate state interests.

Held: New York's prohibition on assisting suicide does not violate the Equal Protection Clause. Pp. 3-14.

(a) The Equal Protection Clause embodies a general rule that States must treat like cases alike but may treat unlike cases accordingly. The New York statutes outlawing assisted suicide neither infringe fundamental rights nor involve suspect classifications, and are therefore entitled to a strong presumption of validity. On their faces, neither the assisted-suicide ban nor the law permitting patients to refuse medical treatment treats anyone differently from anyone else or draws any distinctions between persons. Everyone, regardless of physical condition, is entitled, if competent, to refuse unwanted lifesaving medical treatment; no one is permitted to assist a suicide. Generally, laws that apply evenhandedly to all unquestionably comply with equal protection. This Court disagrees with the Second Circuit's submission that ending or refusing lifesaving medical treatment "is nothing more nor less than assisted suicide." The distinction between letting a patient die and making that patient die is important, logical, rational, and well established: It comports with fundamental legal principles of causation; has been recognized, at least implicitly, by this Court in *Cruzan v. Director, Mo. Dept. of Health*; and has been widely recognized and endorsed in the medical profession, the state courts, and the overwhelming majority of state legislatures, which, like New York's, have permitted the former while prohibiting the latter. The Court therefore disagrees with respondents' claim that the distinction is "arbitrary" and "irrational." The line between the two acts may not always be clear, but certainty is not required, even were it possible. Logic and contemporary practice support New York's judgment that the two acts are different, and New York may therefore, consistent with the Constitution, treat them differently.

(b) New York's reasons for recognizing and acting on the distinction between refusing treatment and assisting a suicide—including prohibiting intentional killing and preserving life; preventing suicide; maintaining physicians' role as their patients' healers; protecting vulnerable people from indifference, prejudice, and psychological and financial pressure to end their lives; and avoiding a possible slide towards euthanasia—are valid and important public interests that easily satisfy the constitutional requirement that a legislative classification bear a rational relation to some legitimate end.

JUDGES: REHNQUIST, C. J., delivered the opinion of the Court, in which O'CONNOR, SCALIA, KENNEDY, and THOMAS, JJ., joined. O'CONNOR, J., filed a concurring opinion, in which GINSBURG and BREYER, JJ., joined in part.

STEVENS, J., SOUTER, J., GINSBURG, J., and BREYER, J., filed opinions concurring in the judgment.

OPINION: CHIEF JUSTICE REHNQUIST delivered the opinion of the Court.

In New York, as in most States, it is a crime to aid another to commit or attempt suicide, but patients may refuse even lifesaving medical treatment. The question presented by this case is whether New York's prohibition on assisting suicide therefore violates the Equal Protection Clause of the Fourteenth Amendment. We hold that it does not.

The Equal Protection Clause commands that no State shall "deny to any person within its jurisdiction the equal protection of the laws." This provision creates no substantive rights. Instead, it embodies a general rule that States must treat like cases alike but may treat unlike cases accordingly. If a legislative classification or distinction "neither burdens a fundamental right nor targets a suspect class, we will uphold [it] so long as it bears a rational relation to some legitimate end."

New York's statutes outlawing assisting suicide affect and address matters of profound significance to all New Yorkers alike. They neither infringe fundamental rights nor involve suspect classifications. These laws are therefore entitled to a "strong presumption of validity."

On their faces, neither New York's ban on assisting suicide nor its statutes permitting patients to refuse medical treatment treat anyone differently than anyone else or draw any distinctions between persons. Everyone, regardless of physical condition, is entitled, if competent, to refuse unwanted lifesaving medical treatment; no one is permitted to assist a suicide. Generally speaking, laws that apply evenhandedly to all "unquestionably comply" with the Equal Protection Clause.

The Court of Appeals, however, concluded that some terminally ill people—those who are on life-support systems—are treated differently than those who are not, in that the former may "hasten death" by ending treatment, but the latter may not "hasten death" through physician-assisted suicide. This conclusion depends on the submission that ending or refusing lifesaving medical treatment "is nothing more nor less than assisted suicide." Unlike the Court of Appeals, we think the distinction between assisting suicide and withdrawing life-sustaining treatment, a distinction widely recognized and endorsed in the medical profession and in our legal traditions, is both important and logical; it is certainly rational.

The distinction comports with fundamental legal principles of causation and intent. First, when a patient refuses life-sustaining medical treatment, he dies from an underlying fatal disease or pathology; but if a patient ingests lethal medication prescribed by a physician, he is killed by that medication.

Furthermore, a physician who withdraws, or honors a patient's refusal to begin, life-sustaining medical treatment purposefully intends, or may so intend, only to respect his patient's wishes and "to cease doing useless and futile or degrading things to the patient when [the patient] no longer stands to benefit from them." The same is true when a doctor provides aggressive palliative care; in some cases, painkilling drugs may hasten a patient's death, but the physician's purpose and intent is, or may be, only to ease his patient's pain. A doctor who assists a suicide, however, "must, necessarily and indubitably, intend primarily that the patient be made dead." Similarly, a patient who commits suicide with a doctor's aid necessarily has the specific intent to end his or her own life, while a patient who refuses or discontinues treatment might not.

The law has long used actors' intent or purpose to distinguish between two acts that may have the same result. Put differently, the law distinguishes actions taken "because of" a given end from actions taken "in spite of" their unintended but foreseen consequences.

Given these general principles, it is not surprising that many courts, including New York courts, have carefully distinguished refusing life-sustaining treatment from suicide. In fact, the first state-court decision explicitly to authorize withdrawing lifesaving treatment noted the "real distinction between the self-infliction of deadly harm and a self-determination against artificial life support." And recently, the Michigan Supreme Court also rejected the argument that the distinction "between acts that artificially sustain life and acts that artificially curtail life" is merely a "distinction without constitutional significance—a meaningless exercise in semantic gymnastics," insisting that "the Cruzan majority disagreed and so do we."

Similarly, the overwhelming majority of state legislatures have drawn a clear line between assisting suicide and withdrawing or permitting the refusal of unwanted lifesaving medical treatment by prohibiting the former and permitting the latter. And "nearly all states expressly disapprove of suicide and assisted suicide either in statutes dealing with durable powers of attorney in health-care situations, or in 'living will' statutes." Thus, even as the States move to protect and promote patients' dignity at the end of life, they remain opposed to physician-assisted suicide.

New York is a case in point. The State enacted its current assisted-suicide statutes in 1965. Since then, New York has acted several times to protect patients' common-law right to refuse treatment. In so doing, however, the State has neither endorsed a general right to "hasten death" nor approved physician-assisted suicide. Quite the opposite: The State has reaffirmed the line between "killing" and "letting die." More recently, the New York State Task Force on Life and the Law studied assisted suicide and euthanasia and, in 1994, unanimously recommended against legalization. In the Task Force's view, "allowing decisions to forego life-sustaining treatment and allowing assisted suicide or euthanasia have radically different consequences and meanings for public policy."

This Court has also recognized, at least implicitly, the distinction between letting a patient die and making that patient die. In *Cruzan v. Director, Mo. Dept. of Health*, we concluded that "the principle that a competent person has a constitutionally protected liberty interest in refusing unwanted medical treatment may be inferred from our prior decisions," and we assumed the existence of such a right for purposes of that case. But our assumption of a right to refuse treatment was grounded not, as the Court of Appeals supposed, on the proposition that patients have a general and abstract "right to hasten death," but on well established, traditional rights to bodily integrity and freedom from unwanted touching. In fact, we observed that "the majority of States in this country have laws imposing criminal penalties on one who assists another to commit suicide." Cruzan therefore provides no support for the notion that refusing life-sustaining medical treatment is "nothing more nor less than suicide."

For all these reasons, we disagree with respondents' claim that the distinction between refusing lifesaving medical treatment and assisted suicide is "arbitrary" and "irrational."* Granted, in some cases, the line between the two may not be clear, but certainty is not required, even were it possible.† Logic and contemporary practice support New York's judgment that the two acts are different, and New York may therefore, consistent with the Constitution, treat them differently. By permitting everyone to refuse unwanted medical treatment while prohibiting anyone from assisting a suicide, New York law follows a longstanding and rational distinction.

New York's reasons for recognizing and acting on this distinction—including prohibiting intentional killing and preserving life; preventing suicide; maintaining physicians' role as their patients' healers; protecting vulnerable people from indifference, prejudice, and psychological and financial pressure to end their lives; and avoiding a possible slide towards euthanasia—are discussed in greater detail in our opinion in Glucksberg. These valid and important public interests easily satisfy the constitutional requirement that a legislative classification bear a rational relation to some legitimate end.‡

The judgment of the Court of Appeals is reversed.

It is so ordered.

---

*Respondents also argue that the State irrationally distinguishes between physician-assisted suicide and "terminal sedation," a process respondents characterize as "inducing barbiturate coma and then starving the person to death." Petitioners insist, however, that " 'although proponents of physician-assisted suicide and euthanasia contend that terminal sedation is covert physician-assisted suicide or euthanasia, the concept of sedating pharmacotherapy is based on informed consent and the principle of double effect.' " Just as a State may prohibit assisting suicide while permitting patients to refuse unwanted lifesaving treatment, it may permit palliative care related to that refusal, which may have the foreseen but unintended "double effect" of hastening the patient's death.

†We do not insist, as JUSTICE STEVENS suggests [in his concurring opinion], that "in all cases there will in fact be a significant difference between the intent of the physicians, the patients or the families [in withdrawal-of-treatment and physician-assisted-suicide cases]." In the absence of omniscience, however, the State is entitled to act on the reasonableness of the distinction.

‡JUSTICE STEVENS observes that our holding today "does not foreclose the possibility that some applications of the New York statute may impose an intolerable intrusion on the patient's freedom." This is true, but, as we observe in Glucksberg, a particular plaintiff hoping to show that New York's assisted-suicide ban was unconstitutional in his particular case would need to present different and considerably stronger arguments than those advanced by respondents here.

CONCUR BY: O'CONNOR; STEVENS; SOUTER; GINSBURG; BREYER

CONCUR: JUSTICE O'CONNOR, concurring.*

*JUSTICE GINSBURG concurs in the Court's judgments substantially for the reasons stated in this opinion. JUSTICE BREYER joins this opinion except insofar as it joins the opinions of the Court.

Death will be different for each of us. For many, the last days will be spent in physical pain and perhaps the despair that accompanies physical deterioration and a loss of control of basic bodily and mental functions. Some will seek medication to alleviate that pain and other symptoms.

The Court frames the issue in this case as whether the Due Process Clause of the Constitution protects a "right to commit suicide which itself includes a right to assistance in doing so," and concludes that our Nation's history, legal traditions, and practices do not support the existence of such a right. I join the Court's opinions because I agree that there is no generalized right to "commit suicide." But respondents urge us to address the narrower question whether a mentally competent person who is experiencing great suffering has a constitutionally cognizable interest in controlling the circumstances of his or her imminent death. I see no need to reach that question in the context of the facial challenges to the New York and Washington laws at issue here. The parties and amici agree that in these States a patient who is suffering from a terminal illness and who is experiencing great pain has no legal barriers to obtaining medication, from qualified physicians, to alleviate that suffering, even to the point of causing unconsciousness and hastening death. In this light, even assuming that we would recognize such an interest, I agree that the State's interests in protecting those who are not truly competent or facing imminent death, or those whose decisions to hasten death would not truly be voluntary, are sufficiently weighty to justify a prohibition against physician-assisted suicide.

Every one of us at some point may be affected by our own or a family member's terminal illness. There is no reason to think the democratic process will not strike the proper balance between the interests of terminally ill, mentally competent individuals who would seek to end their suffering and the State's interests in protecting those who might seek to end life mistakenly or under pressure. As the Court recognizes, States are presently undertaking extensive and serious evaluation of physician-assisted suicide and other related issues. In such circumstances, "the ... challenging task of crafting appropriate procedures for safeguarding ... liberty interests is entrusted to the 'laboratory' of the States ... in the first instance."

In sum, there is no need to address the question whether suffering patients have a constitutionally cognizable interest in obtaining relief from the suffering that they may experience in the last days of their lives. There is no dispute that dying patients in Washington and New York can obtain palliative care, even when doing so would hasten their deaths. The difficulty in defining terminal illness and the risk that a dying patient's request for assistance in ending his or her life might not be truly voluntary justifies the prohibitions on assisted suicide we uphold here.

JUSTICE STEVENS, concurring in the judgments.

The Court ends its opinion with the important observation that our holding today is fully consistent with a continuation of the vigorous debate about the "morality, legality, and practicality of physician-assisted suicide" in a democratic society. I write separately to make it clear that there is also room for further debate about the limits that the Constitution places on the power of the States to punish the practice.

I

Today, the Court decides that Washington's statute prohibiting assisted suicide is not invalid "on its face," that is to say, in all or most cases in which it might be applied. That holding, however, does not foreclose the possibility that some applications of the statute might well be invalid.

As originally filed, this case presented a challenge to the Washington statute on its face and as it applied to three terminally ill, mentally competent patients and to four physicians who treat terminally ill patients. After the District Court issued its opinion holding that the statute placed an undue burden on the right to commit physician-assisted suicide, the three patients died. Although the Court of Appeals considered the constitutionality of the statute "as applied to the prescription of life-ending medication for use by terminally ill, competent adult patients who wish to hasten their deaths," the court did not have before it any individual plaintiff seeking to hasten her death or any doctor who was threatened with prosecution for assisting in the suicide of a particular patient; its analysis and eventual holding that the statute was unconstitutional was not limited to a particular set of plaintiffs before it.

The appropriate standard to be applied in cases making facial challenges to state statutes has been the subject of debate within this Court. Upholding the validity of the federal Bail Reform Act of 1984, the Court stated in *United States* v. *Salerno* that a "facial challenge to a legislative Act is, of course, the most difficult challenge to mount successfully, since the challenger must establish that no set of circumstances exists under which the Act would be valid." I do not believe the Court has ever actually applied such a strict standard, even in Salerno itself, and the Court does not appear to apply Salerno here. Nevertheless, the Court does conceive of respondents' claim as a facial challenge—addressing not the application of the statute to a particular set of plaintiffs before it, but the constitutionality of the statute's categorical prohibition against "aiding another person to attempt suicide." Accordingly, the Court requires the plaintiffs to show that the interest in liberty protected by the Fourteenth Amendment "includes a right to commit suicide which itself includes a right to assistance in doing so."

History and tradition provide ample support for refusing to recognize an open-ended constitutional right to commit suicide. Much more than the State's paternalistic interest in protecting the individual from the irrevocable consequences of an ill-advised decision motivated by temporary concerns is at stake.

There is truth in John Donne's observation that "No man is an island." The State has an interest in preserving and fostering the benefits that every human being may provide to the community—a community that thrives on the exchange of ideas, expressions of affection, shared memories and humorous incidents as well as on the material contributions that its members create and support. The value to others of a person's life is far too precious to allow the individual to claim a constitutional entitlement to complete autonomy in making a decision to end that life. Thus, I fully agree with the Court that the "liberty" protected by the Due Process Clause does not include a categorical "right to commit suicide which itself includes a right to assistance in doing so."

But just as our conclusion that capital punishment is not always unconstitutional did not preclude later decisions holding that it is sometimes impermissibly cruel, so is it equally clear that a decision upholding a general statutory prohibition of assisted suicide does not mean that every possible application of the statute would be valid. A State, like Washington, that has authorized the death penalty and thereby has concluded that the sanctity of human life does not require that it always be preserved, must acknowledge that there are situations in which an interest in hastening death is legitimate. Indeed, not only is that interest sometimes legitimate, I am also convinced that there are times when it is entitled to constitutional protection.

In *Cruzan* v. *Director, Mo. Dept. of Health,* the Court assumed that the interest in liberty protected by the Fourteenth Amendment encompassed the right of a terminally ill patient to direct the withdrawal of life-sustaining treatment. As the Court correctly observes today, that assumption "was not simply deduced from abstract concepts of personal autonomy." Instead, it was supported by the common-law tradition protecting the individual's general right to refuse unwanted medical treatment. We have recognized, however, that this common-law right to refuse treatment is neither absolute nor always sufficiently weighty to overcome valid countervailing state interests. As Justice Brennan pointed out in his Cruzan dissent, we have upheld legislation imposing punishment on persons refusing to be vaccinated, and as JUSTICE SCALIA pointed out in his concurrence, the State ordinarily has the right to interfere with an attempt to commit suicide by, for example, forcibly placing a bandage on a self-inflicted wound to stop the flow of blood. In most cases, the individual's constitutionally protected interest in his or her own physical autonomy, including the right to refuse unwanted medical treatment, will give way to the State's interest in preserving human life.

Cruzan, however, was not the normal case. Given the irreversible nature of her illness and the progressive character of her suffering, Nancy Cruzan's interest in refusing medical care was incidental to her more basic interest in controlling the manner and timing of her death. In finding that her best interests would be served by cutting off the nourishment that kept her alive, the trial court did more than simply vindicate Cruzan's interest in refusing medical treatment; the court, in essence, authorized affirmative conduct that would hasten her death. When this Court reviewed the case and upheld Missouri's requirement that there be clear and convincing evidence establishing Nancy Cruzan's intent to have life-sustaining nourishment withdrawn, it made two important assumptions: (1) that there was a "liberty interest" in refusing unwanted treatment protected by the Due Process Clause; and (2) that this liberty interest did not "end the inquiry" because it might be outweighed by relevant state interests. I agree with both of those assumptions, but I insist that the source of Nancy Cruzan's right to refuse treatment was not just a common-law rule. Rather, this right is an aspect of a far broader and more basic concept of freedom that is even older than the common law. This freedom embraces, not merely a person's right to refuse a particular kind of unwanted treatment, but also her interest in dignity, and in determining the character of the memories that will survive long after her death. In recognizing that the State's interests did not outweigh Nancy Cruzan's liberty interest in refusing medical treatment, Cruzan rested not simply on the common-law right to refuse medical treatment, but—at least implicitly—on the even more fundamental right to make this "deeply personal decision."

Thus, the common-law right to protection from battery, which included the right to refuse medical treatment in most circumstances, did not mark "the outer limits of the substantive sphere of liberty" that supported the Cruzan family's decision to hasten Nancy's death. Those limits have never been precisely defined. They are generally identified by the importance and character of the decision confronted by the individual. Whatever the outer limits of the concept may be, it definitely includes protection for matters "central to personal dignity and autonomy." It includes,

> the individual's right to make certain unusually important decisions that will affect his own, or his family's, destiny. The Court has referred to such decisions as implicating "basic values," as being "fundamental," and as being dignified by history and tradition. The character of the Court's language in these cases brings to mind the origins of the American heritage of freedom—the abiding interest in individual liberty that makes certain state intrusions on the citizen's right to decide how he will live his own life intolerable.

The Cruzan case demonstrated that some state intrusions on the right to decide how death will be encountered are also intolerable. The now-deceased plaintiffs in this action may in fact have had a liberty interest even stronger than Nancy Cruzan's because, not only were they terminally ill, they were suffering constant and severe pain. Avoiding intolerable pain and the indignity of living one's final days incapacitated and in agony is certainly "at the heart of [the] liberty... to define one's own concept of existence, of meaning, of the universe, and of the mystery of human life."

While I agree with the Court that Cruzan does not decide the issue presented by these cases, Cruzan did give recognition, not just to vague, unbridled notions of autonomy, but to the more specific interest in making decisions about how to confront an imminent death. Although there is no absolute right to physician-assisted suicide, Cruzan makes it clear that some individuals who no longer have the option of deciding whether to live or to die because they are already on the threshold of death have a constitutionally protected interest that may outweigh the State's interest in preserving life at all costs. The liberty interest at stake in a case like this differs from, and is stronger than, both the common-law right to refuse medical treatment and the unbridled interest in deciding whether to live or die. It is an interest in deciding how, rather than whether, a critical threshold shall be crossed.

III

The state interests supporting a general rule banning the practice of physician-assisted suicide do not have the same force in all cases. First and foremost of these interests is the "unqualified interest in the preservation of human life," which is equated with "the sanctity of life." That interest not only justifies—it commands—maximum protection of every individual's interest in remaining alive, which in turn commands the same protection for decisions about whether to commence or to terminate life-support systems or to administer pain medication that may hasten death. Properly viewed, however, this interest is not a collective interest that should always outweigh the interests of a person who because of pain, incapacity, or sedation finds her life intolerable, but rather, an aspect of individual freedom.

Many terminally ill people find their lives meaningful even if filled with pain or dependence on others. Some find value in living through suffering; some have an abiding desire to witness particular events in their families' lives; many believe it a sin to hasten death. Individuals of different religious faiths make different judgments and choices about whether to live on under such circumstances. There are those who will want to continue aggressive treatment; those who would prefer terminal sedation; and those who will seek withdrawal from life-support systems and death by gradual starvation and dehydration. Although as a general matter the State's interest in the contributions each person may make to society outweighs the person's interest in ending her life, this interest does not have the same force for a terminally ill patient faced not with the choice of whether to live, only of how to die. Allowing the individual, rather than the State, to make judgments "about the 'quality' of life that a particular individual may enjoy," does not mean that the lives of terminally ill, disabled people have less value than the lives of those who are healthy. Rather, it gives proper recognition to the individual's interest in choosing a final chapter that accords with her life story, rather than one that demeans her values and poisons memories of her.

Similarly, the State's legitimate interests in preventing suicide, protecting the vulnerable from coercion and abuse, and preventing euthanasia are less significant in this context. I agree that the State has a compelling interest in preventing persons from committing suicide because of depression, or coercion by third parties. But the State's legitimate interest in preventing abuse does not apply to an individual who is not victimized by abuse, who is not suffering from depression, and who makes a rational and voluntary decision to seek assistance in dying. Although, as the New York Task Force report discusses, diagnosing depression and other mental illness is not always easy, mental health workers and other professionals expert in working with dying patients can help patients cope with depression and pain, and help patients assess their options.

Relatedly, the State and amici express the concern that patients whose physical pain is inadequately treated will be more likely to request assisted suicide. Encouraging the development and ensuring the availability of adequate pain treatment is of utmost importance; palliative care, however, cannot alleviate all pain and suffering. An individual adequately informed of the care alternatives thus might make a rational choice for assisted suicide. For such an individual, the State's interest in preventing potential abuse and mistake is only minimally implicated.

The final major interest asserted by the State is its interest in preserving the traditional integrity of the medical profession. The fear is that a rule permitting physicians to assist in suicide is inconsistent with the perception that they serve their patients solely as healers. But for some patients, it would be a physician's refusal to dispense medication to ease their suffering and make their death tolerable and dignified that would be inconsistent with the healing role. For doctors who have long-standing relationships with their patients, who have given their patients advice on alternative treatments, who are attentive to their patient's individualized needs, and who are knowledgeable about pain symptom management and palliative care options, heeding a patient's desire to assist in her suicide would not serve to harm the physician-patient relationship. Furthermore, because physicians are already involved in making decisions that hasten the death of terminally ill patients—through termination of life support, withholding of medical treatment, and terminal sedation—there is in fact significant tension between the traditional view of the physician's role and the actual practice in a growing number of cases.*

As the New York State Task Force on Life and the Law recognized, a State's prohibition of assisted suicide is justified by the fact that the "ideal" case in which "patients would be screened for depression and offered treatment, effective pain medication would be available, and all patients would have a supportive committed family and doctor" is not the usual case. Although, as the Court concludes today, these potential harms are sufficient to support the State's general public policy against assisted suicide, they will not always outweigh the individual liberty interest of a particular patient. Unlike the Court of Appeals, I would not say as a categorical matter that these state interests are invalid as to the entire class of terminally ill, mentally competent patients. I do not, however, foreclose the possibility that an individual plaintiff seeking to hasten her death, or a doctor whose

---

*I note that there is evidence that a significant number of physicians support the practice of hastening death in particular situations. A survey published in the *New England Journal of Medicine* found that 56 percent of responding doctors in Michigan preferred legalizing assisted suicide to an explicit ban. In a survey of Oregon doctors, 60 percent of the responding doctors supported legalizing assisted suicide for terminally ill patients. Another study showed that 12 percent of physicians polled in Washington State reported that they had been asked by their terminally ill patients for prescriptions to hasten death, and that, in the year prior to the study, 24 percent of those physicians had complied with such requests.

assistance was sought, could prevail in a more particularized challenge. Future cases will determine whether such a challenge may succeed.

IV

In New York, a doctor must respect a competent person's decision to refuse or to discontinue medical treatment even though death will thereby ensue, but the same doctor would be guilty of a felony if she provided her patient assistance in committing suicide. Today we hold that the Equal Protection Clause is not violated by the resulting disparate treatment of two classes of terminally ill people who may have the same interest in hastening death. I agree that the distinction between permitting death to ensue from an underlying fatal disease and causing it to occur by the administration of medication or other means provides a constitutionally sufficient basis for the State's classification. Unlike the Court, however, I am not persuaded that in all cases there will in fact be a significant difference between the intent of the physicians, the patients, or the families in the two situations.

There may be little distinction between the intent of a terminally ill patient who decides to remove her life-support and one who seeks the assistance of a doctor in ending her life; in both situations, the patient is seeking to hasten a certain, impending death. The doctor's intent might also be the same in prescribing lethal medication as it is in terminating life support. A doctor who fails to administer medical treatment to one who is dying from a disease could be doing so with an intent to harm or kill that patient. Conversely, a doctor who prescribes lethal medication does not necessarily intend the patient's death—rather that doctor may seek simply to ease the patient's suffering and to comply with her wishes. The illusory character of any differences in intent or causation is confirmed by the fact that the American Medical Association unequivocally endorses the practice of terminal sedation. The purpose of terminal sedation is to ease the suffering of the patient and comply with her wishes, and the actual cause of death is the administration of heavy doses of lethal sedatives. This same intent and causation may exist when a doctor complies with a patient's request for lethal medication to hasten her death.*

Thus, although the differences the majority notes in causation and intent between terminating life-support and assisting in suicide support the Court's rejection of the respondents' facial challenge, these distinctions may be inapplicable to particular terminally ill patients and their doctors. Our holding today in Vacco v. Quill that the Equal Protection Clause is not violated by New York's classification, just like our holding in Washington v. Glucksberg that the Washington statute is not invalid on its face, does not foreclose the possibility that some applications of the New York statute may impose an intolerable intrusion on the patient's freedom.

---

*If a doctor prescribes lethal drugs to be self-administered by the patient, it not at all clear that the physician's intent is that the patient "be made dead." Many patients prescribed lethal medications never actually take them; they merely acquire some sense of control in the process of dying that the availability of those medications provides.

There remains room for vigorous debate about the outcome of particular cases that are not necessarily resolved by the opinions announced today. How such cases may be decided will depend on their specific facts. In my judgment, however, it is clear that the so-called "unqualified interest in the preservation of human life" is not itself sufficient to outweigh the interest in liberty that may justify the only possible means of preserving a dying patient's dignity and alleviating her intolerable suffering.

JUSTICE SOUTER, concurring in the judgment.

Even though I do not conclude that assisted suicide is a fundamental right entitled to recognition at this time, I accord the claims raised by the patients and physicians in this case and Washington v. Glucksberg a high degree of importance, requiring a commensurate justification. The reasons that lead me to conclude in Glucksberg that the prohibition on assisted suicide is not arbitrary under the due process standard also support the distinction between assistance to suicide, which is banned, and practices such as termination of artificial life support and death-hastening pain medication, which are permitted. I accordingly concur in the judgment of the Court.

JUSTICE GINSBURG, concurring in the judgments.

I concur in the Court's judgments in these cases substantially for the reasons stated by JUSTICE O'CONNOR in her concurring opinion.

JUSTICE BREYER, concurring in the judgments.

I believe that JUSTICE O'CONNOR's views, which I share, have greater legal significance than the Court's opinion suggests. I join her separate opinion, except insofar as it joins the majority. And I concur in the judgments. I shall briefly explain how I differ from the Court.

I agree with the Court in Vacco v. Quill that the articulated state interest justify the distinction drawn between physician assisted suicide and withdrawal of life-support. I also agree with the Court that the critical question in both of the cases before us is whether "the 'liberty' specially protected by the Due Process Clause includes a right" of the sort that the respondents assert. I do not agree, however, with the Court's formulation of that claimed "liberty" interest. The Court describes it as a "right to commit suicide with another's assistance." But I would not reject the respondents' claim without considering a different formulation, for which our legal tradition may provide greater support. That formulation would use words roughly like a "right to die with dignity." But irrespective of the exact words used, at its core would lie personal control over the manner of death, professional medical assistance, and the avoidance of unnecessary and severe physical suffering—combined.

As JUSTICE SOUTER points out, Justice Harlan's dissenting opinion in *Poe*

v. *Ullman,* offers some support for such a claim. In that opinion, Justice Harlan referred to the "liberty" that the Fourteenth Amendment protects as including "a freedom from all substantial arbitrary impositions and purposeless restraints" and also as recognizing that "certain interests require particularly careful scrutiny of the state needs asserted to justify their abridgment." The "certain interests" to which Justice Harlan referred may well be similar (perhaps identical) to the rights, liberties, or interests that the Court today, as in the past, regards as "fundamental."

Justice Harlan concluded that marital privacy was such a "special interest." He found in the Constitution a right of "privacy of the home"—with the home, the bedroom, and "intimate details of the marital relation" at its heart—by examining the protection that the law had earlier provided for related, but not identical, interests described by such words as "privacy," "home," and "family." The respondents here essentially ask us to do the same. They argue that one can find a "right to die with dignity" by examining the protection the law has provided for related, but not identical, interests relating to personal dignity, medical treatment, and freedom from state-inflicted pain.

I do not believe, however, that this Court need or now should decide whether or not such a right is "fundamental." That is because, in my view, the avoidance of severe physical pain (connected with death) would have to comprise an essential part of any successful claim and because, as JUSTICE O'CONNOR points out, the laws before us do not force a dying person to undergo that kind of pain. Rather, the laws of New York and of Washington do not prohibit doctors from providing patients with drugs sufficient to control pain despite the risk that those drugs themselves will kill. And under these circumstances the laws of New York and Washington would overcome any remaining significant interests and would be justified, regardless.

Medical technology, we are repeatedly told, makes the administration of pain-relieving drugs sufficient, except for a very few individuals for whom the ineffectiveness of pain control medicines can mean, not pain, but the need for sedation which can end in a coma. We are also told that there are many instances in which patients do not receive the palliative care that, in principle, is available, but that is so for institutional reasons or inadequacies or obstacles, which would seem possible to overcome, and which do not include a prohibitive set of laws.

This legal circumstance means that the state laws before us do not infringe directly upon the (assumed) central interest (what I have called the core of the interest in dying with dignity) as, by way of contrast, the state anticontraceptive laws at issue in Poe did interfere with the central interest there at stake—by bringing the State's police powers to bear upon the marital bedroom.

Were the legal circumstances different—for example, were state law to prevent the provision of palliative care, including the administration of drugs as needed to avoid pain at the end of life—then the law's impact upon serious and otherwise unavoidable physical pain (accompanying death) would be more directly at issue. And as JUSTICE O'CONNOR suggests, the Court might have to revisit its conclusions in these cases.

WASHINGTON, ET AL., PETITIONERS v. HAROLD GLUCKSBERG ET AL.

No. 96-110

SUPREME COURT OF THE UNITED STATES

1997 U.S. LEXIS 4039

January 8, 1997, Argued

June 26, 1997, Decided

PRIOR HISTORY: ON WRIT OF CERTIORARI TO THE UNITED STATES COURT OF APPEALS FOR THE NINTH CIRCUIT.

DISPOSITION. *79 F3d 790,* reversed and remanded.

SYLLABUS:

It has always been a crime to assist a suicide in the State of Washington. The State's present law makes "promoting a suicide attempt" a felony, and provides: "A person is guilty of [that crime] when he knowingly causes or aids another person to attempt suicide." Respondents, four Washington physicians who occasionally treat terminally ill, suffering patients, declare that they would assist these patients in ending their lives if not for the State's assisted-suicide ban. They, along with three gravely ill plaintiffs who have since died and a nonprofit organization that counsels people considering physician-assisted suicide, filed this suit against petitioners, the State and its Attorney General, seeking a declaration that the ban is, on its face, unconstitutional. They assert a liberty interest protected by the Fourteenth Amendment's due process clause which extends to a personal choice by a mentally competent, terminally ill adult to commit physician-assisted suicide. Relying primarily on *Planned Parenthood of Southeastern Pa. v. Casey,* 505 U. S. 833, and *Cruzan* v. *Director, Mo. Dept. of Health,* 497 US. 261, the Federal District Court agreed, concluding that Washington's assisted-suicide ban is unconstitutional because it places an undue burden on the exercise of that constitutionally protected liberty interest.

The en banc Ninth Circuit affirmed.

Held: Washington's prohibition against "causing" or "aiding" a suicide does not violate the Due Process Clause.

(a) An examination of our Nation's history, legal traditions, and practices demonstrates that Anglo-American common law has punished or otherwise disapproved of assisting suicide for over 700 years; that rendering such assistance is still a crime in almost every State; that such prohibitions have never contained exceptions for those who were near death; that the prohibitions have in recent years been reexamined and, for the most part, reaffirmed in a number of States; and that the President recently signed the Federal Assisted Suicide Funding Restriction Act of 1997, which prohibits the use of federal funds in support of physician-assisted suicide.

(b) In light of that history, this Court's decisions lead to the conclusion that respondents' asserted "right" to assistance in committing suicide is not a fundamental liberty interest protected by the Due Process Clause. The Court's established method of substantive-due-process analysis has two primary features: First, the Court has regularly observed that the Clause specially protects those fundamental rights and liberties which are, objectively, deeply rooted in this Nation's history and tradition. Second, the Court has required a "careful description" of the asserted fundamental liberty interest. The Ninth Circuit's and respondents' various descriptions of the interest here at stake—e.g., a right to "determine the time and manner of one's death," the "right to die," a "liberty to choose how to die," a right to "control of one's final days," "the right to choose a humane, dignified death," and "the liberty to shape death"—run counter to that second requirement. Since the Washington statute prohibits "aiding another person to attempt suicide," the question before the Court is more properly characterized as whether the "liberty" specially protected by the Clause includes a right to commit suicide which itself includes a right to assistance in doing so. This asserted right has no place in our Nation's traditions, given the country's consistent, almost universal, and continuing rejection of the right, even for terminally ill, mentally competent adults. To hold for respondents, the Court would have to reverse centuries of legal doctrine and practice, and strike down the considered policy choice of almost every State. Respondents' contention that the asserted interest is consistent with this Court's substantive-due-process cases, if not with this Nation's history and practice, is unpersuasive. The constitutionally protected right to refuse lifesaving hydration and nutrition that was discussed in *Cruzan,* was not simply deduced from abstract concepts of personal autonomy, but was instead grounded in the Nation's history and traditions, given the common-law rule that forced medication was a battery, and the long legal tradition protecting the decision to refuse unwanted medical treatment. And although Casey recognized that many of the rights and liberties protected by the Due Process Clause sound in personal autonomy, it does not follow that any and all important, intimate, and personal decisions are so protected. Casey did not suggest otherwise.

(c) The constitutional requirement that Washington's assisted-suicide ban be rationally related to legitimate government interests is unquestionably met here. These interests include prohibiting intentional killing and preserving human life; preventing the serious public-health problem of suicide, especially among the young, the elderly, and those suffering from untreated pain or from depression or other mental disorders; protecting the medical profession's integrity and ethics and maintaining physicians' role as their patients' healers; protecting the poor, the elderly, disabled persons, the terminally ill, and persons in other vulnerable groups from indifference, prejudice, and psychological and financial pressure to end their lives; and avoiding a possible slide toward voluntary and perhaps even involuntary euthanasia. The relative strengths of these various interests need not be weighed exactingly, since they are unquestionably important and legitimate, and the law at issue is at least reasonably related to their promotion and protection.

79 F.3d 790, reversed and remanded.

JUDGES: REHNQUIST, C. J., delivered the opinion of the Court, in which O'CONNOR, SCALIA, KENNEDY, and THOMAS, JJ., joined. O'CONNOR, J., filed a concurring opinion, in which GINSBURG and BREYER, JJ., joined in part. STEVENS, J., SOUTER, J., GINSBURG, J., and BREYER, J., filed opinions concurring in the judgment.

OPINION: CHIEF JUSTICE REHNQUIST delivered the opinion of the Court.

The question presented in this case is whether Washington's prohibition against "causing" or "aiding" a suicide offends the Fourteenth Amendment to the United States Constitution. We hold that it does not.

It has always been a crime to assist a suicide in the State of Washington. In 1854, Washington's first Territorial Legislature outlawed "assisting another in the commission of self-murder." Today, Washington law provides: "A person is guilty of promoting a suicide attempt when he knowingly causes or aids another person to attempt suicide." "Promoting a suicide attempt" is a felony, punishable by up to five years' imprisonment and up to a $10,000 fine. At the same time, Washington's Natural Death Act, enacted in 1979, states that the "withholding or withdrawal of life-sustaining treatment" at a patient's direction "shall not, for any purpose, constitute a suicide."

I

We begin, as we do in all due-process cases, by examining our Nation's history, legal traditions, and practices. In almost every State—indeed, in almost every western democracy—it is a crime to assist a suicide. The States' assisted-suicide bans are not innovations. Rather, they are longstanding expressions of the States' commitment to the protection and preservation of all human life. Indeed, opposition to and condemnation of suicide—and, therefore, of assisting suicide—are consistent and enduring themes of our philosophical, legal, and cultural heritages.

More specifically, for over 700 years, the Anglo-American common-law tradition has punished or otherwise disapproved of both suicide and assisting suicide. In the thirteenth century, Henry de Bracton, one of the first legal-treatise writers, observed that "just as a man may commit felony by slaying another so may he do so by slaying himself." The real and personal property of one who killed himself to avoid conviction and punishment for a crime were forfeit to the king; however, thought Bracton, "if a man slays himself in weariness of life or because he is unwilling to endure further bodily pain... [only] his movable goods [were] confiscated." Thus, "the principle that suicide of a sane person, for whatever reason, was a punishable felony was...introduced into English common law." Centuries later, Sir William Blackstone, whose Commentaries on the Laws of England not only provided a definitive summary of the common law but was also a primary legal authority for eighteenth- and nineteenth-century American lawyers, referred to suicide as "self-murder" and "the pretended heroism, but real cowardice, of the Stoic philosophers, who destroyed themselves to avoid those ills which they had not the fortitude to endure...." Blackstone emphasized that "the law has...ranked [suicide] among the highest crimes," although, anticipating later developments, he conceded that the harsh and shameful punishments imposed for suicide "border a little upon severity."

For the most part the early American colonies adopted the common-law approach. For example, the legislators of the Providence Plantations, which would later become Rhode Island, declared, in 1647, that "self-murder is by all agreed to be the most unnatural and it is by this present Assembly declared, to be that, wherein he that doth it kills himself out of a premeditated hatred against his own life or other humor: ... his goods and chattels are the king's custom, but not his debts nor lands; but in case he be an infant, a lunatic, mad or distracted man, he forfeits nothing." Virginia also required ignominious burial for suicides, and their estates were forfeit to the crown.

Over time, however, the American colonies abolished these harsh common-law penalties. William Penn abandoned the criminal-forfeiture sanction in Pennsylvania in 1701, and the other colonies (and later, the other States) eventually followed this example. Zephaniah Swift, who would later become Chief Justice of Connecticut, wrote in 1796 that

> there can be no act more contemptible, than to attempt to punish an offender for a crime, by exercising a mean act of revenge upon lifeless clay, that is insensible of the punishment. There can be no greater cruelty, than the inflicting [of] a punishment, as the forfeiture of goods, which must fall solely on the innocent offspring of the offender.... [Suicide] is so abhorrent to the feelings of mankind, and that strong love of life which is implanted in the human heart, that it cannot be so frequently committed, as to become dangerous to society. There can of course be no necessity of any punishment.

This statement makes it clear, however, that the movement away from the common law's harsh sanctions did not represent an acceptance of suicide; rather, as Chief Justice Swift observed, this change reflected the growing consensus that it was unfair to punish the suicide's family for his wrongdoing. Nonetheless, although States moved away from Blackstone's treatment of suicide, courts continued to condemn it as a grave public wrong.

That suicide remained a grievous, though nonfelonious, wrong is confirmed by the fact that colonial and early state legislatures and courts did not retreat from prohibiting assisting suicide. Swift, in his early-nineteenth-century treatise on the laws of Connecticut, stated that "if one counsels another to commit suicide, and the other by reason of the advice kills himself, the advisor is guilty of murder as principal." This was the well established common-law view, as was the similar principle that the consent of a homicide victim is "wholly immaterial to the guilt of the person who caused [his death]." And the prohibitions against assisting suicide never contained exceptions for those who were near death. Rather, "the life of those to whom life had become a burden—of those who [were] hopelessly diseased or fatally wounded—nay, even the lives of criminals condemned to death, [were] under the protection of law, equally as the lives of those who [were] in the full tide of life's enjoyment, and anxious to continue to live."

The earliest American statute explicitly to outlaw assisting suicide was enacted in New York in 1828, and many of the new States and Territories followed New York's example. Between 1857 and 1865, a New York commission led by Dudley Field drafted a criminal code that prohibited "aiding" a suicide and, specifically, "furnishing another person with any deadly weapon or poisonous drug, knowing that such person intends to use such weapon or drug in taking his own life." By the time the Fourteenth Amendment was ratified, it was a crime in most States to assist a suicide. The Field Penal Code was adopted in the Dakota Territory in 1877, in New York in 1881, and its language served as a model for several other western States' statutes in the late nineteenth and early twentieth centuries. California, for example, codified its assisted-suicide prohibition in 1874, using language similar to the Field Code's. In this century, the Model Penal Code also prohibited "aiding" suicide, prompting many States to enact or revise their assisted-suicide bans. The Code's drafters observed that "the interests in the sanctity of life that are represented by the criminal homicide laws are threatened by one who expresses a willingness to participate in taking the life of another, even though the act may be accomplished with the consent, or at the request, of the suicide victim."

Though deeply rooted, the States' assisted-suicide bans have in recent years been reexamined and, generally, reaffirmed. Because of advances in medicine and technology, Americans today are increasingly likely to die in institutions, from chronic illnesses. Public concern and democratic action are therefore sharply focused on how best to protect dignity and independence at the end of life, with the result that there have been many significant changes in state laws and in the attitudes these laws reflect. Many States, for example, now permit "living wills," surrogate health-care decisionmaking, and the withdrawal or refusal of life-sustaining medical treatment. At the same time, however, voters and legislators continue for the most part to reaffirm their States' prohibitions on assisting suicide.

The Washington statute at issue in this case was enacted in 1975 as part of a revision of that State's criminal code. Four years later, Washington passed its Natural Death Act, which specifically stated that the "withholding or withdrawal of life-sustaining treatment...shall not, for any purpose, constitute a suicide" and that "nothing in this chapter shall be construed to condone, authorize, or approve mercy killing...." In 1991, Washington voters rejected a ballot initiative which, had it passed, would have permitted a form of physician-assisted suicide. Washington then added a provision to the Natural Death Act expressly excluding physician-assisted suicide.

California voters rejected an assisted-suicide initiative similar to Washington's in 1993. On the other hand, in 1994, voters in Oregon enacted, also through ballot initiative, that State's "Death With Dignity Act," which legalized physician-assisted suicide for competent, terminally ill adults. Since the Oregon vote, many proposals to legalize assisted-suicide have been and continue to be introduced in the States' legislatures, but none has been enacted. And just last year, Iowa and Rhode Island joined the overwhelming majority of States explicitly prohibiting assisted suicide. Also, on April 30, 1997, President Clinton signed the Federal Assisted Suicide Funding Restriction Act of 1997, which prohibits the use of federal funds in support of physician-assisted suicide.

Thus, the States are currently engaged in serious, thoughtful examinations of physician-assisted suicide and other similar issues. For example, New York State's Task Force on Life and the Law—an ongoing, blue-ribbon commission composed of doctors, ethicists, lawyers, religious leaders, and interested laymen—was convened in 1984 and commissioned with "a broad mandate to recommend public policy on issues raised by medical advances." Over the past decade, the Task Force has recommended laws relating to end-of-life decisions, surrogate pregnancy, and organ donation. After studying physician-assisted suicide, however, the Task Force unanimously concluded that "legalizing assisted suicide and euthanasia would pose profound risks to many individuals who are ill and vulnerable.... The potential dangers of this dramatic change in public policy would outweigh any benefit that might be achieved."

Attitudes toward suicide itself have changed since Bracton, but our laws have consistently condemned, and continue to prohibit, assisting suicide. Despite changes in medical technology and notwithstanding an increased emphasis on the importance of end-of-life decisionmaking, we have not retreated from this prohibition. Against this backdrop of history, tradition, and practice, we now turn to respondents' constitutional claim.

II

The Due Process Clause guarantees more than fair process, and the "liberty" it protects includes more than the absence of physical restraint. The Clause also provides heightened protection against government interference with certain fundamental rights and liberty interests. In a long line of cases, we have held that, in addition to the specific freedoms protected by the Bill of Rights, the "liberty" specially protected by the Due Process Clause includes the rights to marry, to have children, to direct the education and upbringing of one's children, to marital privacy, to use contraception, to bodily integrity, and to abortion. We have also assumed, and strongly suggested, that the Due Process Clause protects the traditional right to refuse unwanted lifesaving medical treatment.

But we "have always been reluctant to expand the concept of substantive due process because guideposts for responsible decisionmaking in this unchartered area are scarce and open-ended." By extending constitutional protection to an asserted right or liberty interest, we, to a great extent, place the matter outside the arena of public debate and legislative action. We must therefore "exercise the utmost care whenever we are asked to break new ground in this field," lest the liberty protected by the Due Process Clause be subtly transformed into the policy preferences of the members of this Court.

Our established method of substantive-due-process analysis has two primary features: First, we have regularly observed that the Due Process Clause specially protects those fundamental rights and liberties which are, objectively, "deeply rooted in this Nation's history and tradition," and "implicit in the concept of ordered liberty," such that "neither liberty nor justice would exist if they were sacrificed." Second, we have required in substantive due-process cases a "careful description" of the asserted fundamental liberty interest. Our Nation's history, legal traditions, and practices thus provide the crucial "guideposts for responsible decisionmaking," that direct and restrain our exposition of the Due Process Clause. As we stated recently in Flores, the Fourteenth Amendment "forbids the government to infringe...'fundamental' liberty interests at all, no matter what process is provided, unless the infringement is narrowly tailored to serve a compelling state interest."

JUSTICE SOUTER, relying on Justice Harlan's dissenting opinion in Poe v. Ullman, would largely abandon this restrained methodology, and instead ask "whether [Washington's] statute sets up one of those 'arbitrary impositions' or 'purposeless restraints' at odds with the Due Process Clause of the Fourteenth Amendment."* In our view, however, the development of this Court's substantive-due-process jurisprudence, described briefly above, has been a process whereby the outlines of the "liberty" specially protected by the Fourteenth Amendment— never fully clarified, to be sure, and perhaps not capable of being fully clarified— have at least been carefully refined by concrete examples involving fundamental rights found to be deeply rooted in our legal tradition. This approach tends to rein in the subjective elements that are necessarily present in due-process judicial review. In addition, by establishing a threshold requirement—that a challenged state action implicate a fundamental right—before requiring more than a reasonable relation to a legitimate state interest to justify the action, it avoids the need for complex balancing of competing interests in every case.

---

*In JUSTICE SOUTER'S opinion, Justice Harlan's Poe dissent supplies the "modern justification" for substantive-due-process review. But although Justice Harlan's opinion has often been cited in due-process cases, we have never abandoned our fundamental-rights-based analytical method. Just four terms ago, six of the Justices now sitting joined the Court's opinion in Reno v. Flores; Poe was not even cited. And in Cruzan, neither the Court's nor the concurring opinions relied on Poe; rather, we concluded that the right to refuse unwanted medical treatment was so rooted in our history, tradition, and practice as to require special protection under the Fourteenth Amendment. True, the Court relied on Justice Harlan's dissent in Casey, but, as Flores demonstrates, we did not in so doing jettison our established approach. Indeed, to read such a radical move into the Court's opinion in Casey would seem to fly in the face of that opinion's emphasis on stare decisis.

Turning to the claim at issue here, the Court of Appeals stated that "properly analyzed, the first issue to be resolved is whether there is a liberty interest in determining the time and manner of one's death," or, in other words, "is there a right to die?" Similarly, respondents assert a "liberty to choose how to die" and a right to "control of one's final days," and describe the asserted liberty as "the right to choose a humane, dignified death," and "the liberty to shape death." As noted above, we have a tradition of carefully formulating the interest at stake in sub-stantive-due-process cases. For example, although Cruzan is often described as a "right to die" case, we were, in fact, more precise: we assumed that the Constitution granted competent persons a "constitutionally protected right to refuse life-saving hydration and nutrition." The Washington statute at issue in this case prohibits "aiding another person to attempt suicide," and, thus, the question before us is whether the "liberty" specially protected by the Due Process Clause includes a right to commit suicide which itself includes a right to assistance in doing so.

We now inquire whether this asserted right has any place in our Nation's traditions. Here, as discussed above, we are confronted with a consistent and almost universal tradition that has long rejected the asserted right, and continues explicitly to reject it today, even for terminally ill, mentally competent adults. To hold for respondents, we would have to reverse centuries of legal doctrine and practice, and strike down the considered policy choice of almost every State.

Respondents contend, however, that the liberty interest they assert is consistent with this Court's substantive-due-process line of cases, if not with this Nation's history and practice. Pointing to Casey and Cruzan, respondents read our jurisprudence in this area as reflecting a general tradition of "self-sovereignty," and as teaching that the "liberty" protected by the Due Process Clause includes "basic and intimate exercises of personal autonomy." According to respondents, our liberty jurisprudence, and the broad, individualistic principles it reflects, protects the "liberty of competent, terminally ill adults to make end-of-life decisions free of undue government interference." The question presented in this case, however, is whether the protections of the Due Process Clause include a right to commit suicide with another's assistance. With this "careful description" of respondents' claim in mind, we turn to Casey and Cruzan.

In Cruzan, we considered whether Nancy Beth Cruzan, who had been severely injured in an automobile accident and was in a persistive vegetative state, "had a right under the United States Constitution which would require the hospital to withdraw life-sustaining treatment" at her parents' request. We began with the observation that "at common law, even the touching of one person by another without consent and without legal justification was a battery." We then discussed the related rule that "informed consent is generally required for medical treatment." After reviewing a long line of relevant state cases, we concluded that "the common-law doctrine of informed consent is viewed as generally encompassing the right of a competent individual to refuse medical treatment." Next, we reviewed our own cases on the subject, and stated that "the principle that a competent person has a constitutionally protected liberty interest in refusing unwanted medical treatment may be inferred from our prior decisions." Therefore, "for purposes of [that] case, we assumed that the United States Constitution would grant a competent person a constitutionally protected right to refuse lifesaving hydration and nutrition." We concluded that, notwithstanding this right, the Constitution permitted Missouri to require clear and convincing evidence of an incompetent patient's wishes concerning the withdrawal of life-sustaining treatment.

Respondents contend that in Cruzan we "acknowledged that competent, dying persons have the right to direct the removal of life-sustaining medical treatment and thus hasten death," and that "the constitutional principle behind recognizing the patient's liberty to direct the withdrawal of artificial life support applies at least as strongly to the choice to hasten impending death by consuming lethal medication." Similarly, the Court of Appeals concluded that "Cruzan, by recognizing a liberty interest that includes the refusal of artificial provision of life-sustaining food and water, necessarily recognized a liberty interest in hastening one's own death."

The right assumed in Cruzan, however, was not simply deduced from abstract concepts of personal autonomy. Given the common-law rule that forced medication was a battery, and the long legal tradition protecting the decision to refuse unwanted medical treatment, our assumption was entirely consistent with this Nation's history and constitutional traditions. The decision to commit suicide with the assistance of another may be just as personal and profound as the decision to refuse unwanted medical treatment, but it has never enjoyed similar legal protection. Indeed, the two acts are widely and reasonably regarded as quite distinct. In Cruzan itself, we recognized that most States outlawed assisted suicide—and even more do today—and we certainly gave no intimation that the right to refuse unwanted medical treatment could be somehow transmuted into a right to assistance in committing suicide.

Respondents also rely on Casey. There, the Court's opinion concluded that "the essential holding of Roe v. Wade should be retained and once again reaffirmed." We held, first, that a woman has a right, before her fetus is viable, to an abortion "without undue interference from the State"; second, that States may restrict postviability abortions, so long as exceptions are made to protect a woman's life and health; and third, that the State has legitimate interests throughout a pregnancy in protecting the health of the woman and the life of the unborn child. In reaching this conclusion, the opinion discussed in some detail this Court's substantive-due-process tradition of interpreting the Due Process Clause to protect certain fundamental rights and "personal decisions relating to marriage, procreation, contraception, family relationships, child rearing, and education," and noted that many of those rights and liberties "involve the most intimate and personal choices a person may make in a lifetime."

The Court of Appeals, like the District Court, found Casey "highly instructive" and "almost prescriptive" for determining "what liberty interest may inhere in a terminally ill person's choice to commit suicide":

> Like the decision of whether or not to have an abortion, the decision how and when to die is one of "the most intimate and personal choices a person may make in a lifetime," a choice "central to personal dignity and autonomy."

Similarly, respondents emphasize the statement in Casey that:

> At the heart of liberty is the right to define one's own concept of existence, of
> meaning, of the universe, and of the mystery of human life. Beliefs about these
> matters could not define the attributes of personhood were they formed under
> compulsion of the State.

By choosing this language, the Court's opinion in Casey described, in a general way
and in light of our prior cases, those personal activities and decisions that this Court
has identified as so deeply rooted in our history and traditions, or so fundamental to
our concept of constitutionally ordered liberty, that they are protected by the Fourteenth Amendment. The opinion moved from the recognition that liberty necessarily includes freedom of conscience and belief about ultimate considerations to
the observation that "though the abortion decision may originate within the zone of
conscience and belief, it is more than a philosophic exercise." That many of the
rights and liberties protected by the Due Process Clause sound in personal
autonomy does not warrant the sweeping conclusion that any and all important, intimate, and personal decisions are so protected, and Casey did not suggest otherwise.

The history of the law's treatment of assisted suicide in this country has been
and continues to be one of the rejection of nearly all efforts to permit it. That
being the case, our decisions lead us to conclude that the asserted "right" to assistance in committing suicide is not a fundamental liberty interest protected by the
Due Process Clause. The Constitution also requires, however, that Washington's
assisted-suicide ban be rationally related to legitimate government interests. This
requirement is unquestionably met here. As the court below recognized, Washington's assisted-suicide ban implicates a number of state interests.*

First, Washington has an "unqualified interest in the preservation of human
life." The State's prohibition on assisted suicide, like all homicide laws, both
reflects and advances its commitment to this interest.† This interest is symbolic
and aspirational as well as practical:

"While suicide is no longer prohibited or penalized, the ban against assisted
suicide and euthanasia shores up the notion of limits in human relationships. It
reflects the gravity with which we view the decision to take one's own life or the
life of another, and our reluctance to encourage or promote these decisions."

---

*The court identified and discussed six state interests: (1) preserving life; (2) preventing sui-
cide; (3) avoiding the involvement of third parties and use of arbitrary, unfair, or undue influence; (4)
protecting family members and loved ones; (5) protecting the integrity of the medical profession; and
(6) avoiding future movement toward euthanasia and other abuses.

Respondents also admit the existence of these interests. Brief for Respondents 28–39, but contend that Washington could better promote and protect them through regulation, rather than prohibition of physician-assisted suicide. Our inquiry, however, is limited to the question whether the
State's prohibition is rationally related to legitimate state interests.

†The States express this commitment by other means as well:

"Nearly all states expressly disapprove of suicide and assisted suicide either in statutes dealing
with durable powers of attorney in health-care situations, or in 'living will' statutes. In addition, all
states provide for the involuntary commitment of persons who may harm themselves as the result of
mental illness, and a number of states allow the use of nondeadly force to thwart suicide attempts."

Respondents admit that "the State has a real interest in preserving the lives of those who can still contribute to society and enjoy life." The Court of Appeals also recognized Washington's interest in protecting life, but held that the "weight" of this interest depends on the "medical condition and the wishes of the person whose life is at stake." Washington, however, has rejected this sliding-scale approach and, through its assisted-suicide ban, insists that all persons' lives, from beginning to end, regardless of physical or mental condition, are under the full protection of the law. As we have previously affirmed, the States "may properly decline to make judgments about the 'quality' of life that a particular individual may enjoy." This remains true, as Cruzan makes clear, even for those who are near death.

Relatedly, all admit that suicide is a serious public-health problem, especially among persons in otherwise vulnerable groups. The State has an interest in preventing suicide, and in studying, identifying, and treating its causes.

Those who attempt suicide—terminally ill or not—often suffer from depression or other mental disorders. Research indicates, however, that many people who request physician-assisted suicide withdraw that request if their depression and pain are treated. The New York Task Force, however, expressed its concern that, because depression is difficult to diagnose, physicians and medical professionals often fail to respond adequately to seriously ill patients' needs. Thus, legal physician-assisted suicide could make it more difficult for the State to protect depressed or mentally ill persons, or those who are suffering from untreated pain, from suicidal impulses.

The State also has an interest in protecting the integrity and ethics of the medical profession. In contrast to the Court of Appeals' conclusion that "the integrity of the medical profession would [not] be threatened in any way by [physician-assisted suicide]," the American Medical Association, like many other medical and physicians' groups, has concluded that "physician-assisted suicide is fundamentally incompatible with the physician's role as healer." And physician-assisted suicide could, it is argued, undermine the trust that is essential to the doctor-patient relationship by blurring the time-honored line between healing and harming.

Next, the State has an interest in protecting vulnerable groups—including the poor, the elderly, and disabled persons—from abuse, neglect, and mistakes. The Court of Appeals dismissed the State's concern that disadvantaged persons might be pressured into physician-assisted suicide as "ludicrous on its face." We have recognized, however, the real risk of subtle coercion and undue influence in end-of-life situations. Similarly, the New York Task Force warned that "legalizing physician-assisted suicide would pose profound risks to many individuals who are ill and vulnerable.... The risk of harm is greatest for the many individuals in our society whose autonomy and well-being are already compromised by poverty, lack of access to good medical care, advanced age, or membership in a stigmatized social group." If physician-assisted suicide were permitted, many might resort to it to spare their families the substantial financial burden of end-of-life health-care costs.

The State's interest here goes beyond protecting the vulnerable from coercion: it extends to protecting disabled and terminally ill people from prejudice, negative and inaccurate stereotypes, and "societal indifference." The State's assisted-suicide ban reflects and reinforces its policy that the lives of terminally ill, disabled, and elderly people must be no less valued than the lives of the young and healthy, and that a seriously disabled person's suicidal impulses should be interpreted and treated the same way as anyone else's.

Finally, the State may fear that permitting assisted suicide will start it down the path to voluntary and perhaps even involuntary euthanasia. The Court of Appeals struck down Washington's assisted-suicide ban only "as applied to competent, terminally ill adults who wish to hasten their deaths by obtaining medication prescribed by their doctors." Washington insists, however, that the impact of the court's decision will not and cannot be so limited. If suicide is protected as a matter of constitutional right, it is argued, "every man and woman in the United States must enjoy it." The Court of Appeals' decision, and its expansive reasoning, provide ample support for the State's concerns. The court noted, for example, that the "decision of a duly appointed surrogate decision maker is for all legal purposes the decision of the patient himself"; that "in some instances, the patient may be unable to self-administer the drugs and ... administration by the physician ... may be the only way the patient may be able to receive them"; and that not only physicians, but also family members and loved ones, will inevitably participate in assisting suicide. Thus, it turns out that what is couched as a limited right to "physician-assisted suicide" is likely, in effect, a much broader license, which could prove extremely difficult to police and contain.* Washington's ban on assisting suicide prevents such erosion.

This concern is further supported by evidence about the practice of euthanasia in the Netherlands. The Dutch government's own study revealed that in 1990, there were 2,300 cases of voluntary euthanasia (defined as "the deliberate termination of another's life at his request"), 400 cases of assisted suicide, and more than 1,000 cases of euthanasia without an explicit request. In addition to these latter 1,000 cases, the study found an additional 4,941 cases where physicians administered lethal morphine overdoses without the patients' explicit consent. This study suggests that, despite the existence of various reporting procedures, euthanasia in the Netherlands has not been limited to competent, terminally ill adults who are enduring physical suffering, and that regulation of the practice may not have prevented abuses in cases involving vulnerable persons, including severely disabled neonates and elderly persons suffering from dementia. The New York Task Force, citing the Dutch experience, observed that "assisted suicide and euthanasia are closely linked," and concluded that the "risk of ... abuse is neither

*JUSTICE SOUTER concludes that "the case for the slippery slope is fairly made out here, not because recognizing one due process right would leave a court with no principled basis to avoid recognizing another, but because there is a plausible case that the right claimed would not be readily containable by reference to facts about the mind that are matters of difficult judgment, or by gatekeepers who are subject to temptation, noble or not." We agree that the case for a slippery slope has been made out, but—bearing in mind Justice Cardozo's observation of "the tendency of a principle to expand itself to the limit of its logic"—we also recognize the reasonableness of the widely expressed skepticism about the lack of a principled basis for confining the right.

speculative nor distant." Washington, like most other States, reasonably ensures against this risk by banning, rather than regulating, assisting suicide.

We need not weigh exactingly the relative strengths of these various interests. They are unquestionably important and legitimate, and Washington's ban on assisted suicide is at least reasonably related to their promotion and protection. We therefore hold that Wash. Rev. Code § 9A.36.060(1) (1994) does not violate the Fourteenth Amendment, either on its face or "as applied to competent, terminally ill adults who wish to hasten their deaths by obtaining medication prescribed by their doctors."

Throughout the Nation, Americans are engaged in an earnest and profound debate about the morality, legality, and practicality of physician-assisted suicide. Our holding permits this debate to continue, as it should in a democratic society. The decision of the en banc Court of Appeals is reversed, and the case is remanded for further proceedings consistent with this opinion.

It is so ordered.

CONCURBY: O'CONNOR; STEVENS; SOUTER; GINSBURG; BREYER

CONCUR: JUSTICE O'CONNOR, concurring.*

*JUSTICE GINSBURG concurs in the Court's judgments substantially for the reasons stated in this opinion. JUSTICE BREYER joins this opinion except insofar as it joins the opinions of the Court.

JUSTICE SOUTER, concurring in the judgment.

Three terminally ill individuals and four physicians who sometimes treat terminally ill patients brought this challenge to the Washington statute making it a crime "knowingly... [to] aid another person to attempt suicide," claiming on behalf of both patients and physicians that it would violate substantive due process to enforce the statute against a doctor who acceded to a dying patient's request for a drug to be taken by the patient to commit suicide. The question is whether the statute sets up one of those "arbitrary impositions" or "purposeless restraints" at odds with the Due Process Clause of the Fourteenth Amendment. I conclude that the statute's application to the doctors has not been shown to be unconstitutional, but I write separately to give my reasons for analyzing the substantive due process claims as I do, and for rejecting this one.

I

Although the terminally ill original parties have died during the pendency of this case, the four physicians who remain as respondents here continue to request declaratory and injunctive relief for their own benefit in discharging their obligations to other dying patients who request their help. The case reaches us on an order granting summary judgment, and we must take as true the undisputed allegations that each of the patients was mentally competent and terminally ill, and that each made a knowing and voluntary choice to ask a doctor to prescribe "medications...to be self-administered for the purpose of hastening...death." The State does not dispute that each faced a passage to death more agonizing both mentally and physically, and more protracted over time, than death by suicide with a physician's help, or that each would have chosen such a suicide for the sake of personal dignity, apart even from relief from pain. Each doctor in this case claims to encounter patients like the original plaintiffs who have died, that is, mentally competent, terminally ill, and seeking medical help in "the voluntary self-termination of life." While there may be no unanimity on the physician's professional obligation in such circumstances, I accept here respondents' representation that providing such patients with prescriptions for drugs that go beyond pain relief to hasten death would, in these circumstances, be consistent with standards of medical practice. Hence, I take it to be true, as respondents say, that the Washington statute prevents the exercise of a physician's "best professional judgment to prescribe medications to [such] patients in dosages that would enable them to act to hasten their own deaths."

In their brief to this Court, the doctors claim not that they ought to have a right generally to hasten patients' imminent deaths, but only to help patients who have made "personal decisions regarding their own bodies, medical care, and, fundamentally, the future course of their lives," and who have concluded responsibly and with substantial justification that the brief and anguished remainders of their lives have lost virtually all value to them. Respondents fully embrace the notion that the State must be free to impose reasonable regulations on such physician assistance to ensure that the patients they assist are indeed among the competent and terminally ill and that each has made a free and informed choice in seeking to obtain and use a fatal drug.

In response, the State argues that the interest asserted by the doctors is beyond constitutional recognition because it has no deep roots in our history and traditions. But even aside from that, without disputing that the patients here were competent and terminally ill, the State insists that recognizing the legitimacy of doctors' assistance of their patients as contemplated here would entail a number of adverse consequences that the Washington Legislature was entitled to forestall. The nub of this part of the State's argument is not that such patients are constitutionally undeserving of relief on their own account, but that any attempt to confine a right of physician assistance to the circumstances presented by these doctors is likely to fail.

First, the State argues that the right could not be confined to the terminally ill. Even assuming a fixed definition of that term, the State observes that it is not always possible to say with certainty how long a person may live. It asserts that "there is no principled basis on which [the right] can be limited to the prescription of medication for terminally ill patients to administer to themselves" when the right's justifying principle is as broad as "merciful termination of suffering." Second, the State argues that the right could not be confined to the mentally competent, observing that a person's competence cannot always be assessed with certainty, and suggesting further that no principled distinction is possible between a competent patient acting independently and a patient acting through a duly appointed and competent surrogate. Next, according to the State, such a right might entail a right to or at least merge in practice into "other forms of life-ending assistance," such as euthanasia. Finally, the State believes that a right to physician assistance could not easily be distinguished from a right to assistance from others, such as friends, family, and other health-care workers. The State thus argues that recognition of the substantive due process right at issue here would jeopardize the lives of others outside the class defined by the doctors' claim, creating risks of irresponsible suicides and euthanasia, whose dangers are concededly within the State's authority to address.

II

When the physicians claim that the Washington law deprives them of a right falling within the scope of liberty that the Fourteenth Amendment guarantees against denial without due process of law, they are not claiming some sort of procedural defect in the process through which the statute has been enacted or is administered. Their claim, rather, is that the State has no substantively adequate justification for barring the assistance sought by the patient and sought to be offered by the physician. Thus, we are dealing with a claim to one of those rights sometimes described as rights of substantive due-process and sometimes as unenumerated rights, in view of the breadth and indeterminacy of the "due process" serving as the claim's textual basis. The doctors accordingly arouse the skepticism of those who find the Due Process Clause an unduly vague or oxymoronic warrant for judicial review of substantive state law, just as they also invoke two centuries of American constitutional practice in recognizing unenumerated, substantive limits on governmental action.

The principal significance of this history in the State of Washington, according to respondents, lies in its repudiation of the old tradition to the extent of eliminating the criminal suicide prohibitions. Respondents do not argue that the State's decision goes further, to imply that the State has repudiated any legitimate claim to discourage suicide or to limit its encouragement. The reasons for the decriminalization, after all, may have had more to do with difficulties of law enforcement than with a shift in the value ascribed to life in various circumstances or in the perceived legitimacy of taking one's own. Thus it may indeed make sense for the State to take its hands off suicide as such, while continuing to prohibit the sort of assistance that would make its commission easier. Decriminalization does not, then, imply the existence of a constitutional liberty interest in suicide as such; it simply opens the door to the assertion of a cognizable liberty interest in bodily integrity and associated medical care that would otherwise have been inapposite so long as suicide, as well as assisting suicide, was a criminal offense.

This liberty interest in bodily integrity was phrased in a general way by then-Judge Cardozo when he said, "every human being of adult years and sound mind has a right to determine what shall be done with his own body" in relation to his medical needs. The familiar examples of this right derive from the common law of battery and include the right to be free from medical invasions into the body, as well as a right generally to resist enforced medication. Thus "it is settled now ... that the Constitution places limits on a State's right to interfere with a person's most basic decisions about ... bodily integrity." Constitutional recognition of the right to bodily integrity underlies the assumed right, good against the State, to require physicians to terminate artificial life support, and the affirmative right to obtain medical intervention to cause abortion.

It is, indeed, in the abortion cases that the most telling recognitions of the importance of bodily integrity and the concomitant tradition of medical assistance have occurred. In Roe v. Wade, the plaintiff contended that the Texas statute making it criminal for any person to "procure an abortion" for a pregnant woman was unconstitutional insofar as it prevented her from "terminating her pregnancy by an abortion 'performed by a competent, licensed physician, under safe, clinical conditions,' " and in striking down the statute we stressed the importance of the relationship between patient and physician.

The analogies between the abortion cases and this one are several. Even though the State has a legitimate interest in discouraging abortion, the Court recognized a woman's right to a physician's counsel and care. Like the decision to commit suicide, the decision to abort potential life can be made irresponsibly and under the influence of others, and yet the Court has held in the abortion cases that physicians are fit assistants. Without physician assistance in abortion, the woman's right would have too often amounted to nothing more than a right to self-mutilation, and without a physician to assist in the suicide of the dying, the patient's right will often be confined to crude methods of causing death, most shocking and painful to the decedent's survivors.

There is, finally, one more reason for claiming that a physician's assistance here would fall within the accepted tradition of medical care in our society, and the abortion cases are only the most obvious illustration of the further point. While the Court has held that the performance of abortion procedures can be restricted to physicians, the Court's opinion in Roe recognized the doctors' role in yet another way. For, in the course of holding that the decision to perform an abortion called for a physician's assistance, the Court recognized that the good physician is not just a mechanic of the human body whose services have no bearing on a person's moral choices, but one who does more than treat symptoms, one who ministers to the patient. This idea of the physician as serving the whole person is a source of the high value traditionally placed on the medical relationship. Its value is surely as apparent here as in the abortion cases, for just as the decision about abortion is not directed to correcting some pathology, so the decision in which a dying patient seeks help is not so limited. The patients here sought not only an end to pain (which they might have had, although perhaps at the price of stupor) but an end to their short remaining lives with a dignity that they believed would be denied them by powerful pain medication, as well as by their consciousness of dependency and helplessness as they approached death. In that period when the end is imminent, they said, the decision to end life is closest to decisions that are generally accepted as proper instances of exercising autonomy over one's own body, instances recognized under the Constitution and the State's own law, instances in which the help of physicians is accepted as falling within the traditional norm.

Respondents argue that the State has in fact already recognized enough evolving examples of this tradition of patient care to demonstrate the strength of their claim. Washington, like other States, authorizes physicians to withdraw life-sustaining medical treatment and artificially delivered food and water from patients who request it, even though such actions will hasten death. The State permits physicians to alleviate anxiety and discomfort when withdrawing artificial life-supporting devices by administering medication that will hasten death even further. And it generally permits physicians to administer medication to patients in terminal conditions when the primary intent is to alleviate pain, even when the medication is so powerful as to hasten death and the patient chooses to receive it with that understanding.

The argument supporting respondents' position thus progresses through three steps of increasing forcefulness. First, it emphasizes the decriminalization of suicide. Reliance on this fact is sanctioned under the standard that looks not only to the tradition retained, but to society's occasional choices to reject traditions of the legal past. While the common law prohibited both suicide and aiding a suicide, with the prohibition on aiding largely justified by the primary prohibition on self-inflicted death itself, the State's rejection of the traditional treatment of the one leaves the criminality of the other open to questioning that previously would not have been appropriate. The second step in the argument is to emphasize that the State's own act of decriminalization gives a freedom of choice much like the individual's option in recognized instances of bodily autonomy. One of these, abortion, is a legal right to choose in spite of the interest a State may legitimately invoke in discouraging the practice, just as suicide is now subject to choice, despite a State interest in discouraging it. The third step is to emphasize that respondents claim a right to assistance not on the basis of some broad principle that would be subject to exceptions if that continuing interest of the State's in discouraging suicide were to be recognized at all. Respondents base their claim on the traditional right to medical care and counsel, subject to the limiting conditions of informed, responsible choice when death is imminent, conditions that support a strong analogy to rights of care in other situations in which medical counsel and assistance have been available as a matter of course. There can be no stronger claim to a physician's assistance than at the time when death is imminent, a moral judgment implied by the State's own recognition of the legitimacy of medical procedures necessarily hastening the moment of impending death.

In my judgment, the importance of the individual interest here, as within that class of "certain interests" demanding careful scrutiny of the State's contrary claim, cannot be gainsaid. Whether that interest might in some circumstances, or at some time, be seen as "fundamental" to the degree entitled to prevail is not, however, a conclusion that I need draw here, for I am satisfied that the State's interests described in the following section are sufficiently serious to defeat the present claim that its law is arbitrary or purposeless.

The State has put forward several interests to justify the Washington law as applied to physicians treating terminally ill patients, even those competent to make responsible choices: protecting life generally, discouraging suicide even if knowing and voluntary, and protecting terminally ill patients from involuntary suicide and euthanasia, both voluntary and nonvoluntary.

It is not necessary to discuss the exact strengths of the first two claims of justification in the present circumstances, for the third is dispositive for me. That third justification is different from the first two, for it addresses specific features of respondents' claim, and it opposes that claim not with a moral judgment contrary to respondents', but with a recognized state interest in the protection of nonresponsible individuals and those who do not stand in relation either to death or to their physicians as do the patients whom respondents describe. The State claims interests in protecting patients from mistakenly and involuntarily deciding to end their lives, and in guarding against both voluntary and involuntary euthanasia. Leaving aside any difficulties in coming to a clear concept of imminent death, mistaken decisions may result from inadequate palliative care or a terminal prognosis that turns out to be error; coercion and abuse may stem from the large medical bills that family members cannot bear or unreimbursed hospitals decline to shoulder. Voluntary and involuntary euthanasia may result once doctors are authorized to prescribe lethal medication in the first instance, for they might find it pointless to distinguish between patients who administer their own fatal drugs and those who wish not to, and their compassion for those who suffer may obscure the distinction between those who ask for death and those who may be unable to request it. The argument is that a progression would occur, obscuring the line between the ill and the dying, and between the responsible and the unduly influenced, until ultimately doctors and perhaps others would abuse a limited freedom to aid suicides by yielding to the impulse to end another's suffering under conditions going beyond the narrow limits the respondents propose. The State thus argues, essentially, that respondents' claim is not as narrow as it sounds, simply because no recognition of the interest they assert could be limited to vindicating those interests and affecting no others. The State says that the claim, in practical effect, would entail consequences that the State could, without doubt, legitimately act to prevent.

The mere assertion that the terminally sick might be pressured into suicide decisions by close friends and family members would not alone be very telling. Of course that is possible, not only because the costs of care might be more than family members could bear but simply because they might naturally wish to see an end of suffering for someone they love. But one of the points of restricting any right of assistance to physicians, would be to condition the right on an exercise of judgment by someone qualified to assess the patient's responsible capacity and detect the influence of those outside the medical relationship.

The State, however, goes further, to argue that dependence on the vigilance of physicians will not be enough. First, the lines proposed here (particularly the requirement of a knowing and voluntary decision by the patient) would be more difficult to draw than the lines that have limited other recently recognized due process rights. Limiting a State from prosecuting use of artificial contraceptives by married couples posed no practical threat to the State's capacity to regulate contraceptives in other ways that were assumed at the time of Poe to be legitimate; the trimester measurements of Roe and the viability determination of Casey were easy to make with a real degree of certainty. But the knowing and responsible mind is harder to assess.* Second, this difficulty could become the greater by combining with another fact within the realm of plausibility, that physicians simply would not be assiduous to preserve the line. They have compassion, and those who would be willing to assist in suicide at all might be the most susceptible to the wishes of a patient, whether the patient were technically quite responsible or not. Physicians, and their hospitals, have their own financial incentives, too, in this new age of managed care. Whether acting from compassion or under some other influence, a physician who would provide a drug for a patient to administer might well go the further step of administering the drug himself; so, the barrier between assisted suicide and euthanasia could become porous, and the line between voluntary and involuntary euthanasia as well.† The case for the slippery slope is fairly made out here, not because recognizing one due process right would leave a court with no principled basis to avoid recognizing another, but because there is a plausible case that the right claimed would not be readily containable by reference to facts about the mind that are matters of difficult judgment, or by gatekeepers who are subject to temptation, noble or not.

Respondents propose an answer to all this, the answer of state regulation with teeth. Legislation proposed in several States, for example, would authorize physician-assisted suicide but require two qualified physicians to confirm the patient's diagnosis, prognosis, and competence; and would mandate that the patient make repeated requests witnessed by at least two others over a specified time span; and would impose reporting requirements and criminal penalties for various acts of coercion.

---

*While it is also more difficult to assess in cases involving limitations on life incidental to pain medication and the disconnection of artificial life support, there are reasons to justify a lesser concern with the punctilio of responsibility in these instances. The purpose of requesting and giving the medication is presumably not to cause death but to relieve the pain so that the State's interest in preserving life is not unequivocally implicated by the practice; and the importance of pain relief is so clear that there is less likelihood that relieving pain would run counter to what a responsible patient would choose, even with the consequences for life expectancy. As for ending artificial life support, the State again may see its interest in preserving life as weaker here than in the general case just because artificial life support preserves life when nature would not; and, because such life support is a frequently offensive bodily intrusion, there is a lesser reason to fear that a decision to remove it would not be the choice of one fully responsible. Where, however, a physician writes a prescription to equip a patient to end life, the prescription is written to serve an affirmative intent to die (even though the physician need not and probably does not characteristically have an intent that the patient die but only that the patient be equipped to make the decision). The patient's responsibility and competence are therefore crucial when the physician is presented with the request.

†Again, the same can be said about life support and shortening life to kill pain, but the calculus may be viewed as different in these instances, as noted just above.

But at least at this moment there are reasons for caution in predicting the effectiveness of the teeth proposed. Respondents' proposals, as it turns out, sound much like the guidelines now in place in the Netherlands, the only place where experience with physician-assisted suicide and euthanasia has yielded empirical evidence about how such regulations might affect actual practice. Dutch physicians must engage in consultation before proceeding, and must decide whether the patient's decision is voluntary, well considered, and stable, whether the request to die is enduring and made more than once, and whether the patient's future will involve unacceptable suffering. There is, however, a substantial dispute today about what the Dutch experience shows. Some commentators marshall evidence that the Dutch guidelines have in practice failed to protect patients from involuntary euthanasia and have been violated with impunity. This evidence is contested. The day may come when we can say with some assurance which side is right, but for now it is the substantiality of the factual disagreement, and the alternatives for resolving it, that matter. They are, for me, dispositive of the due process claim at this time.

I take it that the basic concept of judicial review with its possible displacement of legislative judgment bars any finding that a legislature has acted arbitrarily when the following conditions are met: there is a serious factual controversy over the feasibility of recognizing the claimed right without at the same time making it impossible for the State to engage in an undoubtedly legitimate exercise of power; facts necessary to resolve the controversy are not readily ascertainable through the judicial process; but they are more readily subject to discovery through legislative fact-finding and experimentation. It is assumes in this case, and must be, that a State's interest in protecting those unable to make responsible decisions and those who make no decisions at all entitles the State to bar aid to any but a knowing and responsible person intending suicide, and to prohibit euthanasia. How, and how far, a State should act in that interest are judgments for the State, but the legitimacy of its action to deny a physician the option to aid any but the knowing and responsible is beyond question.

The capacity of the State to protect the others if respondents were to prevail is, however, subject to some genuine question, underscored by the responsible disagreement over the basic facts of the Dutch experience. This factual controversy is not open to a judicial resolution with any substantial degree of assurance at this time. It is not, of course, that any controversy about the factual predicate of a due process claim disqualifies a court from resolving it. Courts can recognize captiousness, and most factual issues can be settled in a trial court. At this point, however, the factual issue at the heart of this case does not appear to be one of those. The principal enquiry at the moment is into the Dutch experience, and I question whether an independent front-line investigation into the facts of a foreign country's legal administration can be soundly undertaken through American courtroom litigation. While an extensive literature on any subject can raise the hopes for judicial understanding, the literature on this subject is only nascent. Since there is little experience directly bearing on the issue, the most that can be said is that whichever way the Court might rule today, events could overtake its assumptions, as experimentation in some jurisdictions confirmed or discredited the concerns about progression from assisted suicide to euthanasia.

Legislatures, on the other hand, have superior opportunities to obtain the facts necessary for a judgment about the present controversy. Not only do they have more flexible mechanisms for fact-finding than the Judiciary, but their mechanisms include the power to experiment, moving forward and pulling back as facts emerge within their own jurisdictions. There is, indeed, good reason to suppose that in the absence of a judgment for respondents here, just such experimentation will be attempted in some of the States.

I do not decide here what the significance might be of legislative foot-dragging in ascertaining the facts going to the State's argument that the right in question could not be confined as claimed. Sometimes a court may be bound to act regardless of the institutional preferability of the political branches as forums for addressing constitutional claims. Now, it is enough to say that our examination of legislative reasonableness should consider the fact that the Legislature of the State of Washington is no more obviously at fault than this Court is in being uncertain about what would happen if respondents prevailed today. We therefore have a clear question about which institution, a legislature or a court, is relatively more competent to deal with an emerging issue as to which facts currently unknown could be dispositive. The answer has to be, for the reasons already stated, that the legislative process is to be preferred. There is a closely related further reason as well.

One must bear in mind that the nature of the right claimed, if recognized as one constitutionally required, would differ in no essential way from other constitutional rights guaranteed by enumeration or derived from some more definite textual source than "due process." An unenumerated right should not therefore be recognized, with the effect of displacing the legislative ordering of things, without the assurance that its recognition would prove as durable as the recognition of those other rights differently derived. To recognize a right of lesser promise would simply create a constitutional regime too uncertain to bring with it the expectation of finality that is one of this Court's central obligations in making constitutional decisions.

Legislatures, however, are not so constrained. The experimentation that should be out of the question in constitutional adjudication displacing legislative judgment is entirely proper, as well as highly desirable, when the legislative power addresses an emerging issue like assisted suicide. The Court should accordingly stay its hand to allow reasonable legislative consideration. While I do not decide for all time that respondents' claim should not be recognized, I acknowledge the legislative institutional competence as the better one to deal with that claim at this time.